T0320320

Model-Based Machine Learning

Today, machine learning is being applied to a growing variety of problems in a bewildering variety of domains. A fundamental challenge when using machine learning is connecting the abstract mathematics of a machine learning technique to a concrete, real world problem. This book tackles this challenge through **model-based machine learning** which focuses on understanding the assumptions encoded in a machine learning system and their corresponding impact on the behaviour of the system.

The key ideas of model-based machine learning are introduced through a series of case studies involving real-world applications. Case studies play a central role because it is only in the context of applications that it makes sense to discuss modelling assumptions. Each chapter introduces one case study and works through step-by-step to solve it using a model-based approach. The aim is not just to explain machine learning methods, but also showcase how to create, debug, and evolve them to solve a problem.

Features:

- Explores the assumptions being made by machine learning systems and the effect these assumptions have when the system is applied to concrete problems

- Explains machine learning concepts as they arise in real-world case studies

- Shows how to diagnose, understand and address problems with machine learning systems

- Full source code available, allowing models and results to be reproduced and explored

- Includes optional deep-dive sections with more mathematical details on inference algorithms for the interested reader

John Winn is a Principal Researcher at Microsoft Research, UK.

Model-Based Machine Learning

John Michael Winn
with
Christopher M. Bishop
Thomas Diethe
John Guiver
Yordan Zaykov

CRC Press
Taylor & Francis Group
Boca Raton London New York

CRC Press is an imprint of the
Taylor & Francis Group, an **informa** business

A CHAPMAN & HALL BOOK

Cover image adapted from shutterstock image 1810092946

MATLAB® is a trademark of The MathWorks, Inc. and is used with permission. The MathWorks does not warrant the accuracy of the text or exercises in this book. This book's use or discussion of MATLAB® software or related products does not constitute endorsement or sponsorship by The MathWorks of a particular pedagogical approach or particular use of the MATLAB® software.

First edition published 2024
by CRC Press
6000 Broken Sound Parkway NW, Suite 300, Boca Raton, FL 33487-2742

and by CRC Press
4 Park Square, Milton Park, Abingdon, Oxon, OX14 4RN

CRC Press is an imprint of Taylor & Francis Group, LLC

© 2024 Taylor & Francis Group, LLC

ISBN: 9781498756815 (hbk)
ISBN: 9781032558820 (pbk)
ISBN: 9780429192685 (ebk)

DOI: 10.1201/9780429192685

Typeset in Nimbus
by Deanta Global Publishing Services, Chennai, India

Access the online version of the book here: https://www.mbmlbook.com/index.html

To Ellen, Joshua and Layla

Contents

Preface

Today, machine learning is being applied to a growing variety of problems in a bewildering variety of domains. When doing machine learning, a fundamental challenge is connecting the abstract mathematics of a particular machine learning technique to a concrete, real-world problem. This book tackles this challenge through *model-based machine learning*. Model-based machine learning is an approach which focuses on understanding the assumptions encoded in a machine learning system, and their corresponding impact on the behaviour of the system. The practice of model-based machine learning involves separating out these assumptions being made about a real-world situation from the detailed mathematics of the algorithms needed to do the machine learning. This approach makes it easier to both understand the behaviour of a machine learning system and to communicate this to others. Much more detail on what model-based machine learning is and how it can help are described in the introduction chapter entitled "How can machine learning solve my problem?".

This book is unusual for a machine learning text book in that we do not review categories of algorithms or techniques. Instead, we introduce all of the key ideas through case studies involving real-world applications. Case studies play a central role because it is only in the context of applications that it makes sense to discuss modelling assumptions. Each case study chapter

Only a few building blocks are needed to construct an infinite variety of models.

introduces a real-world application and solves it using a model-based approach. In addition, a first tutorial chapter explores a fictional problem involving a murder mystery.

Each chapter also serves to introduce a variety of machine learning concepts, not as abstract ideas, but as concrete techniques motivated by the needs of the application. You can think of these concepts as the building blocks for constructing models. Although you will need to invest some time to understand these concepts fully, you will soon discover that a huge variety of models can be constructed from a relatively small number of building blocks. By working through the case studies in this book, you will learn what these components are and how to use them. The aim is to give you sufficient appreciation of the power and flexibility of model-based approach to allow *you* to solve *your* machine learning problem.

Who this book is for

This book is intended for any technical person who wants to use machine learning to solve a real-world problem or who wants to understand why an existing machine learning system behave the way it does. The focus of most of the book is on designing models to solve problems arising in real case studies. The final chapter "How to read a model" looks instead at using model-based machine learning to understand existing machine learning techniques.

Some more mathematically minded readers will want to understand the details of how models are turned into runnable algorithms. We have separated these parts of the book, which require more advanced mathematics, into deep-dive sections. Deep-dive sections are marked with panels like the one below. These sections are *optional* – you can read the book without them.

> **⌦ Inference deep-dive**
> Technical sections which dive into the details of algorithms will be marked like this. If you just want to focus on modelling, you can skip these sections.

How to read this book

Each case study in this book describes a journey from problem statement to solution. You probably do not want to follow this journey in a single sitting. To help with this, each case study is split into sections – we recommend reading a section at a time and pausing to digest what you have learned at the end of each section. To help with this, the machine learning concepts introduced in a section will be highlighted **like this** and will be reviewed in a small glossary at the end of each section.

We aim to provide enough details of each concept to allow the case studies to be understood, along with links to external sources, such as Bishop [2006], where you can get more details if you are interested in a particular topic.

Each introductory section of the book also includes a self assessment, consisting of hands-on, practical exercises. You can use these exercises to test your own understanding of the concepts introduced in the corresponding section. Rather than being purely mathematical exercises, these are generally more open-ended assessments with the aim of getting into the right mindset for thinking about assumptions and machine learning model development. Most exercises are designed to allow self-checking, for example by comparing the results of one exercise with another. For some exercises, it can be helpful to work through them with a partner, so you can compare notes on your answers and discuss any assumptions you have made.

Online book and code

This book has an online version at mbmlbook.com which complements the paper version and has additional material and functionality. For example, the online format enables interactive model diagrams, popup definitions of terms and allows the data behind any plot to be downloaded. The online version also includes contact details for providing feedback and reporting errata, and will always be up-to-date with corrections.

In addition, all the results in the book can be reproduced using the accompanying source code. This code is open source and is freely available at github.com/dotnet/mbmlbook.

Acknowledgements

First and foremost, I would like to thank the major contributors without whom this book would not have happened. Christopher Bishop helped develop the initial concept and structure for this book and also contributed several chapters. Each case study chapter was a significant machine learning project in itself, requiring the development of a model to solve a genuine real-world problem – Tom Diethe, John Guiver and Yordan Zaykov took on these projects: gathering data, writing code, running experiments, solving problems and producing all the results that you see in each chapter. They all also provided detailed and thoughtful discussion and feedback on the chapters themselves.

The staff at CRC Press have been hugely supportive and helpful in the final stages of preparing this book for publication. I'd particularly like to thank my editors, first John Kimmel and later Lara Spieker for their unwavering support in guiding this book home.

I am grateful to Microsoft for giving me the freedom to work on this book, as well as providing the stimulating research environment which has allowed me to develop my machine learning skills and understanding for the last twenty years. My Microsoft colleagues have also been invaluable in providing detailed feedback on many aspects of this book. In Cambridge, Tom Minka, Sebastian Blohm, John Bronskill, Andy Gordon, Sam Webster, Alex Spengler, Andrew Fitzgibbon, Elena Pochernina, Matteo Venanzi, Boris Yangel, Jian Li and Jonathan Tims have all provided valuable discussion and feedback on early drafts. I want particularly to thank Pashmina Cameron for her very detailed and thoughtful feedback which really helped improve the quality and clarity of many chapters. More widely across Microsoft, Jim Edelen, Alex Wetmore, Tyler Gill, Max Bovykin, Fedor Zhdanov, Li Deng, Michael Shelton, Emmanuel Gillain and Bahar Bina have provided very useful commentary especially on the early chapters and on the exercises.

Outside of Microsoft, I am indebted to Angela Simpson and Adnan Custovic for their collaboration on the project which led to the Chapter 6 case study on childhood asthma, and also for their comments on that chapter. Other collaborators in the healthcare AI space, Damian Sutcliffe and Andres Floto, have also given much valuable feedback on this chapter and others. Thanks also to Dr Sarah Supp for kindly contributing her photo of baked goods to inspire novel data visualisations in Chapter 2.

The online version of this book was launched early on in the writing process and has been invaluable in gathering feedback throughout. I owe a debt of gratitude to Nick Duffield for the graphic design of the online version and to Andy Slowey, Nathan Jones, Ian Kelly for keeping it up and running over the years. I am also hugely grateful to Dmitry Kats and Alexander Novikov for their hard work in open sourcing the accompanying code, and for making substantial improvements to it in the process.

Very many online readers have corrected typos and provided feedback, questions and positive comments, all of which has been immensely helpful and encouraging. For taking the time to pause reading and write back, I'd like to thank: Yousry Abdallah, Marius Ackerman, Tauheedul Ali, Ali Arslan, Luca Baldassarre, Chethan Bhateja, Marcus Blankenship, Glen Bojsza, Subhash Bylaiah, Aurelien Chauvey, Joh Dokler, Vladislavs Dovgalecs, Peter Dulimov, Daniel Emaasit, Gordon Erlebacher, Hon Fai Choi, Tavares Ford, Eric Fung, Shreyas Gite, Chiraag Gohel, Craig Gua, Guy Hall, Jonathan Holden, Veeresh Inginshetty, Mohammed Jalil, Lin Jia, Brett Jones, Oleg Karandin, Joakim Grahl Knudsen, Veysel Kocaman, Michael Landis, John Lataire, Josh Lawrence, Dustin Lee, Vincent Lefoulon, Ben Lefroy, Mark Legters, MartinaÂăLutterová Štúrova, Andrew MacGinitie, Tegan Maharaj, John Marino, Kyli McKay-Bishop, Arthur Mota Gonçalves, Moritz Münst, Takuya Nakazato, Hiske Overweg, Francisco Pereira, Benjamin Poulain, Venkat Ramakrishnan, Martin Roa Villescas, Marwan Sabih, Hammad Saleem, Lucian Sasu, Yurii Shevchuk, Sphiwe Skhosana, Vivek Srinivasan, David Steinar Asgrimsson, Gijs Stoeldraaijers, Agnieszka Szefer, Yousuke Takada, Matthew E. Taylor, Martin Thøgersen, Udit Tidu, Levente Torok, Benjamin Tran Dinh, Tavi Truman, Edderic Ugaddan, Ron Williams, Ted Willke, Marat Zaynutdinov and Mark Zhukovsky.

Finally, my deepest gratitude to my wife Ellen for her unflagging support and inspiration during the many years it has taken to write this book.

How can machine learning solve my problem?

A s machine learning researchers, there's a question that we get asked in some form almost every day:

"How can machine learning solve my problem?"

In this book we answer this question by example. We do not just list machine learning techniques and concepts – instead we describe a series of case studies, all the way through from problem statement to working solution. Machine learning concepts are explained as they arise in the context of solving each problem. The case studies we present are all real examples from within Microsoft, along with an initial case study which introduces some core concepts. We also look at real problems encountered during each case study, how they were detected, how they were diagnosed and how they were overcome. The aim is to explain not just what machine learning methods are, but also how to create, debug and evolve them to solve your problem.

How does a model-based approach help?

When trying to solve a problem using machine learning, the fundamental challenge is to connect the abstract mathematics of machine learning to the concrete, real-world problem domain. In this book we apply an approach called **model-based machine learning**. which focuses on understanding this connection. This understanding then helps with developing effective machine learning systems, interpreting their behaviour and solving the various problems that arise during the process.

The core idea at the heart of model-based machine learning is that all the *assumptions* about the problem domain are made explicit in the form of a **model**. In fact, a model is just made up of this set of assumptions, expressed in a precise mathematical form. These assumptions effectively build up a description of the world which can then be used to learn or reason about it. For example, in the next chapter, we build a model to help us solve a simple murder mystery. The assumptions of the model include the list of suspects, the possible murder weapons, and the tendency for particular weapons to be preferred by different suspects.

In model-base machine learning, the model is then used to create a bespoke **algorithm** to answer a particular question about the problem domain, such as making a prediction or performing some reasoning. Model-based machine learning can be applied to pretty much any problem, and its general-purpose approach means you don't need to learn a huge number of machine learning algorithms and techniques.

So why do the assumptions of the model play such a key role? Well it turns out that machine learning cannot generate solutions purely from data alone. There are always assumptions built into any machine learning algorithm, although sometimes these assumptions are far from explicit. Different algorithms correspond to different sets of assumptions. In cases when the assumptions are unclear, the only way to decide which algorithm will give the best results is to try each in turn. This is time-consuming and inefficient, and it requires software implementations of all of the algorithms being compared. And if none of the algorithms tried gives good results, it is even harder to work out how to create a better algorithm.

Models versus algorithms

Let's look more closely at the relationship between models and algorithms. We can think of a machine learning algorithm as a monolithic box which takes in data and produces results. The algorithm must necessarily make assumptions, since it is these assumptions that distinguish a particular algorithm from any other. However, given just the algorithm, those assumptions are implicit and opaque.

Now consider the model-based approach. The model comprises the set of assumptions we are making about the problem domain. To get from the model to a set of predictions we need to take the data and compute those variables whose values we wish to know. This computational

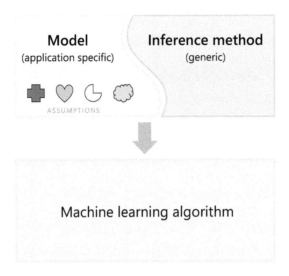

Figure 1 In the model-based view of machine learning, a custom algorithm is created by combining a model and an inference method. Here the coloured shapes within the model represent the assumptions comprising that specific model. Changes to the assumptions give rise to different machine learning algorithms, even when the inference method is kept fixed.

process is called **inference**. There are several techniques available for doing inference, as we shall discuss during the course of this book. The combination of the model and the inference procedure together define a machine learning algorithm, as illustrated in Figure 1.

Although there are various choices for the inference method, by decoupling the model from the inference we are able to apply the same inference method to a wide variety of models. To illustrate this point, every single case study in this book will be solved using just one inference method.

Model-based machine learning can be used to do any machine learning task, such as classification (Chapter 4) or clustering (Chapter 6), whilst providing additional insight and control over how these tasks are performed. Solving these tasks using model-based machine learning provides a way to handle extensions to the task or to improve accuracy, by making changes to the model – we will look at an example of this in Chapter 4. Additionally, the assumptions you are making about the problem domain are laid out clearly in the model, so it is easier to work out why one model works better than another, to communicate to someone else what a model is doing, and to understand what's happening when things go wrong. Using models also makes it easier to share other people's solutions in order to adapt, extend or combine them.

An example: deep learning

In recent years, **deep learning** has become the dominant approach to machine learning to such an extent that, to many people, deep learning *is* machine learning. What is less well known is that deep learning is an example of model-based machine learning, where the model being used is a neural network. Assumptions about the problem domain are encoded in the architecture of the neural network and in the choice of activation function for the neurons. No matter what neural network model is chosen, the same inference methods can be applied. For example, a neural network is usually trained using some kinds of **stochastic gradient descent** (SGD) method. Combining a particular neural network with SGD effectively gives a custom algorithm for training to solve a particular machine learning problem.

Figure 2 illustrates how deep learning has made use of model-based machine learning. One of the first breakthroughs in deep learning was when deep neural networks were used for object recognition in images [Krizhevsky et al., 2012]. The particular architecture of neural network chosen for this task encoded assumptions about the nature of objects in images – for example, that objects look similar no matter where in the image they appear. Combined with a suitable inference method, this gave a custom algorithm for object recognition which achieved unprecedented accuracy. For speech recognition, this assumption does not make sense and so different architectures were used which made more appropriate assumptions – for example, that a particular word may be spoken quickly or slowly. However, other assumptions encoded in the form of the neural network were retained, since they are broadly applicable to many problem domains. The ability to retain many aspects of the neural network while making targeted changes has allowed deep learning to be applied to many different application areas relatively quickly, including machine translation [Sutskever et al., 2014]. Arguably, it is this ability, building on its model-based foundations, that has enabled the deep learning revolution.

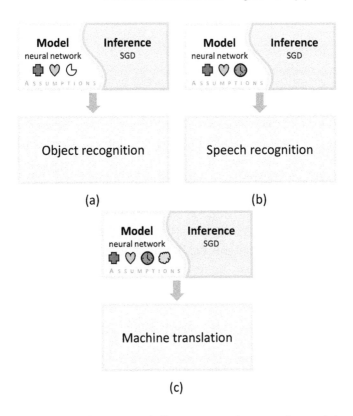

(a)   (b)

(c)

Figure 2 In deep learning, different neural network models encode different assumptions about the task they are used for, illustrated here as different icons within each model. For example, the architecture of a neural network for object recognition encodes the assumption that objects look similar no matter where in the image they appear. Although the neural network models are different for different tasks, the same inference methods can be applied. Here, stochastic gradient descent (SGD) can be applied to train any of these models. Since the models are similar and the inference methods are the same, deep learning can be rapidly applied to new problem domains.

Tools for model-based machine learning

The decomposition of an algorithm into a model and a separate inference method has another powerful consequence. It becomes possible to create a software framework which will generate the machine learning algorithm *automatically*, given only the definition of the model and a choice of inference method. This allows the applications developer to focus on the creation of the model, which is domain-specific, and frees them from needing to be an expert on the inner workings of the inference procedure.

For more than 15 years, we have been working on such a software framework at Microsoft Research, called **Infer.NET** [Minka et al., 2014]. Because a model consists simply of a set of assumptions it can be expressed in very compact code, which is relatively easy to understand and modify. The corresponding code for the algorithm, which is generally much more complex, is then produced automatically. All of the models in this book were created using Infer.NET, and the corresponding model source code is available online. However, these solutions could equally be implemented by hand or by using an alternative model-based framework – they are not specific to Infer.NET. Examples of alternative software frameworks that implement the model-based machine learning philosophy include BUGS [Lunn et al., 2000] and Stan [Stan Development Team, 2014].

As well as these general-purpose software frameworks, there has been enormous effort put in developing software specifically for neural network models, such as Tensorflow [Abadi et al., 2016] and PyTorch [Paszke et al., 2019]. Such frameworks embody the model-based machine learning approach by allowing the neural network to be described through a model description, such as in an ONNX file [Bai et al., 2019]. In this way, a custom neural network model can be trained or applied automatically, by any of the range of tools that support the ONNX format. This portability and ease-of-use are consequences of the model-based approach to machine learning.

Now that we have explained the concept of model-based machine learning, let's see an example of it being used. On to the first case study!

REVIEW OF CONCEPTS

model-based machine learning An approach to machine learning where all the assumptions about the problem domain are made explicit in the form of a model. This model is then used to create a model-specific algorithm to learn or reason about the domain. The algorithm creation part of this process can be automated.

model A set of assumptions about a problem domain, expressed in a precise mathematical form, that is used to create a machine learning solution.

algorithm A series of instructions used to solve a problem or perform a computation. Usually an algorithm is applied to some input data to produce some output.

inference The process of using a machine learning model to perform a task given some data. For example, inference may be applied to a model to make predictions or to learn from, or reason about, data.

deep learning An approach to machine learning which makes use of neural network models with many layers.

stochastic gradient descent A common inference method for training a neural network model.

Infer.NET A software framework developed at Microsoft Research Cambridge which can do model-based machine learning automatically given a model definition. Available for download at dotnet.github.io/infer.

CHAPTER 1

A murder mystery

As the clock strikes midnight in the Old Tudor Mansion, a raging storm rattles the shutters and fills the house with the sound of thunder. The dead body of Mr Black lies slumped on the floor of the library, blood still oozing from the fatal wound. Quick to arrive on the scene is the famous sleuth Dr Bayes, who observes that there were only two other people in the Mansion at the time of the murder. So who committed this dastardly crime? Was it the fine upstanding pillar of the establishment Major Grey? Or was it the mysterious and alluring femme fatale Miss Auburn?

We begin our study of model-based machine learning by investigating a murder. Although seemingly simple, this murder mystery will introduce many of the key concepts that we will use throughout the book. You can reproduce all results in this chapter for yourself using the companion source code [Diethe et al., 2019].

The goal in tackling this mystery is to work out the identity of the murderer. Having only just discovered the body, we are very uncertain as to whether the murder was committed by Miss Auburn or Major Grey. Over the course of investigating the murder, we will use clues discovered at the crime scene to reduce this uncertainty as to who committed the murder.

DOI: 10.1201/9780429192685-2

(a) Major Grey   (b) Miss Auburn

Figure 1.1 Is the murderer Major Grey or Miss Auburn? Probabilities allow us to express how certain we are that a particular suspect is the murderer.

Immediately we face our first challenge, which is that we have to be able to handle quantities whose values are uncertain. In fact the need to deal with uncertainty arises throughout our increasingly data-driven world. In most applications, we will start off in a state of considerable uncertainty and, as we get more data, become increasingly confident. In a murder mystery, we start off very uncertain who the murderer is and then slowly get more and more certain as we uncover more clues. Later in the book, we will see many more examples where we need to represent uncertainty: when two players play each other in Xbox live it is more likely that the stronger player will win, but this is not guaranteed; we can be fairly sure that a user will reply to a particular email but we can never be certain.

Consequently, we need a principled framework for quantifying uncertainty which will allow us to create applications and build solutions in ways that can represent and process uncertain values. Fortunately, there is a simple framework for manipulating uncertain quantities which uses **probability** to quantify the degree of uncertainty. Many people are familiar with the idea of probability as the frequency with which a particular event occurs. For example, we might say that the probability of a coin landing heads is 50% which means that in a long run of flips, the coin will land heads approximately 50% of the time. In this book we will be using probabilities in a much more general sense to quantify uncertainty, even for situations, such as a murder, which occur only once.

Let us apply the concept of probability to our murder mystery. The probability that Miss Auburn is the murderer can range from 0% to 100%, where 0% means we are certain that Miss Auburn is innocent, while 100% means we are certain that she committed the murder. We can equivalently express probabilities on a scale from 0 to 1, where 1 is equivalent to 100%. From what we know about our two characters, we might think it is unlikely that someone with the impeccable credentials of Major Grey could commit such a heinous crime, and therefore our suspicion is directed towards the enigmatic Miss Auburn. Therefore, we might assume that the probability that Miss Auburn committed the crime is 70%, or equivalently 0.7.

To express this assumption, we need to be precise about what this 70% probability is referring to. We can do this by representing the identity of the murderer with a **random variable** – this is a variable (a named quantity) whose value we are uncertain about. We can define a random variable called `murderer` which can take one of two values: it equals either `Auburn` or `Grey`. Given this definition of `murderer`, we can write our 70% assumption in the form

$$P(\texttt{murderer} = \texttt{Auburn}) = 0.7 \tag{1.1}$$

where the notation $P(\ )$ denotes the probability of the quantity contained inside the brackets. Thus, equation (1.1) can be read as "the probability that the murderer was Miss Auburn is 70%". Our assumption of 70% for the probability that Auburn committed the murder may seem rather arbitrary – we will work with it for now, but in the next chapter we shall see how such probabilities can be *learned* from data.

We know that there are only two potential culprits and we are also assuming that only one of these two suspects actually committed the murder (in other words, they did not act together). Based on this assumption, the probability that Major Grey committed the crime must be 30%. This is because the two probabilities must add up to 100%, since one of the two suspects must be the murderer. We can write this probability in the same form as above:

$$P(\texttt{murderer} = \texttt{Grey}) = 0.3. \tag{1.2}$$

We can also express the fact that the two probabilities add up to 1.0:

$$P(\texttt{murderer} = \texttt{Grey}) + P(\texttt{murderer} = \texttt{Auburn}) = 1. \tag{1.3}$$

This is an example of the **normalisation constraint** for probabilities, which states that the probabilities of all possible values of a random variable must add up to 1.

If we write down the probabilities for all possible values of our random variable murderer, we get:

$$P(\text{murderer} = \text{Grey}) = 0.3$$
$$P(\text{murderer} = \text{Auburn}) = 0.7. \qquad (1.4)$$

Written together, this is an example of a **probability distribution**, because it specifies the probability for every possible state of the random variable murderer. We use the notation $P(\text{murderer})$ to denote the distribution over the random variable murderer. This can be viewed as a shorthand notation for the combination of $P(\text{murderer} = \text{Auburn})$ and $P(\text{murderer} = \text{Grey})$. As an example of using this notation, we can write the general form of the normalisation constraint:

$$\sum_{\text{murderer}} P(\text{murderer}) = 1 \qquad (1.5)$$

where the symbol $\sum$ means "sum" and the subscript "murderer" indicates that the sum is over the states of the random variable murderer, i.e. Auburn and Grey. Using this notation, the states of a random variable do not need to be listed out – very useful if there are a lot of possible states!

At this point, it is helpful to introduce a pictorial representation of a probability distribution that we can use to explain some of the later calculations. Figure 1.2 shows a square of area 1.0 which has been divided in proportion to the probabilities of our two suspects being the murderer. The square has a total area of 1.0 because of the normalisation constraint, and is divided into two regions. The region on the left has an area of 0.3, corresponding to the probability that Major Grey is the murderer, while the region on the right has an area of 0.7, corresponding to the probability that Miss Auburn is the murderer. The diagram therefore provides a simple visualisation of these probabilities. If we pick a point at random within the square, then the probability that it will land in the region corresponding to Major Grey is 0.3 (or equivalently 30%) and the probability that it will land in the region corresponding to Miss Auburn is 0.7 (or equivalently 70%). Randomly choosing a value such that the probability of picking any particular value is given by a proba-

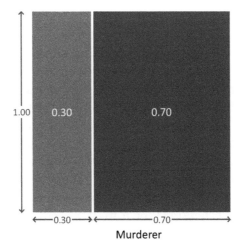

Figure 1.2 Representation of probabilities using areas. The grey area represents the probability that Major Grey is the murderer and the red area represents the probability that Miss Auburn is the murderer.

bility distribution, is known as **sampling**. Sampling can be very useful for understanding a probability distribution or for generating synthetic data sets – later in this book, we will see examples of both of these.

The Bernoulli distribution

The technical term for this type of distribution over a two-state random variable is a **Bernoulli distribution**, which is usually defined over the two states `true` and `false`. For our murder mystery, we can use `true` to mean `Auburn` and `false` to mean `Grey`. Using these states, a Bernoulli distribution over the variable `murderer` with a 0.7 probability of `true` (`Auburn`) and a 0.3 probability of `false` (`Grey`) is written $Bernoulli(\text{murderer}; 0.7)$. More generally, if the probability of `murderer` being `true` is some number p, we can write the distribution of `murderer` as $Bernoulli(\text{murderer}; p)$.

Often when we are using probability distributions, it will be unambiguous which variable the distribution applies to. In such situations we can simplify the notation, and instead of writing $Bernoulli(\text{murderer}; p)$ we just write $Bernoulli(p)$. It is important to appreciate that is just a shorthand notation and does not represent a distribution over p. Since we will be referring to distributions frequently throughout this book, it is very useful to have this kind of shorthand to keep notation clear and concise.

We can use the Bernoulli distribution with different values of the probability to represent different judgements or assessments of uncertainty, ranging from complete ignorance through to total certainty. For example, if we had absolutely no idea which of our suspects was guilty, we could assign $P(\texttt{murderer}) = Bernoulli(\texttt{murderer}; 0.5)$ or equivalently $P(\texttt{murderer}) = Bernoulli(0.5)$. In this case, both states have probability 50%. This is an example of a **uniform distribution** in which all states are equally probable. At the other extreme, if we were absolutely certain that Auburn was the murderer, then we would set $P(\texttt{murderer}) = Bernoulli(1)$, or if we were certain that Grey was the murderer then we would have $P(\texttt{murderer}) = Bernoulli(0)$. These are examples of a **point mass**, which is a distribution where all of the probability is assigned to one value of the random variable. In other words, we are certain about the value of the random variable.

So, using this new terminology, we have chosen the probability distribution over $\texttt{murderer}$ to be $Bernoulli(0.7)$. Next, we will show how to relate different random variables together to start solving the murder.

REVIEW OF CONCEPTS

probability   A measure of uncertainty which lies between 0 and 1, where 0 means impossible and 1 means certain. Probabilities are often expressed as percentages (such as 0%, 50% and 100%).

random variable   A variable (a named quantity) whose value is uncertain.

normalisation constraint   The constraint that the probabilities given by a probability distribution must add up to 1 over all possible values of the random variable. For example, for a $Bernoulli(p)$ distribution, the probability of true is p and so the probability of the only other state false must be $1 - p$.

probability distribution   A function which gives the probability for every possible value of a random variable. Written as $P(\texttt{A})$ for a random variable $\texttt{A}$.

sampling   Randomly choosing a value such that the probability of picking any particular value is given by a probability distribution. This is known as sampling from the distribution. For example, here are 10 samples from a *Bernoulli*(0.7) distribution: `false`, `true`, `false`, `false`, `true`, `true`, `true`, `false`, `true` and `true`. If we took a very large number of samples from a *Bernoulli*(0.7) distribution, then the percentage of the samples equal to `true` would be very close to 70%.

Bernoulli distribution   A probability distribution over a two-valued (binary) random variable. The Bernoulli distribution has one parameter p which is the probability of the value `true` and is written as *Bernoulli*(p). As an example, *Bernoulli*(0.5) represents the uncertainty in the outcome of a fair coin toss.

uniform distribution   A probability distribution where every possible value is equally probable. For example, *Bernoulli*(0.5) is a uniform distribution since `true` and `false` both have the same probability (of 0.5) and these are the only possible values.

point mass   A distribution which gives probability 1 to one value and probability 0 to all other values, which means that the random variable is certain to have the specified value. For example, *Bernoulli*(1) is a point mass indicating that the variable is certain to be `true`.

SELF ASSESSMENT 1.1

The following exercises will help embed the concepts you have learned in this section. It may help to refer back to the text or the review of concepts.

1. To get familiar with thinking about probabilities, estimate the probability of the following events, expressing each probability as a percentage.

   a. After visiting a product page on Amazon, a user chooses to buy the product.

   b. After receiving an email, a user chooses to reply to it.

   c. It will rain tomorrow where you live.

   d. When a murder is committed, the murderer turns out to be a member of the victim's family.

   Given your estimates, what is the probability of these events not happening? Remember the normalisation constraint. If you can, compare your estimates for these probabilities with someone else's and discuss where and why you disagree.

2. Write your answers to question 1 as Bernoulli distributions over suitably named random variables, using both the long and short forms.

3. Suppose I am certain that it will rain tomorrow where you live. What Bernoulli distribution represents my belief? What would the distribution be if instead I am certain that it will *not* rain tomorrow? What if I am completely unsure if it would rain or not?

4. For one of the events in question 1, write a program to print out 100 samples from a Bernoulli distribution with your estimated probability of the event happening (if you're not a programmer, you can use a spreadsheet instead). To sample from a *Bernoulli*(p), you first need a random number between 0 and 1 (RAND in Excel or random number functions in any programming language can give you this). To get one sample, you then see if the random number is less than p - in which case the sample is true, otherwise false. What proportion of the samples are true? You should find this is close to the parameter p. If you increase to 1,000 or 10,000 samples, you should find that the proportion gets closer and closer to p. We'll see why this happens later in the book.

1.1 INCORPORATING EVIDENCE

Dr Bayes searches the mansion thoroughly. She finds that the only weapons available are an ornate ceremonial dagger and an old army revolver. "One of these must be the murder weapon", she concludes.

So far, we have considered just one random variable: murderer. But now that we have some new information about the possible murder weapons, we can introduce a new random variable, weapon, to represent the choice of murder weapon. This new variable can take two values: revolver or dagger. Given this new variable, the next step is to use probabilities to express its relationship to our existing murderer variable. This will allow us to reason about how these variables affect each other and to make progress in solving the murder.

Suppose Major Grey were the murderer. We might believe that the probability of his choosing a revolver rather than a dagger for the murder is, say, 90% on the basis that he would be familiar with the use of such a gun from his time in the army. But if instead Miss Auburn were the murderer, we might think the probability of her using a revolver would be much smaller, say 20%, since she might be unfamiliar with the operation of a weapon which went out of use before she was born. This means that the probability distribution over the random variable weapon depends on whether the murderer is Major Grey or Miss Auburn. This is known as a **conditional probability distribution** because the probability values it gives vary depending on another random variable, in this case murderer. If Major Grey were the murderer, the conditional probability of choosing the revolver can be expressed like so:

$$P(\texttt{weapon} = \texttt{revolver}|\texttt{murderer} = \texttt{Grey}) = 0.9. \qquad (1.6)$$

Here the quantity on the left side of this equation is read as "the probability that the weapon is the revolver *given* that the murderer is Grey". It describes a probability distribution over the quantity on the left side of the vertical 'conditioning' bar (in this case the value of weapon), which depends on the value of any quantities on the right-hand side of the bar (in this case the value of murderer). We also say that the distribution over weapon is *conditioned* on the value of murderer.

Since the only other possibility for the weapon is a dagger, the probability that Major Grey would choose the dagger must be 10%,

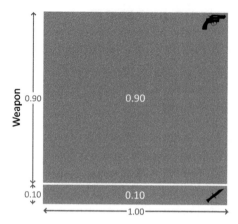

Figure 1.3 Representation of the probabilities for the two weapons, conditional on Major Grey being the murderer.

and hence

$$P(\texttt{weapon} = \texttt{dagger}|\texttt{murderer} = \texttt{Grey}) = 0.1. \qquad (1.7)$$

Again, we can also express this information in pictorial form, as shown in Figure 1.3. Here we see a square with a total area of 1.0. The upper region, with area 0.9, corresponds to the conditional probability of the weapon being the revolver, while the lower region, with area 0.1, corresponds to the conditional probability of the weapon being the dagger. If we pick a point at random uniformly from within the square (in other words, sample from the distribution), there is a 90% probability that the weapon will be the revolver.

Now suppose instead that it was Miss Auburn who committed the murder. Recall that we considered the probability of her choosing the revolver was 20%. We can therefore write

$$P(\texttt{weapon} = \texttt{revolver}|\texttt{murderer} = \texttt{Auburn}) = 0.2. \qquad (1.8)$$

Again, the only other choice of weapon is the dagger and so

$$P(\texttt{weapon} = \texttt{dagger}|\texttt{murderer} = \texttt{Auburn}) = 0.8. \qquad (1.9)$$

This conditional probability distribution can be represented pictorially as shown in Figure 1.4.

We can combine all of the above information into the more compact form

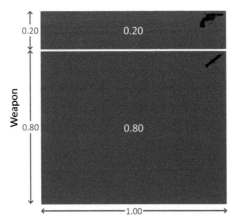

Figure 1.4 Representation of the probabilities for the two weapons, conditional on Miss Auburn being the murderer.

$$P(\texttt{weapon} = \texttt{revolver}|\texttt{murderer}) = \begin{cases} 0.9 & \text{if } \texttt{murderer} = \texttt{Grey} \\ 0.2 & \text{if } \texttt{murderer} = \texttt{Auburn}. \end{cases} \quad (1.10)$$

This can be expressed in an even more compact form as $P(\texttt{weapon}|\texttt{murderer})$. As before, we have a normalisation constraint which is a consequence of the fact that, for each of the suspects, the weapon used must have been either the revolver or the dagger. This constraint can be written as

$$\sum_{\texttt{weapon}} P(\texttt{weapon}|\texttt{murderer}) = 1 \quad (1.11)$$

where the sum is over the two states of the random variable `weapon`, that is for `weapon=revolver` and for `weapon=dagger`, with `murderer` held at any fixed value (`Grey` or `Auburn`). Notice that we do not expect that the probabilities add up to 1 over the two states of the random variable `murderer`, which is why the two numbers in equation (1.10) do not add up to 1. These probabilities do not need to add up to 1, because they refer to the probability that the revolver was the murder weapon in two different circumstances: if Grey was the murderer and if Auburn was the murderer. For example, the probability of choosing the revolver could be high in both circumstances or low in both circumstances – so the normalisation constraint does not apply.

Conditional probabilities can be written in the form of a **conditional probability table** (CPT) – which is the form we will often

Table 1.1 The conditional probability table for $P(\text{weapon}|\text{murderer})$. Table columns correspond to values of the conditioned variable weapon, rows correspond to values of the conditioning variable murderer, and table cells contain the conditional probability values. The normalisation constraint means that the values in any row must add up to 1. We have also added blue bars to the table to provide a visual indication of the probability values.

murderer	weapon=revolver	weapon=dagger
Auburn	0.200	0.800
Grey	0.900	0.100

use in this book. For example, the conditional probability table for $P(\text{weapon}|\text{murderer})$ looks like this: As we just discussed, the normalisation constraint means that the probabilities in the rows of Table 1.1 must add up to 1, but not the probabilities in the columns.

Independent variables

We have assumed that the probability of each choice of weapon changes depending on the value of murderer. We say that these two variables are *dependent*. More commonly, we tend to focus on what variables do not affect each other, in which case we say they are **independent variables**. Consider for example, whether it is raining or not outside the Old Tudor Mansion at the time of the murder. It is reasonable to assume that this variable raining has no effect whatsoever on who the murderer is (nor is itself affected by who the murderer is). So we have assumed that the variables murderer and raining are independent. You can test this kind of assumption by asking the question "Does learning about the one variable, tell me anything about the other variable?". So in this case, the question is "Does learning whether it was raining or not tell me anything about the identity of the murderer?", for which a reasonable answer is "No".

If we tried to write down a conditional probability for $P(\text{raining}|\text{murderer})$, then it would give the same probability for raining whether murderer was Grey or Auburn. If this were not true, learning about one variable would tell us something about the other variable, through a change in its probability distribution. We can express independence between these two variables mathematically.

$$P(\text{raining}|\text{murderer}) = P(\text{raining}) \qquad (1.12)$$

What this equation says is that the probability of raining given knowledge of the murderer is exactly the same as the probability of raining without taking into account murderer. In other words, the two variables are independent. This also holds the other way around:

$$P(\text{murderer}|\text{raining}) = P(\text{murderer}) \qquad (1.13)$$

Independence is an important concept in model-based machine learning, since any variable we do not explicitly include in our model is assumed to be independent of all variables in the model. We will see further examples of independence later in this chapter.

Let us take a moment to recap what we have achieved so far. In the first section, we specified the probability that the murderer was Major Grey (and therefore the complementary probability that the murderer was Miss Auburn). In this section, we also wrote down the probabilities for different choices of weapon for each of our suspects. In the next section, we will see how we can use all these probabilities to incorporate evidence from the crime scene and reason about the identity of the murderer.

REVIEW OF CONCEPTS

conditional probability distribution A probability distribution over some random variable A which changes its value depending on some other variable B, written as $P(\text{A}|\text{B})$. For example, if the probability of choosing each murder weapon (weapon) depends on who the murderer is (murderer), we can capture this in the conditional probability distribution $P(\text{weapon}|\text{murderer})$. Conditional probability distributions can also depend on more than one variable, for example $P(\text{A}|\text{B}, \text{C}, \text{D})$.

conditional probability table A table which defines a conditional probability, where the columns correspond to values of the conditioned variable and rows correspond to the values of the conditioning variable(s). For any setting of the conditioning variable(s), the probabilities over the conditioned variable must add up to 1 – so the values in any row must add up to 1. For example, here is a conditional probability table capturing the conditional probability of weapon given murderer:

murderer	weapon=revolver	weapon=dagger
Auburn	0.200	0.800
Grey	0.900	0.100

independent variables Two random variables are independent if learning about one does not provide any information about the other. Mathematically, two variables A and B are independent if

$$P(A|B) = P(A)$$
$$P(B|A) = P(B)$$

This is an important concept in model-based machine learning, since all variables in the model are assumed to be independent of any variable not in the model.

SELF ASSESSMENT 1.2

The following exercises will help embed the concepts you have learned in this section. It may help to refer back to the text or the review of concepts.

1. To get familiar with thinking about conditional probabilities, estimate conditional probability tables for each of the following.

   a. The probability of being late for work, conditioned on whether or not traffic is bad.

   b. The probability a user replies to an email, conditioned on whether or not he knows the sender.

   c. The probability that it will rain on a particular day, conditioned on whether or not it rained on the previous day.

   Ensure that the rows of your conditional probability tables add up to one. If you can, compare your estimates for these probabilities with someone else's and discuss where and why you disagree.

2. Pick an example, like one of the ones above, from your life or work. You should choose an example where one binary (two-valued) variable affects another. Estimate the conditional probability table that represents how one of these variables affects the other.

3. For one of the events in question 1, write a program to print out 100 samples of the conditioned variable for each value of the conditioning variable. Print the samples side by side and compare the proportion of samples in which the event occurs for when the conditioning variable is true to when it is false. Does the frequency of events look consistent with your common sense in each case? If not, go back and refine your conditional probability table and try again.

1.2   UPDATING OUR BELIEFS

Searching carefully around the library, Dr Bayes spots a bullet lodged in the book case. "Hmm, interesting", she says, "I think this could be an important clue".

So it seems that the murder weapon was the revolver, not the dagger. Our intuition is that this new evidence points more strongly towards Major Grey than it does to Miss Auburn, since the Major, due to his age and military background, is more likely to have experience with a revolver than Miss  Auburn. But how can we use this information?

A convenient way to think about the probabilities we have looked at so far is as a description of the process by which we believe the murder took place, taking account of the various sources of uncertainty. So, in this process, we first pick the murderer with the help of Figure 1.2. This shows that there is a 30% chance of choosing Major Grey and a 70% chance of choosing Miss Auburn. Let us suppose that Miss Auburn was the murderer. We can then refer to Figure 1.4 to pick which weapon she used. There is a 20% chance that she would have used the revolver and an 80% chance that she would have used the dagger. Let's consider the event of Miss Auburn picking the revolver. The probability of choosing Miss Auburn *and* the revolver is therefore 70% × 20% = 14%. This is the **joint probability** of choosing Auburn and revolver. If we repeat this exercise for the other three combinations of murderer and weapon, we obtain the joint probability distribution over the two random variables, which we can illustrate pictorially as seen in Figure 1.5.

Figure 1.6 shows how this joint distribution was constructed from the previous distributions we have defined. We have taken the left-hand slice of the $P(\texttt{murderer})$ square corresponding to Major Grey, and divided it vertically in proportion to the two regions of the conditional probability square for Grey. Likewise, we have taken the right-hand slice of the $P(\texttt{murderer})$ square corresponding Miss Auburn, and divided it vertically in proportion to the two regions of the conditional probability square for Auburn.

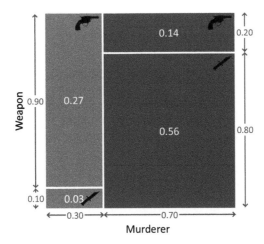

Figure 1.5 Representation of the joint probabilities for the two random variables `murderer` and `weapon`.

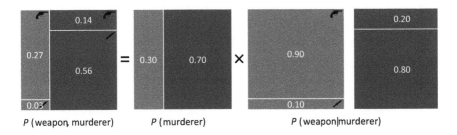

Figure 1.6 The joint distribution for our two-variable model, shown as a product of two factors.

We denote this joint probability distribution by $P(\mathtt{weapon}, \mathtt{murderer})$, which should be read as "the probability of `weapon` *and* `murderer`". In general, the joint distribution of two random variables A and B can be written $P(\mathtt{A}, \mathtt{B})$ and specifies the probability for each possible combination of settings of A and B. Because probabilities must sum to one, we have

$$\sum_{\mathtt{A}} \sum_{\mathtt{B}} P(\mathtt{A}, \mathtt{B}) = 1. \qquad (1.14)$$

Here the notation $\sum_{A}$ denotes a sum over all possible states of the random variable A, and likewise for B. This corresponds to the total area of the square in Figure 1.5 being 1, and arises because we assume the world consists of one, and only one, combination of murderer and weapon. Picking a point randomly in this new square corresponds to sampling from the joint probability distribution.

1.2.1 Two rules for working with joint probabilities

We'd like to use our joint probability distribution to update our beliefs about who committed the murder, in the light of this compelling new evidence. To do this, we need to introduce two important rules for working with joint distributions.

From the discussion above, we see that our joint probability distribution is obtained by taking the probability distribution over murderer and multiplying by the conditional distribution of weapon. This can be written in the form

$$P(\texttt{weapon}, \texttt{murderer}) = P(\texttt{murderer})P(\texttt{weapon}|\texttt{murderer}). \quad (1.15)$$

Equation (1.15) is an example of a very important result called the **product rule of probability**. The product rule says that the joint distribution of A and B can be written as the product of the distribution over A and the conditional distribution of B conditioned on the value of A, in the form

$$P(\texttt{A}, \texttt{B}) = P(\texttt{A})P(\texttt{B}|\texttt{A}). \quad (1.16)$$

Now suppose we sum up the values in the two left-hand regions of Figure 1.5 corresponding to Major Grey. Their total area is 0.3, as we expect because we know that the probability of Grey being the murderer is 0.3. The sum is over the different possibilities for the choice of weapon, so we can express this in the form

$$\sum_{\texttt{weapon}} P(\texttt{weapon}, \texttt{murderer} = \texttt{Grey}) = P(\texttt{murderer} = \texttt{Grey}). \quad (1.17)$$

Similarly, the entries in the second column, corresponding to the murderer being Miss Auburn, must add up to 0.7. Combining these together, we can write

$$\sum_{\texttt{weapon}} P(\texttt{weapon}, \texttt{murderer}) = P(\texttt{murderer}). \quad (1.18)$$

This is an example of the **sum rule of probability**, which says that the probability distribution over a random variable A is obtained by summing the joint distribution $P(\texttt{A}, \texttt{B})$ over all values of B

$$P(\mathtt{A}) = \sum_{\mathtt{B}} P(\mathtt{A}, \mathtt{B}). \tag{1.19}$$

In this context, the distribution $P(\mathtt{A})$ is known as the **marginal distribution** for $\mathtt{A}$ and the act of summing out $\mathtt{B}$ is called **marginalisation**. We can equally apply the sum rule to marginalise over the murderer to find the probability that each of the weapons was used, irrespective of who used them. If we sum the areas of the top two regions of Figure 1.5, we see that the probability of the weapon being the revolver was $0.27 + 0.14 = 0.41$ or 41%. Similarly, if we add up the areas of the bottom two regions, we see that the probability that the weapon was the dagger is $0.03 + 0.56 = 0.59$ or 59%. The two marginal probabilities then add up to 1, which we expect since the weapon must have been either the revolver or the dagger.

The sum and product rules are very general. They apply not just when $\mathtt{A}$ and $\mathtt{B}$ are binary random variables, but also when they are multi-state random variables, and even when they are continuous (in which case the sums are replaced by integrations). Furthermore, $\mathtt{A}$ and $\mathtt{B}$ could each represent sets of several random variables. For example, if $\mathtt{B} \equiv \{\mathtt{C}, \mathtt{D}\}$, then from the product rule (1.16) we have

$$P(\mathtt{A}, \mathtt{C}, \mathtt{D}) = P(\mathtt{A})P(\mathtt{C}, \mathtt{D}|\mathtt{A}) \tag{1.20}$$

and similarly the sum rule (1.19) gives

$$P(\mathtt{A}) = \sum_{\mathtt{C}} \sum_{\mathtt{D}} P(\mathtt{A}, \mathtt{C}, \mathtt{D}). \tag{1.21}$$

The last result is particularly useful since it shows that we can find the marginal distribution for a particular random variable in a joint distribution by summing over all the other random variables, no matter how many there are.

Together, the product rule and sum rule provide the two key results that we will need throughout the book in order to manipulate and calculate probabilities. It is remarkable that the rich and powerful complexity of probabilistic reasoning is all founded on these two simple rules.

1.2.2 Inference using the joint distribution

We now have the tools that we need to incorporate the fact that the weapon was the revolver. Intuitively, we expect that this should increase the probability that Grey was the murderer, but to confirm this,

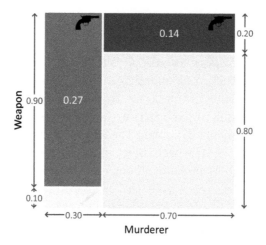

Figure 1.7 This shows the joint distribution from Figure 1.5 in which the regions corresponding to the dagger have been eliminated.

we need to calculate that updated probability. The process of computing revised probability distributions after we have observed the values of some of the random variables is called **probabilistic inference**. Inference is the cornerstone of model-based machine learning – it can be used for reasoning about a situation, learning from data, making predictions – in fact any machine learning task can be achieved using inference.

We can do inference using the joint probability distribution shown in Figure 1.5. Before we observe which weapon was used to commit the crime, all points within this square are equally likely. Now that we know the weapon was the revolver, we can rule out the two lower regions corresponding to the weapon being the dagger, as illustrated in Figure 1.7.

Because all points in the remaining two regions are equally likely, we see that the probability of the murderer being Major Grey is given by the fraction of the remaining area given by the grey box on the left,

$$P(\texttt{murderer} = \texttt{Grey}|\texttt{weapon} = \texttt{revolver}) = \frac{0.27}{0.27 + 0.14} \simeq 0.66$$

in other words, a 66% probability. This is significantly higher than the 30% probability we had before observing that the weapon used was the revolver. We see that our intuition is therefore correct and it now looks more likely that Grey is the murderer rather than Auburn.

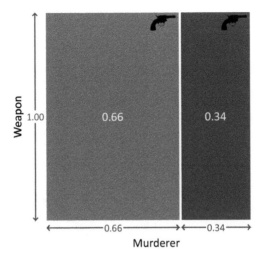

Figure 1.8 Representation of the posterior probabilities that Grey or Auburn was the murderer, given that the weapon is the revolver.

The probability that we assigned to Grey being the murderer *before* seeing the evidence of the bullet is sometimes called the **prior probability** (or just the *prior*), while the revised probability *after* seeing the new evidence is called the **posterior probability** (or just the *posterior*).

The probability that Miss Auburn is the murderer is similarly given by

$$P(\texttt{murderer} = \texttt{Auburn}|\texttt{weapon} = \texttt{revolver}) = \frac{0.14}{0.27 + 0.14} \simeq 0.34.$$

Because the murderer is either Grey or Auburn these two probabilities again sum to 1. We can capture this pictorially by re-scaling the regions in Figure 1.7 to give the diagram shown in Figure 1.8.

We have seen that, as new data, or evidence, is collected, we can use the product and sum rules to revise the probabilities to reflect changing levels of uncertainty. The system can be viewed as having *learned* from that data.

So, after all this hard work, have we finally solved our murder mystery? Well, given the evidence so far it appears that Grey is more likely to be the murderer, but the probability of his guilt currently stands at 66% which feels too small for a conviction. But how high a probability would we need? To find an answer, we turn to William Blackstone's principle [Blackstone, 1765]:

> *"Better that ten guilty persons escape than one innocent suffer."*

We therefore need a probability of guilt for our murderer which exceeds $\frac{10}{10+1} \approx 91\%$. To achieve this level of proof, we will need to gather more evidence from the crime scene, and to make a corresponding extension to our joint probability in order to incorporate this new evidence. We'll look at how to do this in the next section.

REVIEW OF CONCEPTS

joint probability A probability distribution over multiple variables which gives the probability of the variables jointly taking a particular configuration of values. For example, $P(A, B, C)$ is a joint distribution over the random variables A, B and C.

product rule of probability The rule that the joint distribution of A and B can be written as the product of the distribution over A and the conditional distribution of B conditioned on the value of A, in the form

$$P(A, B) = P(A)P(B|A).$$

sum rule of probability The rule that the probability distribution over a random variable A is obtained by summing the joint distribution $P(A, B)$ over all values of B

$$P(A) = \sum_B P(A, B).$$

marginal distribution The distribution over a random variable computed by using the sum rule to sum a joint distribution over all other variables in the distribution.

marginalisation The process of summing a joint distribution to compute a marginal distribution.

probabilistic inference The process of computing probability distributions over certain specified random variables, usually after observing the value of other random variables.

prior probability The probability distribution over a random variable before seeing any data. Careful choice of prior distributions is an important part of model design.

posterior probability The updated probability distribution over a random variable after some data has been taken into account. The aim of inference is to compute posterior probability distributions over variables of interest.

SELF ASSESSMENT 1.3

The following exercises will help embed the concepts you have learned in this section. It may help to refer back to the text or the review of concepts.

1. Check for yourself that the joint probabilities for the four areas in Figure 1.5 are correct and confirm that their total is 1. Use this figure to compute the posterior probability over **murderer**, if the murder weapon had been the dagger rather than the revolver.

2. Choose one of the following scenarios (continued from the previous self assessment) or choose your own scenario

   a. Whether you are late for work, depending on whether or not traffic is bad.

   b. Whether a user replies to an email, depending on whether or not he knows the sender.

   c. Whether it will rain on a particular day, depending on whether or not it rained on the previous day.

   For your selected scenario, pick a suitable prior probability for the conditioning variable (for example, whether the traffic is bad, whether the user knows the sender, whether it rained the previous day). Recall the conditional probability table that you estimated in the previous self assessment. Using the prior and this conditional distribution, use the product rule to calculate the joint distribution over the two variables in the scenario. Draw this joint distribution pictorially, like the example of Figure 1.5. Make sure you label each area with the probability value, and that these values all add up to 1.

3. Now assume that you know the value of the conditioned variable, for example, assume that you are late for work on a particular day. Now compute the posterior probability of the conditioning variable, for example, the probability that the traffic was bad on that day. You can achieve this using your diagram from the previous question, by crossing out the areas that don't apply and finding the fraction of the remaining area where the conditioning event happened.

4. For your joint probability distribution, write a program to print out 1,000 joint samples of both variables. Compute the fraction of samples that have each possible pair of values. Check that this is close to your joint probability table. Now change the program to only print out those samples which are consistent with your known value from the previous question (for example, samples where you are late for work). What fraction of these samples have each possible pair of values now? How does this compare to your answer to the previous question?

1.3   A MODEL OF A MURDER

To solve the murder, we need to incorporate more evidence from the crime scene. Each new piece of evidence will add another random variable into our joint distribution. To manage this growing number of variables, we will now introduce the central concept of this book: the **probabilistic model**. A probabilistic model consists of:

- A set of random variables,

- A joint probability distribution over these variables (i.e. a distribution that assigns a probability to every configuration of these variables such that the probabilities add up to 1 over all possible configurations).

Once we have a probabilistic model, we can reason about the variables it contains, make predictions, learn about the values of some random variables given the values of others, and in general, answer any possible question that can be stated in terms of the random variables included in the model. This makes a probabilistic model an incredibly powerful tool for doing machine learning.

We can think of a probabilistic model as a set of assumptions we are making about the problem we are trying to solve, where any assumptions involving uncertainty are expressed using probabilities. The best way to understand how this is done, and how the model can be used to reason and make predictions, is by looking at example models. In this chapter, we give the example of a probabilistic model of a murder. In later chapters, we shall build a variety of more complex models for other applications. All the machine learning applications in this book will be solved solely through the use of probabilistic models.

So far we've constructed a model with two random variables: `murderer` and `weapon`. For this two-variable model, we were able to write the joint distribution pictorially, like so:

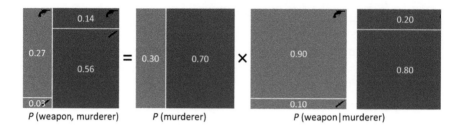

Figure 1.9 The joint distribution for our two-variable model, shown as a product of two factors.

Unfortunately, if we increase the number of random variables in our model beyond two (or maybe three), we cannot represent the joint distribution using this pictorial notation. But in real models, there will typically be anywhere from hundreds to hundreds of millions of random variables. We need a different notation to represent and work with such large joint distributions.

The notation that we will use exploits the fact that most joint distributions can be written as a product of a number of terms or **factors** each of which refers to only a small number of variables. For example, our joint distribution above is the product of two factors: $P(\texttt{murderer})$ which refers to one variable and $P(\texttt{weapon}|\texttt{murderer})$ which refers to two variables. Even for joint distributions with millions of variables, the factors which make up the distribution usually refer to only a few of these variables. As a result, we can represent a complex joint distribution using a **factor graph** [Kschischang et al., 2001] that shows which factors make up the distribution and what variables those factors refer to.

Figure 1.10 shows a factor graph for the two-variable joint distribution above. There are two types of nodes in the graph: a **variable node** for each variable in the model and a **factor node** for each factor in the joint distribution. Variable nodes are shown as white ellipses (or rounded boxes) containing the name of the variable. Factor nodes are small black squares, labelled with the factor that they represent. We connect each factor node to the variable nodes that it refers to. For example, the $P(\texttt{murderer})$ factor node is connected only to the murderer variable node since that is the only variable it refers to, whilst $P(\texttt{weapon}|\texttt{murderer})$ connects to both the weapon and murderer variable nodes, since it refers to both variables. Finally, if the factor defines a distribution over one of its variables, we draw an arrow on the edge

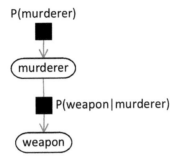

Figure 1.10 Factor graph for the murder mystery model. The model contains two random variables murderer and weapon, shown as white nodes, and two factors $P(\text{murderer})$ and $P(\text{weapon}|\text{murderer})$, shown as black squares.

pointing to that variable (the **child variable**). If the factor defines a conditional distribution, the other edges from that factor connect to the variables being conditioned on (the **parent variables**) and do not have arrows.

The factor graph of Figure 1.10 provides a complete description of our joint probability, since it can be found by computing the product of the distributions represented by the factor nodes. As we look at more complex factor graphs throughout the book, it will always hold that the joint probability distribution over the random variables (represented by the variable nodes) can be written as the product of the factors (represented by the factor nodes). The joint distribution gives a complete specification of a model, because it defines the probability for every possible combination of values for all of the random variables in the model. Notice that in Figure 1.9 the joint distribution was represented explicitly, but in the factor graph it is represented only indirectly, via the factors.

Since we want our factor graphs to tell us as much as possible about the joint distribution, we should label the factors as precisely as possible. For example, since we know that $P(\text{murderer})$ defines a prior distribution of $Bernoulli(0.7)$ over murderer, we can label the factor "Bernoulli(0.7)". We do not need to mention the murderer variable in the factor label since the factor is only connected to the murderer variable node, and so the distribution must be over murderer. This allows more informative labelling of the factor graph, like so:

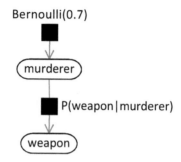

Figure 1.11 Factor graph representation of the murder mystery model with the *Bernoulli* prior over `murderer` labelled explicitly.

In this book, we will aim to label factors in our factor graphs so that the function represented by each factor is as clear as possible.

There is one final aspect of factor graph notation that we need to cover. When doing inference in our two-variable model, we observed the random variable `weapon` to have the value `revolver`. This step of observing random variables is such an important one in model-based machine learning that we introduce a special graphical notation to depict it. When a random variable is observed, the corresponding node in the factor graph is shaded (and sometimes also labelled with the observed value), as shown for our murder mystery in Figure 1.12.

Representing a probabilistic model using a factor graph gives many benefits:

- It provides a simple way to visualise the structure of a probabilistic model and see which variables influence each other.

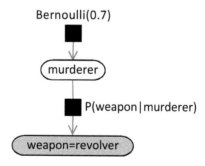

Figure 1.12 The factor graph for the murder mystery, with the `weapon` node shaded to indicate that this random variable has been observed, and is fixed to the value `revolver`.

- It can be used to motivate and design new models, by making appropriate modifications to the graph.

- The assumptions encoded in the model can be clearly seen and communicated to others.

- Insights into the properties of a model can be obtained by operations performed on the graph.

- Computations on the model (such as inference) can be performed by efficient algorithms that exploit the factor graph structure.

We shall illustrate these points in the context of specific examples throughout this book.

1.3.1 Inference without computing the joint distribution

Having observed the value of weapon, we previously computed the full joint distribution and used it to evaluate the posterior distribution of murderer. However, for most real-world models, it is not possible to do this, since the joint distribution would be over too many variables to allow it to be computed directly. Instead, now that we have our joint distribution represented as a product of factors, we can arrive at the same result by using only the individual factors – in a way which is typically far more efficient to compute. The key lies in applying the product and sum rules of probability in an appropriate way. From the product rule (1.15), we have

$$P(\text{weapon}, \text{murderer}) = P(\text{weapon}|\text{murderer})P(\text{murderer}). \quad (1.22)$$

However, by symmetry, we can equally well write

$$P(\text{weapon}, \text{murderer}) = P(\text{murderer}|\text{weapon})P(\text{weapon}). \quad (1.23)$$

Equating the right-hand sides of these two equations and re-arranging, we obtain

$$P(\text{murderer}|\text{weapon}) = \frac{P(\text{weapon}|\text{murderer})P(\text{murderer})}{P(\text{weapon})}. \quad (1.24)$$

This is an example of **Bayes' theorem** or *Bayes' rule* [Bayes, 1763], which plays a fundamental role in many inference calculations (see Panel 1.1). Here $P(\text{murderer})$ is the prior probability distribution

Panel 1.1: Bayes' Theorem

Bayes' theorem allows us to express a conditional probability distribution such as $P(\mathsf{A}|\mathsf{B})$ in terms of the "reversed" conditional distribution $P(\mathsf{B}|\mathsf{A})$:

$$P(\mathsf{A}|\mathsf{B}) = \frac{P(\mathsf{A})P(\mathsf{B}|\mathsf{A})}{P(\mathsf{B})}. \tag{1.25}$$

Bayes' theorem is particularly useful when we want to update the distribution of some uncertain quantity A when we are given some new information represented by the random variable B. For instance, in the murder mystery, we want to know the identity of the murderer A and we have just discovered the choice of weapon B. If we didn't know B, then our knowledge of A would be described by $P(\mathsf{A})$, which we call the *prior*. Once we know the value of B, we can compute the revised distribution $P(\mathsf{A}|\mathsf{B})$ known as the *posterior*. They are related by the reversed conditional distribution $P(\mathsf{B}|\mathsf{A})$ which is known as the *likelihood*. Note that the likelihood should not be viewed as a probability distribution over B, because the value of B is assumed to be known, but rather as a function of the random variable A, and for this reason it is also known as the *likelihood function*. Note also that its sum over A does not necessarily equal 1.

We can also write Bayes' theorem in words:

$$\text{posterior} = \frac{\text{prior} \times \text{likelihood}}{\text{normaliser}}. \tag{1.26}$$

Here the 'normaliser' is just the value of $P(\mathsf{B})$ and is the quantity which ensures that the posterior distribution is normalised. From the sum rule (1.19), it is given by

$$P(\mathsf{B}) = \sum_{\mathsf{A}} P(\mathsf{A})P(\mathsf{B}|\mathsf{A}) \tag{1.27}$$

and can therefore be computed from the prior and the likelihood function.

over the random variable `murderer` and is one of the things we specified when we defined our model for the murder mystery. Similarly, $P(\texttt{weapon}|\texttt{murderer})$ is also something we specified, and is called the **likelihood function** and should be viewed as a function of the random variable murderer. The quantity on the left-hand side $P(\text{murderer}|\text{weapon})$ is the posterior probability distribution over the murderer random variable, i.e. the distribution *after* we have observed the evidence of the revolver.

The denominator $P(\text{weapon})$ in equation (1.24) plays the role of a normalisation constant and ensures that the left-hand side of Bayes' theorem is correctly normalised (i.e. adds up to 1 when summed over all possible states of the random variable murderer). It can be computed from the prior and the likelihood using

$$P(\text{weapon}) = \sum_{\text{murderer}} P(\text{weapon}|\text{murderer})P(\text{murderer}) \quad (1.28)$$

which follows from the product and sum rules. When working with Bayes' rule, it is sometimes useful to drop this denominator $P(\text{weapon})$ and instead write

$$P(\text{murderer}|\text{weapon}) \propto P(\text{weapon}|\text{murderer})P(\text{murderer}) \quad (1.29)$$

where $\propto$ means that the left-hand side is proportional to the right-hand side (i.e. they are equal up to a constant that does not depend on the value of murderer). We do not need to compute the denominator because the normalisation constraint tells us that the conditional probability distribution $P(\text{murderer}|\text{weapon})$ must add up to one across all values of murderer. Once we have evaluated the right-hand side of (1.29) to give a number for each of the two values of murderer, we can scale these two numbers so that they sum up to one, to get the resulting posterior distribution.

Now let us apply Bayes' rule to the murder mystery problem. We know that weapon=revolver, so we can evaluate the right-hand side of equation (1.29) for both murderer=Grey and murderer=Auburn giving:

$$P(\text{murderer} = \text{Grey}|\text{weapon} = \text{revolver}) \quad \propto \quad 0.3 \times 0.9 = 0.27$$
$$P(\text{murderer} = \text{Auburn}|\text{weapon} = \text{revolver}) \quad \propto \quad 0.7 \times 0.2 = 0.14.$$

These numbers sum to 0.41. To get probabilities, we need to scale both numbers to sum to 1 (by dividing by 0.41) which gives:

$$P(\text{murderer} = \text{Grey}|\text{weapon} = \text{revolver}) = \frac{0.27}{0.41} \simeq 0.66$$
$$P(\text{murderer} = \text{Auburn}|\text{weapon} = \text{revolver}) = \frac{0.14}{0.41} \simeq 0.34.$$

This is the same result as before. Although we have arrived at the same result by a different route, this latter approach using Bayes' theorem is preferable as we did not need to compute the joint distribution. With only two random variables so far in our murder mystery this might not look like a significant improvement, but as we go to more complex problems we will see that successive applications of the rules of probability allow us to work with small sub-sets of random variables – even in models with millions of variables!

REVIEW OF CONCEPTS

probabilistic model   A set of random variables combined with a joint distribution that assigns a probability to every configuration of these variables.

factors   Functions (usually of a small number of variables) which are multiplied together to give a joint probability distribution (which may be over a large number of variables). Factors are represented as small black squares in a factor graph.

factor graph   A representation of a probabilistic model which uses a graph with factor nodes (black squares) for each factor in the joint distribution and variable nodes (white, rounded) for each variable in the model. Edges connect each factor node to the variable nodes that it refers to.

variable node   A node in a factor graph that represents a random variable in the model, shown as a white ellipse or rounded box containing the variable name.

factor node   A node in a factor graph that represents a factor in the joint distribution of a model, shown as a small black square labelled with the factor name.

child variable   For a factor node, the connected variable that the arrow points to. This indicates that the factor defines a probability distribution over this variable, possibly conditioned on the other variables connected to this factor. The child variable for a factor is usually drawn directly below the factor.

parent variables   For a factor node, the connected variable(s) with edges that do not have arrows pointing to them. When a factor defines a conditional probability distribution, these are the variables that are conditioned on. The parent variables for a factor are usually drawn above the factor.

Bayes' theorem The fundamental theorem that lets us do efficient inference in probabilistic models. It defines how to update our belief about a random variable A after receiving new information B, so that we move from our prior belief $P(A)$ to our posterior belief given B, $P(A|B)$.

$$P(A|B) = \frac{P(A)P(B|A)}{P(B)}.$$

See Panel 1.1 for more details.

likelihood function A conditional probability viewed as a function of its conditioned variable. For example, $P(B|A)$ can be viewed as a function of A when B is observed and we are interested in inferring A. It is important to note that this is not a distribution over A, since $P(B|A)$ does not have to sum to 1 over all values of A. To get a distribution over A from a likelihood function, you need to apply Bayes' theorem (see Panel 1.1).

SELF ASSESSMENT 1.4

The following exercises will help embed the concepts you have learned in this section. It may help to refer back to the text or the review of concepts.

1. Use Bayes' theorem to compute the posterior probability over `murderer`, for the case that the murder weapon was the dagger rather than the revolver. Compare this to your answer from the previous self-assessment.

2. For the scenario you chose in the previous self assessment, draw the factor graph corresponding to the joint distribution. Ensure that you label the factors as precisely as possible. Verify that the product of factors in the factor graph is equal to the joint distribution.

3. Repeat the inference task from the previous self-assessment (computing the posterior probability of the conditioning variable) using Bayes' theorem rather than using the joint distribution. Check that you get the same answer as before.

1.4 EXTENDING THE MODEL

Dr Bayes pulls out her trusty magnifying glass and contin-ues her investigation of the crime scene. As she examines the floor near Mr Black's body she discovers a hair lying on top of the pool of blood. "Aha" exclaims Dr Bayes "this hair must belong to someone who was in the room when the murder took place!" Looking more closely at the hair, Dr Bayes sees that it is not the lustrous red of Miss Auburn's vibrant locks, nor indeed the jet black of the victim's hair, but the distinguished silver of Major Grey!

Now that we are equipped with the concept of factor graphs, we can extend our model to incorporate this addi-tional clue from the crime scene. The hair is powerful evidence in-dicating that Major Grey was present at the time of the mur-der, but there is also the possi-bility that the hair was stolen by Miss Auburn and planted at the crime scene to mislead our perceptive sleuth. As before, we can capture these thoughts quantitatively using a conditional probability distribu-tion. Let us denote the new information by the random variable `hair`, which takes the value `true` if Major Grey's hair is discovered at the scene of the crime, and `false` otherwise. Clearly the discovery of the hair points much more strongly to Grey than to Auburn, but it does not rule out Auburn completely.

Suppose we think there is a 50% chance that Grey would acciden-tally leave one of his hairs at the crime scene if he were the murderer, but that there is only a 5% chance that Auburn would think to plant a grey hair if she were the murderer. The conditional probability dis-tribution would then be

$$P(\texttt{hair} = \texttt{true}|\texttt{murderer}) = \begin{cases} 0.5 & \text{if } \texttt{murderer} = \texttt{Grey} \\ 0.05 & \text{if } \texttt{murderer} = \texttt{Auburn}. \end{cases} \quad (1.30)$$

As we have seen before, this is the conditional probability of `hair` being `true` given two different values of `murderer`, not a probability distribution over `hair`, and so the numbers in (1.30) do not have to add up to one.

In writing the conditional probability this way, we have actually made an additional assumption: that the probability of one of Major Grey's hairs being found at the scene of the crime only depends on who committed the murder, and not anything else – including the choice of weapon that was used to commit the murder. This assumption has arisen because the conditional probability in (1.30) does not include `weapon` in the variables being conditioned on. Mathematically, this assumption can be expressed as

$$P(\texttt{hair}|\texttt{weapon}, \texttt{murderer}) = P(\texttt{hair}|\texttt{murderer}), \qquad (1.31)$$

which says that the distribution of `hair` is independent of the value of `weapon` once we have conditioned on the value of `murderer`. For this reason, it is known as a **conditional independence** assumption. Notice that (1.31) has a similar form to the equations which hold when two variables are independent, e.g. (1.12), but has an additional conditioning variable on both sides.

The question to ask when considering a conditional independence assumption is "Does learning about one variable tell me anything about the other variable if I knew the value of the conditioning variable?" In this case that would be "Does learning about the hair tell me anything about the choice of weapon if I already knew who the murderer was?" Reasonably, the answer in this case might be that you could learn a little (for example, the dagger might mean the murderer had to get closer to the victim and so was more likely to drop a hair). However, for the sake of simplicity, we assume that this conditional independence assumption holds.

Figure 1.13 shows the factor graph corresponding to our expanded model with the new `hair` variable and a new factor representing this conditional distribution. Our conditional independence assumption has a simple graphical interpretation, namely that there is no edge connecting the `weapon` node directly to the factor representing the conditional distribution $P(\texttt{hair}|\texttt{murderer})$. The only way to get from the `weapon` node to the `hair` node is via the `murderer` node. We see that the *missing* edges in the factor graph capture independence assumptions built into the model.

There is an alternative graphical representation of a model called a **Bayesian network** or *Bayes net* that emphasises such independence assumptions, at the cost of hiding information about the factors. It

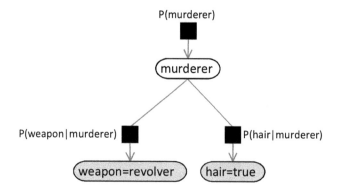

Figure 1.13 The factor graph for the murder mystery after the addition of the new evidence. Both the `weapon` node and the `hair` node are shaded to indicate that these random variables have been set to their observed values. Note the absence of an edge connecting the `weapon` random variable with the factor node representing $P(\texttt{hair}|\texttt{murderer})$.

provides less detail about the model than a factor graph, but gives a good "big picture" view of which variables directly and indirectly affect each other. See Panel 1.2 for more details.

Given the factor graph of Figure 1.13, we can write down the joint distribution as the product of three terms, one for each factor in the factor graph:

$$P(\texttt{murderer}, \texttt{weapon}, \texttt{hair})$$
$$= P(\texttt{murderer})P(\texttt{weapon}|\texttt{murderer})$$
$$P(\texttt{hair}|\texttt{murderer}). \qquad (1.32)$$

Check for yourself that each term on the right of equation (1.32) corresponds to one of the factor nodes in Figure 1.13.

1.4.1 Incremental inference

We want to compute the posterior distribution over `murderer` in this new model, given values of `weapon` and `hair`. Given that we have the result from the previous model, we'd like to make use of it – rather than start again from scratch. To get our posterior distribution in the previous model, we conditioned on the value of `weapon`. To perform incremental inference in this new model, we can write down Bayes' rule but condition each term on the variable `weapon`:

Panel 1.2: Bayesian Networks

A Bayesian network is a different way of using a graph to represent a probabilistic model [Pearl, 1985, 1988]. In a Bayes net, there are variable nodes corresponding to each variable in the model, but there are no factor nodes. Parent variables of a factor are connected directly to the child variable of the factor, using directed edges (arrows). For example, the Bayes net corresponding to the factor graph of our murder (Figure 1.13) looks like this:

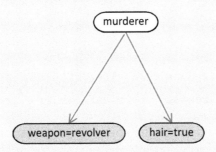

As this figure shows, by hiding the factors, a Bayes net emphasises which variables there are and how they influence each other (directly or indirectly). Bayes nets can be very useful in the early stages of model design when you want to focus on what variables to include and which will affect each other, without yet getting into details of precisely *how* they affect each other.

The disadvantage of using a Bayes net is that it is an incomplete specification of a model – you also have to write down all the factor functions externally to the graph and consider the two together as making up the model. For this reason, we have chosen to use factor graphs in this book, since they provide a stand-alone description of the model.

$$P(\texttt{murderer}|\texttt{hair},\texttt{weapon})$$
$$= \frac{P(\texttt{murderer}|\texttt{weapon})P(\texttt{hair}|\texttt{murderer},\texttt{weapon})}{P(\texttt{hair}|\texttt{weapon})}. \quad (1.33)$$

We can use exactly the same trick as we did back in equation (1.29) to drop the denominator and replace the equals sign with a proportional sign $\propto$:

$$P(\texttt{murderer}|\texttt{weapon}, \texttt{hair}) \propto P(\texttt{murderer}|\texttt{weapon})$$
$$P(\texttt{hair}|\texttt{murderer}, \texttt{weapon}). \quad (1.34)$$

Remembering that `hair` and `weapon` are conditionally indepedent given `murderer`, we can use equation (1.31) and drop `weapon` from the last term:

$$P(\texttt{murderer}|\texttt{weapon}, \texttt{hair}) \propto P(\texttt{murderer}|\texttt{weapon})$$
$$P(\texttt{hair}|\texttt{murderer}). \quad (1.35)$$

Since we know the values of `weapon` and `hair`, we can write in these observations:

$$P(\texttt{murderer}|\texttt{weapon} = \texttt{revolver}, \texttt{hair} = \texttt{true}) \propto$$
$$P(\texttt{murderer}|\texttt{weapon} = \texttt{revolver})P(\texttt{hair} = \texttt{true}|\texttt{murderer}).(1.36)$$

We can now compute the new posterior distribution for `murderer`. As before, each term depends only on the value of `murderer` and the overall normalisation can be evaluated at the end. Substituting in the posterior we obtained in Section 1.2.2 and our new conditional probability from equation (1.30) gives:

$$P(\texttt{murderer} = \texttt{Grey}|\texttt{weapon} = \texttt{rev.}, \texttt{hair} = \texttt{true}) \propto 0.66 \times 0.50 = 0.33$$
$$P(\texttt{murderer} = \texttt{Auburn}|\texttt{weapon} = \texttt{rev.}, \texttt{hair} = \texttt{true}) \propto 0.34 \times 0.05 = 0.017.$$

The sum of these two numbers is 0.347, and dividing both numbers by their sum we obtain the normalised posterior probabilities in the form

$$P(\texttt{murderer} = \texttt{Grey}|\texttt{weapon} = \texttt{rev.}, \texttt{hair} = \texttt{true}) \simeq 0.95$$
$$P(\texttt{murderer} = \texttt{Auburn}|\texttt{weapon} = \texttt{rev.}, \texttt{hair} = \texttt{true}) \simeq 0.05.$$

Taking account of all of the available evidence, the probability that Grey is the murderer is now 95%.

As a recap, we can plot how the probability distribution over `murderer` changed over the course of our murder investigation (Figure 1.14). Notice how the probability of `Grey` being the murderer started out low and increased as each new piece of evidence stacked against him. Similarly, notice how the probability of `Auburn` being the murderer evolved in exactly the opposite direction, due to the normalisation constraint and the assumption that either one of the two suspects was the murderer. We could seek further evidence, in

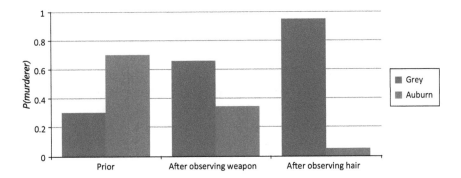

Figure 1.14 The evolution of $P(murderer)$ over the course of the murder investigation.

the hope that this would change the probability distribution to be even more confident (although, of course, evidence implicating Auburn would have the opposite effect). Instead, we will stop here – since 95% is greater than our threshold of 91% and so enough for a conviction!

The model of the murder that we built up in this chapter contains various prior and conditional probabilities that we have set by hand. For real applications, however, we will usually have little idea of how to set such probability values and will instead need to *learn* them from data. In the next chapter, we will see how such unknown probabilities can be expressed as random variables, whose values can be learned using the same probabilistic inference approach that we just used to solve a murder.

REVIEW OF CONCEPTS

conditional independence Two variables A and B are conditionally independent given a third variable C, if learning about A tells us nothing about B (and vice-versa) in the situation where we know the value of C. Put another way, it means that the value of A does not directly depend on the value of B, but only indirectly via the value of C. If A is conditionally independent of B given C, then this can be exploited to simplify its conditional probability like so:

$$P(\mathsf{A}|\mathsf{B},\mathsf{C}) = P(\mathsf{A}|\mathsf{C}).$$

For example, the knowledge that a big sporting event is happening nearby (B) might lead you to expect congestion on your commute (C), which might increase your belief that you will be late for work (**A**). However, if you listen to the radio and find out that there is no congestion (so now you know **C**), then the knowledge of the sporting event (**B**) no longer influences your belief in how late you will be (**A**). This also applies the other way around, so someone observing whether you were late (**A**), who had also learned that there was no congestion (**C**), would be none the wiser as to whether a sporting event was happening (**B**).

Bayesian network   A graphical model where nodes correspond to variables in the model and where edges show which variables directly influence each other. Factors are not shown, but the parent variables in a factor are connected directly to the child variable, using directed edges (arrows); see Panel 1.2.

SELF ASSESSMENT 1.5

The following exercises will help embed the concepts you have learned in this section. It may help to refer back to the text or the review of concepts.

1. Continuing your chosen scenario from previous self assessments, choose an additional variable that is affected by the conditioning variable. For example, if the conditioning variable is "the traffic is bad", then an affected variable might be "my boss is late for work". Draw a factor graph for a larger model that includes this new variable, as well as the two previous variables. Define a conditional probability table for the new factor in the factor graph. Write down any conditional independence assumptions that you have made in choosing this model, along with a sentence justifying that choice of assumption.

2. Assume that the new variable in your factor graph is observed to have some particular value of your choice (for example, "my boss is late for work" is observed to be true). Infer the posterior probability of the conditioning variable ("the traffic is bad") taking into account both this new observation and the observation of the other conditioned variable used in previous self assessments (for example, the observation that I am late for work).

3. Write a program to print out 1,000 joint samples of all three variables in your new model. Write down ahead of time how often

you would expect to see each triplet of values and then verify that this approximately matches the fraction of samples given by your program. Now change the program to only print out those samples which are consistent with your both observations from the previous question (for example, samples where you are late for work AND your boss is late for work). What fraction of these samples have each possible triplet of values now? How does this compare to your answer to the previous question?

4. Consider some other variables that might influence the three variables in your factor graph. For example, whether or not the traffic is bad might depend on whether it is raining, or whether there is an event happening nearby. Without writing down any conditional probabilities or specifying any factors, draw a Bayes net showing how the new variables influence your existing variables or each other. Each arrow in your Bayes net should mean that "the parent variable directly affects the child variable" or "the parent variable (partially) causes the child variable". If possible, present your Bayes network to someone else, and discuss it with them to see if they understand (and agree with) the assumptions you are making in terms of what variables to include in the model and what conditional independence assumptions you have made.

CHAPTER 2

Assessing people's skills

Throughout our lives, we are constantly assessing the skills and abilities of those around us. Who should I hire? Who should play on the team? Who can I ask for help? How can I best teach this person? Taking all that we know about someone and working out what they can and cannot do comes naturally to most of us. But how can we use model-based machine learning to do this automatically?

I n this chapter, we will develop our first model of some real-world data. We will address the problem of assessing candidates for a job that requires certain skills. The idea is that candidates will take a multiple-choice test and we will use model-based machine learning to determine which skills each candidate has (and with what probability) given their answers in the test. We can then use this for tasks such as selecting a shortlist of candidates very likely to have a set of essential skills.

Each question in a test requires certain skills to answer. For a software development job, these skills might be knowledge of the programming language C# or the database query language SQL. Some of the questions might require multiple skills in order to be answered correctly. Figure 2.1 gives some

DOI: 10.1201/9780429192685-3

Software Development Skills Assessment

1. Which line of code creates a new Shape in C#? *C#*

```
a. Shape shape = new Shape();
b. Shape shape = Shape.new();
c. new Shape shape = Shape();
d. Shape shape = new Shape;
e. Shape shape = Shape();
```

2. Which SQL command is used to append a new row to a table in a database? *SQL*

```
a. ADD
b. INSERT
c. UPDATE
d. SET
e. INPUT
```

C#, SQL

3. After an SQL connection has been established using a SqlConnection object called "sql", which of the following will retrieve any rows in the "people" table with the name "bob"?

```
a. SqlCommand cmd = new SqlCommand("SELECT 'bob' FROM people", sql);
b. SqlCommand cmd = new SqlCommand("SELECT * FROM people WHERE name = 'bob'", sql);
c. SqlCommand cmd = new SqlCommand("SELECT * FROM people WHERE 'bob' IN name", sql);
d. SqlCommand cmd = sql.SqlCommand("SELECT * FROM people WHERE name = 'bob'");
e. SqlCommand cmd = sql.SqlCommand("SELECT 'bob' FROM people");
```

4. A developer wants to write a piece of software which

Figure 2.1 Part of a certification test used to assess software development skills. The questions have been annotated with the skills needed to answer them.

example questions which have been marked with the skills required to answer them. Because our model could be used for many different types of job, it must work with different tests and different skills, as long as these skill annotations are provided. It is important that the system should only use these annotations when presented with a new test – it must not require any additional information, for example, sample answers from people with known skills.

In order to assess which skills a candidate has, we will need to analyse their answers to the test. Since we know the skills needed for each question, this may appear straightforward: we just need to check whether they are getting all the SQL questions right or all the C# questions wrong. But the real world is more complicated than this – even if someone knows C# they may make a mistake or misread a question; even if they do not know SQL they may guess the right answer by pure luck. In some cases, the test questions may be badly written or even outright wrong.

The situation is even more complicated for questions that need two (or more) skills. If someone gets a question that needs two skills right, it suggests that they are likely to have both skills. If they get it wrong, there are several possibilities: they could have one skill or the other (but probably not both) or they could have neither. Assessing which of these is the case requires looking at their answers to other questions and trying to find a consistent set of skills that is likely to give rise to all of the answers considered together. To do this kind of complex reasoning automatically, we need to design a model of how a person with particular skills answers a set of questions.

You can recreate all results in this chapter using the companion source code [Diethe et al., 2019].

2.1 A MODEL IS A SET OF ASSUMPTIONS

When designing a model of some data, we must make assumptions about the process that gave rise to the data. In fact, we can say that the model *is* the set of assumptions and the set of assumptions *is* the model. The relationship between a model and the assumptions that it represents is so important that it is worth emphasising:

> **A model = A set of assumptions about the data**

Selecting which assumptions to include in your model is a crucial part of model design. Incorrect assumptions will lead to models that give inaccurate predictions due to these faulty assumptions. However, it is impossible to build a model without making at least *some* assumptions.

As you have seen in Chapter 1, in this book we will use factor graphs to represent our models. As you progress through the book, you will learn how to construct the factor graph that encodes a chosen set of assumptions. Similarly, you will learn to look at a factor graph and work out which assumptions it represents. You can think of a factor graph as being a precise mathematical representation of a set of assumptions. For example, in Chapter 1, we built up a factor graph that represented a precise set of assumptions about a murder mystery. For this application, we need to make assumptions about the process of a candidate answering some test questions if they have a particular skill set. This will define the relationship between a candidate's underlying skills and their test answers, which we can then invert to infer their skills from the test answers.

When designing a factor graph, we start by choosing which variables we want to have in the graph. At the very least, the graph must contain variables representing the data we actually have (whether the candidate got each question right) and any variables that we want to learn about (the skills). As we shall see, it is often useful to introduce other, intermediate, variables. Having chosen the variables, we can start adding factors to our graph to encode how these variables affect each other in the question-answering process. It is usually helpful to start with the variables we want to learn about (the skills) and work through the process to finish with the variables that we can actually measure (whether the candidate got the questions right).

So, starting with the skill variables, here is our first assumption:

① A candidate has either mastered each skill or not.

Assumption ① means that we can represent a candidate's skill as a binary (true/false) variable, which is `true` if the candidate has mastered the skill and `false` if they haven't. Variables which can take one of a fixed set of values (like all the variables we have seen so far) are called **discrete variables**. Later in the chapter, we will encounter **continuous variables** which can take any value in a continuous range of values, such as any real number between 0 and 1. As we shall see, continuous variables are useful for learning the probability of events, amongst many other uses.

We next need to make an assumption about the prior probability of a candidate having each of these skills.

② Before seeing any test results, it is equally likely that a candidate does or doesn't have any particular skill.

Assumption ② means that the prior probability for each skill variable should be set neutrally to 50%, which is *Bernoulli*(0.5). To keep our factor graph small, we will start by considering a single candidate answering the three questions of Figure 2.1.

The above two assumptions, applied to the `csharp` and `sql` skills needed for these questions, give the following minimal factor graph:

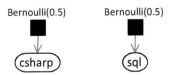

Figure 2.2 Factor graph showing priors for the binary skill variables `csharp` and `sql`.

Remember that every factor graph represents a joint probability distribution over the variables in the graph. The joint distribution for this factor graph is:

$$P(\texttt{csharp}, \texttt{sql}) = \text{Bernoulli}(\texttt{csharp}; 0.5)\ \text{Bernoulli}(\texttt{sql}; 0.5). \quad (2.1)$$

Note that there is a term in the joint probability for every factor (black square) in the factor graph.

Continuing with the question-answering process, we must now make some assumptions about how a candidate's test answers relate to their skills. Suppose they have all the skills for a question, we should still allow that they may get it wrong some of the time. If we gave some

SQL questions to a SQL expert, how many should we expect them to get right? Probably not all of them, but perhaps they would get 90% or so correct. We could check this assumption by asking some real experts to do such a quiz and seeing what scores they get, but for now we'll assume that getting one in ten wrong is reasonable:

③ If a candidate has all of the skills needed for a question, then they will usually get the question right, except one time in ten they will make a mistake.

For questions where the candidate lacks a necessary skill, we may assume that they guess at random:

④ If a candidate doesn't have all the skills needed for a question, they will pick an answer at random. Because this is a multiple-choice exam with five answers, there's a one in five chance that they get the question right.

Assumption ③ and Assumption ④ tell us how to extend our factor graph to model the first two questions of Figure 2.1. We need to add in variables for each question that are **true** if the candidate got the question right and **false** if they got it wrong. Let's call these variables **isCorrect1** for the first question and **isCorrect2** for the second question. Based on our assumptions, if **csharp** is **true**, we expect **isCorrect1** to be **true** unless the candidate makes a mistake (since the first question only needs the **csharp** skill). Since we assume that mistakes happen only one time in ten, the probability that **isCorrect1** is **true** in this case is 90%. If **csharp** is **false**, then we assume that the candidate will only get the question right by one time in five, which is 20%. This gives us the following conditional probability table:

Table 2.1 Conditional probability table showing the probability of each value of **isCorrect1** conditioned on each of the two values of **csharp**.

csharp	isCorrect1=true	isCorrect1=false
true	0.900	0.100
false	0.200	0.800

We will call the factor representing this conditional probability table *AddNoise* since the output is a "noisy" version of the input. Because our assumptions apply equally to all skills, we can use the same factor to relate sql to isCorrect2. This gives the following factor graph for the first two questions:

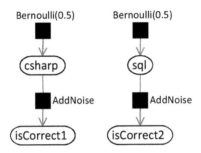

Figure 2.3 Factor graph for the first two questions in our test.

We can write down the joint probability distribution represented by this graph by including the two new terms for the *AddNoise* factors:

$$P(\texttt{csharp}, \texttt{sql}, \texttt{isCorrect1}, \texttt{isCorrect2}) = \qquad (2.2)$$

$$\text{Bernoulli}(\texttt{csharp}; 0.5) \ \text{Bernoulli}(\texttt{sql}; 0.5)$$

$$\text{AddNoise}(\texttt{isCorrect1}|\texttt{csharp}) \ \text{AddNoise}(\texttt{isCorrect2}|\texttt{sql}).$$

Modelling the third question is more complicated since this question requires both the csharp and sql skills. Assumption ③ and Assumption ④ refer to whether a candidate has "all the skills needed for a question". So for question 3, we need to include a new intermediate variable to represent whether the candidate has both the csharp and sql skills. We will call this binary variable hasSkills, which we want to be true if the candidate has both skills needed for the question and false otherwise. We achieve this by putting in an *And* factor connecting the two skill variables to the hasSkills variable. The *And* factor is defined so that $And(\texttt{C}|\texttt{A}, \texttt{B})$ is 1 if C is equal to A AND B and 0 otherwise. In other words, it forces the child variable C to be equal to (A AND B). A factor like *And*, where the child has a unique value given the parents, is called a **deterministic factor** (see Panel 2.1).

Panel 2.1: Deterministic factors

When building a model, we often want to include a variable which is a fixed function of some other variables in the model. For example, we may want a binary variable to be true if all of some other binary variables are true (AND) or if any of them are true (OR). For a continuous variable, we may want it to be the sum or product of some other continuous variables.

We can achieve this by putting a *deterministic* factor in our factor graph. The conditional probability distribution for a deterministic factor always has a value of either 1 or 0. It is 1 if the child variable is equal to the desired function of the parent variables and 0 otherwise. For example, if we want to add a variable C which is to be equal to A AND B, we can add a deterministic factor whose conditional probability distribution is:

A	B	C=false	C=true
false	false	1.000	0.000
false	true	1.000	0.000
true	false	1.000	0.000
true	true	0.000	1.000

Notice that whenever C is equal to A AND B, the conditional probability is 1 and it is 0 elsewhere. Since the overall joint probability includes this factor as one of its terms, the probability of any configuration of variables where C is not equal to A AND B must be zero. So the deterministic factor acts as a constraint that ensures C=(A AND B) is always true.

Throughout this book you will see that deterministic factors play a vital role in a wide variety of models.

Here's a partial factor graph showing how the *And* factor can be used to make the `hasSkills` variable that we need:

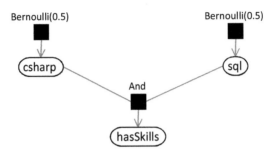

Figure 2.4 The *And* factor is a deterministic factor which constrains `hasSkills` to be true if `csharp` and `sql` are both true and to be false in all other cases.

The joint probability distribution for this factor graph is:

$$P(\texttt{csharp}, \texttt{sql}, \texttt{hasSkills}) = \text{Bernoulli}(\texttt{csharp}; 0.5) \qquad (2.3)$$
$$\text{Bernoulli}(\texttt{sql}; 0.5) \ \text{And}(\texttt{hasSkills}|\texttt{csharp}, \texttt{sql}).$$

The new *And* factor means that we now have a new *And* term in the joint probability distribution.

Now we can put everything together to build a factor graph for all three questions. We just need to connect `hasSkills` to our `isCorrect3` variable, once again using an *AddNoise* factor:

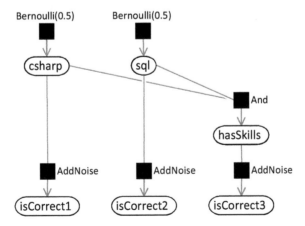

Figure 2.5 Factor graph for the three multiple choice questions of Figure 2.1.

The joint probability distribution for this factor graph is quite long because we now have a total of six factor nodes, meaning that it contains six terms:

$$P(\texttt{csharp}, \texttt{sql}, \texttt{hasSkills}, \texttt{isCorrect1}, \texttt{isCorrect2}, \texttt{isCorrect3}) = \quad (2.4)$$
$$\text{Bernoulli}(\texttt{csharp}; 0.5) \; \text{Bernoulli}(\texttt{sql}; 0.5)$$
$$\text{AddNoise}(\texttt{isCorrect1}|\texttt{csharp}) \; \text{AddNoise}(\texttt{isCorrect2}|\texttt{sql})$$
$$\text{And}(\texttt{hasSkills}|\texttt{csharp}, \texttt{sql}) \; \text{AddNoise}(\texttt{isCorrect3}|\texttt{hasSkills}).$$

Because joint probability distributions like this one are big and awkward to work with, it is usually easier to use factor graphs as a more readable and manageable way to express a model.

It is essential that any model contains variables corresponding to the observed data, and that these variables are of the same type. This allows the data to be attached to the model by fixing these variables to the corresponding observed data values. An inference calculation can then be used to find the marginal distributions for any other (unobserved) variable in the model. For our model, we need to ensure that we can attach our test results data to the model, which consists of a yes/no result for each question depending on whether the candidate got that question right. We can indeed attach this data to our model, because we have binary variables (isCorrect1, isCorrect2, isCorrect3) which we can set to be true if the candidate got the question right and false otherwise.

There is one more assumption being made in this model that has not yet been mentioned. In fact, it is normally one of the biggest assumptions made by any model! It is the assumed *scope* of the model: that is, the assumption that only the variables included in the model are relevant. For example, our model makes no mention of the mental state of the candidate (tired, stressed), or of the conditions in which they were performing the test, or whether it is possible that cheating was taking place, or whether the candidate even understands the language the questions are written in. By excluding these variables from our model, we have made the strong assumption that they are independent from (do not affect) the candidate's answers.

Poor assumptions about scope often lead to unsatisfactory results of the inference process, such as reduced accuracy in making predictions. The scope of a model is an assumption that should be critically assessed during the model design process, if only to identify aspects of the problem that are being ignored. So to be explicit, the last assumption for our learning skills model is:

⑤ Whether the candidate gets a question right depends only on what skills that candidate has and not on *anything* else.

We will not explicitly call out this assumption in future models, but it is good practice to consider carefully what variables are being ignored, whenever you are designing or using a model.

2.1.1 Questioning our assumptions

Having constructed the factor graph, let us pause for a moment and review the assumptions we have made so far. They are all shown together in Table 2.2.

Table 2.2 The five assumptions encoded in our model.

① Each candidate has either mastered each skill or not.
② Before seeing any test results, it is equally likely that each candidate does or doesn't have any particular skill.
③ If a candidate has all of the skills needed for a question then they will get the question right, except one time in ten they will make a mistake.
④ If a candidate doesn't have all the skills needed for a question, they will pick an answer at random. Because this is a multiple-choice exam with five answers, there's a one in five chance that they get the question right.
⑤ Whether the candidate gets a question right depends only on what skills that candidate has and not on anything else.

It is very important to review all modelling assumptions carefully to ensure that they are reasonable. For example, Assumption ① is a simplifying assumption which reduces the degree of skill that a candidate has into a simple yes/no variable. It is usual to have to make such simplifying assumptions, which are not exactly incorrect but which make the model less precise. Simplifying assumptions can be made as long as you keep in mind that these may reduce the accuracy of the results. Assumption ② seems apparently safe since it is just assuming ignorance. However, it is also assuming that each of the skill variables are independent, that is, knowing that someone has one particular skill doesn't tell you anything about whether they have any of the other skills. If some of the skills are related in some way, this may well not be the case. To keep the model simple, we will work with this assumption for now, but bear it in mind as a candidate for refinement later on. Assumption ③ and Assumption ④ are more subtle: is it really true that if the candidate has, say, two out of three skills needed for a question, then they are reduced to guesswork? We will continue to use these assumptions for now – later in the chapter we will show how to diagnose whether our model assumptions are causing problems and see how to revise them. Assumption ⑤, that no other variables are relevant, is reasonable assuming that there is a conscientious examiner administering the test. A good examiner will make sure that a candidate's answers genuinely reflect their skills and are not affected by external conditions or cheating.

Having reviewed our assumptions by eye, we can now try the model out to ensure that the assumptions continue to make sense when applied to realistic example data.

REVIEW OF CONCEPTS

---

discrete variables   Variables which can take one of a fixed set of values. For example, a binary variable can take only two values `true` or `false`.

continuous variables   Variables which can take any value in a continuous range of values, for example, any real number between 0 and 1.

deterministic factor   A factor defining a conditional probability which is always either 0 or 1. This means that the value of child variable can always be uniquely determined (i.e. computed) given the value of the parent variables. For example, a factor representing the AND operation is a deterministic factor. See Panel 2.1 for more details.

SELF ASSESSMENT 2.1

The following exercises will help embed the concepts you have learned in this section. It may help to refer back to the text or the review of concepts.

1. Write down the conditional probability table for a deterministic factor which represents the OR function. The child variable C should be true if either of the parent variables A and B are true. Panel 2.1 should help.

2. Write down all the independence and conditional independence assumptions that you can find in Figure 2.5. For each assumption ask yourself whether it is reasonable – as discussed in Chapter 1, for independence assumptions you need to ask yourself the question "does learning about A tell me anything about B?" and for conditional independence assumptions you need to ask "if I know X, does learning about A tell me anything about B?".

3. As mentioned above, there may be many other variables that affect the test outcomes (e.g. cheating, candidate's state of mind). Draw a Bayesian network that includes one or more of these additional variables, as well as all the variables in our current model. Your Bayes net should only include edges between variables that directly affect each other. It may be helpful to introduce intermediate variables as well. If possible, present your Bayes net to someone else and discuss whether they agree with the assumptions you have made.

2.2 TESTING OUT THE MODEL

Having constructed a model, the first thing to do is to test it out with some simple example data to check that its behaviour is reasonable. Suppose a candidate knows C# but not SQL – we would expect them to get the first question right and the other two questions wrong. So let's test the model out for this case and see what skills it infers for that pattern of answers. For convenience, we'll use isCorrect to refer to the array [isCorrect1,isCorrect2,isCorrect3] and so we will consider the case where isCorrect is [true,false,false].

We want to infer the probability that the candidate has the csharp and sql skills, given this particular set of isCorrect values. This is an example of an **inference query** which is defined by the variables we want to infer (csharp, sql) and the variables we are conditioning on (isCorrect) along with their observed values. Because this example is quite small, we can work out the answer to this inference query by hand.

2.2.1 Doing inference by hand

To get started, let's look at how to infer the probability for the csharp skill given the answer to just the first question. Dropping other variables gives the simplified factor graph shown in Figure 2.6.

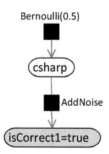

Figure 2.6 Factor graph for just the first question and the csharp skill.

This factor graph now looks just like the one for the murder mystery in Section 1.3 and, just like for the murder mystery, we can apply Bayes' theorem to solve it:

$$P(\mathbf{csharp}|\mathrm{isCorrect1} = \mathrm{true}) \;\propto\; P(\mathrm{isCorrect1} = \mathrm{true}|\mathrm{csharp})$$
$$P(\mathrm{csharp}). \qquad (2.5)$$

In equation (2.5), we have colour coded some of the terms to help track them through the calculation. Putting in numbers for csharp being true and false gives:

$$P(\texttt{csharp} = \texttt{true}|\text{isCorrect1} = \texttt{true}) \ \propto \ 0.9 \times 0.5 \ = \ 0.45$$
$$P(\texttt{csharp} = \texttt{false}|\text{isCorrect1} = \texttt{true}) \ \propto \ 0.2 \times 0.5 \ = \ 0.10.$$

These numbers sum to 0.55. To get probabilities, we need to scale both numbers to sum to 1 (by dividing by 0.55) which gives:

$$P(\texttt{csharp} = \texttt{true}|\text{isCorrect1} = \texttt{true}) = \frac{0.45}{0.55} \simeq 0.818$$
$$P(\texttt{csharp} = \texttt{false}|\text{isCorrect1} = \texttt{true}) = \frac{0.10}{0.55} \simeq 0.182$$

So, given just the answer to the first question, the probability of having the csharp skill is 81.8%.

Performing inference manually for all three questions is a more involved calculation. If you want to explore this calculation, please read the following deep-dive section. If not, skip over it to see how we can automate this inference calculation.

⚓ Inference deep-dive

In this optional section, we perform inference manually in our three-question model by marginalising the joint distribution. Feel free to skip this section.

As we saw in Chapter 1, we can perform inference by marginalising the joint distribution (summing it over all the variables except the one we are interested in) while fixing the values of any observed variables. For the three-question factor graph, we wrote down the joint probability distribution in equation (2.4). Here it is again:

$$P(\texttt{csharp}, \texttt{sql}, \texttt{hasSkills}, \texttt{isCorrect}) = \qquad\qquad (2.6)$$
$$\text{Bernoulli}(\texttt{csharp}; 0.5) \ \text{Bernoulli}(\texttt{sql}; 0.5)$$
$$\text{AddNoise}(\texttt{isCorrect1}|\texttt{csharp}) \ \text{AddNoise}(\texttt{isCorrect2}|\texttt{sql})$$
$$\text{And}(\texttt{hasSkills}|\texttt{csharp}, \texttt{sql}) \ \text{AddNoise}(\texttt{isCorrect3}|\texttt{hasSkills}).$$

Before we start this inference calculation, we need to show how to compute a **product of distributions**. Suppose for some variable x, we know that:

$$P(\mathbf{x}) \propto \text{Bernoulli}(\mathbf{x}; 0.8) \, \text{Bernoulli}(\mathbf{x}; 0.4). \tag{2.7}$$

This may look odd since we normally only associate one distribution with a variable but, as we'll see, products of distributions arise frequently when performing inference. Evaluating this expression for the two values of x gives:

$$P(\mathbf{x}) \propto \begin{cases} 0.8 \times 0.4 = 0.32 & \text{if } \mathbf{x} = \texttt{true} \\ 0.2 \times 0.6 = 0.12 & \text{if } \mathbf{x} = \texttt{false}. \end{cases} \tag{2.8}$$

Since we know that $P(\mathbf{x} = \texttt{true})$ and $P(\mathbf{x} = \texttt{false})$ must add up to one, we can divide these values by $0.32 + 0.12 = 0.44$ to get:

$$P(\mathbf{x}) = \begin{cases} 0.727 & \text{if } \mathbf{x} = \texttt{true} \\ 0.273 & \text{if } \mathbf{x} = \texttt{false} \end{cases} = \text{Bernoulli}(\mathbf{x}; 0.727). \tag{2.9}$$

This calculation may feel familiar to you – it is very similar to the inference calculations that we performed in Chapter 1.

In general, if we want to multiply two Bernoulli distributions, we can use the rule that:

$$\text{Bernoulli}(\mathbf{x}; a) \, \text{Bernoulli}(\mathbf{x}; b)$$

$$\propto \text{Bernoulli} \left(\mathbf{x} \; ; \; \frac{ab}{ab + (1-a)(1-b)} \right). \tag{2.10}$$

If, say, the second distribution is uniform ($b{=}0.5$), the result of the product is $\text{Bernoulli}(\mathbf{x}; a)$. In other words, the distribution $\text{Bernoulli}(\mathbf{x}; a)$ is unchanged by multiplying by a uniform distribution. In general, multiplying *any* distribution by the uniform distribution leaves it unchanged.

Armed with the ability to multiply distributions, we can now compute the probability that our example candidate has the csharp skill. The precise probability we want to compute is $P(\texttt{csharp}|\texttt{isCorrect} = [\text{T}, \text{F}, \text{F}])$, where we have abbreviated true to T and false to F. As before, we can compute this by marginalising the joint distribution and fixing the observed values:

$$P(\texttt{csharp}|\texttt{isCorrect} = [\text{T}, \text{F}, \text{F}]) \propto \tag{2.11}$$

$$\sum_{\texttt{sql}} \sum_{\texttt{hasSkills}} P(\texttt{csharp}, \texttt{sql}, \texttt{hasSkills}, \texttt{isCorrect} = [\text{T}, \text{F}, \text{F}]).$$

As we saw in Chapter 1, we use the proportional sign $\propto$ because we do not care about the scaling of the right-hand side, only the ratio of its value when csharp is true to the value when csharp is false.

Now we put in the full expression for the joint probability from (2.6) and fix the values of all the observed variables. We can ignore the $Bernoulli(0.5)$ terms since, as we just learned, multiplying a distribution by a uniform distribution leaves it unchanged. So the right-hand side of (2.11) becomes

$$\propto \sum_{\text{sql}} \sum_{\text{hasSkills}} \text{AddNoise}(\text{isCorrect1} = \text{T}|\text{csharp}) \qquad (2.12)$$

$$\text{AddNoise}(\text{isCorrect2} = \text{F}|\text{sql})$$
$$\text{And}(\text{hasSkills}|\text{csharp}, \text{sql})$$
$$\text{AddNoise}(\text{isCorrect3} = \text{F}|\text{hasSkills}).$$

Terms inside of each summation $\sum$ that do not mention the variable being summed over can be moved outside of the summation, because they have the same value for each term being summed. You can also think of this as moving the summation signs in towards the right:

$$\propto \text{AddNoise}(\text{isCorrect1} = \text{T}|\text{csharp}) \qquad (2.13)$$

$$\sum_{\text{sql}} \text{AddNoise}(\text{isCorrect2} = \text{F}|\text{sql})$$

$$\sum_{\text{hasSkills}} \text{And}(\text{hasSkills}|\text{csharp}, \text{sql})$$

$$\text{AddNoise}(\text{isCorrect3} = \text{F}|\text{hasSkills}).$$

If you look at the first term here, you'll see that it is a function of csharp only, since isCorrect1 is observed to be true. When csharp is true, this term has the value 0.9. When csharp is false, this term has the value 0.2. Since we only care about the relative sizes of these two numbers, we can replace this term by a *Bernoulli* term where the probability of true is $\frac{0.9}{0.9+0.2} = 0.818$ and the probability of false is therefore $1-0.818=0.182$. Note that this has preserved the true/false ratio $0.818/0.182 = 0.9/0.2$.

Similarly the second *AddNoise* term has value 0.1 when sql is true and the value 0.8 when sql is false, so can be replaced by a *Bernoulli* term where the probability of true is $\frac{0.1}{0.1+0.8} = 0.111$. The final *AddNoise* term can also be replaced, giving:

$$\propto \text{Bernoulli}(\texttt{csharp}; 0.818) \tag{2.14}$$

$$\sum_{\texttt{sql}} \text{Bernoulli}(\texttt{sql}; 0.111)$$

$$\sum_{\texttt{hasSkills}} \text{And}(\texttt{hasSkills}|\texttt{csharp}, \texttt{sql}) \, \text{Bernoulli}(\texttt{hasSkills}; 0.111).$$

For the deterministic *And* factor, we need to consider the four cases where the factor is not zero (which we saw in Panel 2.1) and plug in the *Bernoulli*(0.111) distributions for $\texttt{sql}$ and $\texttt{hasSkills}$ in each case, as shown in Table 2.3.

Table 2.3 Evaluation of the last three terms in (2.14). Each row of the table corresponds to one of the four cases where the *And* factor is 1 (rather than 0). The first three columns give the values of $\texttt{csharp}$, $\texttt{sql}$ and $\texttt{hasSkills}$, which is just the truth table for AND. The next two columns give the corresponding values of the *Bernoulli* distributions for $\texttt{sql}$ and $\texttt{hasSkills}$ and the final column multiplies these together.

csharp	sql	hasSkills	Bern(sql|0.111)	Bern(hasSkills|0.111)	Product
false	false	false	1 − 0.111	1 − 0.111	0.790
false	true	false	0.111	1 − 0.111	0.099
true	false	false	1 − 0.111	1 − 0.111	0.790
true	true	true	0.111	0.111	0.012

Looking at Table 2.3, we can see that when $\texttt{csharp}$ is $\texttt{true}$, either both $\texttt{sql}$ and $\texttt{hasSkills}$ are $\texttt{false}$ (with probability 0.790) or both $\texttt{sql}$ and $\texttt{hasSkills}$ are $\texttt{true}$ (with probability 0.012). The sum of these is 0.802. When $\texttt{csharp}$ is $\texttt{false}$, the corresponding sum is $0.790 + 0.099 = 0.889$. So we can replace the last three terms by a *Bernoulli* term with parameter $\frac{0.802}{0.802+0.889} = 0.474$.

$$\propto \text{Bernoulli}(\texttt{csharp}; 0.818) \, \text{Bernoulli}(\texttt{csharp}; 0.474) \tag{2.15}$$

Now we have a product of Bernoulli distributions, so we can use (2.10) to multiply them together. When $\texttt{csharp}$ is $\texttt{true}$, this product has value $0.818 \times 0.474 = 0.388$. When $\texttt{csharp}$ is $\texttt{false}$, the value is $(1 - 0.818) \times (1 - 0.474) = 0.096$. Therefore, the product of these two distributions is a *Bernoulli* whose parameter is $\frac{0.388}{0.388+0.096}$:

$$= \text{Bernoulli}(\texttt{csharp}; 0.802) \tag{2.16}$$

So we have calculated that the posterior probability that our candidate has the `csharp` skill to be 80.2%. If we work through a similar calculation for the `sql` skill, we find the posterior probability is 3.4%. Together these probabilities say that the candidate is likely to know C# but is unlikely to know SQL, which seems like a very reasonable inference given that the candidate only got the C# question right.

2.2.2 Doing inference by passing messages on the graph

Doing inference calculations manually takes a long time and it is easy to make mistakes. Instead, we can do the same calculation mechanically by using a **message passing algorithm**. This works by passing messages along the edges of the factor graph, where a message is a probability distribution over the variable that the edge is connected to. We will see that using a message passing algorithm lets us do the inference calculations automatically – a huge advantage of the model-based approach!

To understand how message passing works, take another look at equation (2.6):

$$P(\texttt{csharp} = \texttt{true}|\text{isCorrect1} = \text{true}) \quad \propto \quad 0.9 \times 0.5 \quad = \quad 0.45$$
$$P(\texttt{csharp} = \texttt{false}|\text{isCorrect1} = \text{true}) \quad \propto \quad 0.2 \times 0.5 \quad = \quad 0.10.$$

Figure 2.7 shows these colour-coded terms as *messages* being passed from one node to another node in the graph. For example, the factor node for the prior over `csharp` sends this prior distribution as a message to the `csharp` node (in blue). The observed `isCorrect1` node sends an upwards message which is a point mass at the observed value (in red). The *AddNoise* factor transforms this message using Bayes' theorem and outputs its own upwards message (in green). Each of these messages can be computed from information available at the node they are sent from.

At this point, the two messages arriving at the `csharp` node provide all the information we need to compute the posterior distribution for the `csharp` variable, as we saw in equation (2.6). This method of using message passing to compute posterior distributions is called **belief propagation** [Pearl, 1982, 1988; Lauritzen and Spiegelhalter, 1988].

If you would like to see how to use belief propagation to compute posterior distributions in our three-question model, read the next section. Otherwise, you can skip straight to the results.

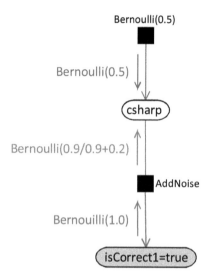

Figure 2.7 Factor graph with probability distributions used for inference.

⚓ **Inference deep-dive**
In this optional section, we show how belief propagation can be used to perform inference in our three-question model. Feel free to skip this section.

Let us redo the inference calculation for the `csharp` skill using message passing – we'll describe the message passing process for this example first, and then look at the general form later on. The first step in the manual calculation was to fix the values of the observed variables. Using message passing, this corresponds to each observed variable sending out a message which is a point mass distribution at the observed value. In our case, each `isCorrect` variable sends the point mass $Bernoulli(0)$ if it is observed to be `false` or the point mass $Bernoulli(1)$ if it is observed to be `true`. This means that the three messages sent are as shown in Figure 2.8.

These point mass messages then arrive at the *AddNoise* factor nodes. The outgoing messages at each factor node can be computed separately as follows:

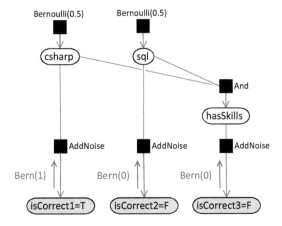

Figure 2.8 The messages sent from the observed variable nodes, which are shown shaded and labelled with their observed values. The message on any edge is a distribution over the variable that the edge is connected to. For example, the left hand *Bern*(1) is short for *Bernoulli*(isCorrect1; 1).

- The message up from the first *AddNoise* factor to csharp can be computed by writing AddNoise(isCorrect1 = T|csharp) as a Bernoulli distribution over csharp. As we saw in the last section, the parameter of the Bernoulli is $p = \frac{0.9}{0.9+0.2} = 0.818$, so the upward message is *Bernoulli*(0.818).

- The message up from the second *AddNoise* factor to sql can be computed by writing AddNoise(isCorrect2 = F|sql) as a Bernoulli distribution over sql. The parameter of the Bernoulli is $p = \frac{0.1}{0.1+0.8} = 0.111$, so the upward message is *Bernoulli*(0.111).

- The message up from the third *AddNoise* factor to hasSkills is the same as the second message, since it is computed for the same factor with the same incoming message. Hence, the third upward message is also *Bernoulli*(0.111).

Note that these three messages are exactly the three Bernoulli distributions we saw in (2.14). Rather than working on the entire joint distribution, we have broken down the calculation into simple, repeatable message computations at the nodes in the factor graph.

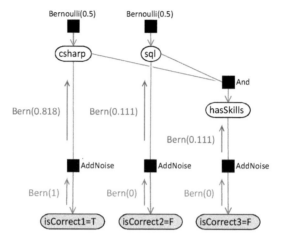

Figure 2.9 Outgoing messages from the *AddNoise* factor nodes.

The messages down from the *Bernoulli*(0.5) prior factors are just the prior distributions themselves:

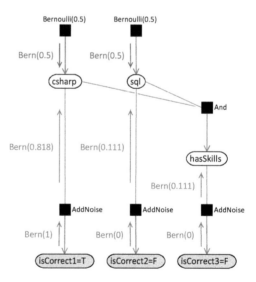

Figure 2.10 Messages from the *Bernoulli* prior factor nodes.

The outgoing message for any variable node is the product of the incoming messages on the other edges connected to that node. For the sql variable node, we now have incoming messages on two edges, which means we can compute the outgoing message towards the *And* factor.

This is *Bernoulli*(0.111) since the upward message is unchanged by multiplying by the uniform downward message *Bernoulli*(0.5). The `hasSkills` variable node is even simpler: since there is only one incoming message, the outgoing message is just a copy of it.

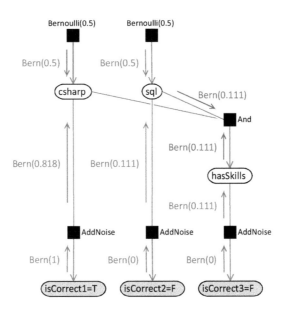

Figure 2.11 Messages out of the `sql` and `hasSkills` variable nodes.

Finally, we can compute the outgoing message from the *And* factor to the `csharp` variable. This is computed by multiplying the incoming messages by the factor function and summing over all variables other than the one being sent to (so we sum over `sql` and `hasSkills`):

$$\sum_{\texttt{sql}} \sum_{\texttt{hasSkills}} \text{And}(\texttt{hasSkills}|\texttt{csharp},\texttt{sql}) \quad (2.17)$$

$$\text{Bernoulli}(\texttt{sql}; 0.111) \, \text{Bernoulli}(\texttt{hasSkills}; 0.111).$$

The summation gives the message *Bernoulli*(0.474), as we saw in equation (2.15), as shown in Figure 2.12.

We now have all three incoming messages at the `csharp` variable node, which means we are ready to compute its posterior marginal. This is achieved by multiplying together the three messages – this is

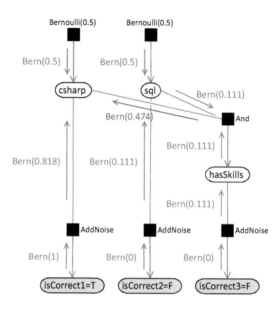

Figure 2.12 The final message toward the `csharp` variable node.

the calculation we performed in equation (2.15) and hence gives the same result *Bernoulli*(0.802) or 80.2%.

To compute the marginal for `sql`, we can re-use most of the messages we just calculated and so only need to compute two additional messages (shown in Figure 2.13). The first message, from `csharp` to the *And* factor, is the product of *Bernoulli*(0.818) and the uniform distribution *Bernoulli*(0.5), so the result is also *Bernoulli*(0.818).

The second message is from the *And* factor to `sql`. Again, we compute it by multiplying the incoming messages by the factor function and summing over all variables other than the one being sent to (so we sum over `csharp` and `hasSkills`):

$$\sum_{\text{csharp}} \sum_{\text{hasSkills}} \text{And}(\text{hasSkills}|\text{csharp}, \text{sql}) \tag{2.18}$$

$$\text{Bernoulli}(\text{csharp}; 0.818) \ \text{Bernoulli}(\text{hasSkills}; 0.111).$$

The summation gives the message *Bernoulli*(0.221), so the two new messages we have computed are those shown in Figure 2.13.

Multiplying this message into `sql` with the upward message from the *AddNoise* factor gives *Bernoulli*(0.111) × *Bernoulli*(0.221) ∝ *Bernoulli*(0.034) or 3.4%, the same result as before. Note that again

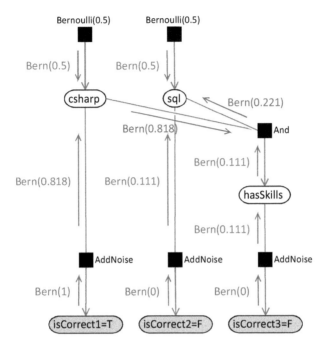

Figure 2.13 Additional messages needed to compute the marginal for the **sql** variable.

we have ignored the uniform *Bernoulli*(0.5) message from the prior, since multiplying by a uniform distribution has no effect.

The message passing procedure we just saw arises from applying the general belief propagation algorithm. In belief propagation, messages are computed in one of three ways, depending on whether the message is coming from a factor node, an observed variable node or an unobserved variable node. The algorithm is summarised in Algorithm 2.1 – a complete derivation of this algorithm can be found in Bishop [2006]. Belief propagation for factor graphs is also discussed in Kschischang et al. [2001].

2.2.3 Using belief propagation to test out the model

The belief propagation algorithm allows us to do inference calculations entirely automatically for a given factor graph. This means that it is possible to completely automate the process of answering an inference query without writing any code or doing any hand calculation!

Algorithm 2.1: Belief Propagation

Input: factor graph, list of target variables to compute marginal distributions for.

Output: marginal distributions for target variables.

repeat

    foreach *node in the factor graph* **do**

        foreach *edge connected to the node* **do**

            If all needed incoming messages are available send the appropriate outgoing message below:

            - Variable node message: the product of all messages received on the other edges;

            - Factor node message: the product of all messages received on the other edges, multiplied by the conditional probability distribution for the factor and summed over all variables except the one being sent to;

            - Observed node message: a point mass at the observed value;

        end

    end

until *target variables have received incoming messages on all edges*

Compute marginal distributions as the product of all incoming messages at each target variable node.

Using belief propagation, we can test out our model fully by automatically inferring the marginal distributions for the skills for every possible configuration of correct and incorrect answers. The results of doing this are shown in Table 2.4. Inspecting this table, we can see that the results appear to be sensible – the probability of having the `csharp` skill is generally higher when the candidate got the first question correct and similarly the probability of having the `sql` skill is generally higher when the candidate got the second question correct. Also, both probabilities are higher when the third question is correct rather than incorrect.

Interestingly, the probability of having the `sql` skill is actually lower when only the first question is correct than where the candidate got all the questions wrong (first and second rows of Table 2.4). This makes

Table 2.4 The posterior probabilities for the `csharp` and `sql` variables for all possible configurations of `isCorrect` As before, the blue bars give a visual representation of the inferred probabilities.

IsCorrect1	IsCorrect2	IsCorrect3	P(csharp)	P(sql)
☐	☐	☐	0.101	0.101
✓	☐	☐	0.802	0.034
☐	✓	☐	0.034	0.802
✓	✓	☐	0.561	0.561
☐	☐	✓	0.148	0.148
✓	☐	✓	0.862	0.326
☐	✓	✓	0.326	0.862
✓	✓	✓	0.946	0.946

sense because getting the first question right means the candidate probably has the `csharp` skill, which makes it even more likely that the explanation for getting the third question wrong is that they *didn't* have the `sql` skill. This is an example of the kind of subtle reasoning which model-based machine learning can achieve, which can give it an advantage over simpler approaches. For example, if we just used the number of questions needing a particular skill that a person got right as an indicator of that skill, we would be ignoring potentially useful information coming from the other questions. In contrast, using a suitable model, we have exploited the fact that getting a `csharp` question right can actually *decrease* the probability of having the `sql` skill.

REVIEW OF CONCEPTS

inference query   A query which defines an inference calculation to be done on a probabilistic model. It consists of the set of variables whose values we know (along with those values) and another set of variables that we wish to infer posterior distributions for. An example of an inference query is if we may know that the variable `weapon` takes the value `revolver` and wish to infer the posterior distribution over the variable `murderer`.

product of distributions   An operation which multiplies two (or more) probability distributions and then normalises the result to sum to 1, giving a new probability distribution. This operation should not be confused with multiplying two different random variables together (which may happen using a deterministic factor in a model). Instead, a product of distributions involves two distributions over the *same* random variable. Products of distributions are used frequently during inference to combine multiple pieces of uncertain information about a particular variable which have come from different sources.

message passing algorithm An algorithm for doing inference calculations by passing messages over the edges of a graphical model, such as a factor graph. The messages are probability distributions over the variable that the edge is connected to. Belief propagation is a commonly used message passing algorithm.

belief propagation A message passing algorithm for computing posterior marginal distributions over variables in a factor graph. Belief propagation uses two different message computations, one for messages from factors to variables and one for messages from variables to factors. Observed variables send point mass messages; see Algorithm 2.1.

SELF ASSESSMENT 2.2

The following exercises will help embed the concepts you have learned in this section. It may help to refer back to the text or the review of concepts.

1. Compute the product of the following pairs of Bernoulli distributions

   a. $\text{Bernoulli}(x; 0.3) \times \text{Bernoulli}(x; 0.9)$

   b. $\text{Bernoulli}(x; 0.5) \times \text{Bernoulli}(x; 0.2)$

   c. $\text{Bernoulli}(x; 0.5) \times \text{Bernoulli}(x; 0.3)$

   d. $\text{Bernoulli}(x; 1.0) \times \text{Bernoulli}(x; 0.2)$

   e. $\text{Bernoulli}(x; 1.0) \times \text{Bernoulli}(x; 0.3)$

   Why can we not compute $\text{Bernoulli}(x; 1.0) \times \text{Bernoulli}(x; 0.0)$?

2. Write a program (or create a spreadsheet) to print out pairs of samples from two Bernoulli distributions with different parameters a and b. Now filter the output of the program to only show samples pairs which have the same value (i.e. where both sample

are **true** or where both are **false**). Print out the fraction of these samples which are **true**. This process corresponds to multiplying the two Bernoulli distributions together and so the resulting fraction should be close to the value given by equation (2.10).

Use your program to (approximately) verify your answers to the previous question. What does your program do when $a = 0.0$ and $b = 1.0$?

3. Manually compute the posterior probability for the **sql** skill, as we did for the **csharp** skill in Section 2.2.1, and show that it comes to 3.4%.

4. Build this model in Infer.NET and reproduce the results in Table 2.4. For examples of how to construct a conditional probability table, refer to the wet grass/sprinkler/rain example in the Infer.NET documentation. You will also need to use the Infer.NET & operator for the *And* factor. This exercise demonstrates how inference calculations can be performed completely automatically given a model definition.

2.3 LOOPINESS

Let's now extend our model slightly by adding a fourth question which needs both skills. This new factor graph is shown in Figure 2.14, where we have added new isCorrect4 and hasSkills4 variables for the new question. Surely we can also do inference in this, very slightly larger, graph using belief propagation? In fact, we cannot.

The problem is that belief propagation can only send a message out of an (unobserved) node after we have received messages on all other edges of that node (Algorithm 2.1). Given this constraint, we can only send all the messages in a graph if there are no **loops**, where a loop is a path through the graph which starts

Loops can be challenging.

and finishes at the same node (without using the same edge twice). If the graph has a loop, then we cannot send any of the messages along the edges of the loop because that will always require one of the other messages in the loop to have been computed first.

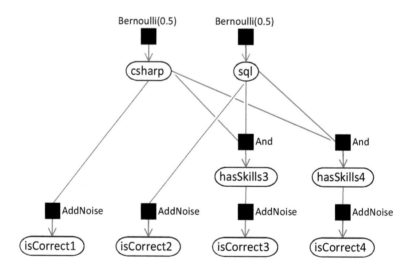

Figure 2.14 Factor graph for a four-question test. This graph contains a loop (shown in red) which means that we cannot apply belief propagation.

If you look back at the old three-question factor graph (Figure 2.5), you'll see that it has no loops (a graph with no loops is called a **tree**) and so belief propagation worked without problems. However, our new graph does have a loop, which is marked in red in Figure 2.14. To do inference in such a **loopy graph**, we need to look beyond standard belief propagation.

To perform inference in loopy graphs, we need to get rid of the loops somehow. In this toy example, we could notice that hasSkills3 and hasSkills4 are the same and remove one of them. Such a simple solution is unlikely to be available in real problems. Instead, there are various general-purpose methods to remove loops, as described in Panel 2.2. Unfortunately, all these methods typically become too slow to use when dealing with large factor graphs. In most real applications, the graphs are very large but inference needs to be performed quickly. The result is that such **exact inference** methods are usually too slow to be useful.

Panel 2.2: Exact inference in loopy graphs

To perform inference calculations exactly in loopy graphs, we need to find a way to remove the loops and so convert the graph into a tree. Once we have a tree, we can run belief propagation as normal. There are two common approaches for removing loops from a loopy graph:

1. **Remove loops by merging variables together**

   In our example, we could replace the variables csharp and sql by a single variable with four states FF, TF, FT, TT. We would also need to modify and in some cases combine all the factors connected to either variable. The resulting factor graph would no longer contain a loop. This approach is the basis of the *junction tree algorithm* [Lauritzen and Spiegelhalter, 1988], which merges variables to create a *junction tree*, on which belief propagation is applied. The junction tree algorithm was used successfully in many early machine learning applications, but it does become unusably slow to run when a large number of variables need to be merged together, as is often the case with today's applications. This is because the number of states in the merged node is the product of the number of states of the individual variables. This product quickly becomes unmanageably large as more variables are merged together.

2. Remove loops by observing a variable in the loop

If we observe `csharp` to be `true`, then the outward messages from the `csharp` variable can be sent, because they are just point masses. This has the effect of cutting the loop. The downside is that to get any marginal you now have to run inference twice, once with `csharp` set to `true` and once with it set to `false` and then combine the two answers. For graphs with many loops, we would need to observe multiple variables to ensure all loops were cut. This is the basis of a method called *cutset conditioning* Pearl [1988]; Suermondt and Cooper [1990], where the *cutset* is the set of variables that are observed (conditioned on) in order to cut all loops. Like the junction tree algorithm, cutset conditioning can be unusably slow when the cutset is large since we need to re-run inference for every configuration of the variables in the cutset. The number of configurations of the cutset is again the product of the number of states of the individual variables, which quickly becomes unmanageably large as the number of variables in the cutset increases.

The alternative is to look at methods that compute an approximation to the required marginal distributions, but which can do so in much less time. In this book, we will focus on such **approximate inference** approaches, since they have proven to be remarkably useful in a wide range of applications. For this particular loopy graph, we will introduce an approximate inference algorithm called **loopy belief propagation**.

2.3.1 Loopy belief propagation

⚓ Inference deep-dive
In this optional section, we define the loopy belief propagation algorithm and use it to perform inference in our loopy model. If you want to focus on modelling, feel free to skip this section.

Loopy belief propagation [Frey and MacKay, 1998] is identical to belief propagation until we come to a message that we cannot compute because it is in a loop. At that point, the loopy belief propagation algorithm computes the message anyway using a suitable initial value for any messages which are not yet available.

So, in loopy belief propagation, when we wish to compute a message m that depends on other messages which are not yet computed, we use a special initial message value for the unavailable messages. This initial value is usually the uniform distribution (such as $Bernoulli(0.5)$), but in some cases, it may be preferable to use some other user-supplied distribution. These initial message values allow us to break the loop and compute m. Once we have computed m, we will be able to compute other messages around the loop and eventually we get back to the original node. At this point, all the incoming messages needed to compute m will have been computed, so we can recompute m using these values instead of the initial ones. But because m has changed in value, we can then go around the loop computing all the messages again. Which will bring us back to recomputing m, and so on. After a number of iterations around the loop, this procedure often leads to the value of message m not changing – we say that it has **converged**. At this point, we can stop sending any further messages, since there will be no further changes to the computed marginal distributions.

The complete loopy belief propagation algorithm is given as Algorithm 2.2 – it requires as input a message-passing schedule, which we will discuss shortly. Loopy belief propagation is not guaranteed to give the exactly correct result but it often gives results that are very close. Unlike exact inference methods, however, loopy belief propagation is still fast when applied to large models, which is a very desirable property in real applications.

Choosing a message-passing schedule

An important consequence of using loopy belief propagation is that we now need to provide a **message-passing schedule**, that is, we need to say the order in which messages will be calculated. This is in contrast to belief propagation where the schedule is fixed, since a message can be sent only at the point when all the incoming messages it depends on are received. A schedule for loopy belief propagation needs to be iterative, in that parts of it will have to be repeated until message passing has converged.

Algorithm 2.2: Loopy Belief Propagation

Input: factor graph, list of target variables to compute
marginals for, message-passing schedule, initial
message values (optional).
Output: marginal distributions for target variables.

Initialise all messages to uniform (or initial values, if
provided).
repeat
    foreach *edge in the message-passing schedule* **do**
        Send the appropriate message below:
        - Variable node message: the product of all messages
        received on the other edges;
        - Factor node message: the product of all messages
        received on the other edges, multiplied by the factor
        function and summed over all variables except the
        one being sent to;
        - Observed node message: a point mass at the
        observed value;
    end
until *all messages have converged*
Compute marginal distributions as the product of all
incoming messages at each target variable node.

The choice of schedule can have a significant impact on the accuracy of inference and on the rate of convergence. Some guidelines for choosing a good schedule are:

- Message computations should use as few initial message values as possible. In other words, the schedule should be as close to the belief propagation schedule as possible and initial message values should only be used where absolutely necessary to break loops. Following this guideline will tend to make the converged marginal distributions more accurate.

- Messages should be sent sequentially around loops within each iteration. Following this guideline will make inference converge faster – if instead it takes two iterations to send a message around any loop, then the inference algorithm will tend to take twice as long to converge.

There are other factors that may influence the choice of schedule: for example, when running inference on a distributed cluster you may want to minimise the number of messages that pass between cluster nodes. Manually designing a message-passing schedule in a complex graph can be challenging – thankfully, there are automatic scheduling algorithms available that can produce good schedules for a large range of factor graphs, such as those used in Infer.NET [Minka et al., 2014].

2.3.2 Applying loopy belief propagation to our model

Let's now apply loopy belief propagation to solve our model of Figure 2.14, assuming that the candidate also gets the fourth question wrong (so that `isCorrect4` is `false`). We'll start by laying out the model a bit differently to make the loop really clear – see Figure 2.15a. Now we need to pick a message-passing schedule for this model. A schedule which follows the guidelines above is:

1. Send messages towards the loop from the `isCorrect` observed nodes and the Bernoulli priors (Figure 2.15b);

2. Send messages clockwise around the loop until convergence (Figure 2.15c). We need to use one initial message to break the loop (shown in green);

3. Send messages anticlockwise around the loop until convergence (Figure 2.15d). We must also use one initial message (again in green).

In fact, the messages in the clockwise and anti-clockwise loops do not affect each other since the messages in a particular direction only depend on incoming messages running in the same direction. So we can execute steps 2 and 3 of this schedule in either order (or even in parallel!).

For the first step of the schedule, the actual messages passed are shown in (Figure 2.15b). The messages sent around the loop clockwise A, B, C, D are shown in Table 2.5 for first five iterations around the loop. By the fourth iteration the messages are no longer changing, which means that they have converged (and so we could have stopped after four iterations).

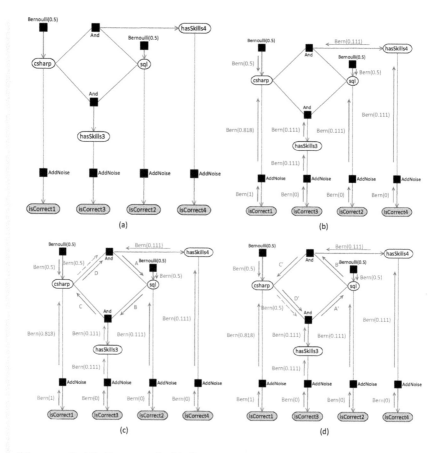

Figure 2.15 Loopy belief propagation in the four-question factor graph (a) The factor graph of Figure 2.14 rearranged to show the loop more clearly. (b) The first stage of loopy belief propagation, showing messages being passed inwards toward the loop. (c,d) The second and third stages of loopy belief propagation where messages are passed clockwise or anti-clockwise around the loop. In each case, the first message (A or A') is computed using a uniform initial message (green dashed arrow).

The messages for the anti-clockwise loop A', B', C', D' turn out to be identical to the corresponding A, B, C, D messages, because the messages from `hasSkills3` and `hasSkills4` are the same. Given these messages, the only remaining step is to multiply together the incoming messages at `csharp` and `sql` to get the marginal distributions.

Table 2.5 The messages sent around the loop in the first five iterations of message passing – the numbers shown are the parameters of the Bernoulli distribution of each message By the fourth iteration, the messages have stopped changing, showing that the algorithm has converged rapidly.

Iteration	A	B	C	D
1	0.360	0.066	0.485	0.809
2	0.226	0.035	0.492	0.813
3	0.224	0.035	0.492	0.814
4	0.224	0.035	0.492	0.814
5	0.224	0.035	0.492	0.814

Loopy belief propagation gives the marginal distributions for csharp and sql as $Bernoulli(0.809)$ and $Bernoulli(0.010)$ respectively. If we use an exact inference method to compute the true posterior marginals, we get $Bernoulli(0.800)$ and $Bernoulli(0.024)$, showing that our approximate answers are reasonably close to the exact solution. For the purposes of this application, we are interested in whether a candidate has a skill or not but can tolerate the predicted probability being off by a percentage point or two, if it can make the system run quickly. This illustrates why approximate inference methods can be so useful when tackling large-scale inference problems. However, it is always worth investigating what inaccuracies are being introduced by using an approximate inference method. Later on, in Section 2.5.1, we'll look at one possible way of doing this.

Another reason for using approximate inference methods is that they let us do inference in much more complex models than is possible using exact inference. The accuracy gain achieved by using a better model, that more precisely represents the data, usually far exceeds the accuracy loss caused by doing approximate inference. Or as the mathematician John Tukey put it,

> "Far better an approximate answer to the right question. . . than an exact answer to the wrong one."

REVIEW OF CONCEPTS

loops A loop is a path through a graph starting and ending at the same node which does not go over any edge more than once. For example, see the loop highlighted in red in Figure 2.15a.

tree A graph which does not contain any loops, such as the factor graphs of Figures 2.4 and 2.5. When a graph is a tree, belief propagation can be used to give exact marginal distributions.

loopy graph A graph which contains at least one loop. For example, the graph of Figure 2.14 contains a loop, which may be seen more clearly when it is laid out as shown in Figure 2.15a. Loopy graphs present greater difficulties when performing inference calculations – for example, belief propagation no longer gives exact marginal distributions.

exact inference An inference calculation which exactly computes the desired posterior marginal distribution or distributions. Exact inference is usually only possible for relatively small models or for models which have a particular structure, such as a tree. See also Panel 2.2.

approximate inference An inference calculation which aims to closely approximate the desired posterior marginal distribution, used when exact inference will take too long or is not possible. For most useful models, exact inference is not possible or would be very slow, so some kind of approximate inference method will be needed.

loopy belief propagation An approximate inference algorithm which applies the belief propagation algorithm to a loopy graph by initialising messages in loops and then iterating repeatedly. The loopy belief propagation algorithm is defined in Algorithm 2.2.

converged The state of an iterative algorithm when further iterations do not lead to any change. When an iterative algorithm has converged, there is no point in performing further iterations and so the algorithm can be stopped. Some convergence criteria must be used to determine whether the algorithm has converged – these usually allow for small changes (for example, in messages) to account for numerical inaccuracies or to stop the algorithm when it has approximately converged, to save on computation.

message-passing schedule The order in which messages are calculated and passed in a message passing algorithm. The result of the message passing algorithm can change dramatically depending on the order in which messages are passed and so it is important to use an appropriate schedule. Often, a schedule will be iterative – in other words, it will consist of an ordering of messages to be computed repeatedly until the algorithm converges.

SELF ASSESSMENT 2.3

The following exercises will help embed the concepts you have learned in this section. It may help to refer back to the text or the review of concepts.

1. Draw a factor graph for a six-question test which assesses three skills. Identify all the loops in your network. If there are no loops, add more questions until there are.

2. For your six-question test, design a message-passing schedule which uses as few initial messages as possible (one per loop). Remember that a message cannot be sent from a node unless messages have been received on all edges connected to that node (except for observed variable nodes).

3. Extend your three question Infer.NET model from the previous self assessment, to include the fourth question of Figure 2.14. Use the TraceMessages attribute to see what messages Infer.NET is sending and confirm that they match the schedule and values shown in Table 2.5. If you get stuck, you can refer to the source code for this chapter [Diethe et al., 2019].

2.4 MOVING TO REAL DATA

Now that we have fully tested out our model on example data, we are ready to work with some real data. We asked 22 volunteers to complete an assessment test consisting of 48 questions, intended to assess seven different development skills. Many of the questions required two skills, because they needed both the knowledge of a software development concept (such as object-oriented programming) and a knowledge of the programming language that the question used (such as C#).

As well as completing the test, we also asked each volunteer to say which development skills they consider that they have. These self-assessed skills will be used as **ground truth** for the skill variables – that is, we will consider them to be the true values of the variables. Such ground truth data will be used to assess the accuracy of our system in inferring the skills automatically from the volunteers' answers. The ground truth data should be reasonably reliable since the volunteers have no incentive to exaggerate their skills: the results were kept anonymous so that the reported skills and answers could not be linked to any particular volunteer. However, it is plausible that some volunteers may over- or under-estimate their own skills and we will need to bear this in mind when using these data to assess our accuracy.

Part of the raw data that we collected is shown in Table 2.6.

Table 2.6 Part of the raw data collected from volunteers completing a real assessment test. This data consists of the self-assessed skills (S1-S7) and the answers to each question (Q1-Q48) The first row of data gives the correct answers to each question. Each subsequent row gives the data for one of the participants.

#	S1	S2	S3	S4	S5	S6	S7	Q1	Q2	Q3	Q4	Q5	Q6	Q7	Q8	Q9	Q10	Q11	Q12	Q13	Q14	Q15	Q16	Q17	Q18	Q19	Q20	Q21	Q22	Q23	Q24	Q25	Q26	Q27
ANS								2	4	3	3	4	1	4	5	1	5	1	1	1	4	3	1	2	3	2	3	4	4	2	2	2	4	
P1	✓	✓	✓	✓	☐	✓	✓	2	4	3	3	4	3	4	5	1	5	1	1	1	4	3	1	2	3	2	3	4	5	2	2	2	4	
P2	✓	✓	✓	✓	☐	☐	✓	1	4	3	3	4	1	4	5	1	5	1	5	1	4	3	3	5	3	2	3	4	5	5	2	2	4	
P3	☐	☐	☐	✓	☐	✓	☐	3	4	5	2	4	5	4	5	1	5	5	3	2	5	5	1	2	1	2	3	1	5	1	1	4	4	
P4	✓	✓	☐	✓	☐	☐	☐	2	4	3	3	4	3	4	5	1	5	1	1	1	4	3	1	2	3	2	3	4	5	2	2	2	4	
P5	✓	✓	☐	☐	☐	☐	✓	2	4	3	3	4	1	4	5	1	5	1	1	1	4	3	1	2	3	2	3	4	5	2	2	2	4	
P6	☐	☐	☐	☐	☐	☐	☐	1	3	3	5	3	4	5	2	5	2	1	4	2	2	4	4	5	1	3	2	1	3	1	2	3	5	
P7	✓	✓	☐	☐	☐	☐	☐	2	4	3	3	4	1	4	5	1	5	1	1	1	2	3	1	2	3	2	3	4	5	2	2	2	4	
P8	✓	✓	☐	☐	☐	☐	✓	2	4	5	2	4	1	4	5	1	5	1	1	1	4	3	1	2	3	2	3	4	4	2	2	2	4	
P9	✓	✓	☐	☐	✓	✓	✓	2	4	1	3	4	1	4	5	1	5	1	1	1	4	3	1	2	3	2	3	4	2	2	1	2	5	
P10	✓	✓	☐	☐	✓	✓	✓	2	4	3	3	4	1	4	5	1	5	1	1	2	4	3	1	2	3	2	2	1	5	2	2	2	4	
P11	✓	✓	☐	☐	☐	☐	✓	1	4	3	3	4	3	4	5	1	5	3	1	1	4	3	1	2	3	2	3	4	5	4	2	2	4	...
P12	☐	☐	☐	☐	✓	☐	☐	1	1	1	3	4	1	4	5	1	5	1	5	5	2	2	1	5	3	2	3	4	5	2	2	2	4	
P13	✓	✓	☐	☐	☐	☐	☐	2	4	3	3	4	3	4	5	1	5	1	1	1	2	3	1	2	3	2	3	4	2	2	2	2	4	
P14	✓	✓	☐	☐	✓	☐	☐	2	5	3	3	5	4	5	1	5	1	1	5	2	3	1	2	3	2	3	2	4	2	3	2	4		
P15	✓	☐	☐	☐	☐	☐	☐	2	4	3	3	4	3	4	5	1	5	4	5	1	2	3	5	2	3	2	4	4	1	2	3	2	4	
P16	✓	✓	☐	☐	✓	✓	✓	2	4	3	5	4	1	4	5	1	5	1	1	1	4	3	1	2	3	2	3	4	5	5	2	2	4	
P17	✓	✓	☐	☐	☐	☐	✓	2	4	3	3	4	1	4	5	1	5	1	1	1	4	3	1	2	3	2	3	4	5	2	2	2	4	
P18	✓	✓	☐	☐	☐	☐	✓	2	4	3	3	4	3	4	5	1	5	1	1	1	4	3	1	2	3	2	3	4	2	2	2	2	4	
P19	✓	✓	☐	✓	☐	☐	✓	2	4	5	3	4	3	4	2	1	5	1	5	1	4	3	1	2	3	2	3	4	3	2	2	2	4	
P20	✓	✓	✓	✓	☐	✓	✓	2	4	3	3	4	1	4	5	1	5	1	1	1	4	3	1	2	3	2	3	4	4	2	2	2	4	
P21	✓	✓	☐	✓	✓	✓	✓	2	4	3	3	4	1	3	5	1	5	1	1	1	4	3	1	2	3	2	3	4	5	2	2	2	4	
P22	✓	✓	✓	✓	☐	✓	☐	2	4	4	3	4	1	4	5	1	5	1	1	1	3	3	1	2	4	2	3	4	5	5	2	2	4	

In this machine learning application, we need the system to be able to work with any test supplied to it, without having to gather new ground truth data for each new test. This means that we cannot use the ground truth data when doing inference in our model, since we will not have this kind of data in practice. Learning without using ground truth data is called **unsupervised learning**. We still need ground truth data when developing our system, however, since we need to evaluate how well the system works. We will evaluate it on this particular test, with the assumption that it will then work with similar accuracy on new, unseen tests.

2.4.1 Visualising the data

When working on a new data set, it is *essential* to spend time looking at the data by visualising it in various ways (see Panel 2.3 for why this is so important). So let's now look at making a **visualisation** of our test answers.

The crucial elements of a good visualisation are (i) it is a faithful representation of the underlying data, (ii) it makes at least one aspect of the data very clear, (iii) it stands alone (does not require any explanatory text) and (iv) it is otherwise as simple as possible. There are entire books on the topic (such as Tufte [1986]), as well as useful websites (these are constantly changing – use your search engine!) and commercial visualisation software (such as Tableau). In addition, most programming languages have visualisation and charting libraries available, particularly those languages focused on data science such as R, Python and Matlab. In this book, we aim to illustrate what makes a good visualisation by example, through the various figures illustrating each case study. For example, in Table 2.4 the use of bars to represent probabilities, as well as numbers, makes it easier to see the relationship between which questions were correct and the inferred skill probabilities.

Photo (and cookies) by Sarah Supp, Dec 2018.

It is good to be creative when visualizing your data.

Panel 2.3: The importance of visualisation

Machine learning algorithms often don't fail when there is an error in the code, but instead continue silently on to give inaccurate results. Visualisations of data, of the inference process, and of results provide a very effective way of detecting and understanding such errors.

Visualisations are also important because:

- They let you discover issues with the data, such as mistakes in the data entry, missing data, mislabelled data, data that was saved in the wrong format or data which is being loaded incorrectly.

- They let you see patterns in the data, even before any model is created or any inference calculations are done. Carefully designed visualisations can expose a useful pattern in much the same way that a carefully designed model can expose one.

- They let you communicate the results of your work to others, to help convince them that your system is working well or to demonstrate that it is extracting useful information from the data.

Rather than asking "do I need to visualise this data?", a better question is "can I afford NOT to visualise this data?" Any time you choose not to visualise some data, some part of the inference process or some results, there is a (high) chance that you are missing something important. **A good rule of thumb is that it is worth spending at least 20% of your time on making visualisations.**

We want to visualise whether each person got each question right or wrong, along with the skills needed for that question (as provided by the person who wrote the test). For the skills needed, we can use a grid where a white square means the skill is needed and a black square means it is not needed (Figure 2.16a). Similarly for the answers, we can use another grid where white means the answer was right and black means it was wrong (Figure 2.16b). To make it easier to spot the relationship between the skills and the answers, we can align the two grids, giving the visualisation of Figure 2.16.

Already this visualisation is telling us a lot about the data: it lets us see which questions are easy (columns that are nearly all white) and which are hard (columns that are nearly all black). Similarly, it lets us identify individuals who are doing well or badly and gives us a sense of the variation between people. Most usefully, it shows us that people often get questions wrong in runs. In our test consecutive questions usually need similar skills, so a run of wrong questions can be explained by the lack of a corresponding skill. These runs are reassuring since this is the kind of pattern we would expect if the data followed the assumptions of our model.

A difficulty with this visualisation is that we have to look back and forth between the two grids to discover the relationship between the answers to a question and the skills needed for a question. It is not

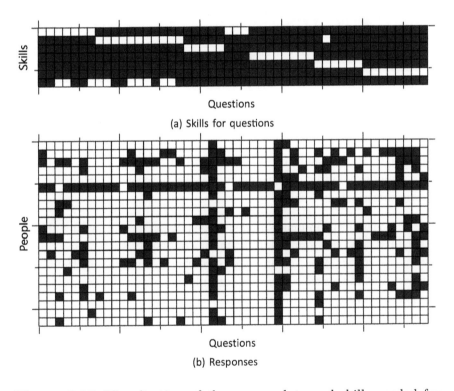

Figure 2.16 Visualisation of the answer data and skills needed for each question. (a) Each row corresponds to a skill and each column to a question. White squares show which skills are needed for each question (b) Each row corresponds to a person and again each column corresponds to a question. Here, white squares show which questions each person got correct.

particularly easy, for example, to identify the set of skills needed for the questions that a particular person got wrong. To address this, we could try to create a visualisation that contains the information in both of the grids. One way to do this is to associate a colour with each skill and colour the wrong answers appropriately, as shown in Figure 2.17:

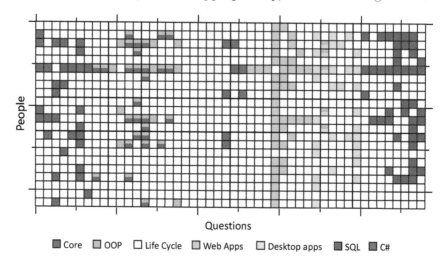

Figure 2.17 A visualisation of the same data as Figure 2.16 but using only a single, coloured grid, to make it easier to see associations between wrong questions and skills.

This visualisation makes it easier to spot patterns of wrong answers associated with the same skill, without constantly switching focus between two grids. We could instead have chosen to highlight the correct answers but in this case it is more useful to focus on the wrong answers since these are rarer, and so more interesting. For example, we can see that those people who got some orange (Object Oriented Programming) questions wrong often got many other orange questions wrong, since orange grid cells often appear in blocks. This is very suggestive of the absence of an underlying skill influencing the answers to all these questions. Conversely for the cyan (Desktop apps) questions, there seems to be less block structure, suggesting that our assumption of one skill influencing all these questions is weaker in this case.

2.4.2 A factor graph for the whole test

Reassured that our data looks plausible, we would now like to run inference on a factor graph for this assessment test. We've already seen factor graphs for three questions (Figure 2.5) and for four questions (Figure 2.14) where there were just two skills being modelled. But if we tried to draw a factor graph for all 48 questions and all seven skills in the same way, it would be huge and not particularly useful. To avoid such overly large factor graphs, we can represent repeated structure in the graph using a **plate**. Here is an example of using a plate used to represent the prior over five skill variables:

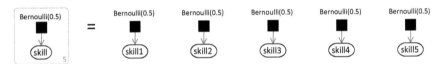

Figure 2.18 Using a plate to represent repeated structure in a factor graph.

The factor graph on the left with a plate is equivalent to the factor graph on the right without a plate. The plate is shown as a rectangle with the number of repetitions in the bottom right corner – which in this case is 5. Variable and factor nodes contained in the plate are considered to be replicated 5 times. Where a variable has been replicated inside a plate, it becomes a **variable array** of length 5 – so in this example skill is an array with elements skill[0], skill[1], skill[2], skill[3] and skill[4]. Note that we use index 0 to refer to the first element of an array.

Figure 2.19 shows how we can use plates to draw a compact factor graph for the entire test. There are two plates in the graph, one across the skills and one across the questions. Instead of putting in actual numbers for the number of repetitions, we have used variables called skills and questions. This gives us a factor graph which is configurable for any number of skills and any number of questions and so could be used for any test. For our particular test, we will set skills to 7 and questions to 48.

Figure 2.19 has also introduced the *Subarray* factor connecting two new variables skillsNeeded and relevantSkills, both of which are arrays inside the questions plate. The skillsNeeded array must be provided (indicated by the grey shading) and contains the information of which skills are needed for each question. Each element of skillsNeeded is itself a small array of integers specifying the indices of the skills needed for that question–so for a question that needs the first and third skills this will be [0, 2]. The *Subarray* factor uses

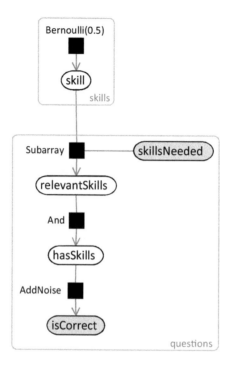

Figure 2.19 A factor graph for the entire test, constructed using plates and the *Subarray* factor.

this information to pull out the relevant subarray of the skill array and put it into the corresponding element of the relevantSkills array. Continuing our example, this would mean that the element of relevantSkills would contain the subarray [skill[0], skill[2]]. From this point on, the factor graph is as before: hasSkills is an AND of the elements of relevantSkills and isCorrect is then a noisy version of hasSkills.

2.4.3   Our first results

We are now ready to get our first results on a real data set. It's taken a while to get here, because of the time we have spent testing out the model on small examples and visualising the data. But, by doing these tasks, we can be confident that our inference results will be meaningful from the start.

We can apply loopy belief propagation to the factor graph of Figure 2.19 separately for each person, with isCorrect set to that

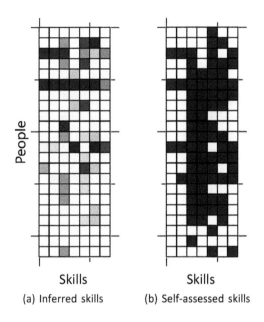

Skills   Skills

(a) Inferred skills   (b) Self-assessed skills

Figure 2.20 Initial results of applying our model to real assessment data. (a) Computed probability of each person having each skill, where white corresponds to probability 1.0, black to probability 0.0 and shades of grey indicate intermediate probability values. (b) Ground truth self-assessed skills where white indicates that the person assessed that they have the skill and black indicates that they do not. Unfortunately, the inferred skills have little similarity to the self-assessed skills.

person's answers. For each skill, this will give the probability that the person has that skill. Repeating this for each person leads to a matrix of results which is shown in the visualisation on the left of Figure 2.20, where the rows correspond to different people and the columns correspond to different skills. For comparison, we include the self-assessed skills for the same people on the right of the figure.

There is clearly something very wrong with these inference results! The inferred skills show little similarity to the self-assessed skills. There are a couple of people where the inferred skills seem reasonable – such as the people on the 3rd and 6th rows. However, for most people, the system has inferred that they have almost all the skills, whether they do or not. How can this happen after all our careful testing and preparation?

In fact, the first time a machine learning system is applied to real data, it is very common that the results are not as intended. The challenge is to find out what is wrong and to fix it.

REVIEW OF CONCEPTS

ground truth A data set which includes values for variables which we want to predict or infer, used for evaluating the prediction accuracy of a model and/or for training a model. Ground truth data is usually expensive or difficult to collect and so is a valuable and scarce commodity in most machine learning projects.

unsupervised learning Learning which doesn't use labelled (ground truth) data but instead aims to discover patterns in unlabelled data automatically, without manual guidance.

visualisation A pictorial representation of some data or inference result which allows patterns or problems to be detected, understood, communicated and acted upon. Visualisation is a very important part of machine learning, as discussed in Panel 2.3.

plate A container in a factor graph which compactly represents a number of repetitions of the contained nodes and edges. The plate is drawn as a rectangle and labelled in the bottom right-hand corner with the number of repetitions. For example, see Figure 2.18.

variable array An ordered collection of variables where individual variables are identified by their position in the ordering (starting at zero). For example, a variable array called `skill` of length 5 would contain five variables: `skill[0]`, `skill[1]`, `skill[2]`, `skill[3]`, and `skill[4]`.

SELF ASSESSMENT 2.4

The following exercises will help embed the concepts you have learned in this section. It may help to refer back to the text or the review of concepts.

1. Create an alternative visualisation of the data set of Table 2.6 which shows which people get the most questions right and which questions the most people get right. For example, you could sort the rows and columns of Figure 2.16 or Figure 2.17. What does

your new visualisation show that was not apparent in the visualisations used in this section? Note: The data set can be downloaded in Excel or CSV form using the buttons by the online version of the table.

2. Implement the factor graph with plates from Figure 2.19 using Infer.NET [Minka et al., 2014]. You will need to use Variable arrays, ForEach loops and the Subarray factor. Apply your factor graph to the data set and verify that you get the results shown in Figure 2.20a.

2.5 DIAGNOSING THE PROBLEM

When a machine learning system is not working, there are generally three possible reasons: bad data, bad model or bad inference. Here are some common causes of problems under each of these three headings:

Bad data: Data items have been entered, stored or loaded incorrectly; the data items are incomplete or mislabelled; data values are too noisy to be useful; the data is biased or unrepresentative of how the system will be used; it is the wrong data for the task; there is insufficient data to make accurate predictions.

Bad model: One or more of the modelling assumptions are wrong – that is, not consistent with the actual process that generated the data; the model makes too many simplifying assumptions; the model contains insufficient assumptions to make accurate predictions given the amount of available data.

Bad inference: The inference code contains a bug; the message-passing schedule is bad; the inference has not converged; there are numerical problems (e.g. rounding, overflow); the approximate inference algorithm is not accurate enough.

In our case, we can be fairly confident that the data is good because we have inspected and visualised it carefully. So it seems likely that either the model or the inference is causing the problem. We'll start by checking that the inference algorithm, loopy belief propagation, is working correctly.

2.5.1 Checking the inference algorithm

To see if inference is working correctly, we need to be able to separate out any problems caused by inference issues from any problems caused by our model not matching the data. To achieve this separation, we can generate a new *synthetic* data set which is guaranteed to match the model exactly. If we get poor results using this data set it suggests that there is an inference problem. We will create this synthetic data set by sampling from the joint distribution specified by the model, which guarantees that the data is consistent with the model (refer to Chapter 1 for a reminder of what sampling is). We can generate samples by running the data generation process specified by the model – a

---

Algorithm 2.3: Ancestral sampling

Input: factor graph
Output: sampled values for each variable in the graph

Order variables from top to bottom so that parent variables
come before child variables.
foreach *variable v in this ordering* **do**

> If **v** has parent variables, retrieve their sampled values
> (which must already exist due to the ordering).
> Sample a value for **v** from the parent factor function,
> conditioned on the retrieved parent values, if any. If the
> parent factor is deterministic (such as an *And* factor) this
> simplifies to just computing the child value from the
> parent values.
> Store the sampled value.

end

---

process called **ancestral sampling**, as defined by Algorithm 2.3 (see
also Bishop [2006]).

Looking at the factor graph of Figure 2.19, we run ancestral sampling following the arrows from top to bottom (from ancestor to de-
scendent), by sampling a value for each variable given its parents in the
graph. If a variable is the child variable of a deterministic factor, then
we just compute its value from the values of its parent variables using the function encoded by the deterministic factor (such as the AND
function).

So, starting at the top, we sample a value for each element of
the skill array from a *Bernoulli*(0.5) distribution – in other words,
we pick **true** with 50% probability and **false** otherwise. For the
relevantSkills array element, for a question we just pull out the
already-sampled values of the skill array that are relevant to that
question. These values are then ANDed together to give hasSkills.
Figure 2.21 gives an example set of 22 samples for the skill and
hasSkills arrays. To get a data set with multiple rows, we just repeat the entire sampling process for each row. Notice how, for each
row, hasSkills is always the same for questions that require the same
skills (are the same colour).

The final stage of ancestral sampling in our model requires
sampling each element of isCorrect, given its parent element of

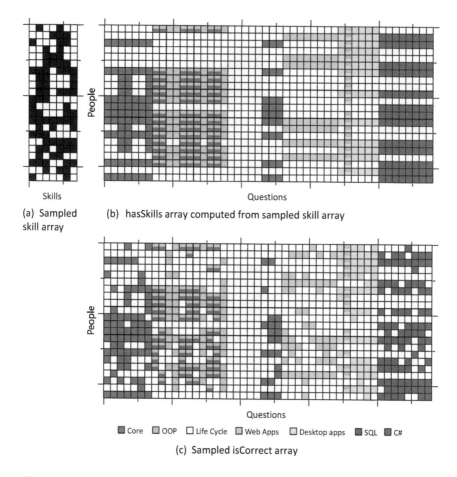

(a) Sampled skill array

(b) hasSkills array computed from sampled skill array

☐ Core ☐ OOP ☐ Life Cycle ☐ Web Apps ☐ Desktop apps ■ SQL ■ C#

(c) Sampled isCorrect array

Figure 2.21 Synthetic data set created using ancestral sampling. First the skill array was sampled and then the hasSkill array was computed from it. The isCorrect array was then sampled given the hasSkill array, which has the effect of making it a noisy version of hasSkill.

hasSkills. Where hasSkills is true we sample from $Bernoulli(0.9)$ and where hasSkills is false we sample from $Bernoulli(0.2)$ (following Table 2.1). The result of performing this step gives the isCorrect samples of Figure 2.21c. Notice that these samples end up looking like a noisy version of the hasSkills samples – about one in ten white squares has been flipped to colour and about one in five coloured squares has been flipped to white.

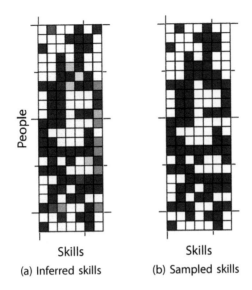

(a) Inferred skills   (b) Sampled skills

Figure 2.22 Skills inferred from a sample data set shown next to the actual sampled skills for that data set. The inferred skills are close to the actual skills, suggesting that the inference algorithm is working well.

We now have an entire sampled data set, which we can run our inference algorithm on to test if it is working correctly. The inferred skill probabilities are shown in Figure 2.22 next to the actual skills that we sampled. Unlike with the real data, the results are pretty convincing: the inferred skills look very similar to the actual sampled skills. So, when we run inference on a data set that conforms perfectly to our model, the results are good. This suggests that the inference algorithm is working well and the problem must instead be that our model does not match the real data.

An important and subtle point is that the inferred skills are close *but not identical* to the sampled skills, even though the data is perfectly matched to the model. This is because there is still some remaining uncertainty in the skills even given all the answers in the test. For example, the posterior probability of skill 7 (C#) is uncertain in the cases where the individual does not have skill 1 (Core) or skill 2 (OOP). This makes sense because the C# skill is only tested in combination with these first two skills – if a person does not have them, then they will get the associated questions wrong, whether or not they know C#. So in this case, the inference algorithm is correct to be uncertain about whether or not the person has the C# skill. We could use this information to improve the test, such as by adding questions that directly test the C# skill by itself.

2.5.2   Working out what is wrong with the model

We have determined that our model assumptions are not matching the data – now we need to identify which assumption(s) are at fault. We can again use sampling to achieve this but rather than sampling the skill array, we can set it to the true (self-assessed) values. If we then sample the isCorrect array, it will show us which answers the model is expecting people to get wrong if they had these skills. By comparing this to the actual isCorrect array from our data set, we can see where the model's assumptions differ from reality. Figure 2.23 shows that the actual isCorrect data looks quite different to the sampled data. The biggest difference appears to be that our volunteers got many more questions right than our model is predicting, given their stated skills. This suggests that they are able to guess the answer to a question much more often than the 1-in-5 times that our model assumes. On reflection, this makes sense – even if someone doesn't have the skill to answer a question they may be able to eliminate some answers on the basis of general knowledge or intelligent guesswork.

We can investigate this further by computing the fraction of times that our model predicts our volunteers should get each question right, given their self-assessed skills, and then compare it to the fraction of times they actually got it right (Figure 2.24).

For a few questions, the fraction of people who got them correct matches that predicted by the model – but for most questions the actual fraction is higher than the predicted fraction. This suggests that some questions are easier to guess than others and that they can be guessed correctly more often than 1-in-5 times. So we need to change our assumptions (and our model) to allow different guess probabilities for different questions. We can modify our fourth assumption as follows:

④ If a candidate doesn't have all the skills needed for a question, they will ~~pick an answer at random~~ guess an answer, where the probability that they guess correctly is about 20% for most questions but could vary up to about 60% for very guessable questions.

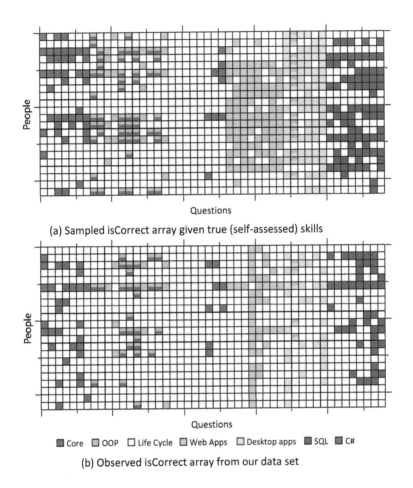

(a) Sampled isCorrect array given true (self-assessed) skills

Questions

■ Core ◻ OOP ◻ Life Cycle ◼ Web Apps ◻ Desktop apps ◼ SQL ◼ C#

(b) Observed isCorrect array from our data set

Figure 2.23 The modelling problem can be diagnosed by comparing (a) the `isCorrect` data sampled from the model given the self-assessed skills and (b) the observed `isCorrect` data showing which questions the volunteers actually got wrong.

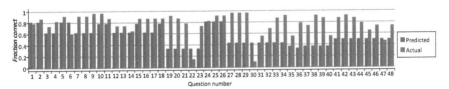

Figure 2.24 The fraction of people the model predicts will get each question right given their self-assessed skills (blue) compared to the fraction that actually got it right (red), for each of the 48 questions in the test.

This assumption means that, rather than having a fixed guess probability for all questions, we need to extend our model to *learn* a different guess probability for each question.

REVIEW OF CONCEPTS

ancestral sampling   A process of producing samples from a probabilistic model by first sampling variables which have no parents using their prior distributions, then sampling their child variables conditioned on these sampled values, then sampling the children's child variables similarly and so on. Ancestral sampling is defined in Algorithm 2.3. For an example of ancestral sampling, see Section 2.5.1.

SELF ASSESSMENT 2.5

The following exercises will help embed the concepts you have learned in this section. It may help to refer back to the text or the review of concepts.

1. Make a check list of the causes of problems with machine learning systems (either data problems, model problems or inference problems). Rank the causes in the order which you think are most likely to occur. Now if you are working on a machine learning problem in the future, this check list could be useful when diagnosing the root cause of the problem.

2. Write a program to implement ancestral sampling in the skills model, as was described in this section, and use it to make a synthetic data set. Visualise this data set, for example, using the visualisation you developed in the previous self assessment. Check that your samples look similar to the samples from Figure 2.21.

3. Try changing a couple of the probability values that we have chosen in the model, such as the prior probability of having a skill or the probability of guessing the answer. Run your sampling program again and see how the synthetic data set changes. You could imagine repeating this procedure until the synthetic data looks as much like the real data as possible given the model assumptions. This would be quite inefficient, so we instead learn these probability values as part of the inference algorithm, as we shall see in the next section.

2.6   LEARNING THE GUESS PROBABILITIES

You might expect that inferring the guess probabilities would require very different techniques than we have used so far. In fact, our approach will be exactly the same: we add the probability values we want to learn as new continuous random variables in our model and use probabilistic inference to compute their posterior distributions. This demonstrates the power of the model-based approach – whenever we want to know something, we introduce it as a random variable in our model and compute it using a standard inference algorithm.

Let's see how to modify our model to include the guess probabilities as random variables. To keep things consistent, we'll also add in a variable for the mistake probability (actually the no-mistake probability) but we'll keep this fixed at a 10% chance of making a mistake. To start with, we'll change how we write the *AddNoise* factor. Figure 2.25 shows how the existing *AddNoise* factor (which has the guess and no-mistake probabilities hard-coded at 0.2 and 0.9, respectively) can be replaced by a general *Table* factor which takes these probabilities as additional arguments. We can then set these arguments using two new random variables, which we name as `probGuess` and `probNoMistake`. Inferring the posterior distribution over the variable `probGuess` will allow us to learn the guess probability for a question. But before we can do this, we must first see what kind of distribution we can use to represent the uncertainty in such a variable.

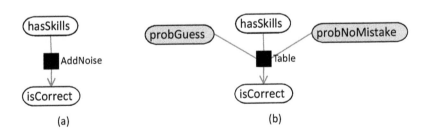

Figure 2.25 Two ways of writing the *AddNoise* factor: (a) As a custom factor with the guess and mistake probabilities 'built-in'. (b) Using a general purpose *Table* factor which has arguments for the probability that the child is `true` given that the parent is `false` (left argument) or given the parent is `true` (right argument). This way of writing the factor allows the arguments to be included as variables in the graph.

2.6.1 Representing uncertainty in continuous values

The two new variables probGuess and probNoMistake have a different type to the ones we have encountered so far: previously all of our variables have been binary (two-valued), whereas these new variables are continuous (real-valued) in the interval 0.0 to 1.0 inclusive. This means we cannot use a Bernoulli distribution to represent their uncertainty. In fact, because our variables are continuous, we need to use a distribution based on a **probability density function** – if you are not familiar with this term, read Panel 2.4.

We need a distribution whose density function can represent both our prior assumption "the probability that they guess correctly is about 20% for most questions but could vary up to about 60% for very guessable questions" and also the posterior over the guess probabilities, once we have learned from the data. The distribution should also be restricted to the range 0.0 to 1.0 inclusive. A suitable function would be one that could model a single "bump" that lies in this range, since the bump could be broad from 20% to 60% for the prior and then could become narrow around a particular value for the learned posterior. A distribution called the **beta distribution** meets these requirements. It has the following density function:

$$Beta(x; \alpha, \beta) = \frac{x^{\alpha-1}(1-x)^{\beta-1}}{B(\alpha, \beta)} \tag{2.19}$$

where $B()$ is the beta function that the distribution is named after, which is used to ensure the area under the function is 1.0. The beta density function has two parameters, α and β that between them control the position and width of the bump – Figure 2.26a shows a set of beta pdfs for different values of these parameters. The parameters α and β must be positive, that is, greater than zero. The mean value $\frac{\alpha}{\alpha+\beta}$ dictates where the centre of mass of the bump is located and the sum $\alpha + \beta$ controls how broad the bump is – larger $\alpha + \beta$ means a narrower bump. We can configure a beta distribution to encode our prior assumption by choosing $\alpha = 2.5$ and $\beta = 7.5$, which gives the density function shown in Figure 2.26b.

We want to extend our factor graph so that the prior probability of each probGuess variable is:

$$p(\text{probGuess}) = Beta(\text{probGuess}; 2.5, 7.5) \tag{2.20}$$

Notice the notation here: we use a lower-case p to denote a probability _density_ for a continuous variable, where previously we have used an

Panel 2.4: Probability density functions

When we want to represent the uncertainty in a continuous variable, such as a person's height, apparently reasonable statements like "There is an 80% chance that his height is 1.84 m" don't actually make sense. To see why, consider the mathematically equivalent statement "There is an 80% chance that his height is 1.840000000...m". This statement seems very unreasonable, because it suggests that no matter how many additional decimal places we measure the height to, we will always get zeroes. In fact, the more decimal places we measure, the more likely it is that we will find a non-zero. If we could keep measuring to infinite precision, the probability of getting exactly 1.84000...(or any particular value) would effectively vanish to nothing.

So rather than refer to the probability of a continuous variable taking on a particular value, we instead refer to the probability that its value lies in a particular range, such as the range from 1.835 m to 1.845 m. In everyday language, we convey this by the accuracy with which we express a number, so when we say "1.84 m", we often mean "1.84 m to the nearest centimetre", that is, anywhere between 1.835 m and 1.845 m. We could represent a distribution over a continuous value, by giving a set of such ranges along with the probability that the value lies in each range, such that the probabilities add up to one. For example:

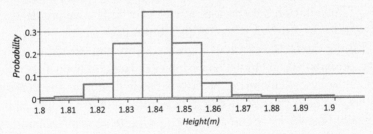

This approach can be useful but often also causes problems: it introduces a lot of parameters to learn (one per range); it can be difficult to choose a sensible set of ranges; there are discontinuities as we move from one range to another; and it is hard to impose smoothness, that is, probabilities associated with neighbouring ranges should be similar. A better solution is to define a function, such that the area under the function between any two values gives the probability of being in that range of values. Such a function is called a **probability density function** (pdf). For example, this plot shows a Gaussian pdf (we'll learn much more about Gaussians in Chapter 3):

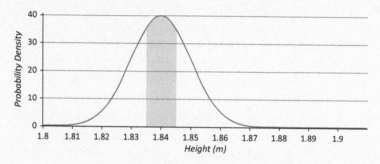

Notice that the y-axis now goes up well above 1, since a probability density is not limited to be between 0 and 1. Instead, the total area under the function is required to be 1.0. The area of the shaded region between 1.835 m and 1.845 m is 0.383, which gives the probability that the height lies between these two values. Similarly, computing the area under the pdf between *any* two points gives the probability that the height lies between those points.

upper-case P to denote the probability *distribution* for a discrete variable. This notation acts as a reminder of whether we are dealing with continuous densities or discrete distributions.

Taking the factor graph of Figure 2.19, we can extend it to have the guess probabilities included as variables in the graph with this distribution as the prior. One other change is needed: to infer the guess probabilities, we need to look at the data across as many people as possible (it would be very inaccurate to try to estimate a guess probability from just one person's answer!). So we must now extend the factor graph to model everyone's results at once, that is, the entire dataset. To do this, we add a new plate to our factor graph which replicates all variables that are specific to each person (which are: skill, relevantSkills, hasSkills and isCorrect). Since we are assuming that the guess probabilities for a question are the same for everyone, probGuess is placed outside the new plate, but inside the questions plate. Since the no-mistake probability is assumed to be the same for everyone and for all questions, `probNoMistake` is placed outside of all plates. The final factor graph, of the entire data set, is shown in Figure 2.27.

We can run inference on this graph to learn the guess probabilities. Even now that we have continuous variables, we can essentially run loopy belief propagation on the graph. The only modification we need is a change to ensure that the uncertainty in our guess probabilities is always represented as a beta distribution (this modified form is called expectation propagation and will be described fully in the next chapter). After running inference, we get a beta distribution for each question representing the uncertain value of the guess probability for that question. The beta distributions for some of the questions are shown in Figure 2.28 (we show only every fifth question, so that the figure is not overwhelmed by too many curves). The first thing to note is that the distributions are all still quite wide, indicating that there is still substantial uncertainty in the guess probabilities. This is not too surprising since the data set contains relatively few people and we only learn about question's guess probability from the subset of those people who are inferred not to have the skills needed for a question. For question 1, where we assume pretty much everyone has the (Core) skill needed, the posterior distribution is very close to the prior (compare the curve to Figure 2.26b) since there is hardly any data to learn

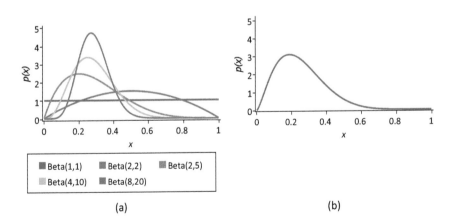

(a)

(b)

Figure 2.26 (a) Example beta distributions for different values of the parameters α and β. (b) The $Beta(2.5,7.5)$ distribution which we can use as a prior for the probability of guessing a question correctly. The peak of the distribution is at around 0.2, but it extends to the right up to around 0.6 to allow for questions that are easier to guess.

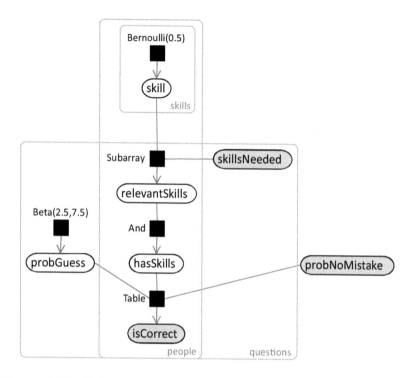

Figure 2.27 A factor graph for the entire data set, for all people who took the test. The guess probabilities for each question appear as a variable array with an appropriate beta prior.

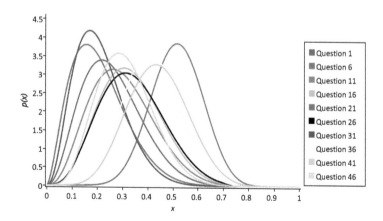

Figure 2.28 Posterior beta distributions over `probGuess` for every fifth question.

the guess probability from, as almost no one is guessing this question. Several of the questions (such as 11, 16 and 26) have posteriors that are shifted slightly to the right from the prior, suggesting that these are a bit easier to guess than 1-in-5. Most interestingly, the guess probabilities for some questions have been inferred to be either quite low (questions 6, 31) or quite high (question 21, 36, 41). We can plot the posteriors over the guess probabilities for all of the questions by plotting the mean (the centre of mass) of each along with error bars showing the uncertainty (Figure 2.29). This shows that a substantial number have a guess probability which is higher than 0.2.

Just as a reminder – we have learned these guess probabilities without knowing which people had which skills, that is, without using any ground truth data. Since it doesn't have ground truth, the model has had to use all the assumptions that we built into it, in order to infer the guess probabilities.

We can now investigate whether learning the guess probabilities has improved the accuracy of the skills we infer for each person. Figure 2.30 shows the inferred skill posteriors for the old model and for the new

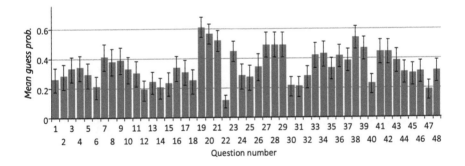

Figure 2.29 The inferred guess probabilities. The blue bar shows the mean of the posterior distribution over the guess probability for each question. The black lines are called error bars and indicate the uncertainty in the inferred guess probabilities. The top and bottom of the error bars show the upper and lower quartiles of the posterior distribution, that is, the values where there is 25% chance of the guess probability being above or below the value respectively. As we suspected, the variation in the mean shows that some questions are much easier to guess than others.

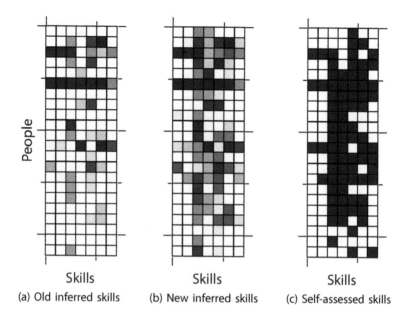

(a) Old inferred skills (b) New inferred skills (c) Self-assessed skills

Figure 2.30 Skill posteriors for (a) the original model and (b) the new model with learned guess probabilities, as compared to (c) the ground truth skills. Qualitatively, the skills inferred by the new model are closer to the self-assessed skills.

model with learned guess probabilities. Visually, it is clear that the new probabilities are closer to the ground truth skills, which is great news!

2.6.2 Measuring progress

As well as visually inspecting the improvements, it is also important to measure the improvements numerically. To do this, we must choose an **evaluation metric** which we will use to measure how well we are doing. For the task of inferring an applicant's skills, our evaluation metric should measure how close the inferred skill probabilities are to the ground truth skills.

A common metric to use is the probability of the ground truth values under the inferred distributions, since this will be high when the correct value has high probability (which we want) and low when the correct value has low probability (which we do not want). These probabilities can often get very small, which makes them hard to work with.

Instead we can take the logarithm of the probability, since logarithms allow small probabilities to be compared more easily – this metric is referred to as the **log probability**.

If the inferred probability of a person having a particular skill is p, then the log probability metric equals $\log p$ if the person has the skill and $\log(1 - p)$ if they don't. If the person does have the skill, then the best possible prediction is $p = 1.0$, which gives log probability of $\log 1.0 = 0$ (the logarithm of one is zero). A less confident prediction, such as $p = 0.8$, will give a log probability with a negative value, in this case $\log 0.8 = -0.223$. The worst possible prediction of $p = 0.0$ gives a log probability of negative infinity. This tells us two things about this metric:

1. Since the perfect log probability is zero and real systems are less than perfect, the log probability will in practice have a negative value. For this reason, it is common to use the negative log probability and consider lower values (values closer to 0) to be better.

2. This metric penalises confidently wrong predictions very heavily, because the logarithm gives very large negative values when the probability of the ground truth is very close to zero. This should be taken into account particularly where there are likely to be errors in the ground truth.

It is useful to combine the individual log probability values into a single overall metric. To do this, the log probabilities for each skill and each person can be either averaged or added together to get an overall log probability – we will use averaging since it makes the numbers more manageable. Notice that the best possible overall score (zero) is achieved by having $p = 1$ where the person has the skill and $p = 0$ where they don't – in other words, by having the inferred skill probability matrix exactly match the ground truth skill matrix.

Figure 2.31a shows the negative log probability averaged across skills and people for the original and improved models. The score for the improved model is substantially lower, indicating that it is making quantitatively much better predictions of the skill probabilities. We can investigate this further by breaking down the overall negative log probability into the contributions for the different skills (Figure 2.31b). This shows that learning the guess probabilities improves the log probability metric for all skills except the Core skill where it is about the same. This is because almost everyone has the Core skill and so the original

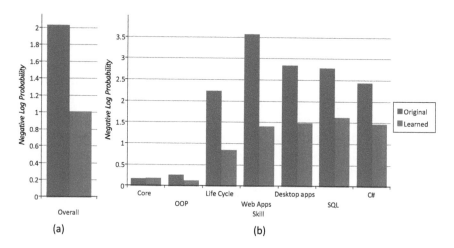

Figure 2.31 (a) Overall negative log probability for the original model and the model with learned guess probabilities. The lower red bar indicates that learning the guess probabilities gives a substantially better model, according to this metric. (b) Negative log probability for each skill, showing that the improvement varies from skill to skill.

model (which predicted that everyone has every skill) actually did well for this skill. But in general, in terms of log probability our new results are a substantial improvement over the original inferred skills.

2.6.3 A different way of measuring progress

It is good practice to use more than one evaluation metric when assessing the accuracy of a machine learning system. This is because each metric will provide different information about how the system is performing and there will be less emphasis on increasing any particular metric. No metric is perfect – focusing too much on increasing any one metric is a bad idea since it can end up exposing flaws in the metric rather than actually improving the system. This is succinctly expressed by **Goodhart's law** which can be stated as

> "When a measure becomes a target, it ceases to be a good measure".

Using multiple evaluation metrics will help us avoid becoming victims of Goodhart's law.

When deciding on a second evaluation metric to use, we need to think about how our system is to be used. One scenario is to use the system to select a short list of candidates very likely to have a particular skill. Another is to filter out candidates who are very unlikely to have the skill, to make a "long list". For both of these scenarios, we might only care about the ordering of people by their skill probabilities, not on the actual value of these probabilities. In each case, we would select the top N people, but for the shortlist N would be small, whereas for the long list N would be large. For any number of selected candidates, we can compute:

- the fraction of candidates who have the skill that are correctly selected – this is the **true positive rate** or TPR,

- the fraction of candidates who don't have the skill that are incorrectly selected – this is the **false positive rate** or FPR.

The terminology of true and false positive predictions and their corresponding rates is summarised in Table 2.7.

In general, there is a trade-off between having a high TPR and a low FPR. For a shortlist, if we want everyone on the list to have the skill (FPR=0), we would have to tolerate missing a few people with the skill (TPR less than 1). For a long list, if we want to include all people with the skill (TPR=1), we would have to tolerate including some people without the skill (FPR above 0). A **receiver operating characteristic curve**, or ROC curve [Fawcett, 2006], lets us visualise this trade-off by plotting TPR against FPR for all possible lengths of list N. The ROC curves for the original and improved models are shown

Table 2.7 The terms *positive* and *negative* are used for the predicted and ground truth values to avoid confusion with *true* and *false* which are used to say if the prediction was correct or not True and false positive rates are calculated for a particular set of predictions (the # means 'number of').

		Prediction		
		Positive	Negative	
Ground truth	Positive	True positive (TP)	False negative (FN)	True positive rate $\frac{\#TP}{\#TP + \#FN}$
	Negative	False positive (FP)	True negative (TN)	False positive rate $\frac{\#FP}{\#FP + \#TN}$

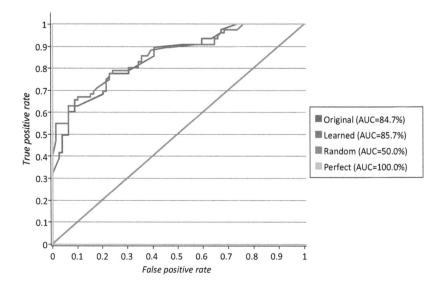

Figure 2.32 Receiver operating characteristic curves for all skills combined for the original model and the model with learned guess probabilities. Surprisingly, the original model has only a slightly worse ROC curve than the improved one. For comparison, curves for the best possible results (Perfect) and for a random prediction (Random) are also shown.

in Figure 2.32, where the TPR and FPR have been computed across all skills merged together. We could also have plotted ROC curves for individual skills but, since our data set is relatively small, the curves would be quite bumpy, making it hard to interpret and compare them.

Figure 2.32 immediately reveals something surprising that the log probability metric did not: the original model does very well and our new model only has a slightly higher ROC curve. It appears that whilst the skill probabilities computed by the first model were generally too high, they were still giving a good *ordering* on the candidates. That is, the people who had a particular skill had higher inferred skill probabilities than the people who did not, even though the probabilities themselves were not very accurate. A system which gives inaccurate probabilities is said to have poor **calibration**. The log probability metric is sensitive to bad calibration while the ROC curve is not. Using both metrics together, lets us see that learning the guess probabilities improved the calibration of the model substantially but improved the predicted ordering only slightly. We will discuss calibration in more detail in Chapter 4, particularly in Panel 4.3.

The ROC curve can be used as an evaluation metric by computing the area under the curve (AUC), since in general a higher area implies a better ranking. A perfect ranking would have an AUC of 1.0 (see the "Perfect" line of Figure 2.32). It is usually a good idea to look at the ROC curve as well as computing the AUC since it gives more detail about how well a system would work in different scenarios, such as for making a short or long list.

Our improved system has a very respectable AUC of 0.86, substantially improved log probability scores across all skills and has been visually checked to give reasonable results. It would now be ready to be tried out for real.

2.6.4 Finishing up

In this chapter, we've gone through the process of building a model-based machine learning system from scratch. We've seen how to build a model from a set of assumptions, how to run inference, how to diagnose and fix a problem and how to evaluate results. As it happens, the model we have developed in this chapter has been used previously in the field of psychometrics (the science of measuring mental capacities and processes). For example, Junker and Sijtsma [2001] consider two models DINA (Deterministic Inputs, Noisy And) which is essentially the same as our model and NIDA (Noisy Inputs, Deterministic And) which is a similar model but the *AddNoise* factors are applied to the inputs of the *And* factor rather than the output. Using this second model has the effect of increasing a person's chance of getting a question right if they have some, but not all, of the skills needed for the question.

Of course, there is always room for improving our model. For example, we could learn the probability of making a mistake for each question, as well as the probability of guessing the answer. We could investigate different assumptions about what happens when a person has some but not all of the skills needed for a question (like the NIDA model mentioned above). We could consider modelling whether having certain skills makes it more likely to have other skills. Or we could reconsider the simplifying assumption that the skills are binary and instead model them as a continuous variable representing the degree of skill that a person has. In the next case study, we will do exactly that and represent skills using continuous variables, to solve a very different problem – but first, we will have a short interlude while we look at the *process* of solving machine learning problems.

REVIEW OF CONCEPTS

probability density function   A function used to define the probability distribution over a continuous random variable. The probability that the variable will take a value within a given range is given by the area under the probability density function in that range. See Panel 2.4 for more details.

beta distribution   A probability distribution over a continuous random variable between 0 and 1 (inclusive) whose probability density function is

$$Beta(x; \alpha, \beta) = \frac{x^{\alpha-1}(1-x)^{\beta-1}}{B(\alpha, \beta)}.$$

The beta distribution has two parameters α and β which control the position and width of the peak of the distribution. The mean value $\frac{\alpha}{\alpha+\beta}$ gives the position of the centre of mass of the distribution and the sum $\alpha + \beta$ controls how spread out the distribution is (larger $\alpha + \beta$ means a narrower distribution).

evaluation metric   A measurement of the accuracy of a machine learning system used to assess how well the machine learning system is performing. An evaluation metric can be used to compare two different systems, to compare different versions of the same system or to assess if a system meets some desired target accuracy.

log probability (or *log-prob*)   The logarithm of the probability of the ground truth value of a random variable, under the inferred distribution for that variable. Used as an evaluation metric for evaluating uncertain predictions made by a machine learning system. Larger log-prob values mean that the prediction is better, since it gives higher probability to the correct value. Since the log-prob is a negative number (or zero), it is common to use the negative log-prob, in which case smaller values indicate better accuracy. For example, see Figure 2.31.

Goodhart's law   A law which warns about focusing too much on any particular evaluation metric and which can be stated as "When a measure becomes a target, it ceases to be a good measure".

true positive rate   The fraction of positive items that are correctly predicted as positive. Higher true positive rates indicate better prediction accuracy. See also Table 2.7.

false positive rate   The fraction of negative items that are incorrectly predicted as positive. Higher false positive rates indicate worse prediction accuracy. See also Table 2.7.

receiver operating characteristic curve   A receiver operating characteristic (ROC) curve is a plot of true positive rate against false positive rate which indicates the accuracy of predicting a binary variable. A perfect predictor has an ROC curve that goes vertically up the left–hand side of the plot and then horizontally across the top (see plot in Figure 2.32), whilst a random predictor has an ROC curve which is a diagonal line (again, see plot). In general, the higher the area under the ROC curve, the better the predictor.

calibration   The accuracy of probabilities predicted by a machine learning system. For example, in a well-calibrated system, a prediction made with 90% probability should be correct roughly 90% of the time. Calibration can be assessed by looking at repeated predictions by the same system.

In a poorly calibrated system, the predicted probabilities will not correspond closely to the actual fractions of predictions that are correct. Being poorly calibrated is usually a sign of an incorrect assumption in the model and so is always worth investigating – even if the system is being used in a way that is not sensitive to calibration (for example, if we are ranking by predicted probability rather than using the actual value of the probability). See Panel 4.3 for more details.

SELF ASSESSMENT 2.6

The following exercises will help embed the concepts you have learned in this section. It may help to refer back to the text or the review of concepts.

1. *[This exercise shows where the beta distribution shape comes from and is well worth doing!]* Suppose we have a question which has an actual guess probability of 30%, but we do not know this. To try and find it out, we take $N = 10$ people who do not have the skills needed for that question and see how many of them get it right through guesswork.

   a. Write a program to sample the number of people that get the question right (T). You should sample 10 times from a

Bernoulli(0.3) and count the number of `true` samples. Before you run your sampler, what sort of samples would you expect to get from it?

b. In reality, if we had the answers from only 10 people, we would have only one sample count to use to work on the guess probability. For example, we might know that three people got the question right, so that $T = 3$. How much would this tell us about the actual guess probability? We can write another sampling program to work it out. First, sample a possible guess probability between 0.0 and 1.0. Then, given this sampled guess probability, compute a sample of the number of people that would get the question right, had this been the true guess probability. If your sampled count matches the true count T (in other words, is equal to 3), then you "accept it" and store the sampled guess probability. Otherwise you "reject it" and throw it away. Repeat the process until you have 10,000 accepted samples.

c. Plot a histogram of the accepted samples using 50 bins between 0.0 and 1.0. You should see that the histogram has the shape of a beta distribution!! In fact, your program is sampling from a $Beta(T + 1, (N - T) + 1)$ distribution.

d. Using this information, change N and T in your program to recreate the beta distributions of Figure 2.26a. Explore what happens when you increase N whilst keeping T/N fixed (your beta distribution should get narrower). This should match the intuition that the more people you have data for, the more accurately you can assess the guess probability.

2. Plot a receiver operating characteristic curve for the results you got for the original model in the previous self assessment. You will need to sort the predicted skill probabilities whilst keeping track of the ground truth for each prediction. Then scan down the sorted list computing the true positive rate and false positive rate at each point. Verify that it looks like the original ROC curve of Figure 2.32. Now make a perfect predictor (by cheating and using the ground truth). Plot the ROC curve for this perfect predictor and check that it looks like the Perfect line of Figure 2.32. If you want, you can repeat this for a random predictor (the results should approximate the diagonal line of Figure 2.32).

Interlude: the machine learning life cycle

In tackling our murder mystery back in Chapter 1, we first gathered evidence from the crime scene and then used our own knowledge to construct a probabilistic model of the murder. We incorporated the crime scene evidence into the model, in the form of observed variables, and performed inference to answer the query of interest: what is the probability of each suspect being the murderer? We then assessed whether the results of inference were good enough – that is, was the probability high enough to consider the murder solved? When it was not, we then gathered additional data, extended the model, re-ran inference and finally reached our target probability.

In assessing skills of job candidates in Chapter 2, we gathered data from people taking a real test and visualised this data. We then built a model based on our knowledge of how people take tests. We ran inference and assessed that the results were not good enough. We diagnosed the problem, extended the model and then evaluated both the original and the extended models to quantify the improvement and check that the improved model met our success criteria.

We can generalise from these two examples to define the steps needed for any model-based machine learning application:

1. **Gather data** for training and evaluating the model.

2. **Gather knowledge** to help make appropriate modelling assumptions.

3. **Visualise** the data to understand it better, check for data issues and gain insight into useful modelling assumptions.

4. **Construct a model** which captures knowledge about the problem domain, consistent with your understanding of the data.

5. **Perform inference** to make predictions over the variables of interest using the data to fix the values of other variables.

6. **Evaluate results** using some evaluation metric to see if they meet the success criteria for the target application.

In the (usual) case that the system does not meet the success criteria the first time around, there are then two additional steps needed:

7. **Diagnose issues** which are reducing prediction accuracy. Visualisation is a powerful tool for bringing to light problems with data, models or inference algorithms. Inference issues can also be diagnosed using synthetic data sampled from the model (as we saw in Chapter 2). At this stage, is may also be necessary to diagnose performance issues if the inference algorithm is taking too long to complete.

8. **Refine the system** – this could mean refining the data, model, visualisations, inference or evaluation.

These two stages need to be repeated until the system is performing at a level necessary for the intended application. Model-based machine learning can make this repeated refinement process much quicker when using automatic inference software, since it is easy to extend or modify a model and inference can then be immediately applied to the modified model. This allows for rapid exploration of a number of models, each of which would be very slow to code up by hand.

The stages of this *machine learning life cycle* can be illustrated in a flow chart:

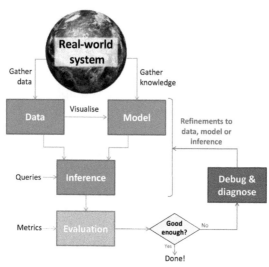

As we move on to our next case study, keep this life cycle flowchart in mind – it will continue to be useful as a template for solving machine learning problems.

CHAPTER 3

Meeting your match

Every day, millions of players around the world log in to Xbox Live® to play against each other in hundreds of different games. Their enjoyment depends on being matched to other players of comparable skill, so that they get a good gaming experience. So how can we use model-based machine learning to automatically match players of similar ability?

One of the great advantages of the online world for gaming is the ready availability of opponents at any time of day or night. An important requirement for Xbox Live is the capability to find opponents with comparable skill levels, in order that players have an enjoyable gaming experience. This requirement means the system must have a way of estimating the skills of players. However, achieving this presents some significant challenges – in particular, a game is not always won by the stronger player. Many games involve an element of chance, and in a particular game luck may favour the weaker player. More generally, a player's performance can vary from one game to the next due to factors such as tiredness or fluctuating enthusiasm. We therefore cannot assume that the winner of a particular game has a higher skill level than the loser. On the other hand, we do expect a stronger player to win against a weaker player more often than they lose, so the game outcome does give us useful information about the players' relative skills.

Another challenge concerns new players to the game. We have little idea of their ability until we see the outcomes of some games. New players are not always poor players – they may have played under different identities or have experience of other similar games. Either way, it is essential to have reasonably reliable assessments of their skills after only a few games so that they can be matched against players of

DOI: 10.1201/9780429192685-4

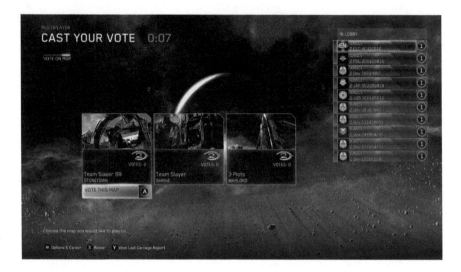

Figure 3.1 Xbox Live® provides a real-time matchmaking service for online gaming.

comparable skill. This ensures that new players have a good gaming experience and so are more likely to continue to subscribe to Xbox Live. Rapid assessment of skills is therefore important to the commercial success of the service.

A final challenge arises when we have games played by teams of players. We observe that one team wins and the other loses, and we must use this information to learn about the skills of the individual players. At first, it might seem impossible to solve this "credit assignment" problem. But we can make use of the fact that, particularly in online games, the composition of teams changes frequently and so over the course of multiple games we can disambiguate the contributions of individual players to the successes and failures of the teams in which they play.

We will need to work with the data available in Xbox Live, when doing match-making amongst the players. Table 3.1 shows a sample of the kind of data that we need to work with, in this case from the Xbox game Halo 2.

In summary, our goal is to use data of the above form to infer the skills of individual players, in order to match players against others of a similar skill level in future games. A secondary goal is to use the inferred skill levels in order to create "leader boards" showing the ranking of players within a tournament or league. The system must also allow

Table 3.1 Sample of the available data, showing ten games in the "Head to Head" variant of Halo2 The columns give the anonymised player ids, their scores, the game outcome, the game id and the variant of the game that was played.

Player1	Player2	Player1Score	Player2Score	Outcome	Id	Variant
Gamer00123	Gamer00103	0	2	Player2Win ⌄	282203	Slayer
Gamer00044	Gamer00094	2	4	Player2Win ⌄	282201	Slayer
Gamer00139	Gamer00074	2	5	Player2Win ⌄	282205	Slayer
Gamer00095	Gamer00140	2	2	Draw ⌄	282211	Slayer
Gamer00120	Gamer00141	5	1	Player1Win ⌄	282209	Slayer
Gamer00142	Gamer00143	5	2	Player1Win ⌄	282208	Slayer
Gamer00144	Gamer00122	1	1	Draw ⌄	282212	Slayer
Gamer00116	Gamer00145	5	0	Player1Win ⌄	282207	Slayer

for the fact that players may play one-on-one or may work together in teams. Furthermore, we must solve this problem in a way that makes efficient use of the game outcome results so that we can arrive at an accurate assessment of a player's skill after observing a relatively small number of games involving that player.

The models developed in this chapter are based on the Trueskill model from Herbrich et al. [2007]. You can recreate all results in this chapter using the companion source code [Diethe et al., 2019].

3.1 MODELLING THE OUTCOME OF GAMES

Our goal is to build a system which can assess the skills of players in online gaming. As a first step towards this, we need to look at the simpler problem of predicting the outcome of a game where we already know the skills of the players involved. This will allow us to develop many of the concepts required to solve the more complex problem of determining skills.

Suppose that Jill is going to play a game of Halo against Fred on Xbox Live. In Chapter 2, we represented a person's software development skills by using a binary variable for each skill, indicating whether the person possessed that particular skill or not. This approach is insufficient when we consider a person's skill at a typical Xbox game such as Halo, since there is a wide spectrum of possible skill levels. Instead, it is more appropriate to represent a person's skill using a continuous value. The first of our modelling assumptions is therefore:

① Each player has a skill value, represented by a continuous variable.

The stronger player is not always the winner.

We denote the skill of Jill by `Jskill` and the skill of Fred by `Fskill`. Let us suppose that Fred has a skill level of `Fskill` = 12.5 while Jill has a skill of `Jskill` = 15. These numbers appear to be completely arbitrary, and the scale on which we measure skill is indeed arbitrary. What matters, however, is how the skill values compare between players, and we shall see in a moment how to give meaning to such numbers. We have given Jill a higher skill value to indicate that she is the stronger player.

Now we run into the first of our challenges, which is that the stronger player in a game such as Halo is not always the winner. If Jill and Fred were to play lots of games against each other, we would expect Jill to win more than half of them, but not necessarily to win them all. We can capture this variability in the outcome of a game by introducing the notion of a *performance* for each player, which expresses how well they played on a particular game. The player with the higher performance for a specific game will be the winner of that game. A player with a high skill level will tend to have a high performance, but their actual performance will vary from one game to another. As with skill, the performance is most naturally expressed using a continuous quantity. We denote Jill's performance by `Jperf` and Fred's performance by `Fperf`. Figure 3.2 shows `Jperf` plotted against `Fperf`. For points lying in the region above the diagonal line Jill is the winner, while below the diagonal line Fred is the winner.

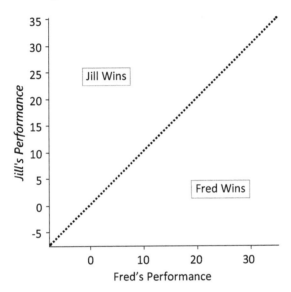

Figure 3.2 Schematic illustration of the values of Jill's performance and Fred's performance showing the areas in which Jill would be the winner and in which Fred would be the winner.

3.1.1 Modelling how well someone plays

We can think of a person's skill as their average performance across many games. For example, Jill's skill level of 15 means her performance will have an average value of 15, but on a particular game it might be higher or lower. Once again we have to deal with uncertainty, and we shall do this using a suitable probability distribution. We anticipate that larger departures of performance from the average will be less common, and therefore have lower probability than values which are close to the average. Intuitively, the performance should therefore take

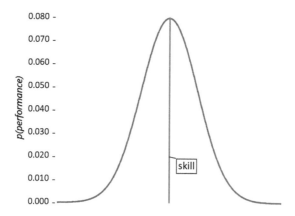

Figure 3.3 Illustration of a "bell curve" showing how the performance of a player can vary randomly around their skill value.

the form of a "bell curve" as illustrated in Figure 3.3 in which the probability of a given performance value falls off on either side of the skill value.

Because performance is a continuous quantity, this bell curve is an example of a probability density, which we encountered previously in Panel 2.4. Although we have sketched the general shape of the bell curve, to make further progress we need to define a specific form for this curve. There are many possible choices, but there is one which stands out as special in having some very useful mathematical properties. It is called the *Gaussian probability density* and is the density function for the **Gaussian distribution**.

In fact, the Gaussian distribution has so many nice properties that it is one of the most widely used distributions in the fields of machine learning and statistics. A particular Gaussian distribution is completely characterised by just two numbers: the **mean**, which sets the position of the centre of the curve, and the **standard deviation**, which determines how wide the curve is (see Panel 3.1 for discussion of these concepts). Figure 3.4 shows a Gaussian distribution, illustrating the interpretation of the mean and the standard deviation.

To understand the scale of the values on the vertical axis of Figure 3.4, remember that the total area under a probability distribution curve must be one. Note that the distribution is symmetrical about its maximum point – because there is equal probability of being on either side of this point, the performance at this central point is also the mean performance.

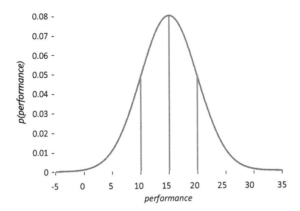

Figure 3.4 Plot of the Gaussian distribution having mean of 15 and standard deviation of 5, showing the mean (red line) and the values which differ from the mean by plus-or-minus one standard deviation (green lines). There is roughly a 68.2% probability of a random variable with this distribution having a value lying within one standard deviation of the mean (i.e. between the two green lines), a 95.4% probability of the value lying within two standard deviations of the mean (i.e. between 5 and 25), and a 99.7% probability of the value lying within three standard deviations of the mean (i.e. between 0 and 30).

In standard notation, we write the mean as μ and the standard deviation as σ. Using this notation, the Gaussian density function can be written as

$$Gaussian(x; \mu, \sigma^2) = \frac{1}{(2\pi)^{1/2}\sigma} \exp\left\{-\frac{(x-\mu)^2}{2\sigma^2}\right\}. \qquad (3.1)$$

The left-hand side says that $Gaussian(x; \mu, \sigma^2)$ is a probability distribution over x whose value is dependent on the values of μ and σ. It is often convenient to work with the square of the standard deviation, which we call the **variance** and which we denote by σ^2 (see Panel 3.1). We shall also sometimes use the inverse of the variance $\tau = 1/\sigma^2$ which is known as the **precision**. For the most part, we shall use standard deviation since this lives on the same scale (i.e. has the same units) as x.

Sometimes when we are using a Gaussian distribution, it will be clear which variable the distribution applies to. In such cases, we can simplify the notation and instead of writing $Gaussian(x; \mu, \sigma^2)$ we sim-

Panel 3.1: Mean, variance and standard deviation

Suppose we make multiple measurements of some quantity x, resulting in a set of values $x_1, x_2, \ldots, x_N$. For example, we might measure the heights of adults in the population. It can be very useful to summarise the properties of this set of values by computing some simple **statistics**. One well-known statistic is called the *mean* and is defined by

$$\text{mean} = \frac{x_1 + x_2 + \cdots + x_N}{N}$$

$$= \frac{1}{N} \sum_{n=1}^{N} x_n. \tag{3.2}$$

The mean is therefore simply the average of the values. Another useful statistic is the variance which measures how much the values vary around the mean value and is defined by

$$\text{variance} = \frac{(x_1 - \text{mean})^2 + \cdots + (x_N - \text{mean})^2}{N}$$

$$= \frac{1}{N} \sum_{n=1}^{N} (x_n - \text{mean})^2. \tag{3.3}$$

If heights are measured in metres, then the units of the mean height would again be metres, whereas the variance would have the units of metres-squared. It is usually more useful to measure variation from the mean in the same units that we measure the mean in, and so we can instead use the standard deviation, which is given by the square root of the variance

$$\text{standard deviation} = \sqrt{\text{variance}}. \tag{3.4}$$

The standard deviation would then have the units of metres, and would be a more easily interpretable quantity because it would tell us directly about the variability of heights within the population. For example, in a particular population of people, the mean height might be 1.64 metres and the standard deviation might be 0.35 metres.

There is an important connection between the statistics of a data set and the parameters of the probability distribution that gave rise to that data set. Consider the Gaussian distribution in equation (3.1).

If we take a very large number of samples from this distribution, then the mean and variance statistics of the samples will be almost exactly equal to the mean and variance parameters of the distribution (see Bishop [2006]). In fact, this is why the parameters of the Gaussian distribution are called the "mean" and "variance" parameters. In general, the statistics of a very large set of samples from any distribution can be computed directly from the distribution's parameters, without actually having to do any sampling.

ply write $Gaussian(\mu, \sigma^2)$. It is important to appreciate that is simply a shorthand notation and does not represent a distribution over μ and σ^2.

Now let's see how we can apply the Gaussian distribution to model a single game of Halo between Jill and Fred. Figure 3.5 shows the Gaussian distributions which describe the probabilities of various performances being achieved by Jill and Fred in their Halo game. Here we have chosen the standard deviations of the two Gaussians to be the same, with perfSD = 5 (where "perfSD" denotes the standard deviation of the performance distribution). We shall discuss the significance of this choice shortly. The first question we can ask is: "What is the probability that Jill will be the winner?" Note that there is considerable overlap between the two distributions, which implies that there

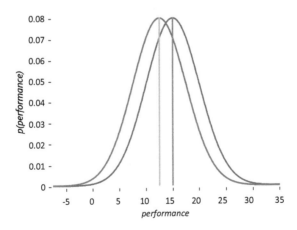

Figure 3.5 Plot of the Gaussian distributions of performance for Jill (blue) and Fred (red).

is a significant chance that the performance value for Fred would be higher than that for Jill and hence that he will win the game, even though Jill has a higher skill. You can also see that if the curves were more separated (for example, if Jill had a skill of 30), then the chance of Fred winning would be much reduced.

We have introduced two further assumptions into our model, and it is worth making these explicit:

② Each player has a performance value for each game, which is independent from game to game and has an average value equal to the skill of that player. The variation in performance, which is the same for all players, is symmetrically distributed around the mean value and is more likely to be close to the mean than to be far from the mean.

③ The player with the highest performance value wins the game.

As written, Assumption ② expresses the qualitative knowledge that a domain expert in online games might possess, and corresponds to a bell-shaped performance distribution. This needs to be refined into a specific mathematical form and for this we choose the Gaussian, although we might anticipate that other bell-shaped distributions would give qualitatively similar results.

This is a good moment to introduce our first factor graph for this chapter. To construct this graph we start with the variable nodes for each random variable in our problem. So far we have two variables: the performance of Fred, which we denote by the continuous variable Fperf, and the performance for Jill, denoted by Jperf. Each of these is described by a Gaussian distribution whose mean is the skill of the corresponding player, and with a common standard deviation of 5, and therefore a variance of 5^2:

$$\begin{aligned}
p(\texttt{Jperf}) &= \text{Gaussian}(\texttt{Jperf}; 15, 5^2) \\
p(\texttt{Fperf}) &= \text{Gaussian}(\texttt{Fperf}; 12.5, 5^2).
\end{aligned} \tag{3.5}$$

Note that, as in Section 2.6, we are using a lower-case p to denote a probability <u>density</u> for a continuous variable, and will use an upper-case P to denote the probability <u>distribution</u> for a discrete variable.

The other uncertain quantity is the winner of the game. For this we can use a binary variable JillWins which takes the value true if Jill is the winner and the value false if Fred is the winner. The value of this variable is determined by which of the two variables `Jperf` and `Fperf` is larger – it will be `true` is `Jperf` is larger or otherwise `false`. Using T for `true` and F for `false` as before, we can express this distribution by

$$P(\texttt{JillWins} = \texttt{T}|\texttt{Jperf}, \texttt{Fperf}) = \begin{cases} 1 & \text{if } \texttt{Jperf} > \texttt{Fperf}, \\ 0 & \text{otherwise.} \end{cases} \quad (3.6)$$

Since probabilities sum to one, we then have

$$P(\texttt{JillWins} = \texttt{F}|\texttt{Jperf}, \texttt{Fperf})$$
$$= 1 - P(\texttt{JillWins} = \texttt{T}|\texttt{Jperf}, \texttt{Fperf}). \quad (3.7)$$

We shall refer to the conditional probability in equation (3.6) as the *GreaterThan* factor, which we shall denote by "¿" when drawing factor graphs. Note that this is a deterministic factor since the value of the child variable is fixed if the values of both parent variables are known. Using this factor, we are now ready to draw the factor graph. This has three variable nodes, each with a corresponding factor node, and is shown in Figure 3.6.

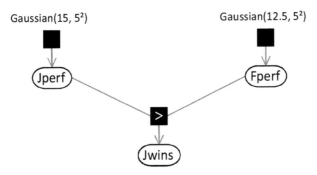

Figure 3.6 Factor graph for a game between two players, Fred and Jill, with known skills.

3.1.2 Computing the probability of winning

We asked for the probability that Jill would win this game of Halo. We can find an approximate answer to this question by using ancestral sampling – refer back to Section 2.5.1 for a reminder of what this is. To apply ancestral sampling in our factor graph, we must first sample from the parent variables `Jperf` and `Fperf` and then compute the value of the child variable `Jwins`.

Consider first the sampling of the performance `Jperf` for Jill. There are standard numerical techniques for generating random numbers having a Gaussian distribution of specified mean and variance. If we generate five samples from $Gaussian(x; 15, 5^2)$ and plot them as a histogram, we obtain the result shown in Figure 3.7a. Note that we have divided the height of each bar in the histogram by the total number of samples (in this case 5) and set the width of the histogram bins to be one. This ensures that the total area under the histogram is one. If we increase the number of samples to 50, as seen in Figure 3.7b, we see that the histogram roughly approximates the bell curve of a Gaussian. By increasing the number of samples we obtain a more accurate approximation, as shown in Figure 3.7c for the case of 500 samples, and in Figure 3.7d for 5,000 such samples. We see that we need to draw a relatively large number of samples in order to obtain a good approximation to the Gaussian. When using ancestral sampling,

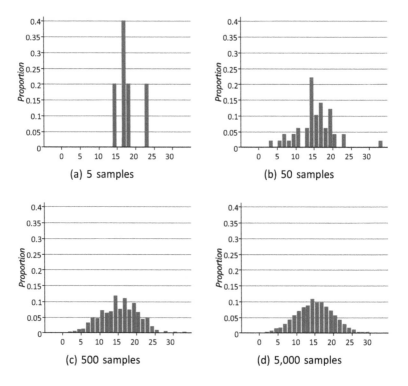

Figure 3.7 Histograms of samples drawn from the Gaussian distribution shown in Figure 3.4, with a mean of 15 and a standard deviation of 5.

we therefore need to use a lot of samples in order to obtain reasonably accurate results. This makes ancestral sampling computationally very inefficient, although it is a straightforward technique which provides a useful way to help understand a model or generate synthetic data sets.

Having seen how to sample from a single Gaussian distribution, we can now consider ancestral sampling from the complete graph in Figure 3.6 representing a single game of Halo between Jill and Fred. We first select a performance Jperf for Jill on this specific game, corresponding to the top-level variable node on the factor graph, by drawing a value from the Gaussian distribution

$$p(\texttt{Jperf}) = \text{Gaussian}(\texttt{Jperf}; 15, 5^2). \tag{3.8}$$

Independently, we choose a performance value Fperf for Fred, which is also a top-level variable node, by drawing a sample from the Gaussian distribution

$$p(\texttt{Fperf}) = \text{Gaussian}(\texttt{Fperf}; 12.5, 5^2). \tag{3.9}$$

We then compute the value of the remaining variable JillWins using these sampled values. This involves comparing the two performance values, and if Jperf is greater than Fperf then JillWins is true, otherwise JillWins is false. If we repeat this sampling process many times, then the fraction of times that JillWins is true gives (approximately) the probability of Jill winning a game. The larger the number of samples over which we average, the more accurate this approximation will be. Figure 3.8 shows a scatter plot of the performances of our two players across 1,000 samples.

For each game, we independently select the performance of each player by generating random values according to their respective Gaussian distributions. Each of these games is shown as a point on the scatter plot. Also shown is the diagonal line along which the two performances are equal. Points lying below this line represent games in which Fred is the winner, while points lying above the line are those for which Jill is the winner. We see that the majority of points lie above the line, as we expect because Jill has a higher skill value. By simply counting the number of points, we find that Jill wins 63.1% of the time.

Of course this is only an approximate estimate of the probability of Jill winning. We can find the exact result mathematically by making

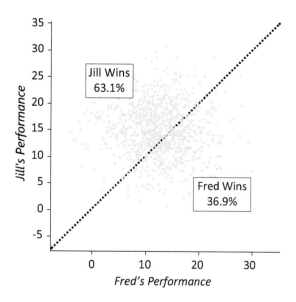

Figure 3.8 Samples of Jill and Fred's performances overlaid on the schematic illustration from Figure 3.2. The cloud of samples is vertically centred on Jill's skill of 15 and horizontally centred on Fred's skill of 12.5. The centre of the cloud is therefore above the diagonal and so more samples correspond to Jill winning than to Fred winning.

use of the equation for the Gaussian distribution (3.1), which tells us that the probability of Jill being the winner is given by

$$P(\texttt{Jperf} > \texttt{Fperf} | \texttt{Jskill}, \texttt{Fskill})$$

$$= CumGauss \left(\frac{\texttt{Jskill} - \texttt{Fskill}}{\sqrt{2}\texttt{perfSD}} \right). \tag{3.10}$$

Here *CumGauss* denotes the **cumulative Gaussian function** which is illustrated in Figure 3.9.

Using a numerical evaluation of this function, we find that the probability of Jill winning the game is 63.8%, which is close to the value of 63.1% that we obtained by ancestral sampling.

We noted earlier that the scale on which skill is measured is essentially arbitrary. If we add a fixed number to the skills of all the players, this would leave the probabilities of winning unchanged since, from equation (3.10), they depend only on the difference in skill values. Likewise, if we multiplied all the skill values by some fixed number,

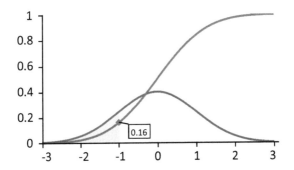

Figure 3.9 The blue curve shows a Gaussian distribution with mean of zero and a standard deviation of one. The area under this Gaussian up to the point x is known as the cumulative Gaussian distribution and is shown by the red curve, as a function of x. For example, at $x = -1$, the area of the shaded region has the value 0.16, as indicated.

and at the same time we multiplied the parameter `perfSD` by the same number, then again the probabilities of winning would be unchanged. All that matters is the difference in skill values measured in relation to the value of `perfSD`.

We have now built a model which can predict the outcome of a game for two players of known skills. In the next section, we will look at how to extend this model to go in the opposite direction: to predict the player skills given the outcome of one or more games.

REVIEW OF CONCEPTS

Gaussian distribution   A specific form of probability density over a continuous variable that has many useful mathematical properties. It is governed by two parameters – the mean and the standard deviation. The mathematical definition of a Gaussian is given by equation (3.1)

mean   The average of a set of values. See Panel 3.1 for a more detailed discussion of the mean and related concepts.

standard deviation   The square root of the variance.

variance   A measure of how much a set of numbers vary around their average value. The variance and related quantities are discussed in Panel 3.1.

precision   The inverse of the variance.

statistics A statistic is a function of a set of data values. For instance, the mean is a statistic whose value is the average of a set of values. Statistics can be useful for summarising a large data set compactly.

cumulative Gaussian function The value of the cumulative Gaussian function at a point x is equal to the area under a zero-mean unit-variance Gaussian from minus infinity up to the point x. It follows from this definition that the gradient of the cumulative Gaussian function is given by the Gaussian distribution.

SELF ASSESSMENT 3.1

The following exercises will help embed the concepts you have learned in this section. It may help to refer back to the text or the review of concepts.

1. Write a program or create a spreadsheet which produces 10,000 samples from a Gaussian with zero mean and a standard deviation of 1 (most languages/spreadsheets have built in functions or available libraries for sampling from a Gaussian). Compute the percentage of these samples which lie between −1 and 1, between −2 and 2 and between −3 and 3. You should find that these percentages are close to those given in the caption of Figure 3.4.

2. Construct a histogram of the samples created in the previous exercise (like the ones in Figure 3.7) and verify that it resembles a bell-shaped curve.

3. Compute the mean, standard deviation and variance of your samples, referring to Panel 3.1. The mean should be close to zero and the standard deviation and variance should both be close to 1 (since $1^2 = 1$).

4. Produce 10,000 samples from the Gaussian prior for Jill's performance with mean 15 and standard deviation 5. Then produce a second set of samples for Fred's performance using mean 12.5 and standard deviation 5. Plot a scatter plot like Figure 3.8 where the Y co-ordinate of each point is a sample from the first set and the X co-ordinate is the corresponding sample from the second set (pairing the first sample from each set, the second sample from each set and so on). Compute the fraction of samples which lie above the diagonal line where X=Y and check that this is close

to the value in Figure 3.8. Explore what happens to this fraction when you change the standard deviations – for example, try reducing both to 2 or increasing both to 10.

5. Using Infer.NET create double variables Y and X with priors of $Gaussian(15, 5^2)$ and $Gaussian(12.5, 5^2)$, respectively, to match the previous exercise. Define a third random variable Ywins equal to Y > X. Compute the posterior distribution over Ywins and verify that it is close to the fraction of samples above the diagonal from the previous exercise.

3.2 INFERRING THE PLAYERS' SKILLS

So far we have assumed that we know the skills of Jill and Fred, and we have used these skills to compute the probability that each of the players would be the winner. In practice, we have to reason backwards: we observe who wins the game and need to use this information to learn about the skill values of the players. We therefore turn to the problem of learning player skills.

Given the outcome of a game, it would seem reasonable to increase the skill value for the winner and decrease the skill value for the loser. What is less clear, however, is how big an adjustment we should make. Intuitively, we can reason as follows. Suppose that Jill is the winner of the game. If Jill's skill is significantly higher than

In any game, seeing who wins and who loses tells us about the skill of the players.

Fred's, then it is unsurprising that Jill should be the winner, and so the change in skill values should be relatively small. If the skills are similar, then a larger change would be justified. However, if Jill's skill is significantly less than Fred's, then the game outcome is very surprising. The outcome suggests that our current assessments of the skill values are not very accurate, and therefore that we should make a much larger adjustment in skill values. Put concisely, the degree of surprise gives an indication of how big a change in skill values should be made. We will see that performing inference in a suitable model automatically gives this kind of behaviour.

3.2.1 Modelling skills

We have already noted that skill is an uncertain quantity, and should therefore be included in the model as a random variable. We need to define a suitable prior distribution for this variable. This distribution captures our prior knowledge about a player's skill before they have played this particular game. For a new player, this distribution would need to be broad and cover the full range of skills that the player might have. For a more established player, we may already have a good idea of their skill and so the distribution would be narrower. Because skill is a continuous variable, we can once again use a Gaussian distribution to define this prior. This represents a modification to our first modelling assumption, which becomes:

① Each player has a skill value, represented by a continuous variable with a Gaussian prior distribution.

Let us return to our game of Halo between Jill and Fred. So far we have assumed that the skill values for Jill and Fred are known and have values of 15 and 12.5, respectively. For the remainder of the chapter, we shall instead assume that the skills for Jill and Fred are not known, but have uncertainty represented by a Gaussian distribution. For Jill, we will now assume a mean skill of 120 with a standard deviation of 40 – this would typically arise if Jill is a relatively new player and so there is a lot of uncertainty in her skill . For Fred, we will now assume a mean skill of 100 with a standard deviation of 5 which would be reasonable if Fred is a more established player whose skill is more precisely known. We must therefore extend our model by introducing two more uncertain variables `Jskill` and `Fskill`: the skills of Jill and Fred. Each of these variables will have its own Gaussian distribution and therefore its own factor in the factor graph. The factor graph for our extended model is shown in Figure 3.10.

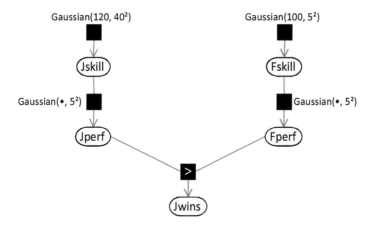

Figure 3.10 TrueSkill model for two players in a game, with uncertain skills. Here we have used the notation $Gaussian(\cdot, 5^2)$ to describe a factor whose distribution is Gaussian with a mean given by the parent variable, in this case the corresponding skill variable, and a standard deviation of 5.

---

① Each player has a skill value, represented by a continuous variable with a broad Gaussian distribution.

② Each player has a performance value for each game, which is independent from game to game and has an average value equal to the skill of that player. The variation in performance, which is the same for all players, is symmetrically distributed around the mean value and is more likely to be close to the mean than to be far from the mean.

③ The player with the higher performance value wins the game.

Figure 3.11 The three assumptions encoded in our model.

The model in Figure 3.10 was developed by Herbrich et al. [2007] who called it the TrueSkill model. As a reminder, the assumptions that are encoded in the model are all shown together in Figure 3.11.

Having stated our modelling assumptions explicitly, it is worth taking a moment to review them. Assumption ① says that a player's ability at a particular type of game can be expressed as a single continuous variable. This seems reasonable for most situations, but we could imagine a more complex description of a player's abilities which, for example, distinguishes between their skill in attack and their skill at defence. This might be important in team games (discussed later) where a strong team may require a balance of players with strong attack skills and those with good defensive skills. We also assumed a Gaussian prior for the skill variable. This is the simplest probabilistic model we could have for a continuous skill variable, and it brings some nice analytical and engineering properties. However, if we looked at the skills of a large population of players we might find a rather non-Gaussian distribution of skills, for example, new players may often have low skill but, if they have played a similar game before, may occasionally have a high skill.

Similarly, Assumption ② considers a single performance variable and again assumes it has a Gaussian distribution. It might well be the case that players can sometimes have a seriously "off" day when their performance is way below their skill value, while it would be very unlikely for a player to perform dramatically higher than their skill value. This suggests that the performance distribution might be non-symmetrical. Another aspect that could be improved is the assumption that the variance is the same for all players – it is likely that some players are more consistent than others and so would have correspondingly lower variance.

Finally, Assumption ③ says that the game outcome is determined purely by the performance values. If we had introduced multiple variables to characterise the skill of a player, there would presumably each have a corresponding performance variable (such as how the player performed in attack or defence), and we would need to define how these would be combined in order to determine the outcome of a game.

3.2.2   Inference in the TrueSkill model

Once a game has been played, we aim to use the outcome of the game to infer the updated skill distribution for the players. This involves solving a probabilistic inference problem to calculate the posterior distribution of each player's skill, taking account of the new information provided by the result of the game. Although the prior distribution is Gaussian, it turns out that the corresponding posterior distribution is not Gaussian. The following section shows how to compute the posterior distribution for the skill and why it is not Gaussian – feel free to skip it or return to it later if you prefer.

> ⛵ **Inference deep-dive**
>
> In this optional section, we see how to do exact inference in the model as defined so far, and then we see why exact inference is not useable in practice. If you want to focus on modelling, feel free to skip this section.

Now that we have the factor graph describing our model, we can set the variable `Jwins` according to the observed game outcome and run inference in order to compute the marginal posterior distributions of the skill variables `Jskill` and `Fskill`. The graph has a tree structure (there are no loops) and so we have already seen in Chapter 2 that we can solve this problem using belief propagation.

Consider the evaluation of the posterior distribution for `Jskill` in the case where Jill won the game (`Jwins` is `true`). Using the belief propagation algorithm, we have to evaluate the messages shown in Figure 3.12. Message (1) is just given by the Gaussian factor itself. Similarly, message (2) is just the product of all incoming messages on other edges of the `Fskill` node, and since there is only one incoming message this is just copied to the output message. These first two messages are summarised in Figure 3.13.

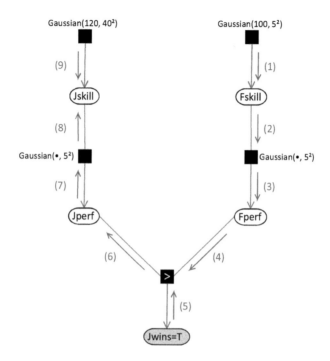

Figure 3.12 The messages which arise in the application of belief propagation to the evaluation of the updated distribution for `Jskill`.

Next we have to compute message (3) in Figure 3.12. The belief propagation algorithm tells us to multiply the incoming message (2) by the Gaussian factor and then sum over the variable `Fskill`. In this case, the summation becomes an integration because `Fskill` is a continuous variable. We can gain some insight into this step by once again considering a generative viewpoint based on sampling. Imagine that we draw samples from the Gaussian distribution over `Fskill`. Each sample is a specific value of `Fskill` and forms the mean of a Gaussian distribution over `Fperf`. In Figure 3.14a, we consider three samples of `Fskill` and plot the corresponding distributions over `Fperf`. To compute the desired outgoing message we then average these samples, giving the result shown in Figure 3.14b. This represents an approximation to the marginalisation over `Fskill`, and would become exact if we considered an infinite number of samples instead of just three.

The sampling approximation becomes more accurate as we increase the number of samples, as shown in Figure 3.14c and Figure 3.14d. In this final figure, the resulting distribution looks

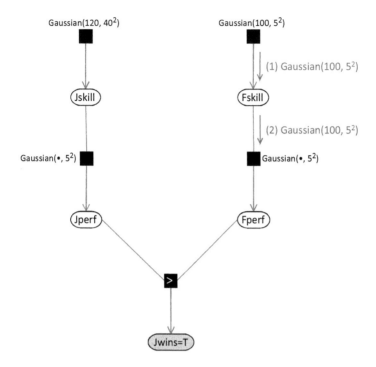

Figure 3.13 Messages (1) and (2) in the application of belief propagation to the evaluation of the updated distribution for `Jskill`.

almost Gaussian. This is not a coincidence, and in fact the calculation of the outgoing message can be worked out exactly (see equation (2.115) in Bishop [2006]) with the result that the outgoing message is also a Gaussian whose mean is the mean of the distribution of `Fskill` and whose variance is the sum of the variances of `Fskill` and `Fperf`: $5^2 + 5^2$. This process of "smearing" out one Gaussian using the other Gaussian is an example of a mathematical operation called **convolution**. Message (4) is just a copy of message (3) as there is only one incoming message to the `Fperf` node. Since we observe that `Jwins` is `true`, message (5) is a Bernoulli point mass at the value `true`. These three messages are illustrated in Figure 3.15.

Now let's turn to computing message (6). The observation that Jill wins (`Jwins=true`) applies a constraint that the performance of Jill must be higher than that of Fred, so `Jperf > Fperf`. This constraint is applied when we multiply in the *GreaterThan* factor with the value of `Jwins` set to `true`. Figure 3.16 shows the effect of multiplying in

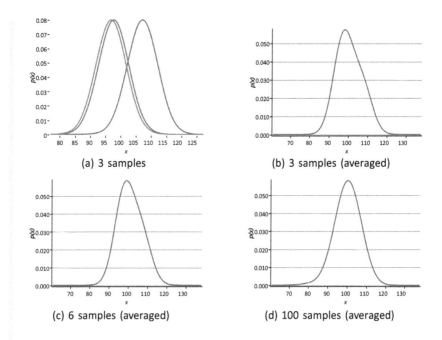

Figure 3.14 Illustration of the sampling approximation to the computation of message (3) in Figure 3.12. Panel (a) shows three Gaussians whose means have themselves been sampled from *Gaussian*$(100, 5^2)$, while panel (b) shows the average of these three samples. As we increase the number of samples, so the average gets progressively closer to being Gaussian, as seen in panels (c) and (d).

this constraint to the Gaussian message coming from Fperf. In the figure, the product is always zero below the diagonal line – in other words, where Jpref $<=$ Fperf. This area is set to zero because it corresponds to Fred winning, which has zero probability because it contradicts our observation that Jill won. So we end up with a Gaussian "bump" truncated at the diagonal.

To compute message (6), we have to integrate the product in Figure 3.16 over Fperf, to give a message which is a function of Jperf. You can visualise this message by imagining looking the truncated Gaussian bump from the direction of the axis for Jill's performance and summing over what can be seen from each point. The resulting message is zero below about 80, and then curves up to near one at about 120 and then remains there up to infinity, as shown in Figure 3.17.

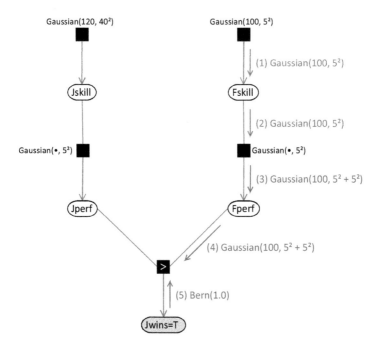

Figure 3.15 Messages (3), (4) and (5) in the application of belief propagation to the evaluation of the updated distribution for `Jskill`.

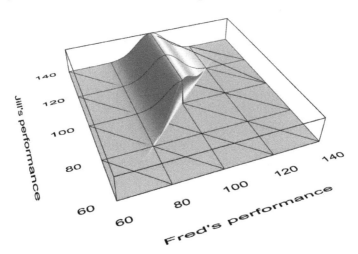

Figure 3.16 Plot of the result of multiplying the *GreaterThan* factor by messages (4) and (5) and then summing over message (5). Note that this plot represents an un-normalised distribution, and so no vertical scale has been shown.

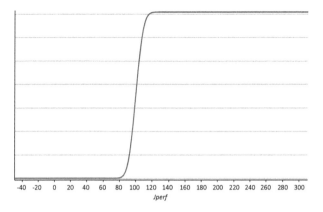

-40 -20 0 20 40 60 80 100 120 140 160 180 200 220 240 260 280 300

Jperf

Figure 3.17 The exact Belief Propagation message (6) from the *GreaterThan* factor to the `Jperf` variable, which is given by a cumulative Gaussian.

The reader should take a moment to confirm that shape of this function is what would be expected from integrating Figure 3.16 over the variable `Fperf`. Mathematically, for each value of `Jperf` a truncated Gaussian distribution is being integrated, this is equivalent to the evaluation of the cumulative Gaussian that we introduced back in equation (3.10), and so this message can be evaluated analytically (indeed, this is how Figure 3.17 was plotted).

For another interpretation of the shape of this message, suppose we knew that `Fperf` was exactly 100. Given that Jill won, this tells us that Jill's performance `Jperf` must be some number greater than 100. This would mean a message in the form of a step, with the value zero below 100 and some positive constant above it. Since, we don't know that `Fperf` is exactly 100, but only know that it is likely to be near 100, this smears out the step into the smooth function of Figure 3.17.

Because message (6) continues up to infinity, it forms what we call an **improper distribution**, which is a distribution whose area cannot be normalised to sum to one. In belief propagation, messages are allowed to be improper, provided that they do not cause posterior marginal distributions to become improper. For example, in this case, the improper message will be multiplied by a proper normalised message, giving a posterior which can be normalised and so is proper.

Message (7) is just a copy of message (6) since there is only one incoming message to the `Jperf` node. These messages are illustrated in Figure 3.18.

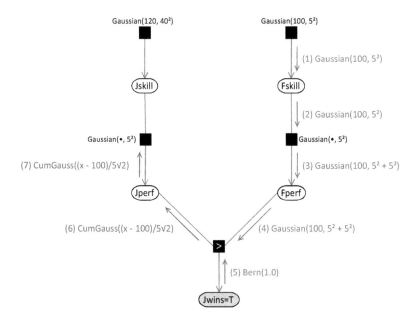

Figure 3.18 Messages (6) and (7) in the application of belief propagation to the evaluation of the updated distribution for Jskill.

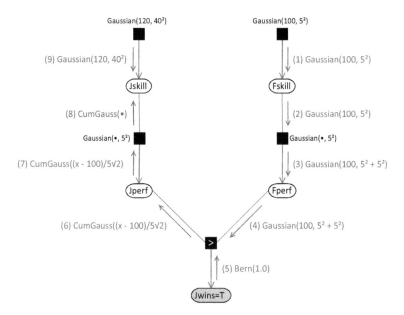

Figure 3.19 Messages (8) and (9) in the application of belief propagation to the evaluation of the updated distribution for Jskill.

Message (8) is found by multiplying the Gaussian factor describing the performance variability by the incoming message (7) and then integrating over `Jperf`. This again is a convolution, and has an exact solution again in the form of a cumulative Gaussian. Effectively it is a blurred version of the incoming cumulative Gaussian message which has been smeared out by the variance of the Gaussian performance factor. Finally, message (9) is the Gaussian distribution for the skill prior. These messages are summarised in Figure 3.19.

To obtain the marginal distribution of `Jskill`, we then multiply messages (8) and (9). Because this is the product of a Gaussian and a cumulative Gaussian, the result is a bump-like distribution which is not symmetrical, and therefore is not a Gaussian. These messages, and the resulting marginal distribution for `Jskill`, are shown in Figure 3.20.

We seem to have solved the problem of finding the posterior distribution for `Jskill`. We can also pass messages in the opposite direction around the graph to obtain the corresponding posterior distribution for `Fskill`. These posterior distributions can be expressed exactly as the product of a Gaussian and a cumulative Gaussian and so require four parameters to describe them, where the two additional parameters come from the cumulative Gaussian.

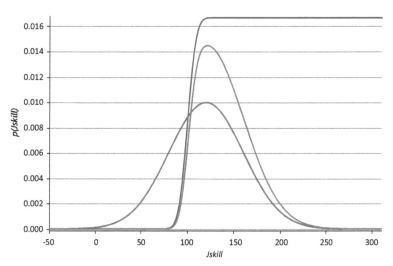

Figure 3.20 Plot of the exact message (8) in blue, the exact message (9) in red. Also shown in green is the product of these two messages, which gives the exact marginal over `Jskill`. Note that this exact marginal is non-Gaussian.

3.2.3 A problem with using exact inference

We now have a way to compute posterior distributions over the skills of our players. The problem is that these posterior distributions are not Gaussian. Instead, they have a more complex form of distribution which requires four numbers to express, instead of two for a Gaussian. This difference causes a major problem if we imagine, say, Jill going on to play another game with a new player. Before the game with Fred, our uncertainty in the value of `Jskill` was expressed as a Gaussian distribution, which has two parameters (the mean and the variance). After she has played against Fred, the corresponding posterior distribution is expressed as a more complex distribution with four parameters. Now suppose that Jill plays another game of Halo against Alice. We can again represent this by a factor graph similar to Figure 3.10, except that the factor describing our current uncertainty in `Jskill` is now the posterior distribution resulting from the game against Fred. When we run inference in this new graph, to take account of the outcome of the game against Alice, the new posterior marginal will be an even more complex distribution which requires six parameters (to be specific, a product of a Gaussian and two different cumulative Gaussians). Each time Jill plays a game of Halo the distribution over her skill value requires two additional parameters to represent it, and the number of parameters continues to grow as she plays more and more games. This is not a practical approach to use in an engineering application.

Notice that this problem would not arise if the posterior distribution for the variable of interest had the same form as the prior distribution. In some probabilistic models we are able to choose a form of prior distribution, known as a **conjugate** prior, such that the posterior ends up having the same form as the prior. Take a look at Panel 3.2 to learn more about conjugate distributions.

From a message-passing perspective, conjugacy means that the product of all messages arriving at a variable node has the same form as the prior message. This general means that all the incoming messages have the same form as the prior message. In our model, the upwards message from the *GreaterThan* factor is not Gaussian, and so nor is the one up to the `Jskill` variable. This means that the prior Gaussian distribution is not a conjugate distribution for `Jskill`.

Panel 3.2: Conjugate distributions

We can illustrate the idea of a conjugate distribution by considering the following example. Suppose we are selling items through a web page and we want to know the probability that a user will click on the "buy" button. Let us denote this probability by x. The probability that they won't click is then $1 - x$. Note that this is just the Bernoulli distribution that we saw in Chapter 1.

Suppose we collect data from multiple visitors to our web page, and we find that N of them click on the button and M of them do not. If we assume that the visits to the web page are independent, then the conditional probability of seeing this data, given the value of x, is obtained by multiplying the probabilities of each click/non-click event, so that

$$P(\text{data}|x) = x^N (1 - x)^M. \tag{3.11}$$

If we wish to learn the value of x from this data, we need to define a prior probability density $p(x)$. There is a particular form for this prior which makes the calculation especially easy, namely if we choose $p(x)$ to have the same form as equation (3.11), that is:

$$p(x) \propto x^A (1 - x)^B \tag{3.12}$$

where A and B are parameters. In this case, the corresponding posterior distribution is then, from Bayes' rule,

$$
\begin{aligned}
p(x|\text{data}) \;&\propto\; P(\text{data}|x) \times p(x) \\
&\propto\; x^{A+N}(1 - x)^{B+M}
\end{aligned}
\tag{3.13}
$$

and so the posterior distribution has the same functional form as the prior distribution, but with A replaced by $A + N$ and B replaced by $B + M$. The prior distribution (3.12) is said to be *conjugate* to the Bernoulli distribution. In fact, you can see that this prior distribution is exactly the beta distribution that we introduced in Section 2.6.

There are many other examples of conjugate distributions [Bishop, 2006]. For instance, the conjugate prior for the mean of a Gaussian is just another Gaussian, while the conjugate prior for the precision of a Gaussian is called a Gamma distribution, which we will meet in Chapter 4. For the simple murder mystery of Chapter 1, the prior distribution was a Bernoulli, which is conjugate to the conditional distribution representing the probability of the murder weapon given the identity of the murderer.

When running inference on a factor graph, we can think of conjugacy as a local property between pairs of nodes. To prevent message complexity from growing, we will need to find an approximation to an outgoing message whenever we have a non-conjugate relationship between a parent distribution and the corresponding child distribution.

Without conjugacy, it is necessary to introduce some form of approximation, to allow the posterior of `Jskill` to remain Gaussian. In the next section, we will describe a powerful algorithm that extends belief propagation by allowing messages to be approximated even when they are not conjugate. This algorithm will not only solve the inference problem with this model, but turns out to be applicable to a wide variety of other probabilistic models as well - including every single model in this book!

REVIEW OF CONCEPTS

convolution The convolution of a function f with a function g measures the overlap between f and a version of g which is translated by an amount a. It is expressed as a function of a. For more information see Wikipedia.

improper distribution A distribution whose area does not sum to one.

conjugate For a given likelihood function, a prior distribution is said to be conjugate if the corresponding posterior distribution has the same functional form as the prior.

SELF ASSESSMENT 3.2

The following exercises will help embed the concepts you have learned in this section. It may help to refer back to the text or the review of concepts.

1. Reproduce Figure 3.14 by plotting the average of K Gaussian distributions each with a standard deviation of 5 and with mean given by a sample from a $Gaussian(100, 5^2)$. Do this for $K = 3$, $K = 6$ and $K = 100$.

2. Referring to Panel 3.2, use Bayes' theorem to compute the posterior distribution over x (the probability of clicking on the buy button) given that $N = 20$ people do click on the button but $M = 100$ people do not click on it. Assume a $Beta(1, 1)$ prior distribution. Notice that this is a conjugate prior and so the posterior distribution is also a beta distribution.

3. *[Advanced]* Show that the convolution of two Gaussian distributions is also a Gaussian distribution whose variance is the sum of the variances of the two original distributions. Section 2.3.3 in Bishop [2006] should help.

3.3 A SOLUTION: EXPECTATION PROPAGATION

We have seen that belief propagation allows us to calculate the exact marginal posterior distribution for the variable `Jskill` in the model of Figure 3.10. Whereas the prior distribution for `Jskill` is a Gaussian described by two parameters, the posterior distribution is not Gaussian but is a more complex distribution requiring four parameters. To stop the number of parameters increasing after every game, we need a way to approximate this true posterior by a distribution having a fixed number of parameters, and for this we choose the Gaussian. The posterior distribution will then have the same functional form as the prior, mimicking the behaviour of a conjugate prior. If we can achieve this, we will be able to treat the resulting approximate posterior distribution as the prior distribution for the next game. Then the skill for each player will always be represented by a Gaussian distribution governed by just two parameters.

The first question is how to approximate a non-Gaussian distribution by a Gaussian. A simple solution is to find the mean and the variance of the non-Gaussian distribution and then to choose as our approximation a Gaussian having the same mean and variance. This turns out to be a sensible approximation, which can be derived formally by optimising a measure of the dissimilarity of two probability distributions [Bishop, 2006; Minka, 2005].

We might be tempted then just to approximate the exact posterior distribution for `Jskill` by a Gaussian. Although this will work satisfactorily for the factor graph of Figure 3.10, it will break down again as we go to more complex factor graphs (such as those we will encounter later in this chapter). Messages with simple functional forms tend to become more complex as a result of passing through factors. As we extend our model to larger and more sophisticated graphs, we quickly arrive at situations where messages cannot be evaluated exactly. Such problems can be avoided by making our approximations *locally* at each factor node, so that all messages have the desired distribution type. This ensures that factors can be composed together into arbitrary graphs, as long as each factor is capable of sending approximate messages to all neighbouring variable nodes using the appropriate types of distribution.

The following section goes into the mathematical details of this kind of approximate inference algorithm. If you want to skip these details, feel free to go to the next section.

⚓ Inference deep-dive

In this optional section, we introduce the approximate inference technique of expectation propagation, which we will use extensively in this book. If you want to focus on modelling, feel free to skip this section.

Returning to Figure 3.12 (which is reproduced in Figure 3.21 for convenience), we see that message (6) was the first message that we encountered which was non-Gaussian.

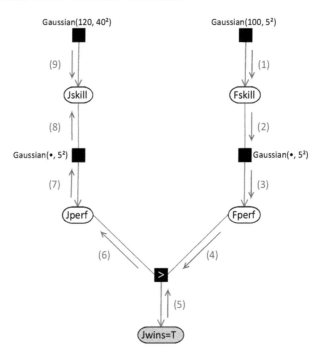

Figure 3.21 The messages which arise in the application of belief propagation to the evaluation of the updated distribution for `Jskill`. (Reproduced from Figure 3.12.)

Our goal is therefore to approximate message (6) by a Gaussian, thereby ensuring that all subsequent messages will also be Gaussian distributions.

While this seems like a desirable goal, there also seems to be a significant obstacle – the exact form of message (6) as seen in Figure 3.17 does not look at all Gaussian! In fact, its mean and variance are not even well defined (they are both infinite). The key to finding a sensible Gaussian approximation is to notice that the approximate version of message (6) will subsequently be passed through the graph as modified forms of messages (7) and (8) and will then be multiplied by the downward message (9) in order to determine the (approximate) posterior distribution of Jskill. Our goal will therefore be to make the Gaussian approximation to message (6) over Jperf be most accurate in those regions which are considered more probable by the information coming from other parts of the graph. As we have just discussed, however, we need to keep our approximation local to the region of the graph where the message is generated. Message (6) is sent to the node Jperf and so we can choose our approximation so as to maximise the accuracy of the marginal distribution of Jperf. This is obtained by multiplying message (6) by the downward message on the same edge in the graph, which can be evaluated as shown in Figure 3.22. Note that these same messages are needed to find the posterior marginal for Fskill, so there is no additional overhead introduced by evaluating them.

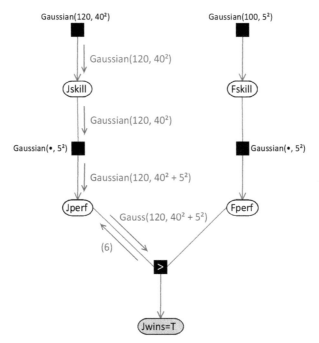

Figure 3.22 Evaluation of the context message that will be used to find a Gaussian approximation for message (6).

Let's consider the piece of the factor graph close to the `Jperf` node in more detail, as seen in Figure 3.23.

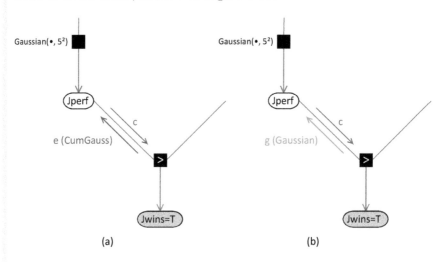

(a)   (b)

Figure 3.23 Detail of the factor graph around the `Jperf` node, showing the messages involved: (a) when running belief propagation and (b) when making a local Gaussian approximation to the upward message from the *GreaterThan* factor.

Here e denotes the exact message (6) as seen in Figure 3.20, c denotes the downward "context" message and g denotes our desired Gaussian approximation to message e. These messages are all just functions of the variable `Jperf`. We have already seen that we cannot simply approximate message e by a Gaussian since message e has infinite mean and variance. Instead we make a Gaussian approximation for the marginal distribution of `Jperf`. The exact marginal is given by the product of incoming messages ce. We therefore define our approximate message g to be such that the product of the messages c and g gives a marginal distribution for `Jperf` which is a best Gaussian approximation to the true marginal, so that

$$cg = \text{Proj}\,(ce). \tag{3.14}$$

Here Proj() denotes "projection" and represents the process of replacing a non-Gaussian distribution with a Gaussian having the same mean and variance. This can be viewed as projecting the exact message onto the "nearest" message within the family of Gaussian distributions. Dividing both sides by c, we then obtain

$$g = \frac{\text{Proj}\,(ce)}{c}. \tag{3.15}$$

Details of the mathematics of how to do this are discussed in Herbrich et al. [2007].

We therefore find a Gaussian approximation g to the exact e message (6) as follows. First, we compute the exact outgoing message (6) as before. This is shown in blue in Figure 3.24. Then we multiply this by the incoming message context message c which is shown in red in Figure 3.24. This gives a distribution, shown in green in Figure 3.24 which is non-Gaussian but which is localised and therefore has finite mean and variance and so can be approximated by a Gaussian. This curve is repeated in Figure 3.25 which also shows the Gaussian distribution which has the same mean and variance.

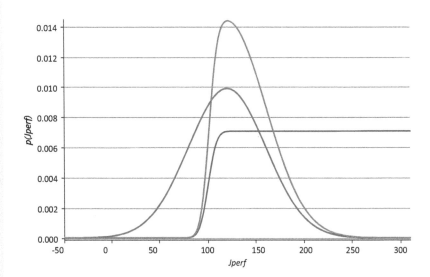

Figure 3.24 Plot of the exact outgoing message (6) in blue, the incoming $Gaussian(120, 40^2 + 5^2)$ context message in red and the product of these two messages in green.

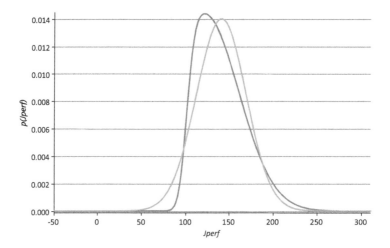

Figure 3.25 In green, the product of the true belief propagation and incoming context messages copied from Figure 3.24. In orange, the Gaussian approximation to this product, which is $Gaussian(140.4, 28.5^2)$.

Finally, we divide this Gaussian distribution by the incoming Gaussian context message c to generate our approximate outgoing g message. Because the ratio of two Gaussians is itself a Gaussian [Bishop, 2006], the resulting outgoing message will also be Gaussian, which was our original goal. For our specific example, this message is a Gaussian with a mean of 160.8 and a standard deviation of 40.2. The computation of the approximate message is summarised in Figure 3.26.

We see that overall we multiplied by the incoming context message, then made the Gaussian approximation, then finally divided out the context message again. The evidence provided by the incoming message is therefore used only to determine the region over which the Gaussian approximation should be accurate, but is not directly incorporated into the approximated message. If we happened to have a conjugate distribution, then the projection operation would be unnecessary and the context message would have no effect.

Now that we have found a suitable Gaussian approximation to the outgoing message (6), we can continue to pass messages along the graph to give the corresponding approximate message (7) as shown in Figure 3.27.

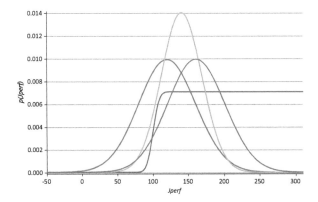

Figure 3.26 The steps involved in computing the Gaussian approximation to message (6). The blue curve shows the exact message (6), the red curve shows the incoming context message $Gaussian(120, 40^2 + 5^2)$, the orange curve shows the Gaussian approximation to the product of true message and context message which is $Gaussian(140.4, 28.5^2)$. Finally, the purple curve shows the result of dividing the orange curve by the red context message to give $Gaussian(160.8, 40.2^2)$. This Gaussian is then used as message (6).

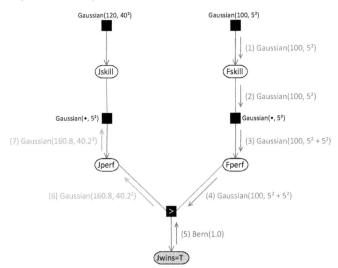

Figure 3.27 Messages (5), (6) and (7) in the evaluation of the updated distribution for `Jskill`. Note that messages (6) and (7), which are highlighted in orange, differ from the exact messages in Figure 3.18.

Evaluation of the new (approximate) version of message (8) again involves the convolution of a Gaussian with a Gaussian, with the result shown in Figure 3.28.

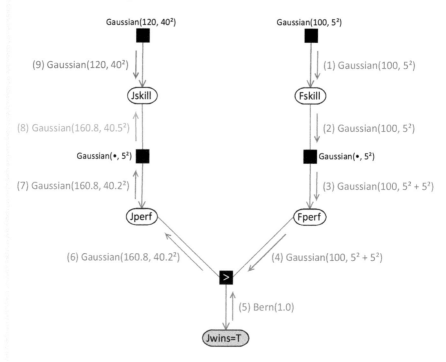

Figure 3.28 Messages (8) and (9) in the evaluation of the updated distribution for `Jskill`. Note that in addition to messages (6) and (7), message (8) (in orange) also differs from the exact message from Figure 3.19.

The downward message (9) is unchanged, and so we can finally compute the Gaussian approximation to the posterior distribution of `Jskill` as the product of two Gaussians, which gives the final result of a Gaussian with a mean of 140.1 and a standard deviation of 28.5.

This approach to locally approximate messages during the message-passing process is known as **expectation propagation** (or EP) and was developed by Minka [2001]. The approximation is being made locally at the factor node, and in a way that is independent of the structure of the remainder of the graph. This technique can therefore be applied to arbitrarily structured graphs, so long as each factor is consistently sending and receiving messages with the required distribution types, in this case Gaussians. The expectation propagation algorithm is summarised in Algorithm 3.1 with the differences to loopy belief propagation highlighted in red.

Algorithm 3.1: Expectation Propagation

Input: factor graph, list of target variables to compute marginals for, message-passing schedule, initial message values (optional), choice of approximating distributions for each edge.

Output: marginal distributions for target variables.

Initialise all messages to uniform (or initial values, if provided).

repeat

    foreach *edge in the message-passing schedule* **do**

        Send the appropriate message below:

        - Variable node message: the product of all messages received on the other edges;

        - Factor node message: Compute the belief propagation message (see Algorithm 2.1). Multiply by the context message (the message coming towards the factor on this edge). Project into the desired distribution type for this edge using moment matching. Divide out the context message.

        - Observed node message: a point mass at the observed value;

    end

until *all messages have converged*

Compute marginal distributions as the product of all incoming messages at each target variable node.

3.3.1 Applying expectation propagation

Let's see what happens to the skill distributions when we apply expectation propagation to our game of Halo between Jill and Fred. First, we suppose that Jill is the winner of the game. In Figure 3.29, we see the prior (dashed) and posterior (solid) distributions of skill for Jill and Fred. Because Jill is the winner, the mean of the skill distribution for Jill increases, while the mean of the skill distribution for Fred decreases. The increase in mean is quite large for Jill, whereas the mean

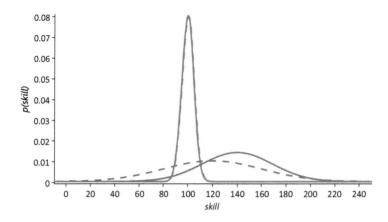

Figure 3.29 The result of applying the TrueSkill model for a game between Jill (blue) and Fred (red) for the case where Jill is the winner. The prior distributions are shown as dashed curves, and the corresponding posterior distributions are shown as solid curves. Jill's initial broad skill distribution says that, before the game, we did not know if Jill was more or less skilled than Fred. After seeing that she won the game, her skill distribution shifts so that most of the area is to the right of Fred's curve, meaning that we now think it is likely that Jill is more skilled than Fred. Because we were already relatively confident about Fred's skill level, his distribution barely changes at all.

for Fred hardly decreases at all. This difference is due to the greater certainty in `Fskill` as compared to `Jskill`. Intuitively we are using the more certain skill of Fred to estimate the skill of Jill. We also see from Figure 3.29 that the standard deviation for Jill's skill distributions decreases as a result of this game. This is because we have learned something about her skill and therefore the degree of uncertainty is reduced.

Alternatively, if Fred were to have won the game, we have the results shown in Figure 3.30. This result is slightly more surprising, since we believed Jill to be the stronger player, although we were not confident about this. Intuitively we would expect the adjustments of the skill distributions therefore to be slightly greater, which is indeed the case. We see that the shift in the means of the distributions is larger than that in Figure 3.29. In fact, the change in the mean of the distribution of `Jskill` is so large that it is now less than the mean of `Fskill`. Again, the standard deviations of Jill's skill has decreased, reflecting a reduc-

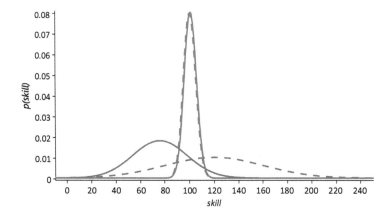

Figure 3.30 As in Figure 3.29 but for the case where Fred is the winner. The prior distributions (dashed lines) are the same as before. Again our belief about Fred's skill barely changes. But now Jill's posterior skill distribution is shifted so that most of the area is to the left of Fred's curve, meaning that we now think Jill is less skilled than Fred.

tion in uncertainty due to the incorporation of new evidence. Because the skill updates in TrueSkill model depend on the variance of the skill distribution, TrueSkill is able to make relatively large changes to the distributions of new players. Furthermore, this happens automatically as a consequence of running inference in our model.

3.3.2 Multiple games

So far in this section, we have developed a probabilistic model for a single game of Halo between Jill and Fred. In practice, we will have a large pool of players, and individual games will take place between pairs of players from within that pool. When we try to assess the skill of a player, we potentially have the results available for all the games ever played by that player against a range of different opponents. We might also have the results available for all the games played by those opponents, many of which might involve yet other players, and so on. In principle, all of this information is relevant and could help us to assess the original player's skill. Furthermore, every time there is a new game outcome we could include this additional information and update the skill of the player even if they themselves haven't played any new games. This new information could be relevant even if it involves a game between other players since it could influence the assessment of their skills, and hence the relative skill of our player.

We could in principle handle this by constructing a very large factor graph expressing all of the games played so far. Each player would have a single variable representing their skill value, but multiple variables (one for each game they have played) representing their performances on each of the games. This would be a complex graph with multiple loops, and we could run (loopy) expectation propagation, to keep the messages within the Gaussian family of distributions, until a suitable convergence criterion is satisfied. This would give a posterior skill distribution for each of the players, taking account of all of the games played. If a new game is then played, we would start again with a new, larger factor graph and re-run inference in order to obtain the new posterior distributions of every player. This approach would be complex to implement and would get increasingly slow with each new game added. With millions of games being played each day, it is completely infeasible.

Instead we can use an approximate inference approach known as **online learning** (sometimes called *filtering*) in which each player's skill distribution gets updated only when a game outcome, is obtained which involves that player. We therefore need only to store the mean and variance of the Gaussian skill distribution for each player. When a player plays a new game, we run inference using this current Gaussian skill distribution as the prior, and the resulting posterior distribution is then stored and forms the prior for the next game. Each single game is therefore described by a graph of the form shown in Figure 3.10.

This particular form of online inference algorithm, based on local projection onto the Gaussian distribution in which each data point (i.e. game outcome) is used only once, is also known as *Gaussian Density Filtering* Maybeck [1982]; Opper [1998]. It can be viewed as a special case of expectation propagation in which a specific choice is made for the message-passing schedule: namely that messages are only passed forwards in time from older games to newer games, but never in the reverse direction.

It is worth noting that if we consider the full factor graph describing all games played so far, then the order in which those games had been played would have been irrelevant. When doing online learning, however, the ordering becomes significant and can influence the assessed skills. We have to live with this, however, as only online learning would be feasible in a practical system.

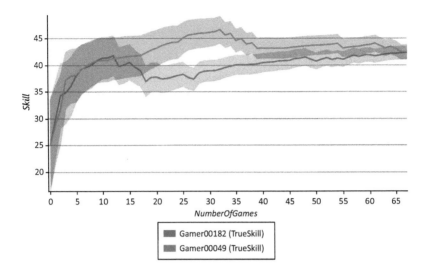

Figure 3.31 Trajectories of skill distributions of two of the top players in the Halo2 head-to-head data set, showing the mean and the one-standard-deviation envelopes. The horizontal axis shows the number of games played by the corresponding player.

We can illustrate the behaviour of online learning in our model using data taken from the game *Halo 2* on Xbox Live. We use a data set involving 1,650 players which contains the outcomes of 5,915 games. Each game is a head-to-head contest in which a pair of players play against each other. Figure 3.31 shows how the skill distributions for two of the top players varies as a function of the number of game outcomes played by each of the two players. To fit our model, these results ignore games which ended in a draw – we will see how to handle drawn games later in the chapter. We see that the initial skill distributions are the same, because all player skills have the same prior distribution before any games are played. As an increasing number of games are played, we see that the standard deviation of the skill distributions decreases. This reduction in uncertainty as a result of observing the outcome of games is the effect we saw earlier in Figures 3.29 and 3.30.

The model we have constructed in this section represents a single game between two players. However, many games on Xbox Live have a more elaborate structure, and so we turn next to a number of model extensions which allow for these additional complexities.

REVIEW OF CONCEPTS

---

expectation propagation   An approximate message-passing algorithm that extends belief propagation by allowing messages to be approximated by the closest distribution in a particular family, such as a Gaussian distribution. This approximation is done either to ensure that the inference algorithm remains tractable or to speed up the inference process. See Algorithm 3.1.

online learning   An approach to machine learning in which data points are considered one at a time, with model parameter distributions updated after each data point.

SELF ASSESSMENT 3.3

The following exercises will help embed the concepts you have learned in this section. It may help to refer back to the text or the review of concepts.

1. Reproduce Figure 3.24 by evaluating the (red) Gaussian context message and the (blue) exact CumGauss message at Jperf values of -50, $-49 \ldots 0$, 1, $2 \ldots 299$, 300. Plot the two lines you get with Jperf on the x-axis and the evaluated messages on the y-axis. You will need to rescale the CumGauss message to get it to fit (remember that the scale of this message does not matter since it is an improper distribution). To get the (green) product message corresponding to the exact marginal for Jperf, first multiply your two messages together at each Jperf value. Then rescale the result so that the area under the line is 1 (you can achieve this roughly by rescaling to make the sum of the value at each point equal to 1). Plot this result as a third line on your axes.

2. Compute the mean and standard deviation of the exact marginal product message that you just computed. The mean can be well approximated by summing the product of the message at each point times the Jperf value at each point. The variance, which is the square of the standard deviation, can be approximated similarly using the mnemonic "the mean of the square minus the square of the mean". First, you need to compute the "mean of the square" which can be approximated by sum of the product of the message at each point times the *square of* the Jperf value

at each point. Then subtract off "the square of the mean" which refers to the mean you just computed. This gives the variance, which you can take the square root of to get the standard deviation. You have now computed the mean and standard deviation of the Gaussian approximation to the marginal for Jperf. You can check your result against the Gaussian in Figure 3.25.

3. Finally, we need to divide this Gaussian distribution (whose mean and standard deviation you just found in the previous exercise) by the Gaussian context message. You can refer to Bishop [2006] for how to do this. You can check your result against message (6) in Figure 3.27. Congratulations! You have now successfully calculated an expectation propagation message!

4. Now we can use Infer.NET to do the expectation propagation calculations for us. Implement the Trueskill model in Infer.NET, setting the skill distributions for Jill and Fred to the ones used in this section. Refer to the guide on how to represent large irregular graphs in the Infer.NET documentation. Compute the posterior marginal distributions for Jill and Fred for the two outcomes where Jill wins the game and where Fred wins the game. Plot your results and check them against Figures 3.29 and 3.30.

3.4 EXTENSIONS TO THE CORE MODEL

So far, we have constructed a probabilistic model of a game played between two players which results in a win for one of the players. To handle the variety of games needed by Xbox Live, we need to extend our model to deal with a number of additional complexities. In particular, real games can end in draws, can involve more than two players and can be played between teams of people. We will now show how our initial model can be extended to take account of these complexities. This flexibility nicely illustrates the power of a model-based approach to machine learning.

Specifically, we need to extend our model so that it can:

- update the skills when the outcome is a draw;

- update the skills of individual team members, for team games;

- apply to games with more than two players.

A model-based approach allows such extensions to be incorporated in a transparent way, giving rise to a solution which can handle all of the above complexities – whilst remaining both understandable and maintainable.

3.4.1 What if a game can end in a draw?

In our current model, the player with the higher performance value on a particular game is the winner of that game. For games which can also end in a draw, we can modify this assumption by introducing the concept of a *draw margin*, such that a player is the winner only if their performance exceeds that of the other player by at least the value of the draw margin. Mathematically this can be expressed as

$$
\begin{aligned}
\text{if} \quad & \texttt{Jperf} > \texttt{Fperf} + \texttt{drawMargin} \quad \text{Jill wins} \\
\text{else if} \quad & \texttt{Fperf} > \texttt{Jperf} + \texttt{drawMargin} \quad \text{Fred wins} \\
\text{else} \quad & \text{game drawn.} \quad (3.16)
\end{aligned}
$$

This is illustrated in Figure 3.32.

We have therefore modified Assumption ③ to read:

③ The player with the higher performance value wins the game, unless the difference between their performance and that of their opponent is less than the draw margin, in which case the game is drawn.

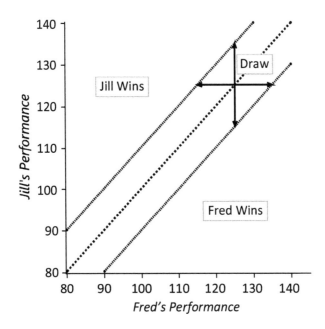

Figure 3.32 Illustration of the regions in performance space where Jill is the winner, where Fred is the winner, and where the game ends in a draw.

The value of the draw margin represents a new parameter in our model, and we may not know the appropriate value. This is particularly true if we introduce a new type of game, or if we modify the rules for an existing game, where we have yet to see any game results. To solve this problem, we simply treat the draw margin as a new random variable drawMargin whose value is to be learned from data. Because drawMargin is a continuous variable, it is chosen to be a Gaussian. This can be expressed as a factor graph, as shown in Figure 3.33. The variable Jwins is replaced by outcome which is a discrete variable that takes one of the values JillWins, Draw or FredWins. The *WinLoseDraw* factor is simply a function whose value is 1 if the three values of Jperf, drawMargin and Fperf are consistent with the value of outcome and is 0 otherwise. With this updated factor, we need to make corresponding modifications to the messages sent out from the factor node. These will not be discussed in detail here, and instead the interested reader can refer to Herbrich et al. [2007] and also an excellent blog post by Moser [2010].

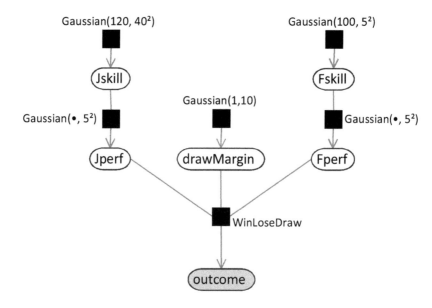

Figure 3.33 TrueSkill model for a game between two players which includes the possibility of a draw.

In order to simplify the subsequent discussion of other extensions to the core model, we will ignore the draw modification in the remaining factor graphs in this chapter, although all subsequent models can be similarly modified to include draws if required.

3.4.2 What if we have more than two players in a game?

Suppose we now have more than two players in a game, such as in the Halo game "Free for All" in which eight players simultaneously play against each other. The outcome of such a game is an ordering amongst the players involved in the game. With our model-based approach, incorporating a change such as this just involves making a

Games with more than two players require a more complex model.

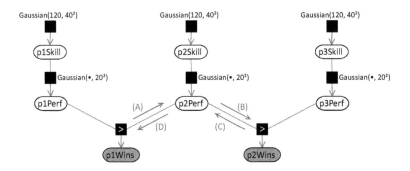

Figure 3.34 Factor graph for a game involving three players. Also shown are some of the messages which arise in the use of expectation propagation applied to this graph.

suitable assumption, constructing the corresponding factor graph and then running expectation propagation again. Our new Assumption ③ can be stated as

③ The order of players in the game, outcome is the same as the ordering of their performance values in that game.

If there are N players in the game then this assumption can be captured in a factor graph using $N-1$ *GreaterThan* factors to describe the player ordering. This is illustrated for the case of three players in Figure 3.34. Note that we could have introduced a separate "greater-than" factor for each possible pair of players. For N players there are $N(N-1)/2$ such factors. However, these additional factors contain only redundant information and lead to an unnecessarily complex graph. The ordering of N players can be expressed using $N-1$ greater than factors, provided these are chosen to connect the pairs of adjacent players in the ordering sequence. In effect, because we know the outcome of the game, we can choose a relatively simple graph which captures this.

⚓ Inference deep-dive
In this optional section, we show why the use of expectation propagation, even for a tree-structured graph, can require iterative solution. If you want to focus on modelling, feel free to skip this section.

The extension to more than two players introduces an interesting effect related to our expectation propagation algorithm. We saw in section 2.2.2 that if our factor graph has a tree structure, then belief propagation gives exact marginal distributions after a single sweep through the graph (with one message passed in each direction across every link). Similarly, if we now apply expectation propagation to the two-player graph of Figure 3.10, this again requires only a single pass in each direction. This is because the "context" messages for the expectation propagation approximation are fixed. However, the situation becomes more complex when we have more than two players. The graph of Figure 3.34 has a tree structure, with no loops, and so exact belief propagation would require only a single pass. However, consider the evaluation of outgoing message (A) using expectation propagation. This requires the incoming message (D) to provide the "context" for the approximation. However, message (D) depends on message (C) which itself is evaluated using expectation propagation using message (B) as context, and message (B) in turn depends on message (A). Expectation propagation therefore requires that we iterate these messages until we reach some suitable convergence criterion (in which the changes to the messages fall below some threshold). We therefore modify our message-passing schedule so that we first pass messages downwards from the skill nodes to the performance nodes (as before), then we perform multiple passes back and forth amongst the performance nodes until we achieve convergence, and then finally pass messages upwards to the skill nodes in order to evaluate posterior skill marginals.

Back in Figures 3.29 and 3.30, we saw that the shift of the distributions between prior and posterior was larger in the case where the weaker player (Fred) won the game. Now we repeat the experiment, except with a third player (Steve), whose prior skill distribution is $Gaussian(140, 40^2)$, keeping Jill as $Gaussian(120, 40^2)$ and Fred as $Gaussian(100, 5^2)$ as before. We apply our multi-player TrueSkill model to a game with the outcome Jill 1st, Fred 2nd and Steve 3rd.

The results of this are shown in Figure 3.35. Firstly, note that since Steve was expected to be the strongest player, but in fact came last, his posterior mean has moved markedly downwards (to below the other two players). Secondly, note that the changes in the means of Jill and Fred are in the same direction as in Figure 3.29, but are more pronounced than before. This is again because the overall game result is more surprising.

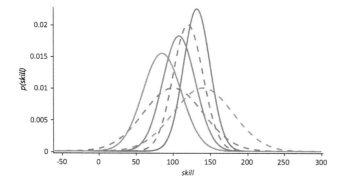

Figure 3.35 The result of applying the TrueSkill model for a three player game between Jill (blue), Fred (red) and Steve (green) for the case where Jill is the winner, Fred comes second and Steve comes last. The prior distributions are shown as dashed curves, and the corresponding posterior distributions are shown as solid curves.

Now let's consider a different outcome with Fred and Jill swapped, so that Fred is 1st, Jill is 2nd and Steve is still in 3rd place. Figure 3.36 shows the (same) priors and the new posteriors for the three skill distributions, with this new outcome.

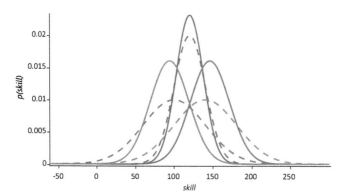

Figure 3.36 As in Figure 3.35 but for the case where Fred is the winner followed by Jill and then Steve came last.

Because there is low uncertainty in Fred's skill, his curve hardly changes given the result of the game. The fact that Fred won is strong evidence that his skill is higher than Jill or Steve's. As a result, both Jill and Steve's skill curves move to the left of Fred's. Because Jill beat Steve, her curve moved less than his did, so that now Steve has the lowest mean, whereas before it was the highest. What is even more interesting, if we compare Steve's posterior skill curve in Figure 3.36 to that in Figure 3.35 is that it is even further to the left with this outcome, even though Steve came last in both cases. This is because we now have to fit Jill's skill between that of Steve and Fred, whereas in the first outcome, Steve's skill just had to move to the left of Fred's. So in this multi-player game, the relative ordering of the *other* players has an effect on our estimate of Steve's skill!

3.4.3   What if the games are played by teams?

Many of the games available on Xbox Live can be played by teams of players. For example, in Halo, another type of game is played between two teams each consisting of eight players. The outcome of the game simply says which team is the winner and which team is the loser. Our challenge is to use this information to revise the skill distributions for each of the in-

The performance of a team depends on the skills of the individual players.

dividual players. This is an example of a **credit assignment problem** in which we have to work out how the credit for a victory (or blame for a defeat) should be attributed to individual players when only the outcome for the overall team is given. The solution is similar to the last two situations: we make an assumption about how the individual player skills combine to affect the game outcome, we construct a probabilistic model which encodes this assumption and then run inference to update the skill distributions. There is no need to invent new algorithms or design new heuristics.

Here is one suitable assumption which we could use when modelling team games, which would replace Assumption ③:

3. The performance of a team is the sum of the performances of its members, and the team with the highest performance value wins the game.

We can now build a factor graph corresponding to this assumption. For example, consider a game between two teams, each of which involves two players. The factor graph for this is shown in Figure 3.37.

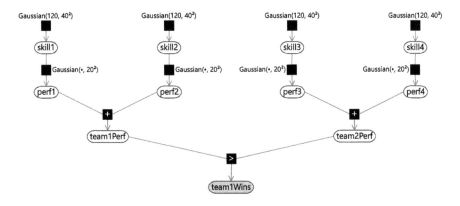

Figure 3.37 A factor graph of the TrueSkill model for two teams. The first team consists of players 1 and 2, and the second team consists of players 3 and 4.

The performance of a team is determined by the performance of the players who comprise that team. Our assumption above was that the team performance is given by the sum of the performances of the individual players. This might be appropriate for collaborative team games such as Halo. However, other assumptions might be appropriate in other kinds of game. For example, in a race where only the fastest player determines the team outcome, we might make the alternative assumption.

③ The performance of a team is equal to the highest performance of any of its members, and the team with the highest performance value wins the game.

In this section, we have discussed various modifications to the core TrueSkill model, namely the inclusion of draws, the extension to multiple players and the extension to team games. These modifications can be combined as required, for example, to allow a game between multiple teams that includes draws, by constructing the appropriate factor graph and then running expectation propagation. This highlights not only the flexibility of the model-based approach to machine learning, but also the ease with which modifications can be incorporated. As long as the model builder is able to describe the process by which the data is generated, it is usually straightforward to formulate the corresponding model. By contrast, when a solution is expressed only as an algorithm, it may be far from clear how the algorithm should be modified to account for changes in the problem specification. In the next section, we conclude our discussion of the online game matchmaking problem by a further modification to the model in which we relax the assumption that the skills of the players are fixed.

REVIEW OF CONCEPTS

credit assignment problem   The problem of allocating a reward amongst a set of entities, such as people, all of which have contributed to the outcome.

SELF ASSESSMENT 3.4

The following exercises will help embed the concepts you have learned in this section. It may help to refer back to the text or the review of concepts.

1. Sketch out a factor graph for a model which allows draws, two-player teams and multiple teams. You will need to combine the factor graphs of Figures 3.33, 3.34 and 3.37. Your sketch can be quite rough – for example, you should name factors (e.g. "Gaussian") but there is no need to provide any numbers for factor parameters.

2. Extend your Infer.NET model from the previous self assessment to have three players and reproduce the results from Figures 3.35 and 3.36.

3. *[Project idea]* There is a wide variety of sports results data available on the web. Find a suitable set of data and build an appropriate model to infer the skills of the teams or players involved. Rank the teams or players by the inferred skill and decide if you think the model has inferred a good ranking. If not, diagnose why not and explore modifications to your model to address the issue.

3.5   ALLOWING THE SKILLS TO VARY

At this point, we seem to have found a comprehensive solution to the problem posed at the start of the chapter. We have a probabilistic model of games between multiple teams of players including draws, in which simpler situations (two players, individuals instead of teams, games without draws) arise as special cases. However, when this system was deployed for real beta testers, it was found that its matchmaking was not always satisfactory. In particular, the skill values for some players seemed to "get stuck" at low values, even as the players played and improved a lot, leading to poor matchmaking.

To understand the reason for this we note that the assumptions encoded in our model do not allow for the skill of a player to change over time. In particular, Assumption ① says that "each player has a skill value" – in other words, each player has a single skill value with no mention of this skill value being allowed to change. Since players' skills do change over time, this assumption will be violated in real data. For example, as a player gains experience in playing a particular type of game, we might anticipate that their skill will improve. Conversely, an experienced player's skill might deteriorate if they play infrequently and get out of practice.

You may think that our online learning process updates our skill distribution for a player over time and so would allow the skill to change. This is a common misconception

Skill increases with practice.

about online learning, but it is not true. Our current model assumes that the skill of a player is a *fixed*, but unknown, quantity. Online learning does not represent the modelling of an evolving skill value, but rather an updating of the uncertainty in this unknown fixed-across-time skill. If a player played for a long time at a particular skill level, then our distribution over their skill would become very narrow. If the player then suddenly improved, perhaps because of some coaching, the current model would struggle to track the player's new skill level because it would be very unlikely under the narrow skill distribution.

3.5.1 Reproducing the problem

To deal with players having changing skills, we will need to change the model. But first, we need to reproduce the problem, so that we can check later that we have fixed it. To do this, we can create a synthetic data set. In this data set, we synthesise the results of games involving a pool of 100 players. The first player, Elliot, has an initial skill fixed at 110, and this skill value is increased in steps as shown by the red line in Figure 3.38. The remaining 99 players have fixed skill values which are drawn from a Gaussian with a mean of 125 and a standard deviation of 10. For each game, two players are selected at random and their performances on this game are evaluated by adding Gaussian noise to their skill values with a standard deviation of 5. This just corresponds to running ancestral sampling on the model in Figure 3.6 (just like we did to create a synthetic data set in Section 2.5.1).

Given this synthetic data set, we can then run online learning using the model in Figure 3.10 in which the game outcomes are known and

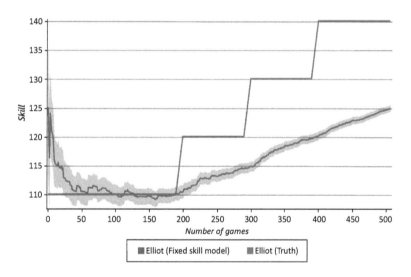

Figure 3.38 The red curve shows the skill value for a player, Elliot, in a synthetic data set drawn from a pool of 100 players. All other players have fixed skills (not shown). The blue line shows the mean of the inferred Gaussian skill distribution for Elliot under our model, which assumes that Elliot's skill is fixed. The blue shaded region shows the plus/minus one-standard-deviation region around the mean of this distribution.

the skills are unknown. Figure 3.38 shows the inferred skill distribution for Elliot under this model. We see that our model cannot account for the changes in Elliot's skill: the estimated skill mean does not match the trajectory of the true skill, and the variances of the estimates are too narrow to include the improving skill value. Due to the small variance, the update to the skill mean is small, and so the evolution of the skill mean is too slow. This is unsurprising as a key assumption of the model, namely that the skill of each player is constant, is incorrect.

To address this problem, we need to change the incorrect assumption in our model. Rather than assuming a fixed skill, we need to allow for the skill to change by a typically small amount from game to game. We can therefore replace Assumption ① with:

① Each player has a skill value, represented by a continuous variable, given by their skill value in their previous game plus some change in skill which has a zero-mean bell-shaped distribution.

Whereas previously a player had a single skill variable, there is now a separate skill variable for each game. We assume that the skill value for a particular player in a specific game is given by the skill value from their previous game with the addition of some change in value having drawn from a zero-mean distribution. Again, we make this assumption mathematically precise by choosing this distribution to be a zero-mean Gaussian. If we denote the skill of a player in their previous game by $\texttt{skill}^{(\text{old})}$ and their skill in the current game by $\texttt{skill}^{(\text{new})}$, then we are assuming that

$$\texttt{skill}^{(\text{new})} = \texttt{skill}^{(\text{old})} + \texttt{skillChange} \tag{3.17}$$

where

$$p(\texttt{skillChange}) = Gaussian(0, \texttt{ChangeVariance}). \tag{3.18}$$

From these two equations, it follows that [Bishop, 2006]

$$p\left(\texttt{skill}^{(\text{new})}\right) = Gaussian\left(\texttt{skill}^{(\text{old})}, \texttt{ChangeVariance}\right). \tag{3.19}$$

This allows us to express our new assumption in the form of a factor graph. For example, in the case of two players who play two successive games against each other, the factor graph would be given by Figure 3.39. The prior distribution for skill of player 1 in the second game, denoted $\texttt{skill1}_{(2)}$, is given by a Gaussian distribution

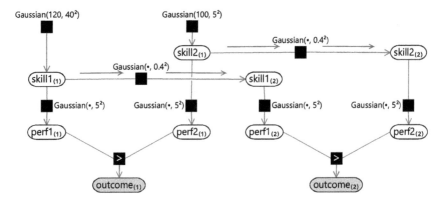

Figure 3.39 A factor graph for two players and two successive games in which the skill values are allowed to change from one game to the next.

whose mean, instead of being fixed, is now given by the skill of that player in the previous game, denoted by $\mathtt{skill1}_{(1)}$. The graph shows a **ChangeVariance** of 0.16 which encodes our belief that the change in skill from one game to the next should be small.

Online inference in this model can be done as follows. We run expectation propagation for the first game using a graph of the form shown in Figure 3.10, to give posterior Gaussian skill distributions for each of the players. Then we send messages through the Gaussian factors connecting the two games, as indicated in blue in Figure 3.39. The incoming messages to these factors are the skill distributions coming from the first game. The subsequent outgoing messages to the new skill variables are broadened versions of these skill distributions, because of the convolution computed for the Gaussian factor. These broadened distributions are then used as the prior skill distribution for this new game. Because we are broadening the prior in the new game, we are essentially saying that we have slightly higher uncertainty about the skill of the player. In turn, this means the new game outcome will lead to a greater change in skill, and so we will be better at tracking changes in skill. It may seem strange that we can improve the behaviour of our system by *increasing* the uncertainty in our skill variable, but this arises because we have modified the model to correspond more closely to reality. In the time since the last game, the player's skill may indeed have changed and we are now correctly modelling this possibility.

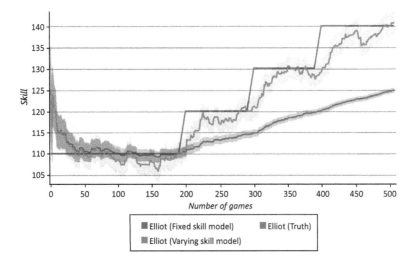

Figure 3.40 This shows the same information as in Figure 3.38 with the addition in green of the distribution of inferred skill for Elliot using a model in which skill values are allowed to evolve over time.

We can now test out this modified model on our synthetic data set. The results are shown by the green curve in Figure 3.40.

We see that the changing skill of Elliot is tracked much better when we allow for varying skills in our model – we have solved the problem of tracking time-varying skills! This model has been applied to the history of chess to work out the relative strengths of different historical chess players, even though they lived decades apart! You can read all about this work in Dangauthier et al. [2007].

3.5.2 The final model

Now that we have adapted the model to cope with varying skills, it meets all the requirements of the Xbox Live team. With all extensions combined, Figure 3.41 shows the full set of assumptions built into our model.

This model encompasses the variety of different game types which arise including teams and multiple players, it allows for draws and it tracks the evolution of player skills over time. As a result, when Xbox 360 launched in November 2005, it used this TrueSkill model as its online skill rating system. Since then, the skill distributions inferred by

① Each player has a skill value, represented by a continuous variable, given by their skill value in their previous game plus some change in skill which has a zero-mean bell-shaped distribution.

② Each player has a performance value for each game, which is independent from game to game and has an average value equal to the skill of that player. The variation in performance, which is the same for all players, is symmetrically distributed around the mean value and is more likely to be close to the mean than to be far from the mean.

③ The performance of a team is given by the sum of the performances of the players within that team.

④ The order of teams in the game outcome is the same as the ordering of their performance values in that game, unless the magnitude of the difference in performance between two teams is below a threshold in which case those teams draw.

Figure 3.41 The four assumptions encoded in our final model.

TrueSkill have been used to perform real-time matchmaking in hundreds of different Xbox games.

The role of the model is to infer the skills, while the decision on how to use those skills to perform matchmaking is a separate question. Typically this is done by selecting players for which the game outcome is most uncertain. Note that this also tends to produce matches whose outcomes are the most informative in terms of learning the skills of the players. The matchmaking process must also take account of the need to provide players with opponents within a reasonably short time, and so there is a natural trade-off between how long a player waits for a game to be set up and the closeness in match to their opponents. One of the powerful aspects of decomposing the matchmaking problem into the two stages of skill inference and matchmaking decision is that changes to the matchmaking criteria are easy to implement and do not require any changes to the more complex modelling and inference code. As discussed in the introduction, the ability to match players against others of similar ability, and to do so quickly and accurately, is a key feature of this very successful service.

The inferred skills produced by TrueSkill are also used for a second, distinct purpose which is to construct leaderboards showing the ranking of players within a particular type of game. For this purpose, we need to define a single skill value for each player based on the inferred Gaussian skill distribution. One possibility would be to use the mean of the distribution, but this fails to take account of the uncertainty, and could lead to a player having an artificially high (or low) position on the leader board. Instead, the displayed skill value for a player is taken to be the mean of their distribution minus three times the standard deviation of their distribution. This is a conservative choice and implies that their actual skill is, with high probability, no lower than their displayed skill. Thus, a player can make progress up the leader board both by increasing the mean of their distribution (by winning games against other players) and by reducing the uncertainty in their skill (by playing lots of games).

There are plenty of ways in which the TrueSkill model can be extended to improve its ability to model particular aspects of the game-playing process. In 2018, a number of such improvements were included in the TrueSkill 2 model [Minka et al., 2018] by making additional assumptions particularly suited to online shooters such as *Gears of War* and *Halo*. For example, the enhanced model made use of the number of kills each player made rather than just their final ranking. It also modelled the correlation of a person's skill in different game modes. Other improvements were made to handle situations, such as a player quitting the game mid-way through, which had previously led to inaccurate skill estimates.

We have seen how TrueSkill continually adapts to track the skill level of individual players. In the next chapter, we shall see another example of a model which adapts to individual users, but in the context of a very different kind of application: helping to de-clutter your email inbox.

CHAPTER 4

Uncluttering your inbox

The sheer volume of email being sent and received means that a typical office worker spends hours each day processing their inbox. The constant stream of new messages can easily become overwhelming. It is also more likely than ever that an important email will get lost amongst the clutter. Can model-based machine learning help to reduce this information overload?

T he average office worker spends almost three hours a day processing their email. About 90% of this time is spent either reading incoming email or managing existing email – only the remaining 10% is spent writing or replying to emails [Outlook team, 2008]. An automatic tool to speed up reading and managing email would free up a lot of people's time, allowing them to focus on important tasks and avoid the stress of information overload.

Microsoft Exchange is an email server used to power more than 300 million mailboxes worldwide [Radicati and Hoang, 2010]. The Exchange team are keen to use machine learning to help people to manage their mail and improve their productivity. In this chapter, we will look at how model-based machine

DOI: 10.1201/9780429192685-5

learning was used by the Exchange team to separate out the clutter from a user's inbox, allowing users to focus on their important emails and reducing the time taken to process incoming email.

The idea was to decide if a user thinks an email was clutter or not, based on the actions the user takes on similar emails. For example, emails that are never read or quickly deleted are likely to be considered as clutter by the user. Now suppose we had a machine learning system that could predict what actions a user would take on a new email – for example, the system would predict whether a user would reply to an email, delete it or leave it unread. Given such a machine learning system we could then hide emails that are unlikely to be read or acted upon. Such clutter emails could then be placed in a separate location where they could be easily reviewed and processed in one go, at a convenient time for the user.

To achieve this goal, the team needed a system that could take a number of older emails that a user had already taken action on and learn which actions the user would be likely to take on emails with different characteristics. The system was to consider many aspects of the email: who sent the email, who was on the To and Cc lines, what the subject was, what was written in the email, whether there were any attachments and so on. The trained system was then to be applied to incoming mails to predict the probability of the user performing various actions on each email. The Exchange team considered it essential that the system make personalised predictions. Unlike junk mail, which emails are clutter is a personal thing: what is clutter for one user might not be clutter for another. For example, a project update email might be clutter for someone not on the project but might be important to read for someone who is working on the project.

In this chapter, we'll use model-based machine learning to develop a personalised system that meets the needs of the Exchange team. We will focus on building a system to predict whether a user will reply to an incoming email. However, the resulting system will be general enough to predict many other kinds of actions and so can be used to predict whether or not a user will consider an email to be clutter. In particular, we will see how to:

- Manage email data and privacy issues;

- Develop a model for predicting actions personalised to each user;

- Use information about an email to drive the model;

- Evaluate the model both in numerical terms and in terms of user experience;

- Extend the model to address various problems as they arise.

You can recreate all results in this chapter using the companion source code [Diethe et al., 2019].

4.1 COLLECTING AND MANAGING EMAIL DATA

For the purposes of writing this chapter, we developed a tool for collecting all of a person's email received in a given time period. We then used the tool to collect emails from 10 volunteers who kindly agreed to share their email data – in an anonymised form, as we shall discuss shortly. This was quite a time-consuming process and so we need to plan carefully about how we are going to use this precious email data. For example, we need to decide which data we will use to train on and which data we will use to evaluate the system's accuracy. It is *very* important that the data used for training is not used for evaluation. If training data is used for evaluation, it can give misleadingly high accuracy results – because it is much easier to make a prediction for an email when you've already been told the correct answer! To avoid this, we need to divide our data into different data sets:

- A **training set** which we will use to train the model;

- A separate **test set** which we will use to assess the prediction accuracy for each user and so indicate what we might expect to achieve for real users.

If you were to evaluate a trained model on its training set, it will tend to give higher accuracy results than on a test set. The amount that the accuracy is higher on the training set indicates how much the model has learned that is specific to the particular data in the training set, rather than to that type of data in general. We say that a model is **overfitting** to the training data, if its accuracy is significantly higher on the training set than on a test set.

If we were only planning to evaluate our system once, these two data sets would be sufficient. However, we expect to make repeated changes to our system, and to evaluate each change to see if it improves prediction accuracy. If we were to evaluate on the test set many times, making only the changes that improve the test set accuracy, we would run the risk of overfitting to the test set. This is because the process of repeatedly making changes that increase the test set accuracy could be picking up on patterns that are specific to the test and training set combined but not to general data of the same type. This overfitting would mean that the accuracy reported on the test set would no longer be representative of what we might expect for real users. To avoid overfitting, we will instead divide our data into three, giving a third data set:

- A **validation set** which we will use to evaluate prediction accuracy during the process of developing the system.

We can evaluate on the validation set as many times as we like to make decisions about which changes to make to our system. Once we have a final system, we will then evaluate once on the test set. If it turns out that the model has been overfitting to the validation set, then the accuracy results on the test set will be lower, indicating that the real user accuracy will be lower than we might have expected from the validation set accuracy numbers.

If the test set accuracy is not yet sufficient, it would then be necessary to make further changes to the system. These can again be assessed on the validation set. At some point, a new candidate system would be ready for test set evaluation. Strictly speaking, a fresh test set should be used at this point. In practice, it is usually okay to evaluate on a test set a small number of times, bearing in mind that the numbers may be slightly optimistic. However, if used too much, a test set can become useless due to the possibility of overfitting, at which point it would then be necessary to gather a fresh test set.

For the email data that we collected, we can divide each user's emails into training, validation and test sets. Since the goal is to make predictions on email arriving in the user's inbox, we exclude emails in the user's Sent Mail and Junk folders from these data sets, since such emails did not arrive in the inbox. We also exclude emails which were automatically moved by a rule, since such emails also did not appear in the inbox. Table 4.1 gives the sizes of the training, validation and test sets for each user, after removing such non-inbox emails.

4.1.1 Learning from confidential data

Table 4.1 highlights another challenge when working with email data – it is highly personal and private data! Email data is an example of **personally identifiable information** (PII), which is information that could be used to identify or learn about a particular person. For an email, personally identifiable information includes the names and email addresses on the email along with the actual words of the subjects and email bodies. Knowing which senders a particular user ignores or replies to, for example, would be very sensitive data. In any system that uses PII, it is essential to ensure that such data is kept confidential.

In a machine learning system, this need for confidentiality appears to conflict with the need to understand the data deeply, monitor the performance of the system, find bugs and make improvements. The main technique used to resolve this conflict is some kind of **anonymisation**, where the data is transformed to remove any PII whilst retaining the underlying patterns that the machine learning system can learn from. For example, names and email addresses can be anonymised by replacing them with arbitrary codes. For this project, we anonymise all user identities using an alphanumeric hash code like "User35CB8E5", as shown in Table 4.1. This type of anonymisation removes PII (or at least makes it extremely difficult to identify the user involved) but preserves information relevant to making predictions, such as how often the user replies to each person.

In some cases, anonymisation is hard to achieve. For example, if we anonymised the subject and body on a word-by-word basis, this anonymisation could potentially be reversed using a word frequency

Table 4.1 Number of emails in the training, validation and test sets for each user and overall.

	Train	Validation	Test	User total
User35CB8E5	1,995	2,005	657	4,657
UserCE3FDB4	1,067	1,067	356	2,490
User6AACED	1,827	1,822	600	4,249
User7E601F9	531	528	173	1,232
User68251CD	600	602	198	1,400
User223AECA	532	532	179	1,243
UserFF0F29E	2,202	2,199	729	5,130
User25C0488	1,181	1,182	393	2,756
User811E39F	1,574	1,565	513	3,652
User10628A6	485	485	163	1,133
Total	11,994	11,987	3,961	27,942
Average	1278.8	1278	422	2978.8

dictionary. For this reason, we have removed the email bodies and subject lines from the data used for this chapter, so that we can make it available for download while protecting the confidentiality of our volunteers. We will retain the lengths of the subject lines and body text, since they are useful for making predictions but do not break confidentiality. If you wish to experiment with a more complete email data set, there are a few such available, an example of which is the Enron email dataset [The CALO Project, 2004]. Notice that, even for this public Enron data set, some emails were deleted "as part of a redaction effort due to requests from affected employees", demonstrating again the sensitive nature of email data! For cases like these where anonymisation cannot easily be achieved, there is an exciting new method under development called *homomorphic encryption* which makes it possible to do machine learning on encrypted data without decrypting the data first. This approach is at the research stage only, so is not yet ready for use in a real application (but read more in Panel 4.1 if you are curious).

Panel 4.1: Homomorphic encryption

Homomorphic encryption is a type of data encryption that allows certain algorithms to run directly on the encrypted data, giving encrypted results, without ever being decrypted! At the moment, there are practical restrictions on the kinds of algorithms that can be run on the data – for example, they may be required to consist only of additions or multiplications (and a limited number of these). There is currently also a significant computational cost to running algorithms this way. Despite these limitations, it is possible to run inference algorithms using homomorphic encryption – for example, Graepel et al. [2013] describe a classification algorithm which runs entirely on encrypted data.

Although still at the research stage, homomorphic encryption has great potential for allowing machine learning algorithms to be run on confidential data.

Using our anonymised and pruned data set means that we can inspect, refine or debug any part of the system without seeing any confidential information. In some cases, this anonymisation can make it hard to understand the system's behaviour or to debug problems. It is therefore useful to have a small non-anonymised data set to work within such cases. For this chapter, we used a selection of our own emails for this purpose. For a deployed system, you can also ask real users to voluntarily supply a very limited amount of what would normally be confidential information, such as a specific email. It is important to allow the user to review exactly what information is being shared and ensure the information is only used for the purpose of debugging the issue they are reporting, for example, an incorrect prediction.

Now that we have training and validation data sets in a suitably anonymised form, we are ready to start developing our model.

REVIEW OF CONCEPTS

training set   The part of the collected data which will be used for model training.

test set   The part of the collected data which will be used to assess a trained model's accuracy. This evaluation should be performed infrequently, ideally only once, to avoid overfitting to the test set.

overfitting   The situation where a trained model has learned too much about patterns in the data that are specific to the training set, rather than patterns relating to general data of the same form. If a model is overfitting, its prediction accuracy on data sets other than the training set is reduced.

validation set   The part of the collected data which will be used to assess a trained model's accuracy as the model is being developed. Typically the validation set is used repeatedly to decide whether or not to make changes to the model. This runs the risk of overfitting to the validation set, which is why it is important also to have a separate test set.

personally identifiable information   Any information about a person which could be used to identify who they are or to learn confidential information about them.

anonymisation   A process where data is transformed to remove any personally identifiable information, whilst retaining enough information to be useful. For example, email addresses can be anonymised by replacing them by a randomly generated string, such that the same address is always replaced by the same string. This allows patterns of email use to be identified without associating those patterns with any given sender or recipient.

4.2 A MODEL FOR CLASSIFICATION

The problem of predicting a label, such as "reply" or "not reply", for a data item is called **classification**. Systems that perform classification are known as **classifiers**, and are probably the most widely used machine learning algorithms today. There are many different classification algorithms available and, for a particular prediction task, some will work better than others. A common approach to solving a classification problem is to try several different classification algorithms and see which one works the best. This approach ignores the underlying reason that the classification algorithms are making different predictions on the same data: that each algorithm is implicitly making different assumptions about the data. Unfortunately, these assumptions are hidden away inside each algorithm.

You may be surprised to learn that many classification algorithms can be interpreted as doing approximate inference in some probabilistic model. So rather than running a classification algorithm, we can instead build the corresponding model and use an inference algorithm to do classification. Why would we do this instead of using the classification algorithm? Because a model-based approach to classification gives us several benefits:

- The assumptions in the classifier are made explicit. This helps us to understand what the classifier is doing, which can allow us to improve how we use it to achieve better prediction accuracy.

- We can modify the model to improve its accuracy or give it new capabilities, beyond those of the original classifier.

- We can use standard inference algorithms to both train the model and to make predictions. This is particularly useful when modifying the model, since the training and prediction algorithms remain in sync with the modified model. Also, different algorithms have different trade-offs between speed and accuracy. We can choose an algorithm that best suits our needs, whilst retaining all of our modelling assumptions.

These are not small benefits – in this chapter, you will see how all three will be crucial in delivering a successful system. We will show how to construct the model for a widely used classifier from scratch, by making a series of assumptions about how the label arises given a data item. We will then show how to extend this initial classification model to achieve various capabilities needed by the email classification system. Throughout the evolution of the model, we will use a standard inference algorithm (expectation propagation) for training and prediction.

Before we construct the model, we need to understand how a classifier with a fixed set of assumptions could possibly be applied to many different problems. This is possible because classifiers require the input data to be transformed into a form which matches the assumptions encoded in the classifier. This transformation is achieved using a set of features (a **feature set**), where a **feature** is a function that acts on a data item to return one or more values, which are usually binary or continuous values. In our model, we will use features that return continuous values in the range 0.0 to 1.0. For example, our first feature will return 1.0 if the user is mentioned on the To line of the email or 0.0 otherwise – we'll call this the *ToLine* feature. It is these feature values, rather than the data item itself, that are fed into the classifier. So, rather than changing the assumptions in the classifier, we use features to transform the data to match the assumptions already built in to the classifier.

Another important simplification that a classifier makes is that it only ever makes predictions about the label variable assuming that the corresponding values for the features are known. Because it always conditions on these known feature values, the model only needs to represent the conditional probability $P(\text{label}|\text{features})$ rather than the joint distribution $P(\text{label}, \text{features})$. Because it represents a conditional probability, this kind of model is called a **conditional model**. It is convenient to build a conditional model because we do not need to model the data being conditioned on (the feature values) but only the probability of the label given these values. This brings us to our first modelling assumption.

① The feature values can always be calculated, for any email.

By always, we mean *always*: during training, when doing prediction, for every single email ever encountered by the system. Although convenient, the assumption that the feature values can always be calculated makes it difficult to handle missing data. For example, if the sender of an email is not known, any features requiring the sender cannot be calculated. Strictly, this would mean we would be unable to make a prediction. In practice, people commonly provide a default feature value if the true value is not available, even though this is not the correct thing to do. For example in the sender case, it is equivalent to treating all emails with missing senders as if they came from a particular "unknown" sender. The correct thing to do would be to make a joint model of the feature values and marginalise over any missing values – but, if data is rarely missing, the simpler approach is often sufficiently good – indeed it is what we shall use here.

4.2.1 A one-feature classification model

We will start by building a model that uses only one feature to predict whether a user will reply to an email: whether the user is on the To line or not (the *ToLine* feature). Since we are building a conditional model, we only need to consider the process of generating the label (whether the user replied to the email or not) from the feature value. The variable we are trying to generate is therefore a binary label that is `true` if the user replied to the mail or `false` otherwise – we will call this variable `repliedTo`. This `repliedTo` variable is the variable that we will observe when training the model and which we will infer when making predictions.

It would be difficult to define the process of generating this binary `repliedTo` variable directly from the continuous feature values, since it is not itself a continuous variable. Instead, we introduce an intermediate variable that is continuous, which we shall call the *score*. We will assume that the score will be higher for emails which having a higher probability of reply and lower for emails which have a lower probability of reply. Here is the assumption:

② Each email has an associated continuous score which is higher when there is a higher probability of the user replying to the email.

Notice that, unlike a probability, the continuous score value is not required to lie between zero and one but can take on any continuous value. This makes it an easier quantity to model since we do not have to worry about keeping its value constrained to be between zero and one.

We are now ready to make an assumption about how the feature value for an email affects its score.

③ If an email's feature value changes by x, then its score will change by *weight* $\times x$ for some fixed, continuous weight.

This assumption says that the score for an email is either always higher if the feature value increases (if the weight is positive) or always lower

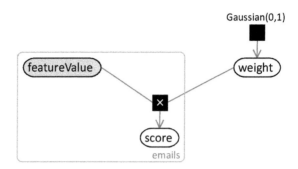

Figure 4.1 Factor graph for a single feature. Each email has a `featureValue` which is multiplied by a single common `weight` to give a `score` for that email. A positive `weight` means that the score increases if the feature value increases. A negative `weight` means that the score decreases if the feature value increases. A higher score corresponds to a higher probability that the email is replied to.

if the feature value increases (if the weight is negative) or is not affected by the feature value (if the weight is zero). The size of any change in score is controlled by the size of the weight: a larger weight means a particular change in feature value produces a larger change in the score. Remember that, according to our previous assumption, a higher score means a higher reply probability and lower score means a lower reply probability.

To build a factor graph to represent Assumption ③, we first need a continuous `featureValue` variable to hold the value of the feature for each email (so it will be inside a plate across the emails). Since this variable will always be observed, we always show it shaded in the factor graph (Figure 4.1). We also introduce a continuous `weight` variable for the feature weight mentioned in the assumption. Because this weight is fixed, it is the same for all emails and so lies outside the emails plate. We can then model Assumption ③ by multiplying the `featureValue` by the `weight`, using a deterministic multiplication factor and storing the result in continuous `score` variable. The factor graph for a single feature modelled in this way is shown in Figure 4.1.

In drawing the factor graph, we've had to assume some prior distribution for `weight`. In this case, we have assumed that the weight is drawn from a Gaussian distribution with zero mean, so that it is equally likely to be positive or negative.

④ The weight for a feature is equally likely to be positive or negative.

We have also the prior distribution to be Gaussian with variance 1.0 (so the standard deviation is also 1.0). This choice means that the weight will most often be in the range from −1.0 to 1.0, occasionally be outside this in the range −2.0 to 2.0 and very occasionally be outside even that range (as we saw in Figure 3.4). We could equally have chosen any value for the variance, which would have led to different ranges of weight values so there is no implied assumption here. The effect of this choice will depend on the feature values which multiply the weight to give the score and also on how we use the score, which we will look at next.

We now have a continuous `score` variable which is higher for emails that are more likely to be replied to and lower for emails that are less likely to be replied to. Next, we need to convert the `score` into a binary `repliedTo` variable. A simple way to do this is to threshold the `score` – if it is above some threshold then `repliedTo` is `true`, otherwise `false`. We can do this by adding a continuous `threshold` variable and use the deterministic *GreaterThan* factor that we met in the previous chapter:

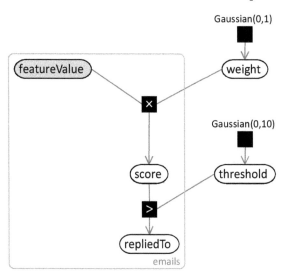

Figure 4.2 Factor graph of Figure 4.1 extended so that if the `score` is greater than a `threshold` the binary `repliedTo` variable is true, otherwise it is false.

Here we've chosen a *Gaussian*(0, 10) prior for the `threshold` – we'll discuss this choice of prior shortly. Now suppose we try to train this one-feature model on the training set for one of our users. We can train the model using probabilistic inference as usual. First, we fix the value of `repliedTo` for each email (by seeing if the user actually did reply to the email) and also the *ToLine* `featureValue` – which is always available since we can calculate it from the email To line. Given these two observed values for each email, we can train by inferring the posterior distributions for `weight` and `threshold`.

Unfortunately, if we attempt to run inference on this model, then any inference algorithm we try will fail. This is because some of the observed values have zero probability under the model. In other words, there is no way that the data-generating process encoded by our model could have generated the observed data values. When your data has zero probability under your model, it is a sure sign that the model is wrong!

The issue is that the model is wildly overconfident. For any `weight` and `threshold` values, it will always predict `repliedTo` to be true with 100% certainty if the `score` is greater than the `threshold` and predict `repliedTo` to be false with 100% certainty otherwise. If we plot the reply probability against the `score`, it abruptly moves from 0% to 100% as the `score` passes the `threshold` (see the blue line in Figure 4.3). We will only be successful in training such a model if we are able to find some `weight` and `threshold` that *perfectly* classifies the training set – in other words gives a `score` above the `threshold` for all replied-to training emails and a score below the `threshold` for all emails that were not replied to. As an example, this would be possible if the user replied to every single email where they were on the To line and did not reply to every single other email. If there is even a single email where this is not the case, then its observed label will have zero probability under the model. For example, suppose a not-replied-to email has a `score` above the `threshold` – the prediction will be that `repliedTo` is `true` with probability 1.0 and so has zero probability of being `false`. But in this case `repliedTo` is observed to be `false`, which has zero probability and is therefore impossible under the model.

Looking back, Assumption ② said that the reply probability would always be higher for emails with a higher score. But in fact, in our current model, this assumption does not hold – if we have two positive scores one higher than the other, they will both have the same 100% probability of reply. So our model is instead encoding the assumption that the reply probability abruptly changes from 0% to 100% as the score increases – it is this overly strong assumption that is causing training to fail.

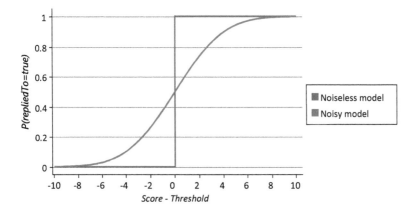

Figure 4.3 Plot of the predicted probability of reply as the score varies relative to the threshold for the noiseless model of Figure 4.2 and a noisy score model which adds Gaussian noise to the score before thresholding it. For the noiseless model, the reply probability abruptly changes from 0.0 to 1.0 as the score passes the threshold. In contrast, for the noisy model, the reply probability varies smoothly from near 0.0 to near 1.0 over a range of score values (from about −8 to +8).

To better represent Assumption ②, we need the reply probability to increase smoothly as the score increases. The red curve in Figure 4.3 shows a much smoother relationship between the score and the reply probability. This curve may look familiar to you, it is the cumulative density function for a Gaussian distribution, like the ones that we saw in Figure 3.9 in the previous chapter. We'd like to change

Adding noise to a model can be helpful when it does not perfectly represent the data.

our model to use this smooth curve. We can achieve this by adding a Gaussian-distributed random value to the **score** before we threshold it. These are called "noise" values, because they take the clean 0% or 100% prediction and make it "noisy". Now, even if the **score** is below the threshold, there is a small probability that the noisy version will be above the threshold (and vice versa) so that the model can tolerate misclassified training examples. The exact probability that this will happen will depend on how far the score is below the threshold and the probability that the added Gaussian noise will push it above the threshold. This probability is given by the cumulative density function for the Gaussian noise, and so you end up with the curve shown in Figure 4.3.

Since the predicted probability varies smoothly from 0.0 to 1.0 over a range of score values, the model can now vary the confidence of its predictions, rather than always predicting 0% or 100%. The range of values that this happens over (the steepness of the curve) is determined by the variance of the Gaussian noise. The plot in Figure 4.3 is for a noise variance of 10, which is the value that we will use in our model, for reasons we will discuss in a moment. So let's add a new continuous variable called `noisyScore` and give it a Gaussian distribution whose mean is at `score` and whose variance is 10. This gives the factor graph of Figure 4.4.

In choosing a variance of 10, we have set how much the score needs to change in order to change the predicted probability. Remember

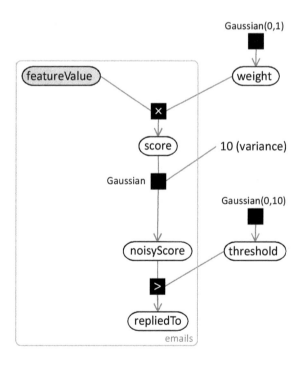

Figure 4.4 Factor graph of a classification model with one feature. The model uses a *Gaussian* factor to introduce uncertainty in the prediction of `repliedTo` for a particular `score`.

that our weights are normally in the range -1.0 to 1.0, sometimes in the range -2.0 to 2.0 and occasionally outside this range. Looking at Figure 4.3, you can see that to change the predicted probability from a "don't know" prediction of 50% to a confident prediction of, say, 85% means that the score needs to change by about 3.0. If we choose feature values in the range -1.0 to 1.0 (which we will), this means that we are making the following assumption:

⑤ A single feature normally has a small effect on the reply probability, sometimes has an intermediate effect and occasionally has a large effect.

This assumption prevents our classification model from becoming too confident in its predictions too quickly. For example, suppose the system sees a few emails with a particular feature value, say *ToLine*=1.0, which are then all replied to. How confident should the system be at predicting reply for the next email with *ToLine*=1.0? The choice of noise variance encodes our assumption of this confidence. Setting the noise variance to a high value means that the system would need to see a lot of emails to learn a large weight for a feature and so would make underconfident predictions. Setting the noise variance too low would have the opposite effect and the system would make confident predictions after only a few training emails. A variance of 10 is a suitable intermediate value that avoids making either under- or over-confident predictions.

We can now try training this new model on the emails of one of our users, say, User35CB8E5. As in Chapter 3, we can use expectation propagation to perform inference. This gives Gaussian distributions over **weight** and **threshold** of $Gaussian(3.77,0.028)$ and $Gaussian(7.63,0.019)$, respectively.

We can now use these Gaussian distributions to make predictions on a new email (or several emails), using online learning, as we saw in Chapter 3. To do this, we replace the priors over **weight** and **threshold** with the learned posterior distributions. Then we fix the feature values for each email and run inference to compute the marginal distribution over **repliedTo**. Since we've only got one feature in our model and it only has two possible values, the model can only make two possible predictions for the reply probability, one for each feature value. Given the above Gaussian distributions for the **weight** and **threshold**, the predicted probability of reply for the two values of the *ToLine* feature are shown in Table 4.2a. As we might have expected, the predicted proba-

Table 4.2 (a) Predicted probability of reply for our one-feature model, for each feature value; (b) for each feature value: the number of emails that were replied to, the number of emails that were not replied to and the fraction of emails that were replied to for the emails of User35CB8E5. Reassuringly, these fractions are close to the predicted probabilities of the learned model.

ToLine	P(repliedTo=true)
0	0.008
1	0.112

(a)

ToLine	Replied to	Not replied to	Fraction replied to
0	19	3,046	0.006
1	111	824	0.119

(b)

bility of reply is higher when the user is on the To line (*ToLine*=1.0) than when the user is not on the To line (*ToLine*=0.0).

To check whether these predicted probabilities are reasonable, we can compute the actual fraction of emails with each feature value that were replied to in the training set. The predicted probabilities should be close to these fractions. The counts of replied-to and not-replied-to emails with each feature value are shown in Table 4.2b, along with the fraction replied to computed from these counts.

These computed fractions are very close to the predicted probabilities, which gives us some reassurance that we have learned correctly from our data set. Effectively, we have provided a long-winded way of learning the conditional probability table given in Table 4.2a! However, if we want to use multiple features in our model, then we cannot use a conditional probability table, since it would become unmanageably large as the number of features increased. Instead, we will use the score variables to provide a different, scalable approach for combining features, as we will see in the next section.

REVIEW OF CONCEPTS

classification The task of predicting one of a fixed number of labels for a given data item. For example, predicting whether or not a user will reply to a particular email or whether a website visitor will click on a particular link. So, in classification, the aim is to make predictions about a discrete variable in the model.

classifiers Systems that perform classification, in other words, which predict a label for a data item (or a distribution over labels if the classifier is probabilistic). Classifiers are probably the best known and most widely used machine learning systems today.

feature set   A set of features that together are used to transform a data item into a form more suitable to use with a particular model or algorithm. Feature sets are usually used with classifiers but can also be used with many other types of models and algorithms.

feature   A function which computes a value when given a data item. Features can return a single binary or continuous value or can return multiple values. A feature is usually used as part of a feature set to transform a data item into a form more suitable to use with a particular model or algorithm.

conditional model   A model which represents a conditional probability rather than a joint probability. Conditional models require that the values of the variables being conditioned on are always known. The advantage of a conditional model is that the model can be simpler since it does not need to model the variables being conditioned on.

4.3 MODELLING MULTIPLE FEATURES

With just one feature, our classification model is not very accurate at predicting reply, so we will now extend it to handle multiple features. We can do this by changing the model so that multiple features contribute to the `score` for an email. We just need to decide how to do this, which involves making an additional assumption:

⑥ A particular change in one feature's value will cause the same change in score, no matter what the values of the other features are.

Let's consider this assumption applied to the *ToLine* feature and consider changing it from 0.0 to 1.0. This assumption says that the change in score due to this change in feature value is always the same, no matter what the other feature values are. This assumption can be encoded in the model by ensuring that the contribution of the ToLine feature to the score is always added on to the contributions from all the other features. Since the same argument holds for each of the other features as well, this assumption means that the score for an email must be the sum of the score contributions from each of the individual features.

So, in our multi-feature model (Figure 4.5), we have a `featureScore` array to hold the score contribution for each feature for each email. We can then use a deterministic summation factor to add the contributions together to give the total `score`. Since we still want Assumption ③ to hold for each feature, the `featureScore` for a feature can be defined, as before, as the product of the `featureValue` and the feature `weight`. Notice that we have added a new plate across the features, which contains the weight for the feature, the feature value and the feature score. The value and the score are also in the emails plate, since they vary from email to email, whilst the weight is outside since it is shared among all emails.

We now have a model which can combine together an entire set of features. This means we are free to put in as many features as we like, to try to predict as accurately as possible whether a user will reply to an email. More than that, we are assuming that anything we do not put in as a feature is not relevant to the prediction. This is our final assumption:

⑦ Whether the user will reply to an email depends only on the values of the features and not on anything else.

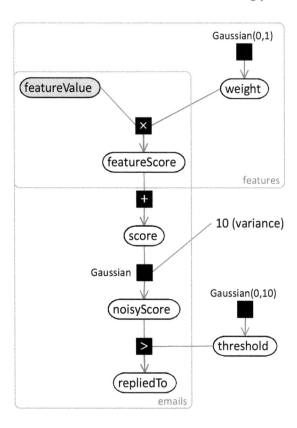

Figure 4.5 Factor graph of a classification model with multiple features. Variables within the features plate are duplicated for each feature, so there is a separate `weight` for each feature and, for each email, a separate `featureValue` and `featureScore`. The `featureScore` values for each feature are summed to give an overall `score` for each email.

As before, now that we have a complete model, it is a good exercise to go back and review all the assumptions that we have made whilst building the model. The full set of assumptions is shown in Table 4.3.

Assumption ① arises because we chose to build a conditional model, and so we need to always condition on the feature values.

In our model, we have used the red curve of Figure 4.3 to satisfy Assumption ②. Viewed as a function that computes the score given the reply probability, this curve is called the *probit function*. It is named this way because the units of the score have historically been called "probability units" or "probits" [Bliss, 1934]. Since **regression** is the term for predicting a continuous value (in this case, the score) from

Table 4.3 The seven assumptions encoded in our classification model.

① The feature values can always be calculated, for any email.

② Each email has an associated continuous score which is higher when there is a higher probability of the user replying to the email.

③ If an email's feature value changes by x, then its score will change by *weight* $\times x$ for some fixed, continuous weight.

④ The weight for a feature is equally likely to be positive or negative.

⑤ A single feature normally has a small effect on the reply probability, sometimes has an intermediate effect and occasionally has a large effect.

⑥ A particular change in one feature's value will cause the same change in score, no matter what the values of the other features are.

⑦ Whether the user will reply to an email depends only on the values of the features and not on *anything* else.

some feature values, the model as a whole is known as a *probit regression* model (or in its fully probabilistic form as the *Bayes Point Machine* [Herbrich et al., 2001]). There are other functions that we could have used to satisfy Assumption ② – the most well known is the **logistic function**, which equals $1/(1 + e^{-x})$ and has a very similar S-shape (see Figure 4.6 to see just how similar!). If we had used the logistic function instead of the probit function, we would have made a *logistic regression* model – a very widely used classifier. In practice, both models are extremely similar – we used a probit model because it allowed us to build on the factors and ideas that you learned about in the previous chapter.

Assumption ③, taken together with Assumption ⑥, means that the score must be a **linear function** of the feature values. For example, if we had two features, the score would be $\texttt{weight}_1 \times \texttt{featureValue}_1 + \texttt{weight}_2 \times \texttt{featureValue}_2$. We use the term linear, because if we plot the first feature value against the second, then points with the same

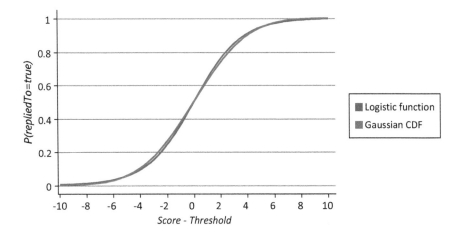

Figure 4.6 The logistic function scaled horizontally to match the Gaussian CDF from Figure 4.3. The similarity of the two functions means that our probit regression model behaves very similarly to a logistic regression model.

score will form a straight line. Any classifier based around a linear function is called a *linear classifier*.

Assumption ④ and Assumption ⑤ are reasonable statements about how features affect the predicted probability. However, Assumption ⑥ places some subtle but important limitations on what the classifier can learn, which are worth understanding. These are explored and explained in Panel 4.2.

Finally, Assumption ⑦ states that our feature set contains all of the information that is relevant to predicting whether a user will reply to an email. We'll see how to develop a feature set to satisfy this assumption as closely as possible in the next section, but first we need to understand better the role that the feature set plays.

4.3.1 Features are part of the model

To use our classification model, we will need to choose a set of features to transform the data, so that it better conforms to the model assumptions of Table 4.3. Another way of looking at this is that the assumptions of the *combined* feature set and classification model must hold in the data. From a model-based machine learning perspective, this means that the feature set combined with the classification model form a larger overall model. In this way of looking at things, the

Panel 4.2: How features combine together

Assumption ⑥ is quite a strong assumption about how features combine together. To investigate the effect of this assumption, consider a two-feature model with the existing *ToLine* feature and a new feature called *FromManager*. This new *FromManager* feature has a value of 1.0 if the sender is the user's manager and 0.0 otherwise. Suppose a particular user replies to 80% of emails from their manager, but only if they are on the To line. If they are not on the To line, then they treat it like any other email where they are on the Cc line. To analyse such a user, we will create a synthetic data set to represent our hypothetical user's email data. For email where *FromManager* is zero, we will take User35CB8E5's data set from Table 4.2. We will then add 500 new synthetic emails where *FromManager* is 1, such that the user is on the To line exactly half of the time, giving the data set in the table below. The final column of this table gives the predicted probabilities for each combination of features, for a model trained on this data.

ToLine	From Manager	Replied to	Not replied to	Fraction replied to	P(repliedTo=true)
0	0	19	3,046	0.006	0.004
1	0	111	824	0.119	0.144
0	1	2	248	0.008	0.108
1	1	200	50	0.800	0.646

There is quite a big difference between the predicted probability of reply and the actual fraction replied to. For example, the predicted probability for emails from the user's manager where the user is on the To line is much too low: 64.6% not 80%. Similarly, the prediction is too high (10.8% not 0.8%) for emails from the user's manager where the user is not on the To line. These inaccurate predictions occur because there is no setting of the `weight` and `threshold` variables that can make the predicted probability match the actual reply fraction. Assumption ⑥ says the change in score for *FromManager* must be the same when *ToLine* is 1.0 as for when *ToLine* is 0.0. But, to match the data, we need the change in score to be higher when *ToLine* is 1.0 than when it is 0.0.

Rather than changing the model to remove Assumption ⑥, we can work around this limitation by adding a new feature that is 1.0 only if *ToLine* and *FromManager* are both 1.0 (an AND of the two features).

This new feature will have its own `weight` associated with it, which means there can now be a different score for manager emails when the user is on the To line to when they are not on the To line. If we train such a three-feature model, we get the new predictions shown here:

ToLine	From Manager	And	Replied to	Not replied to	Fraction replied to	P(repliedTo=true)
0	0	0	19	3,046	0.006	0.007
1	0	0	111	824	0.119	0.119
0	1	0	2	248	0.008	0.024
1	1	1	200	50	0.800	0.766

The predicted probabilities are now much closer to the actual reply fractions in each case, meaning that the new model is making more accurate predictions than the old one. Any remaining discrepancies are due to Assumption ⑤, which controls the size of effect of any single feature.

This problem can be avoided by always using an AND of the values of a subset of features. This is the approach taken in a decision tree model, a non-linear classifier which we will discuss in Section 8.2. When training a decision tree, we are effectively searching for combinations of features like the one above, which lead to good predictions. Unfortunately, decision trees suffer from a different problem, where the values of many features are ignored when making a prediction. A popular solution to both issues is to combine several decision trees together through a linear model into a decision forest – this approach is also discussed in Section 8.2.

feature set is the part of this overall model that is usually easy to change (by changing the feature calculation code), whereas the classification part is the part that is usually hard to change (for example, if you are using off-the-shelf classifier software, there is no easy way to change it).

We can represent this overall combined model in a factor graph by including the feature calculations in the graph, as shown in Figure 4.7. The `email` variable holds all the data about the email itself (you can think of it as an email object). The feature calculations appear as deterministic *ComputeFeature* factors inside of the features plate, each of which computes the feature value for the feature, given the

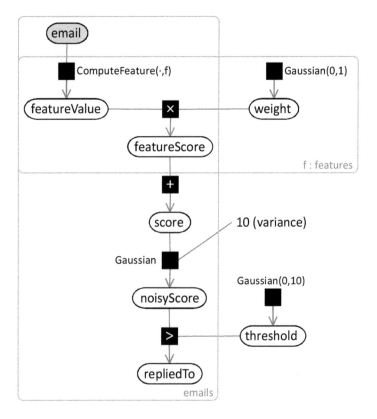

Figure 4.7 Factor graph of a model which includes both feature calculation and classification. The *ComputeFeature* factor takes as arguments the current feature f and the email being considered and computes the value of feature f for that email.

email. Notice that, although only `email` is shown as observed (shaded), `featureValue` is effectively observed as well since it is deterministically computed from `email`.

If the feature set really is part of the model, we must use the same approach for designing a feature set, as for designing a model. This means that we need to visualise and understand the data, be conscious of assumptions being represented, specify evaluation metrics and success criteria, and repeatedly refine and improve the feature set until the success criteria are met (in other words, we need to follow the machine learning life cycle). This is exactly the process we will follow next.

REVIEW OF CONCEPTS

regression The task of predicting a real-valued quantity (for example, a house price or a temperature) given the attributes of a particular data item (such as a house or a city). In regression, the aim is to make predictions about a continuous variable in the model.

logistic function The function $f(x) = 1/(1 + e^{-x})$ which is often used to transform unbounded continuous values into continuous values between 0 and 1. It has an S-shape similar to that of the cumulative Gaussian (see Figure 4.6).

linear function Any function of one or more variables $f(x_1, \ldots, x_k)$ which can be written in the form $f(x_1, \ldots, x_k) = a + b_1 x_1 + \ldots + b_k x_k$. A linear function of just one variable can therefore be written as $f(x) = a + bx$. Plotting $f(x)$ against x for this equation gives a straight line which is why the term *linear* is used to describe this family of functions.

4.4 DESIGNING A FEATURE SET

To use our classification model, we need to design features to transform the data to conform as closely as possible to the assumptions built into the model (Table 4.3). For example, to satisfy Assumption ⑦ (that features contain all relevant information about the user's actions), we need to make sure that our feature set includes all features relevant to predicting reply. Since pretty much any part of an email may help with making such a prediction, this means that we will have to encode almost all aspects of the email in our features. This will include who sent the email, the recipients of the email on the To and Cc lines, the subject of the email and the main body of the email, along with information about the conversation the email belongs to.

When designing a new feature, we need to ensure that:

- the feature picks up on some informative aspect of the data,

- the feature output is of the right form to feed into the model,

- the feature provides new information about the label over and above that provided by existing features.

In this section, we will show how to design several new features for our feature set, while ensuring that they meet the first two of these criteria. In the next section, we will show how to check the third criterion by evaluating the system with and without certain features.

4.4.1 Features with many states

So far, we have represented where the user appears on the email using a *ToLine* feature. This feature has only two states: the user is either on the To line or not. So the feature ignores whether the user is on the Cc line, even though we might expect a user to be more likely to reply to an email if they appear on the Cc line than if they do not appear at all. The feature also ignores the position of the user on the To/Cc line. If the user is first on the To line, we might expect them to be more likely to reply than if they are at the end of a long list of recipients. We can check these intuitions using our data set by finding the actual fraction of all training/validation emails that were replied to in a number of cases: when the user is first, second or later than second on the To line, when the user is first or elsewhere on the Cc line and when the user is not on either the To or Cc lines (for example, if they received the email via a mailing list).

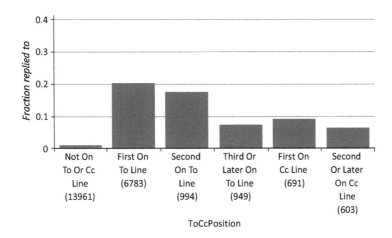

Figure 4.8 Fraction of emails that were replied to, for each of six possible positions of the user on the To or Cc line. The number of emails with the user in each position is shown in brackets (the fraction replied to is a fraction of these emails that were replied to). The plot shows that, for our data set, being first on the To line indicates the highest probability of reply, but that this reduces if the user is second or later. It also shows that if the user is not mentioned on the To or Cc line, the reply probability is very low.

Figure 4.8 plots these fractions, showing that the probability of reply does vary substantially depending on which of these cases applies. This plot demonstrates that a feature that was able to distinguish these cases would indeed pick up on an informative aspect of the data (our first criterion above). When assessing reply fractions, such as those in Figure 4.8, it is important to take into account how many emails the fraction is computed from, since a fraction computed from a small number of emails would not be very accurate. To check this, in Figure 4.8 we show the number of emails in brackets below each bar label, demonstrating that each has sufficient emails to compute the fraction accurately and so we can rely on the computed values.

We can improve our feature to capture cues like this by giving it multiple states, one for each of the bars of Figure 4.8. So the states will be: {NotOnToOrCcLine, FirstOnToLine, SecondOnToLine, ThirdOrLaterOnToLine, FirstOnCcLine, SecondOrLaterOnCcLine}. Now we just need to work out what the output of the feature should be, to be suitable for our model (the second criterion). We could try returning a value of 0.0 for `NotOnToOrCcLine`, 1.0 for `FirstOnToLine` and so on up to a value of 5.0 for `SecondOrLaterOnCcLine`. But, according to Assumption ③ (that the score changes by the weight times the feature value), this would mean that the probability of reply would either steadily increase or steadily decrease as the value changes from 0.0 through to 5.0. Figure 4.8 shows that this is not the case, since the reply fraction goes up and down as we go from left to right. So such an assumption would be incorrect. In general, we want to avoid making assumptions which depend on the ordering of some states that do not have an inherent ordering, like these. Instead we would like to be able to learn how the reply probability is affected separately for each state.

To achieve this, we can modify the feature to output *multiple* feature values, one for each state. We will use a value of 1.0 for the state that applies to a particular email and a value of 0.0 for all other states – this is sometimes called a **one-hot** encoding. So an email where the user is first on the To line would be represented by the feature values $\{0.0, 1.0, 0.0, 0.0, 0.0, 0.0\}$. Similarly an email where the user is first on the Cc line would be represented by the feature values $\{0.0, 0.0, 0.0, 0.0, 1.0, 0.0\}$. By doing this, we have effectively created a group of related binary features – however it is much more convenient to think of them as a single *ToCcPosition* feature which outputs multiple values.

To avoid confusion in terminology, we will refer to the different elements of such a feature as **feature buckets** – so the *ToCcPosition* feature contains six feature buckets. For a particular email, you can imagine the one-hot encoding of a feature to be like throwing a ball that lands in one of the buckets.

Using this terminology, the plate across the features in our factor graph should now be interpreted as being across all buckets of all features, so that each bucket has its own `featureValue` and its own associated `weight`. This means that the `weight` can be different for each bucket of our *ToCcPosition* feature – and so we are no longer assuming that the reply probability steadily increases or decreases across the buckets.

4.4.2 Numeric features

We also need to create features that encode numeric quantities, such as the number of characters in the email body. If we used the number of characters directly as the feature value, we would be assuming that longer emails mean either always higher or always lower reply probability than shorter emails. But in fact we might expect the user to be unlikely to respond to a very short email ("Thanks") or a very long email (such as a newsletter), but may be likely to respond to emails whose length is somewhere in between. Again, we can investigate these beliefs by plotting the fraction of emails replied to for various body lengths. To get a useful plot, it is necessary to group together emails with similar lengths so that we have enough emails to estimate the reply fraction reliably. In Figure 4.9, we label each bar in the bar chart with the corresponding range of body lengths. The range of lengths for each bar is roughly double the size of the previous one, and the final bar is for very long emails (more than 1,023 characters).

There are several aspects of this plot that are worthy of comment. Zero-length emails have a quite high reply probability, probably because these are emails where the message was in the subject. As we anticipated, very short emails have relatively low reply probability and

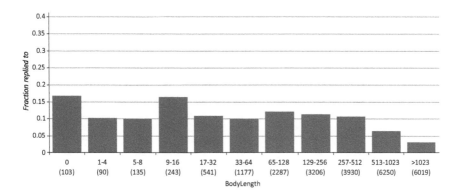

Figure 4.9 Fraction of emails that were replied to, for various ranges of body lengths, given by the number of characters in the email body. The number of emails falling into each length range is shown in brackets. Zero-length emails are likely to have their message in the subject line and so have quite a high reply fraction. For other emails, the reply fraction peaks at around 9–16 characters and then generally decreases, until it is very low for very long emails.

this increases to a peak in the 9–16 characters and is then roughly constant until we get to very long emails of 513 characters or more where the reply probability starts to tail off. To pick up on these changes in the probability of reply, we can use the same approach as we just used for *ToCcPosition* and treat each bar of our plot as a different feature bucket. This gives us a *BodyLength* feature with 11 buckets. Emails whose length fall into a particular length range, such as 33–64 characters, all map to a single bucket. This mapping encodes the assumption that the reply probability does not depend on the exact body length but only on which range that length falls into.

4.4.3 Features with many, many states

We might expect that the sender of an email would be one of the most useful properties for predicting whether a user will reply or not. But why rely on belief, when we can use data? Figure 4.10 shows the fraction of emails replied to for the 20 most frequent senders for User35CB8E5. As you can see, there is substantial variation in reply fraction from one sender to another: some senders have no replies at all, whilst others

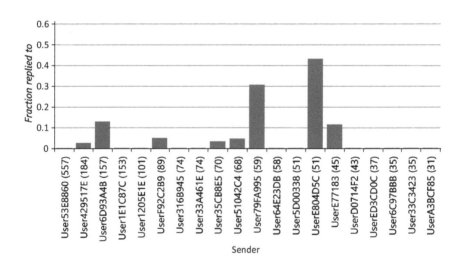

Figure 4.10 Fraction of emails replied to for the 20 most common senders for User35CB8E5 (the number of emails from each sender is shown in brackets). Reply fraction varies significantly from sender to sender, indicating that this is a very useful cue for predicting reply. As discussed in Section 4.1, the sender identities have been anonymised to preserve the privacy of the user.

have a high fraction of replies. A similar pattern holds for the other users in our data set. So indeed, the sender is a very useful cue for predicting reply.

To incorporate the sender information into the feature set, we can use a multi-state *Sender* feature, with one state for each sender in the data set. For example, User35CB8E5 has 658 unique senders in the training and validation sets combined. This would lead to a feature with 658 buckets of which 657 would have value 0.0 and the bucket corresponding to the actual sender would have value 1.0. Since so many of the feature bucket values would be zero, it is much more efficient to change our factor graph to only include the feature buckets that are actually "active" (non-zero). A suitably modified factor graph is shown in Figure 4.11.

In this modified graph, the feature values for an email are represented by the indices of non-zero values (`featureIndices`) along with the corresponding values at these indices (`featureValues`). We use the *Subarray* factor that we introduced back in Section 2.4 to pull out the weights for the active buckets (`featureWeight`) from the full weights array (`weight`). This new factor graph allows features like the *Sender* feature to be added without causing a substantial slow-down in training and classification times. For example, training on User35CB8E5's training set takes 9.2 seconds using the old factor graph but just 0.43 seconds using this new factor graph. This speed up would be even greater if we had trained on more emails, since there would be more unique senders.

4.4.4 An initial feature set

Now that we know how to encode all the different types of data properties, we can complete our initial feature set, ready to start experimenting with. To encode remaining data properties, we add three further features: *FromMe*, *HasAttachments* and *SubjectLength* whose feature buckets and reply fractions are shown in Figure 4.12.

As we discussed back in Section 4.1, we removed the content of the subject lines and email bodies from the data set and so cannot add any features to encode the actual words of the subject or of the email body. To build the classifier for the Exchange project, anonymised subject and body words were used from voluntarily provided data. As you might expect, including such subject and body word features did indeed help substantially with predictive accuracy.

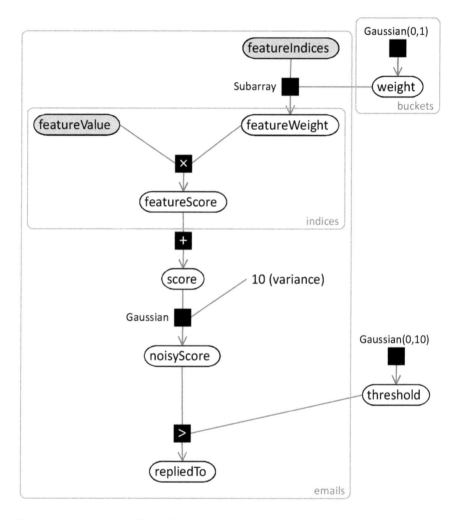

Figure 4.11 Modified factor graph which represents only non-zero feature buckets. The `featureIndices` variable contains the indices of feature buckets that have non-zero values. The `featureValues` variable contains the corresponding values for those buckets. The *Subarray* factor is used to pull out the relevant elements of the `weight` array, which are placed into the `featureWeight` array.

Our initial feature set, with six features, is shown in Table 4.4. Now that we have a classification model and a feature set, we are ready to see how well they work together to predict whether a user will reply to a new email.

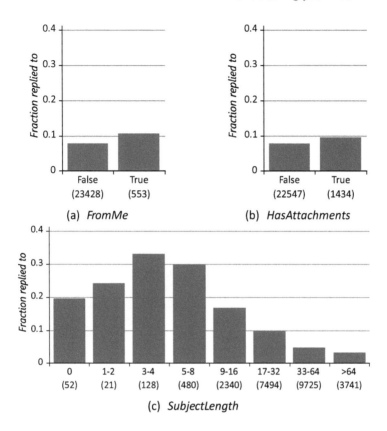

Figure 4.12 Fraction of emails that were replied to for each feature bucket, for the three new features. The number of emails falling into each feature bucket is shown in brackets.

Table 4.4 An initial set of features for predicting reply on an email. For each feature, we show the feature type, a brief description and the number of feature buckets for that feature (where this number is fixed).

	Description	#Buckets
FromMe	Whether the message is from you	1
ToCcPosition	Your position on the To or Cc lines	6
HasAttachments	Whether the message has attachments	1
BodyLength	The number of new characters in the body text	11
SubjectLength	The number of characters in the subject	8
Sender	Who the message is from	(varies)

REVIEW OF CONCEPTS

one-hot A way of encoding a 1-of-N choice using a vector of size N. The vector is zero everywhere except at the position corresponding to the choice, where there is a one. So if there are three options, the first would be encoded by $\{1.0, 0.0, 0.0\}$, the second by $\{0.0, 1.0, 0.0\}$ and the third by $\{0.0, 0.0, 1.0\}$.

feature buckets Labels which identify the values for a feature that returns multiple values. For example, the *ToCcPosition* feature in Figure 4.8 has six feature buckets: `NotOnToOrCcLine`, `FirstOnToLine`, `SecondOnToLine`, `ThirdOrLaterOnToLine`, `FirstOnCcLine` and `SecondOrLaterOnCcLine`. For this feature the value associated with one of the buckets will be 1.0 and the other values will be 0.0, but for other features multiple buckets may have non-zero values.

4.5   EVALUATING AND IMPROVING THE FEATURE SET

Using our newly completed model and feature set, we can train a personalised classifier for each user in our data set. To be precise, for each user's training set, we compute the active feature buckets `featureIndices` for each email, along with their feature values `featureValue`. Given these observed variables, we can then apply expectation propagation to learn a posterior `weight` distribution for each bucket, along with a single posterior distribution over the value of the `threshold`. But first we need to look at how to schedule message passing for our model.

4.5.1   Parallel and sequential schedules

⚓ **Inference deep-dive**
In this optional section, we look at how to schedule the expectation propagation messages for our model. If you want to go straight to look at the results of running expectation propagation, feel free to skip this section.

When running expectation propagation in this model, it is important to choose a good message-passing schedule. In this kind of model, a poor schedule can easily cause the message-passing algorithm to fail to converge or to converge very slowly. When you have a model with repeated structures (such as our classification model), there are two main kinds of message-passing schedule that can be used: sequential or parallel. To understand these two kinds of schedule, let's look at message passing on a simplified form of our model with two features and two weights:

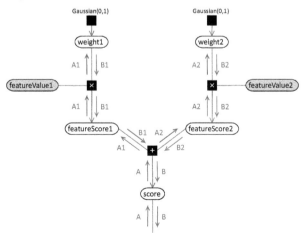

In this figure, rather than using a plate across the buckets, we have instead duplicated the part of the model for each weight. When doing message passing in this model, two choices of schedule are:

- A *sequential schedule* which processes the two weights in turn. For the first weight, this schedule passes messages in the order A, A1, B1, B. After processing this weight, message-passing happens in the bottom piece of the graph (not shown). The schedule then moves on to the second weight, passing messages in the order A, A2, B2, B.

- A *parallel schedule* which processes the two weights at once. In this schedule, first the messages marked A are passed. Then both sets of messages (A1 and B1) and (A2 and B2) are passed, where the messages from the plus factor are computed using the previous B1 and B2 messages. Finally, the messages marked B are passed.

To see the difference between the two schedules, look at how the first A2 message coming out of the plus factor is calculated. In the sequential schedule, it is calculated using the B1 message that has just been updated in this iteration of the schedule. In the parallel schedule, it uses the B1 message calculated in the previous iteration, in other words, an older version of the message. As a result, the parallel schedule converges more slowly than the sequential schedule and is also more likely to fail to converge at all. So why would we ever want to use a parallel schedule? The main reason is if you want to distribute your inference computation in parallel across a number of machines in order to speed it up. In this case, the best option is to use a combined schedule which is sequential on the section of model processed within each machine but which is parallel across machines.

4.5.2 Visualising the learned weights

To ensure this sequential schedule is working well, we can visualise the learned weight distributions to check that they match up to our expectations. Figure 4.13 shows the learned Gaussian distributions over the weights for each feature bucket for User35CB8E5 (to save space, only the 15 most frequent Sender weights are shown).

Looking at each weight in turn, we can see that more positive weights generally correspond to those feature buckets that we would expect to have a higher probability of reply, given the histograms in

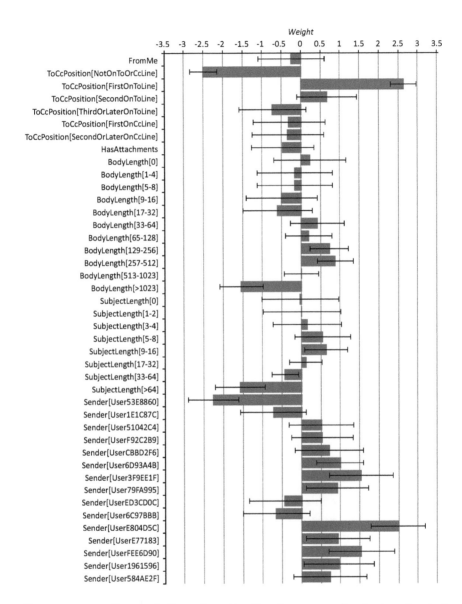

Figure 4.13 Learned Gaussian distributions over the feature bucket weights for User35CB8E5. For each feature bucket, the blue bar indicates the mean of the Gaussian weight distribution showing how much the system expects the feature bucket to increase or decrease the score for an email. The error bars indicate the uncertainty in this learned value by showing plus/minus one standard deviation around the mean.

the previous section. For example, looking at the *SubjectLength* histogram of Figure 4.12c, you can see that the positive and negative learned weights correspond to the peaks and troughs of the histogram. You can also see that the error bars are narrower for common feature buckets like *SubjectLength*[33–64] than for rare feature buckets like *SubjectLength*[1–2]. This is to be expected since, if there are fewer emails with a particular feature bucket active, there is less information about the weight for that bucket and so the learned weight posterior is more uncertain. For very rare buckets, there are so few relevant emails in the training set that we should expect the `weight` posterior to be very close to the *Gaussian*(0,1) prior. You can see this is true for *SubjectLength*[1–2], for example, whose weight mean is close to 0.0 and whose standard deviation is close to 1.0. So, overall, manual inspection of the learned weights is consistent with what we might expect. Inspecting the learned weights of other users also show plausible weight distributions.

Had we found some unexpected weight values here, the most likely explanation would be a bug in the feature calculation. However, unexpected weight values can also uncover faulty intuitions about the kinds of email a user is likely to reply to, or even allow us to discover new types of email reply behaviour that we might not have guessed at.

4.5.3 Evaluating reply prediction

Using the trained model for each user, we can now predict a reply probability for each email in the user's validation set. As we saw in Chapter 2, we can plot an ROC curve to assess the accuracy of these predictions. Doing this for each user, gives the plots in Figure 4.14.

These curves look very promising – there is some variation from user to user, but all the curves are all up in the top left of the ROC plot where we want them to be. But do these plots tell us what we need to know? Given that our aim is to identify emails with particular actions (or lack of actions), we need to know two things:

1. *Out of all replied-to emails, what fraction do we predict will be replied to?*

This is the true positive rate, which the ROC curve is already giving us on its y-axis. In this context, the true positive rate is also referred to as the **recall** since it measures how many of the replied to emails were successfully "recalled" by the system.

2. *Out of emails that we predict will be replied to, what fraction actually are?*

This is a new quantity called the **precision** and is *not* shown on the ROC curve. Note that this is a different meaning of the word *precision* to its use as a parameter describing the inverse variance of a Gaussian – it is usually clear from the context which meaning is intended. To visualise the precision, we must instead use a **precision–recall curve** (P–R curve) which is a plot of precision on the y-axis against recall on the x-axis. Figure 4.15 shows precision–recall curves for exactly the same prediction results as for the ROC curves in Figure 4.14. For more discussion of precision and recall, see Powers [2008].

To get a summary accuracy number for a precision–recall curve, similar to the area under an ROC curve, we can compute the **average precision** (AP) across a range of recalls – these are shown in the legend of Figure 4.15. Precision-recall curves tend to be very noisy at the left-hand end since at this point the precisions are being computed from a very small number of emails – for this reason, we compute the average precision between recalls of 0.1 and 0.9 to give a more stable and reliable accuracy metric. Omitting the right-hand end of the plot as well helps correct for the reduction in average precision caused by ignoring the left hand end of the plot.

Compare the ROC and precision–recall curves – once again we can see the value of using more than one evaluation metric: the precision–recall curves tell a very different story! They show that there is quite a wide variability in the precision we are achieving for different users, and also that the users with the highest precision–recall curves (such as User68251CD) are not the same users that have the highest ROC curves (such as User6AACED). So what's going on?

To help understand the difference, consider a classifier that predicts reply or no-reply at random. The ROC curve for such a classifier is the diagonal line labelled "Random" in Figure 4.14. To plot the P–R curve for a random classifier, we need to consider that it will classify some random subset of emails as being positives, so the fraction of these that are true positives (the precision) is just the fraction of emails that the user replies to in general. So if a user replies to 20% of their emails, we would expect a random classifier to have a precision of 20%. If another user replies to 2% of their emails, we may expect a random classifier to have a precision of 2%. The fraction of emails that each of our users replies to is given in the legend of Figure 4.15, following the average precision. User68251CD replies to the highest percentage of emails 23.6%

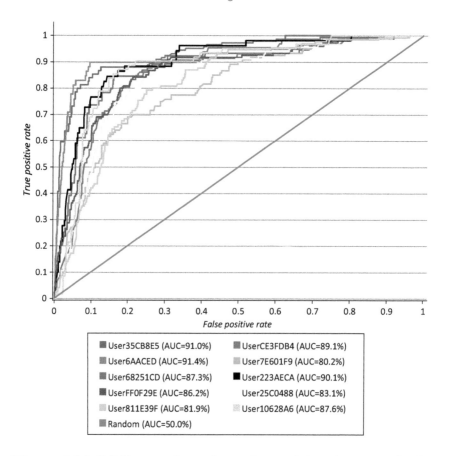

Figure 4.14 ROC curves for each user in our data set computed using predictions on the user's validation set. The legend gives the area under the curve (AUC) for each user.

which means we might expect it to be easier to get higher precisions for that user – and indeed that user has the highest average precision, despite having an intermediate ROC curve. Conversely, User6AACED, who has one of the highest ROC curves, has only a middling P–R curve, because this user only replies to 3.2% of their email. Given that our two error metrics are giving us different information, how can we use them to assess success? How can we set target values for these metrics? The answer lies in remembering that we use metrics like AP and AUC only as a proxy for the things that we really care about – user happiness and productivity. So we need to understand how the values of our metrics map into the users' experience of the system.

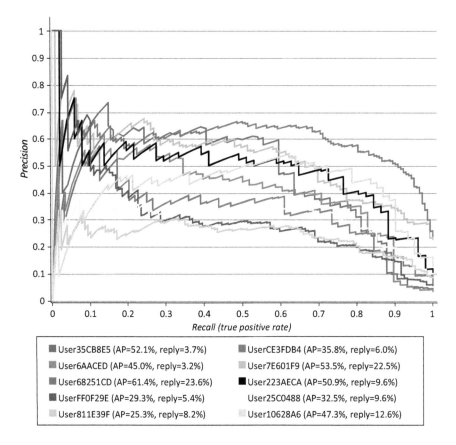

Figure 4.15 Precision–recall curves for the same prediction results as the ROC curves of Figure 4.14. The legend gives the average precision (AP) for each user, along with the percentage of validation set emails that were replied to by that user.

4.5.4 Understanding the user's experience

Once the system is being beta tested by large numbers of users, we can use explicit feedback (for example, questionnaires) or implicit feedback (for example, how quickly people process their email or how many people turn off the feature) to assess how happy/productive users are for particular values of the evaluation metrics. During the early stages of developing

the system, however, we must use our own judgement of how well the system is working on our own emails.

To understand how our evaluation metrics map into a real user's experience, it is *essential* to get some users using the system as soon as possible, even if these users are just team members. To do this, we need a working end-to-end system, including a user interface, that can be used to evaluate qualitatively how well the system is performing. Having a working user interface is particularly important since the choice of user interface imposes requirements on the underlying machine learning system. For example, if emails are to be removed from a user's inbox without giving any visual indication, then a very high precision is essential. Conversely, if emails are just to be gently de-emphasised but left in place, then a lower precision can be tolerated, which allows for a higher recall. These examples show that the user interface and the machine learning system need to be well matched to each other. The user interface should be designed carefully to tolerate any errors made by the machine learning component, whilst maximising its value to the user (see Patil [2012]). A well-designed user interface can easily make the difference between users adopting a particular machine learning system or not.

For our purposes, we need a user interface that emulates an email client but which also displays the reply prediction probability in some visual way. Figure 4.16 shows a suitable user interface created as an evaluation and debugging tool.

The tool has a cut-off reply probability threshold which can be adjusted by a slider – emails with predicted reply probabilities above this threshold are predicted to be replied to and all other emails are predicted as not being replied to. The tool also marks which emails were correctly classified and which were false positives or false negatives, given this cut-off threshold. The use of a threshold on the predicted probability again emphasises the importance of good calibration. If the calibration of the system is poor, or varies from user to user, then it makes it much harder to find a cut-off threshold that gives a good experience. The calibration of our predictions can be plotted and evaluated, as described in Panel 4.3.

For debugging purposes, the tool shows the feature buckets that are active for each email along with the corresponding feature value and learned weight distribution. This is extremely helpful for checking that the feature computation is correct, since the original email and computed features are displayed right next to each other.

reply to?

Order by date | p(ReplyTo) 1 ↓

Test UserF2678D6	07 Jan 14:10	Reply=0.65
Results UserF2678D6, UserF2E2B0F1	14 Nov 2013 16:44	Reply=0.62
First test UserF2678D6, User2E2B0F1	30 Oct 2013 10:33	Reply=0.60
InferGlo UserF2678D6, UserF2E2B0F1	11 Nov 2013 20:41	Reply=0.58
Possible move to 2.35 User790972E, UserF2678D6	03 Oct 2013 10:48	Reply=0.58
Bugs UserF2678D6, User2E2B0F1	10 Oct 2013 16:55	Reply=0.54
Update UserF2678D6, User2E2B0F1	25 Jan 08:06	Reply=0.53
Friday UserF2678D6, User2678D6	24 Sep 2013 20:34	Reply=0.53
Threshold UserF2678D6, User2E2B0F1	12 Feb 18:07	Reply=0.51
Data UserF2678D6, User2E2B0F1	13 Nov 2013 17:59	Reply=0.50
WptChartView UserF2678D6, User2E2B0F1	24 Jan 15:47	Reply=0.49
MBML Weekly Book Meeti... User275C8B8, User2E2B0F1	02 Dec 2013 13:13	Reply=0.49
Emaling: Translations UserF2678D6, User4FE6198	07 Oct 2013 19:37	Reply=0.49
Slides UserA0F8768, User8513018	24 Sep 2013 07:08	Reply=0.48
book UserA0F8768, UserF2678D6, User2E2B0F1	03 Dec 2013 13:31	Reply=0.48
[SubMain] How is your sp...	22 Jan 13:25	Reply=0.47

Feature Set: [Initial]

Use slider below to adjust cut-off

Average Precision 54.7%, Area Under ROC Curve 91.7%, Calibration Error 0.097

Results

UserF2678D6 — Reply=NaN — *Hide details* 14 Nov 2013 16:44
From: user2678d60@example.com
Subject: XX: Xxxxxxx
To: User2E2B0F1
Folder: Sent Items

Xx X'xx xxxxxxx xxx xxxxxxx xxxx. X'xxx xxxxx X'xx xxxxx x xxxxxxx xxx xxxxxx xxxxx xxxxx xxx
xxx X xxxx xxx X xxxx xxxxxxxx xx xxx xxxxxxxxxxxxx xx xxxx Xxx'x xxxxx xxxx – X xxx xxxxxxx xxxxx xxxxx
xxx xxxxx.

User2E2B0F1 — Reply=0.62 — *Hide details* 14 Nov 2013 14:34
From: user2cb0f12@example.com
Subject: XX: Xxxxxxx
To: UserF2678D6
Folder: Inbox

Xxxxx xxxxx xx xx.

Features:

Name	Type	Bucket	Value	WeightMean	WeightVariance
FromMe	BinaryFeature	FromMe	0.0	1.2246	0.6734
ToCcPosition	OneOfNFeature	FirstOnToLine	1.0	2.5105	0.2300
HasAttachments	BinaryFeature	HasAttachments	0.0	-0.4732	0.7904
BodyLength	NumericFeature	17-32	1.0	0.1463	0.8090
SubjectLength	NumericFeature	5-8	1.0	1.0526	0.6661
Sender	OneOfNFeature	User2E2B0F1	1.0	0.9833	0.3852

Figure 4.16 Screenshot of the user interface of the evaluation and debugging tool which allows the accuracy of the system to be assessed on real emails. The tool also exposes the calculated features, learned weights and predicted reply probability for each email, which makes it easier to debug the system. The coloured background of the reply probabilities indicates whether the prediction is a true positive (green), false positive (orange) or true negative or false negative for the current cut-off threshold. To preserve the privacy of the user whose emails are shown here, the content of the emails has been hidden and the identities of all senders and recipients have been anonymised.

Panel 4.3: Calibration

A machine learning system is well-calibrated if the predicted probabilities it gives are accurate [Dawid, 1982]. For example, if a well-calibrated system predicts an event with a probability of 90%, then we should expect this event to happen 90% of the time. It is important to evaluate the calibration of any machine learning system because:

- We often need to be able to trust the probabilities coming from the system. For example, they may be used to drive a user interface which varies with the probability of the prediction (such as only marking emails above a certain probability). Accurate probabilities are especially important if they are to be used as input to another machine learning system.

- If a machine learning system is poorly calibrated, then it suggests a problem either in the model (such as an overly restrictive assumption) or in the approximate inference. Fixing this problem will not only improve calibration but also usually improve prediction accuracy as well.

We can use a calibration plot to evaluate how well-calibrated our email model is. To do this, we take all the validation set predictions made for each user and divide them into bins according to the predicted probability of reply (0–10%,11–20% and so on). For each bin, we then compute the fraction of emails that were actually replied to (we discard bins with too few emails, since then this fraction would be very noisy). Finally, we plot the average of this fraction across users against the predicted probability, as shown below.

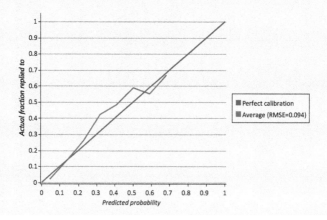

The plot also shows the line for a perfectly calibrated system, which is a diagonal line. Our system is reasonably well-calibrated (within about 0.1 of this diagonal). We can get an overall calibration metric by measuring how far we are from this diagonal using – for example, using a root-mean-squared-error (RMSE) difference, which for our system gives 0.094.

Using this tool, we can assess qualitatively how well the system is working for a particular threshold on the reply probability. Looking at a lot of different emails, we find that the system seems to be working very well, despite the apparently moderate precision. This is because a proportion of the apparent incorrect predictions are actually reasonable, such as:

- False positives where the user "responded" to the email, but not by directly replying. This could be because they responded to the sender without using email (for example, in person, on the phone or via instant messaging) or responding by writing a fresh email to the sender or by replying to a different email.

- False positives where the user intended to reply, but forgot to or didn't have time.

- False negatives where a user replied to an email, as a means of replying to an email earlier in the conversation thread.

- False negatives where a user replied to an email and deleted the contents/subject as a way of starting a new email to the sender.

In all four of these cases, the prediction is effectively correct: in the first two cases this *is* an email that the user would want to reply to and in the last two it is not. The issue is that the "ground truth" label that we have for the item is not correct, since whether or not a user wanted to reply to an email is assumed to be the same as whether they actually did. But in these four cases, it is not. Later in the chapter we will look at how to deal with such noisy ground truth labels.

Since the ground truth labels are used to evaluate the system, such incorrect labels can have a big detrimental effect on the measured accuracy. For example, if 25% of positive emails are incorrectly labelled as negatives, then the measured precision of a perfect classifier would be only 75% rather than 100%. If 5% of negative emails are also incorrectly labelled as positive then, for a user who replies to 10% of their emails, the recall of a perfect classifier would be just 62.5%! To see where this number came from, consider 1,000 emails received by the user. The user would reply to 100 of these emails (10%) and so would not reply to 900 emails. Of the replied-to emails, only 75% (=75 emails) would be labelled positive and of the not-replied-to emails, 5% of 900 = 45 emails would be incorrectly labelled positive. So a perfect classifier would make positive predictions on 75 of the 75+45=120 emails that were labelled as positive, meaning that the measured recall would be $\frac{75}{120} = 62.5\%$.

However, even taking the noisy ground truth labels into account, there are still a number of incorrect predictions that are genuinely wrong. Examples of these are:

1. False negatives where the email is a reply to an email that the user sent, but the sender is new or not normally replied to.

2. False negatives where the email is a forward, but the sender is new or not normally replied to.

3. False negatives for emails to a distribution list that the user owns or manages and so is likely to reply to.

4. False positives for newsletter/marketing/social network emails (sometimes known as "graymail") sent directly to the user, particularly where the sender is new.

We will now look at how to modify the feature set to address some of these incorrect predictions.

4.5.5 Improving the feature set

The first two kinds of incorrect prediction are false negative predictions where the email is a reply to an email from the user or a forward of an email to the user. These mistakes occur because no existing feature distinguishes between these cases and a fresh email coming from the same sender – yet if the email is a reply or forward, there is likely to be a very different reply probability. This violates Assumption ⑦, that is, whether the user will reply or not depends only on the feature values. To fix this issue, we need to introduce a new feature to distinguish these cases. We can detect replies and forwards, by inspecting the prefix on the subject line – whether it is "re:", "fw:", "fwd:" and so on. Figure 4.17

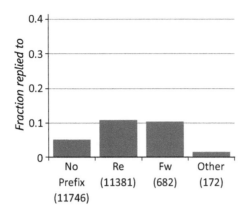

Figure 4.17 Fraction of emails that were replied to where the email had different subject prefixes (re,fw/fwd), an unknown prefix (other) or no prefix at all.

shows the fraction of emails replied to in the training and validation sets for known prefixes, an unknown prefix (other) or no prefix at all. The plot shows that, indeed, users are more likely to reply to messages which are replies or forwards and a *SubjectPrefix* feature might therefore be informative. What this plot does not tell us is whether this new feature gives additional information over the features we already have in our feature set. To check whether it does, we need to evaluate the feature set with and without this new feature. Figure 4.18 gives the area under the ROC curve and the average precision for each user and averaged, for our feature set with and without the *SubjectPrefix* feature.

What these results show is that the new feature sometimes increases accuracy and sometimes reduces accuracy depending on the user (whichever metric you look at). However, on average the accuracy is improved with the feature, which suggests that we should retain it in the feature set. Notice that the average precision is a more sensitive metric than the area under the curve – so it is more helpful when judging a feature's usefulness. It is also worth bearing in mind that either evaluation metric only gives an overall picture. Whilst headline accuracy numbers like these are useful, it is important to always look at the underlying predictions as well. To do this we can go back to the tool and check that adding in this feature has reduced the number of false negatives for reply/forward emails. Using the tool, we find that this is indeed the case, but also that we are now slightly more likely to

UserName	AveragePrecision	AreaUnderCurve
User35CB8E5	52.1%	91.0%
UserCE3FDB4	35.8%	89.1%
User6AACED	45.0%	91.4%
User7E601F9	53.5%	80.2%
User68251CD	61.4%	87.3%
User223AECA	50.9%	90.1%
UserFF0F29E	29.3%	86.2%
User25C0488	32.5%	83.1%
User811E39F	25.3%	81.9%
User10628A6	47.3%	87.6%
Average	43.3%	86.8%

(a) Initial results

UserName	AveragePrecision	AreaUnderCurve
User35CB8E5	54.8%	91.0%
UserCE3FDB4	34.4%	89.1%
User6AACED	46.4%	91.2%
User7E601F9	53.2%	79.9%
User68251CD	62.8%	87.3%
User223AECA	50.2%	89.8%
UserFF0F29E	30.9%	87.2%
User25C0488	31.2%	82.2%
User811E39F	26.4%	82.2%
User10628A6	48.6%	88.6%
Average	43.9%	86.9%

(b) With *SubjectPrefix* feature

Figure 4.18 Evaluation results for each user and overall, for the previous feature set and a feature set with the new *SubjectPrefix* feature added. On average, both the area under the curve and the average precision are slightly improved by adding the *SubjectPrefix* feature.

get false positives for the last email of a conversation. This is because the only difference between the last email of a conversation and the previous ones is the message content, which we have limited access to through our feature set. Although incorrect, such false positives can be quite acceptable to the user, since the user interface will bring the conversation to the user's attention, allowing them to decide whether to continue the conversation or not. So we have removed some false negatives that were quite jarring to the user at the cost of adding a smaller number of false positives that are acceptable to the user. This is a good trade-off – and also demonstrates the risk of paying too much attention to overall evaluation metrics. Here, a small increase in the evaluation metric (or even no increase at all for some users) corresponds to an improvement in user satisfaction.

The next kind of error we found were false negatives for emails received via distribution lists. In these situations, a user is likely to reply to emails received on certain distribution lists, but not on others. The challenge we face with this kind of error is that emails often have multiple recipients and, if the user is not explicitly named, it can be impossible to tell which recipients are distribution lists and which of these distribution lists contain the user. For example, if an email is sent to three different distribution lists and the user is on one of these, it may not be possible to tell which one.

To get around this problem, we can add a *Recipients* feature that captures all of the recipients of the email, on the grounds that one of them (at least) will correspond to the user. Again, this is helping to conform to Assumption ⑦ since we will no longer be ignoring a relevant signal: the identities of the email recipients. We can design this feature similarly to the *Sender* feature, except that multiple buckets of the feature will have non-zero values at once, one for each recipient. We have to be very careful when doing this to ensure that our new *Recipients* feature matches the assumptions of our model. A key assumption is the contribution of a single feature to the overall score is normally in the range −1.0 to 1.0, since the weight for a bucket normally takes values in the range and we have always used feature values of 1.0. But now if we have an email with 20 recipients, then we have 20 buckets active – if each bucket has a feature value of 1.0, then the *Recipients* feature would normally contribute between −20.0 to 20.0 to the overall score. To put it another way, the influence of the *Recipients* feature on the final prediction would be 20 times greater for an email with 20 recipients than for an email with one recipient. Intuitively this does not make sense since we really only care about the single recipient that caused the user to receive the email. Practically this would lead to the feature either dominating all the other features or being ignored depending on the number of recipients – very undesirable behaviour in either case. To rectify this situation, we can simply ensure that, no matter how many buckets of the feature are active, the sum of their feature values is always 1.0. So for an email with five recipients, five buckets are active, each with a feature value of 0.2. This solution is not perfect since there is really only one recipient that we care about and the signal from this recipient will be diluted by the presence of other recipients. A better solution would be to add in a variable to the model to identify the relevant recipient. To keep things simple and to demonstrate the kind of compromises that arise when designing a feature set with a fixed model, we will keep the model the same and use a feature-based solution. As before, we can evaluate our system with and without this new *Recipients* feature.

The comparative results in Figure 4.19 are more clear-cut than the previous ones: in most cases, the accuracy metrics increase with the *Recipients* feature added. Even where a metric does not increase, it rarely decreases by very much. On average, we are seeing a 0.2% increase in AUC and a 0.8% increase in AP. These may seem like small increases in these metrics, but they are in fact quite significant. Using

UserName	AveragePrecision	AreaUnderCurve
User35CB8E5	54.8%	91.0%
UserCE3FDB4	34.4%	89.1%
User6AACED	46.4%	91.2%
User7E601F9	53.2%	79.9%
User68251CD	62.8%	87.3%
User223AECA	50.2%	89.8%
UserFF0F29E	30.9%	87.2%
User25C0488	31.2%	82.2%
User811E39F	26.4%	82.2%
User10628A6	48.6%	88.6%
Average	43.9%	86.9%

UserName	AveragePrecision	AreaUnderCurve
User35CB8E5	57.6%	91.7%
UserCE3FDB4	33.9%	89.0%
User6AACED	46.7%	91.1%
User7E601F9	54.5%	80.2%
User68251CD	63.8%	87.7%
User223AECA	51.5%	89.2%
UserFF0F29E	30.6%	87.2%
User25C0488	32.1%	83.3%
User811E39F	26.4%	82.3%
User10628A6	50.0%	88.9%
Average	44.7%	87.1%

(a) Without *Recipients* feature   (b) With *Recipients* feature

Figure 4.19 Evaluation results for the previous feature set without the *Recipients* feature and for a feature set with the *Recipients* feature included.

the interactive tool tells us that a 1% increase in average precision gives a very noticeable improvement in the perceived accuracy of the system, especially if the change corrects particularly jarring incorrect predictions. For example, suppose a user owns a particular distribution list and replies to posts on the list frequently. Without the *Recipients* feature, the system would likely make incorrect predictions on such emails which would be quite jarring to the user, as the owner of the distribution list. Fixing this problem by adding in the *Recipients* feature would substantially improve the user's experience despite leading to only a tiny improvement in the headline AUC and AP accuracy numbers.

We are now free to go to the next problem on the list and modify the feature set to try to address it. For example, addressing the issue of "graymail" emails would require a feature that looked at the content of the email – in fact a word feature works well for this task. For the project with the Exchange team, we continued to add to and refine the feature set, ensuring at each stage that the evaluation metrics were improving and that mistakes on real emails were being fixed, using the tool. Ultimately we reached the stage where the accuracy metrics were very good and the qualitative accuracy was also good. At this point, you might think we were ready to deploy the system for some beta testers – but in real machine learning systems things are never that easy...

REVIEW OF CONCEPTS

recall   Another term for the true positive rate, often used when we are trying to find rare positive items in a large data set. The recall is the proportion of these items successfully found ("recalled") and is therefore equal to the true positive rate.

precision   The fraction of positive predictions that are correct. Precision is generally complementary to recall in that higher precision means lower recall and vice versa. Precision is often used as an evaluation metric in applications where the focus is on the accuracy of positive predictions. For example, in a search engine the focus is on the accuracy of the documents that are retrieved as results and so a precision metric might be used to evaluate this accuracy.

This kind of precision should not be confused with the inverse variance of a Gaussian which is also known as the precision. In practice, the two terms are used in very different contexts so confusion between the two is rare.

precision–recall curve   A plot of precision against recall for a machine learning system as some parameter of the system is varied (such as the threshold on a predicted probability). Precision–recall curves are useful for assessing prediction accuracy when the probability of a positive prediction is relatively low.

average precision   The average precision across a range of recalls in the precision–recall curve, used as a quantitative evaluation metric. This is effectively the area under the P–R curve if the full range of recalls is used. However, the very left-hand end of the curve is often excluded from this average since the precision measurements are inaccurate, due to being computed from a very small number of data items.

4.6   LEARNING AS EMAILS ARRIVE

So far we've been able to train our model on a large number of emails at once. But for our application, we need to be able to learn from a new email as soon as a user replies to it, or as soon as it becomes clear that the user is not going to reply to it. We cannot wait until we have received a large number of emails, then train on them once and use the trained model forever. Instead, we have to keep training the model as new emails come in and always use the latest trained model to make predictions.

As we saw in Section 3.3 in the previous chapter, we can use online learning to continually update our model, as we receive new training data. In our model online learning is straightforward: for each batch of emails that have arrived since we last trained, we use the previous posterior distributions on `weight` and `threshold` as the priors for training. Once training on the batch is complete, the new posterior distributions over `weight` and `threshold` can be used for making predictions. Later when the next batch of emails is trained on, these posterior distributions will act as the new priors. We can check how well this procedure works by dividing our training data into batches and running online learning as each batch comes in. We can then evaluate this method in comparison to offline training, where all the training data seen up to that point is presented at once. Figure 4.20 shows the AUC and AP averaged across all 10 users using either offline training or online training with different batch sizes.

These results show that online learning gives an accuracy similar to, but slightly lower than offline training, with larger batch sizes giving generally better accuracy. The plots also show that the difference in accuracy decreases as more emails are received. So it seems like online learning could be a suitable solution, once sufficient emails have been received. But this brings us to another problem: it takes around 400 to 500 emails for the average precision to get close to a stable value. For a time before that number is reached, and particularly when relatively few emails have been trained on, the accuracy of the classifier is low. This means that the experience for new users would be poor. Of course, we could wait until the user has received and acted on sufficient emails, but for some users this could take weeks or months. It would be much better if we could give them a good experience straight away. The challenge of making good predictions for new users where there is not yet any training data is known as a **cold start problem**.

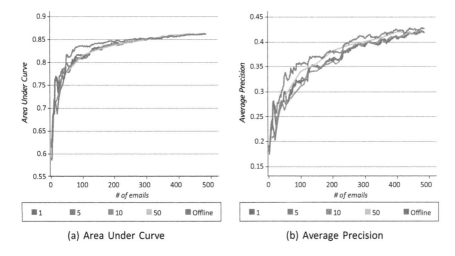

(a) Area Under Curve   (b) Average Precision

Figure 4.20 Prediction accuracy as more and more training emails become available, averaged over all ten users. For each metric, the offline curve shows the accuracy if we retrain the model from scratch on all emails received up to that point. The four other curves show the accuracy if we instead do online training to update the model incrementally after every 1, 5, 10 or 50 emails.

4.6.1   Modelling a community of users

We've already shown that we can solve certain prediction problems by changing the feature set. But in this case, there is no change to the feature set that can help us – we cannot even compute feature values until we have seen at least one email! But since we have a classification model rather than a fixed classification algorithm, we have an additional option available to us: to change the model.

How can we change our model to solve the cold start problem? We can exploit the fact that different users tend to reply to the same kinds of emails. For

Learning from many users will help us to make better predictions for a new user.

example, users tend to be more likely to reply to emails where they are first on the To line or where the email is forwarded to them. This suggests that we might expect the learned weights to be similar across users, at least for those feature buckets that capture behaviours common amongst users. However, there may also be other feature buckets which capture differences in the behaviour from user to user, where we may expect the learned weights to differ between users. To investigate which feature buckets are similar across users, we can plot the learned weights for the first five of our users, for all feature buckets that they have in common (that is, all buckets except those of the *Sender* and *Recipients* features). The resulting plot is shown in Figure 4.21.

As you can see, for many feature buckets, the weights are similar for all five users and even for buckets where there is more variability across users the weights tend to be all positive or all negative. But in a few cases, such as the *FromMe* feature, there is more variability from user to user. This variability suggests that these features capture differences in behaviour between users, such as whether a particular user sends emails to themselves as reminders. Overall, it seems like there is enough similarity between users that we could exploit this similarity to make predictions for a completely new user. To do this, we need to make a new modelling assumption about how the weights vary across multiple users:

⑧ Across many users the variability in the weight for a feature bucket can be captured by a Gaussian distribution.

This assumption says that we can represent how a weight varies across users by an average weight (the mean of the Gaussian distribution) and a measure of how much a typical user's weight deviates from this average (the standard deviation of the Gaussian distribution).

Let's change our model to add in this assumption. Since we are now modelling multiple users, we need to add a plate across users and put our entire existing model inside it. The only variables outside of this new plate will be two new variables per feature bucket: `weightMean` to capture the average weight across users and `weightPrecision` to capture the precision (inverse variance) across users. We then replace the *Gaussian*(0,1) factor inside the plate (that we used to use as a prior) by a Gaussian factor connected to `weightMean` and `weightPrecision`. The resulting factor graph is shown in Figure 4.22.

You'll notice that we have used precision (inverse variance) rather than variance to capture the variability in weights across users. A high `weightPrecision` for a bucket means that its weight tends to be very similar from user to user, whilst a low `weightPrecision` means the

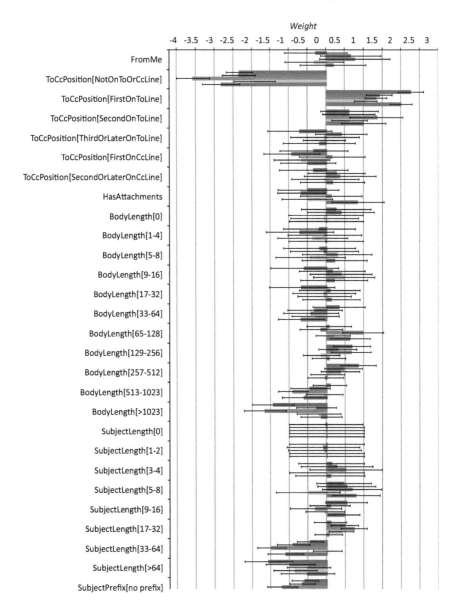

Figure 4.21 Learned Gaussian distributions for the weights for each feature bucket for the first five users in our data set. For most feature buckets the learned weights are similar across users, demonstrating that they reply to emails with similar characteristics.

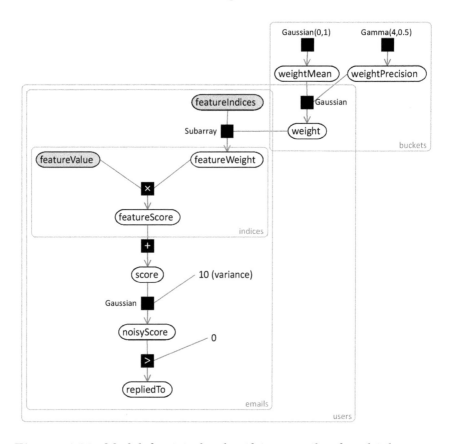

Figure 4.22 Model for jointly classifying emails of multiple users. Our classification model is duplicated for each user by placing it inside a `users` plate. We then introduce two shared variables for each feature bucket: `weightMean` captures the typical (average) weight for that bucket across users and `weightPrecision` captures how much the weight tends to vary across users.

bucket weight tends to vary a lot from user to user. We choose to use precision because we are now trying to learn this variability and it turns out to be much easier to do this using a precision rather than a variance. This choice allows us to use a **gamma distribution** to represent the uncertainty in the `weightPrecision` variable, either when setting its prior distribution or when inferring its posterior distribution. The gamma distribution is a distribution over continuous positive values (that is, values greater than zero). We need to use a new distribution because precisions can only be positive – we cannot use a

Gaussian distribution since it allows negative values, and we cannot use a beta distribution since it only allows values between zero and one. The gamma distribution also has the advantage that it is the conjugate distribution for the precision of a Gaussian (see Panel 3.2 and Bishop [2006]).

The gamma distribution has the following density function:

$$Gamma(x; k, \theta) = \frac{x^{k-1} e^{-\frac{x}{\theta}}}{\theta^k \, \Gamma(k)} \tag{4.1}$$

where $\Gamma()$ is the gamma function, used to ensure the area under the density function is 1.0. The gamma distribution has two parameters: the *shape* parameter k and the *scale* parameter θ – example gamma distributions with different values of these parameters are shown in Figure 4.23a. Confusingly, the gamma distribution is sometimes parameterised by the shape and the *inverse* of the scale, called the *rate*. Since both versions are common, it is important to check which is being used – in this book, we will always use shape and scale parameters.

Since we have relatively few users, we will need to be careful in our choice of gamma prior for `weightPrecision` since it will have a lot of influence on how the model behaves. Usually we expect the precision to be higher than 1.0, since we expect most weights to be similar across users. However, we also need to allow the precision to be around 1.0 for those rarer weights that vary substantially across users. Figure 4.23b shows a *Gamma*(4,0.5) distribution that meets both of these requirements.

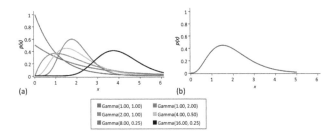

(a)   (b)

■ Gamma(1.00, 1.00)   ■ Gamma(1.00, 2.00)
■ Gamma(2.00, 1.00)   ■ Gamma(4.00, 0.50)
■ Gamma(8.00, 0.25)   ■ Gamma(16.00, 0.25)

Figure 4.23 (a) Example gamma distributions for different values of the shape and scale parameters. (b) The *Gamma*(4, 0.5) distribution which we use as a prior for the precision of the weights.

There is one more point to discuss about the model in Figure 4.22, before we try it out. If you are very observant, you will notice that the `threshold` variable has been fixed to zero. This is because we want to use our communal `weightMean` and `weightPrecision` to learn about how the threshold varies across users as well as how the weights vary. To do this, we can use a common trick which is to fix the threshold to zero and create a new feature which is always on for all emails – this is known as the **bias**. The idea is that changing the score by a fixed value for all emails is equivalent to changing the threshold by the same value. So we can use the bias feature to effectively set the threshold, whilst leaving the actual threshold fixed at 0. Since feature weights have a $Gaussian(0,1)$ prior but the threshold has a $Gaussian(0,10)$ prior, we need to set the value of this new bias feature to be $\sqrt{10}$, in order to leave the model unchanged – if we have a variable whose uncertainty is $Gaussian(0,1)$ and we multiply it by $\sqrt{10}$, we get a variable whose uncertainty is $Gaussian(0,10)$, as required.

4.6.2 Solving the cold start problem

We can now train our communal model on the first five users (the users whose weights were plotted in Figure 4.21). Even though we have substantially changed the model, we are still able to use expectation propagation to do inference tasks like training or prediction. So we do not need to invent a new algorithm to do joint training on multiple users – we can just run the familiar EP algorithm on our extended model.

Figure 4.24 shows the community weight distributions learned: each bar shows the mean of the posterior over `weightMean` and the error bars show a standard deviation given by the mean value of `weightPrecision`. Note the different use of error bars – to show `weightPrecision` (the learned variability across users) rather than the uncertainty in

A hands-on solution to the cold start problem

`weightMean` itself. If you compare the distributions of Figure 4.24 with the individual weights of Figure 4.21, you can see how the learned

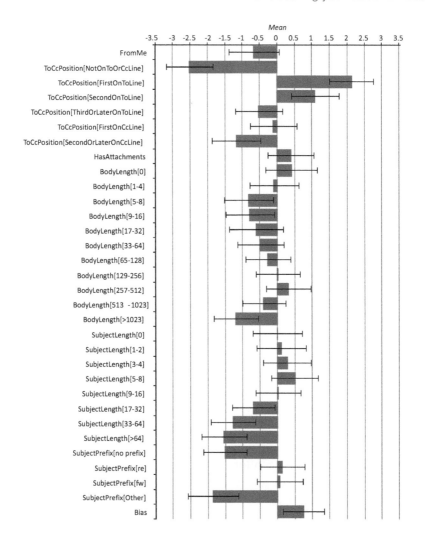

Figure 4.24 Community weight distributions learned from the first five users in our data set. The blue bar shows the expected value of `weightMean` and the errors bars show one standard deviation either side of this corresponding to the expected value of `weightPrecision`. Comparing to Figure 4.21 shows that the learned weight distributions are consistent with the weights learned individually for each user.

distributions have nicely captured the variability in weights across users.

To apply our learned community weight distributions for a new user, we can use the same model configured for a single user with the priors over `weightMean` and `weightPrecision` replaced by the Gaussian and gamma posteriors learned from the first five users. We can use this model to make predictions even when we have not seen any emails for the new user. But we can also use the model to do online training, as we receive emails for a new user. As we do online training using the community model, we can smoothly evolve from making generic predictions that may apply to any user to making personalised predictions specific to the new user. This evolution happens entirely automatically through doing inference in our model – there is no need for us to specify an ad-hoc procedure for switching from community to personalised predictions.

Figure 4.25 shows the accuracy of predictions made using online training in the community model compared to the individual model (using a batch size of 5) for varying amounts of training data. For this plot we again average across all ten users – we make prediction results for the first five users using a separate community model trained on the last five users. The results are very satisfactory – the initial accuracy is high (an average AP of 41.8%) and then it continues to rise smoothly until it reaches an average AP of 43.2% after 500 emails have been trained on. As we might have hoped, our community model is making good predictions from the start, which then become even better as the model personalises to the individual user. The cold start problem is solved!

In the production system used by Exchange, we had a much larger number of users to learn community weights from. In this case, the posteriors over `weightMean` and `weightPrecision` became very narrow. When these posteriors are used as priors, the values of `weightMean` and `weightPrecision` are effectively fixed. This allows us to make a helpful simplification to our system: once we have used the multi-user model to learn community weight distributions, we can go back to the single-user model to do online training and make predictions. All we need to do is replace the *Gaussian*(0,1) prior in the single-user model with a Gaussian prior whose mean and precision are given by the expected values of the narrow `weightMean` and `weightPrecision` distributions. So, in production, the multi-user model is trained once offline on a large number of users and the learned community weight distributions are then used to do training and prediction separately for each user. This separation makes it easier to deploy, manage and debug the behaviour of the system since each user can be considered separately.

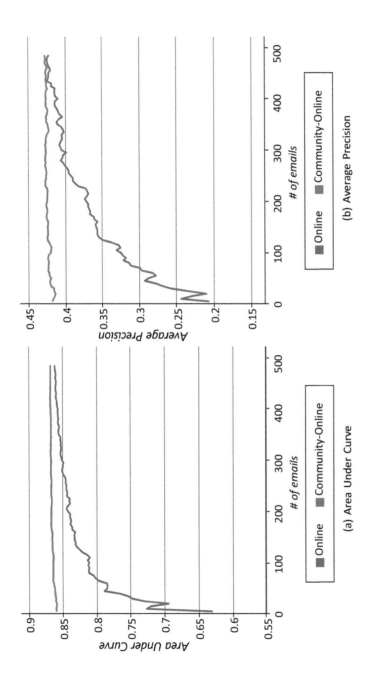

Figure 4.25 Prediction accuracy against amount of training data using individual models or the community model. In both cases, training is done online with batches of five emails. Results are averaged over all ten users – for the first five users prediction uses a community model trained on the second five users, and vice versa for the second five users.

There is one final thing to do before we deploy our system to some beta testers. Remember the test sets of email data that we put to one side at the start of the chapter? Now is the time to break them out and see if we get results on the test sets that are comparable to the results we have seen on our validation sets. Comparative results for the validation and test sets are shown in Table 4.5. The table shows that the AUC measurements for the users' test sets are generally quite similar to those of the validation sets, with no obvious bias favouring one or the other. This suggests that in designing our model and feature set, we have not overfit to the validation data. The AP measurements are more different, particularly for some users – this is because the test sets are quite small and some contain only a few replied-to emails. In such situations, AP measurements become quite noisy and unreliable. However, even if we focus on those users with more replied to emails, it does not appear that the test AP is consistently lower than the validation AP. So both evaluation metrics suggest that there is no fundamental difference between test and validation set accuracies and so we should expect to achieve similar prediction accuracy for real users.

4.6.3   Final testing and changes

At this point, the prediction system was deployed to beta testers for further real-world testing. Questionnaires were used to get feedback on how well the system was working for users. This testing and feedback highlighted two additional issues:

- The predictions appeared to get less accurate over time, as the user's behaviour evolved, for example, when they changed projects or changed teams the clutter predictions did not seem to change quickly enough to match the updated behaviour.

- The calibration of the system, although correct on average, was incorrect for individual users. The predicted probabilities were too high for some users and too low for others.

Investigation of the first issue identified a similar problem to the one we diagnosed in Chapter 3. We have assumed that the weights in the model are fixed across time for a particular user. This assumption does not allow for user behaviour to change. The solution was to change the model to allow the weights to change over time, just as we allowed the skills to change over time in the TrueSkill system. The modified

Table 4.5 Final accuracy results for the validation and test sets for each user and overall the right-hand columns show the number of replied to emails in each data set, which gives an indication of the reliability of the corresponding average precision metric.

UserName	AveragePrecision Validation	AveragePrecision Test	AreaUnderCurve Validation	AreaUnderCurve Test	ValidationReply Count	TestReplyCount
User35CB8E5	57.6%	90.6%	91.7%	92.3%	74	10
UserCE3FDB4	33.9%	38.5%	89.0%	88.2%	64	21
User6AACED	46.7%	46.0%	91.1%	91.7%	58	16
User7E601F9	54.5%	54.2%	80.2%	84.3%	119	36
User68251CD	63.8%	78.8%	87.7%	89.3%	142	62
User223AECA	51.5%	24.3%	89.2%	82.6%	51	12
UserFF0F29E	30.6%	24.3%	87.2%	85.5%	119	40
User25C0488	32.1%	39.4%	83.3%	86.1%	114	44
User811E39F	26.4%	36.9%	82.3%	82.6%	129	64
User10628A6	50.0%	55.5%	88.9%	90.3%	61	24
Average	44.7%	48.9%	87.1%	87.3%	93.1	32.9

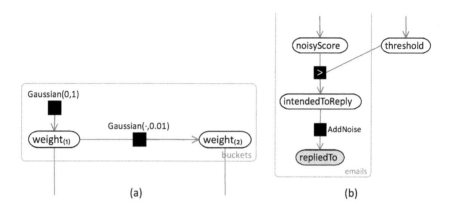

Figure 4.26 Modifications to the model to fix issues found by beta testers (a) Allowing the weights to change over time addresses the issue that action predictions do not evolve as user behaviour changes (b) Explicitly modelling the difference between the intended action label and the actual action label addresses poor calibration that occurs when the intended and actual labels do not match.

model has random variables for each bucket weight for each period of time, such as a variable per week. Figure 4.26a shows an example model segment that contains weights for two consecutive weeks $weight_{(1)}$ and $weight_{(2)}$. To allow the weights to change over time, the weight for the second week is allowed to vary slightly from the weight for the first week, through adding Gaussian noise with very low variance. As with the TrueSkill system, this change allows the system to track slowly-changing user behaviours.

The second issue was harder to diagnose. Investigation of the issue found that the too-high predicted probabilities occurred for users that had a low volume of clutter and the too-low predicted probabilities occurred for users that had a high volume of clutter. It turned out that the problem was the noisy ground truth labels that we encountered in Section 4.5 – for users with a high volume of clutter, a lot of clutter items were incorrectly labelled as not clutter and vice versa for users with a low volume of clutter. Training with these incorrect labels introduced a corresponding bias into the predicted probability of clutter. The solution here is to change the model to represent label noise explicitly. For example, for reply prediction, we can create a new variable in the model `intendedToReply` representing the true label of whether the user truly intended to reply to the message. We then define the observed label `repliedTo` to be a noisy version of this variable, using a factor like the *AddNoise* factor that we used back in Chapter 2. Figure 4.26b shows the relevant piece of a modified model with this change in place. Following this change, the calibration was found to be much closer to ideal across all users and the systematic calibration variation for users with high or low clutter volume disappeared.

In addressing each of these issues, we needed to make changes to the model, something that would be impossible with a black box classification algorithm, but which is central to the model-based machine learning approach. With these model changes in place, the Clutter prediction system is now deployed as part of Office365, helping to remove clutter emails from peoples' inboxes. Figure 4.27 shows a screenshot of the system in action, all using model-based machine learning!

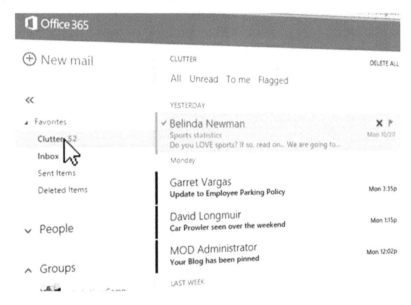

Figure 4.27 The clutter system in action in Office 365.

REVIEW OF CONCEPTS

cold start problem The problem of making good predictions for a new entity (for example, a new user) when there is very little (or no) training data available that is specific to that entity. In general, a cold start problem can occur in any system where new entities are being introduced – for example, in a recommendation system, a cold start problem occurs when trying to predict whether someone will like a newly released movie that has not yet received any ratings.

gamma distribution A probability distribution over a positive continuous random variable whose probability density function is

$$Gamma(x; k, \theta) = \frac{x^{k-1} e^{-\frac{x}{\theta}}}{\theta^k \, \Gamma(k)} \tag{4.2}$$

where $\Gamma()$ is the gamma function, used to ensure the area under the density function is 1.0. The gamma distribution has two parameters *shape* parameter k and the *scale* parameter θ.

bias A feature which is always on for all data items. Since the bias feature is always on, its weight encodes the prior probability of the label. For example, the bias weight might encode probability that a user will reply to an email, before we look at any characteristics of that particular email. Equivalently, use of a bias features allows the `threshold` variable to be fixed to zero, since it is no longer required to represent the prior label probability.

CHAPTER 5

Making recommendations

Whether you're into music, books, films or video games, a good recommendation can be a real joy – and can help less well known works get into the spotlight. But what one person considers a new classic, another will write off as a dud. Can a model be used to understand what someone likes and dislikes well enough to provide tailored recommendations?

Retailers of all kinds are keen to make accurate, personalised recommendations to their customers. But developing an automatic recommendation system requires expertise and investment beyond the means of many retailers, especially smaller ones. Instead, such retailers can turn to the cloud and make use of online recommendation services.

In Microsoft, the Azure Machine Learning team wanted to make it easy for developers and data scientists to embed predictive analytics and machine learning into their applications. The team's solution was a cloud-based platform for building and exploring analytics pipelines, constructed from a number of machine learning building blocks (Figure 5.1). Crucially, the platform also lets these pipelines be deployed as web services which can then be accessed from within an application. With high demand for automated recommendation, the Azure ML team wanted to have building blocks for making recommender systems, flexible enough to meet the needs of different customers.

Potential customers had varying requirements that a recommender system needed to fulfill. Some wanted to make recommendations based

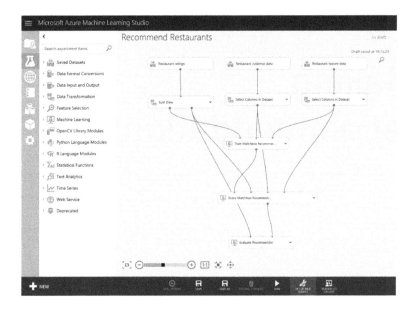

Figure 5.1 The goal: make it possible to construct customised recommendation services in Azure Machine Learning.

solely on other items that a user has liked or disliked. Some had extra information about each item (such as the genre of a movie) that they wanted the system to take into account. Similarly, some had additional data about their users (such as age or gender) that they wanted to use to improve recommendations. Furthermore, while some user feedback came in the form of star ratings, other feedback systems only allowed users to like or dislike items. In addition, the items being recommended varied from traditional retail products like books and films to restaurants and online services.

We needed to construct a model that could meet all of these requirements. In this chapter, we'll show how to develop such a flexible model and how to use it to make personalised recommendations. As an example, we will be using movies as the items to make recommendations for, since these have been very well explored and there are freely available data sets of movie ratings. We will start with an initial model that can predict like or dislike and then extend it to meet the additional customer requirements mentioned above. The model that we will develop in this chapter is closely based on the Matchbox model of Stern et al. [2009].

You can recreate all results in this chapter using the companion source code [Diethe et al., 2019].

5.1 LEARNING ABOUT PEOPLE AND MOVIES

The goal of this chapter is to make personalised movie recommendations to particular people. One way to think about this problem is to imagine a table where the rows are movies and the columns are people. The cells of the table show whether the person likes or dislikes the movie – for example, as shown in Table 5.1. This table is an illustration of the kind of data we might have to train a recommender system, where we have asked a number of people to say whether they like or dislike particular movies.

The empty cells in Table 5.1 show where we do not know whether the person likes the movie or not. There are bound to be such empty cells – we cannot ask every person about every movie and, even if we did, there will be movies that a person has not seen. The goal of our recommender system can be thought of as filling in these empty cells. In other words, given a person and a movie, predict whether they will like or dislike that movie. So how can we go about making such a prediction?

Table 5.1 The kind of data used to train a recommender system Each row is a movie and each column is a person. Filled cells show where a person has said that they liked or disliked a movie. Empty cells show where we do not have any information about whether the person liked the movie, and so are where we could make a like/dislike prediction. Making such a prediction for every empty cell in a person's column would allow us to make a movie recommendation for that person – for example, by recommending the movie with the highest probability that the person would like it.

Movie	Person 1	Person 2	Person 3	Person 4	Person 5
The Lion King	👍			👎	
Lethal Weapon	👎	👍	👍	👍	
The Sound of Music		👍			👎
Amadeus	👍	👎		👍	
When Harry Met Sally	👍	👍		👎	👍

5.1.1 Characterising movies

Let's start by considering how to characterise a movie. Intuitively, we can assume that each movie has some traits, such as whether it is an escapist or realistic, action or emotional, funny or serious. If we consider a particular trait as a line, we can imagine placing movies on that line, like this:

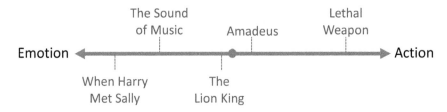

Figure 5.2 Movies placed on a line representing how much each movie is an emotional movie or as an action movie (or neither).

Movies towards the left of the line are emotional movies, like romantic comedies. Movies towards the right of the line are action movies. Movies near the middle of the line are neutral – neither action movies nor emotional movies. Notice that, in defining this trait, we have made the assumption that action and emotional are opposites.

Now let's consider people. A particular person might like emotional movies and dislike action movies. We could place that person towards the left of the line (Figure 5.3). We would expect such a person to like movies on the left-hand end of the line and dislike movies on the right-hand end of the line.

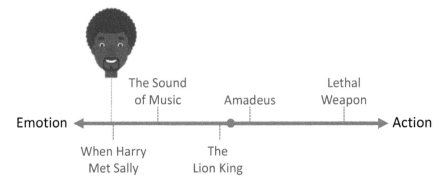

Figure 5.3 A person placed on the left of the line would be expected to like emotional movies and dislike action movies.

Another person may have the opposite tastes: disliking emotional movies and loving action movies. We can place this person towards the right of the line (Figure 5.4). We would expect such a person to dislike movies on the left-hand end of the line and like movies on the right-hand end of the line.

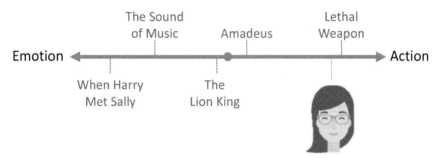

Figure 5.4 A person placed on the right of the line would be expected to like action movies and dislike emotional movies.

It is also perfectly possible a person to like (or dislike) both action and emotional movies. We could consider such a person to be neutral to the action/emotion trait and place them in the middle of the line (Figure 5.5). We would expect that such a person might like or dislike movies anywhere on the line.

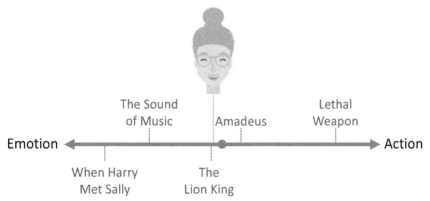

Figure 5.5 A person placed in the middle of the line would be expected to not care whether a movie was an action movie or an emotional one.

We'd like to use an approach like this to make personalised recommendations. The problem is that we do not know where the movies lie on the line *or* where the people lie on the line. Luckily, we can use model-based machine learning to infer both of these using an appropriate model.

5.1.2   A model of a trait

Let's build a model for the action/emotion trait we just described. First, let's state some assumptions that follow from the description above:

① Each movie can be characterised by its position on the trait line, represented as a continuous number.

② A person's preferences can be characterised by a position on the trait line, again represented as a continuous number.

In our model, we will use a `trait` variable to represent the position of each movie on the trait line. Because it is duplicated across movies, this variable will need to lie inside a `movies` plate. We also need a variable for the position of the person on the line, which we will call `preference` since it encodes the person's preferences with respect to the trait. To make predictions, we need a variable showing how much the person is expected to like each movie. We will call this the `affinity` variable and assume that a positive value of this variable means that we expect the person to like the movie and a negative value means that we expect the person to dislike the movie.

We need a way to combine the `trait` and the `preference` to give the behaviour described in the previous section. That is, a person with a negative (left-hand end) `preference` should prefer movies with negative (left-hand end) `trait` values. A person with a positive (right-hand end) `preference` should prefer movies with positive (right-hand end) `trait` values. Finally, a neutral person with a `preference` near zero should not favour any movies, whatever their `trait` values. This behaviour can be summarised as an assumption:

③ A positive preference value means that a person prefers movies with positive values of the trait (and vice versa for negative values). The absolute size of the preference value indicates the strength of preference, where zero means indifference.

This behaviour assumption can be encoded in our model by defining `affinity` to be the product of the `trait` and the `preference`. So we can connect these variables using a product factor, giving the factor graph of Figure 5.6.

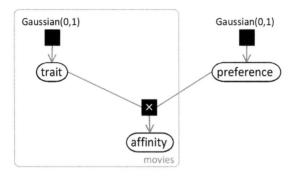

Figure 5.6 Factor graph for a single trait. Each movie has a `trait` value which is multiplied by the person's `preference` to give their `affinity` for that movie. More positive `affinity` values mean that the person is more likely to like the movie.

If you have a very good memory, you might notice that this factor graph is nearly identical to the one for a one-feature classifier (Figure 4.1) from the previous chapter. The only difference is that we have an unobserved `trait` variable where before we had an observed `featureValue`. In a way, we can think of our recommendation model as learning the features of a movie based on people's likes and dislikes – a point we will discuss more later. As we construct our recommendation model, you will see that it is similar in many ways to the classification model from Chapter 4.

Given this factor graph, we want to infer both the movies' `trait` values and the person's `preference` from data about the person's movie likes and dislikes. To do any kind of learning we need to have some variable in the model that we can observe – more specifically, we need a binary variable that can take one of two values (like or dislike). Right now we only have a continuous `affinity` variable rather than a binary one. Sounds familiar? Yes! We encountered exactly this problem back in Section 4.2 of the previous chapter, where we wanted to convert a continuous score into a binary reply prediction. Our solution then was to add Gaussian noise and then threshold the result to give a binary variable. We can use exactly the same solution here by making a noisy version of the affinity (called `noisyAffinity`) and then thresholding this to give a binary `likesMovie` variable. The end result is the factor graph of Figure 5.7 (which closely resembles Figure 4.4 from the last chapter).

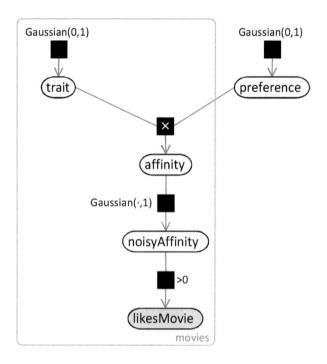

Figure 5.7 Extended factor graph that converts the continuous `affinity` into a binary `likesMovie` variable, which can be observed to train the model.

We could start using this model with one trait and one person, but that wouldn't get us very far – we would only learn about the movies that the person has already rated and so would only be able to recommend movies that they have already seen. In the next section, we will extend our model to handle multiple traits and multiple people so that we can characterise movies more accurately and use information from many peoples' ratings pooled together, to provide better recommendations for everyone.

5.2 MULTIPLE TRAITS AND MULTIPLE PEOPLE

Our model with just one trait is not going to allow us to characterise movies very well. To see this, take another look at Figure 5.4:

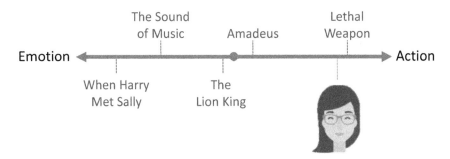

Using just the action/emotion trait, we can hardly distinguish between *The Lion King* and *Amadeus* since these have very similar positions on this trait line. So for the woman in this figure, we would not be able to recommend films like *Amadeus* (which she likes) without also recommending films like *The Lion King* (which she doesn't like).

We can address this problem by using additional traits. If we include a second trait representing how escapist or realist the film is, then each movie will now have a position on this second trait line as well as on the original trait line. This second trait value allows us to distinguish between these two movies. To see this, we can show the movies on a two-dimensional plot where the escapist/realist trait position is on the vertical axis, as shown in Figure 5.8.

In Figure 5.8, the more escapist movies have moved above the emotion/action line and the more realist movies have moved below. The left/right position of these movies has not changed from before (as shown by the dotted lines). This two-dimensional space allows *Amadeus* to move far away from the *The Lion King* which means that the two movies can now be distinguished from each other.

Given this two dimensional plot, we can indicate each person's preference for more escapist or realist movies by positioning them appropriately above or below the emotion/action line, as shown in Figure 5.9. Looking at this figure, you can see that the woman from Figure 5.4 has now moved below the emotion/action line, since she has a preference for more realistic movies. Her preference point is now much closer to *Amadeus* than to *The Lion King* – which means it is now possible for

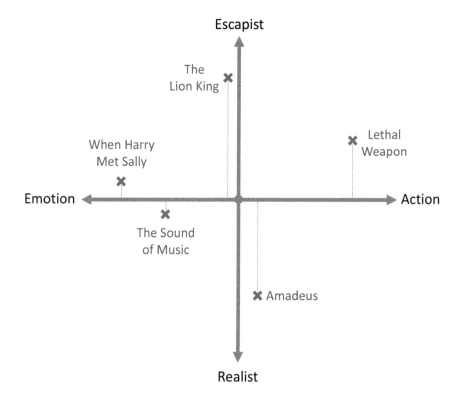

Figure 5.8 Two-dimensional plot where the new vertical axis shows how escapist or realist a movie is. Dotted lines show that the horizontal position of the movies has not changed.

our system to recommend *Amadeus* without also recommending *The Lion King*.

We have now placed movies and people in a two-dimensional space, which we will call **trait space**. If we have three traits, then trait space will be three dimensional, and so on for higher numbers of traits. We can use the concept of trait space to update our first two assumptions to allow for multiple traits:

① Each movie can be characterised by its position ~~on the trait line~~ in trait space, represented as a continuous number for each trait.

② A person's preferences can be characterised by a position ~~on the trait line~~ in trait space, again represented as a continuous number for each trait.

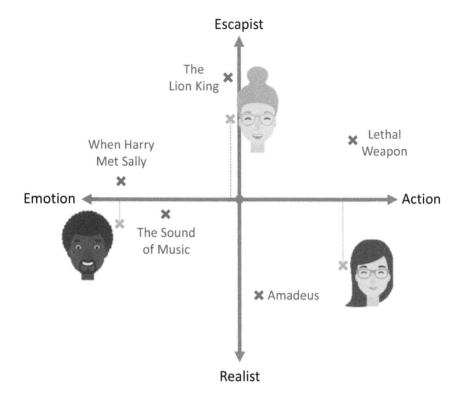

Figure 5.9 Placing people on the two-dimension plot allows us to capture their preferences for escapist/realist movies, whilst still representing their preferences for emotional/action movies.

Assumption ③ does not need to be changed since we are combining each **trait** and **preference** exactly as we did when there was just one trait. However, we do need to make an additional assumption about how a person's preferences for different traits combine together to make an overall affinity.

④ The effect of one trait value on whether a person likes or dislikes a movie is the same, no matter what other trait values that movie has.

We can encode this assumption in our model by computing a separate affinity for each trait (which we will call the **traitAffinity**) and then just add them together to give an overall **affinity**. Figure 5.10 gives the factor graph for this model with a new plate over traits that contains the **trait** value for each movie, the **preference** for each person and

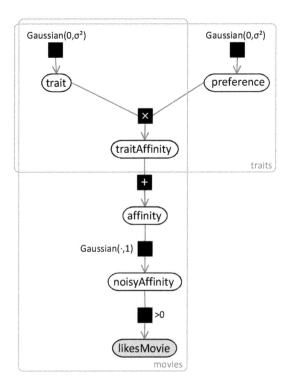

Figure 5.10 Factor graph for combining together multiple traits.

the `traitAffinity`, indicating that all of these variables are duplicated per trait.

This model combines together traits in exactly the same way that we combined together features in the previous chapter. Once again, it leads to a very similar factor graph – to see this, compare Figure 5.10 to Figure 4.5. The main difference again is that we now have an unobserved `trait` variable where before we had an observed `featureValue`. This may seem like a small difference, but the implications of having this variable unobserved are huge. Rather than using features which are hand-designed and provide given values for each item, we are now asking our model to learn the traits and the trait values for itself! Think about this for a moment – we are effectively asking our system to create its own feature set and assign values for those features to each movie – all by just using movie ratings. The fact that this is even possible may seem like magic – but it arises from having a clearly defined model combined with a powerful inference algorithm.

One new complexity arises in this model around the choice of the prior variance σ^2 for the `trait` and `preference` variables. Because we are now adding together several trait affinities, we risk changing the range of values that the `affinity` can take as we vary the number of traits. To keep this range approximately fixed, we set $\sigma^2 = 1/\sqrt{T}$ where T is the number of traits. The intuition behind this choice of variance is that we would then expect the trait affinity to have a variance of approximately $1/\sqrt{T} \times 1/\sqrt{T} = 1/T$. The sum of T of these would have variance of approximately 1, which is the same as the single trait model.

5.2.1 Learning from many people at once

If we try to use this model to infer traits and preferences given data for just one person, we will only be able to learn about movies which that person has rated – probably not very many. We can do much better if we pool together the data from many people, since this is likely to give a lot of data for popular movies and at least a little data for the vast majority of movies. This approach is called **collaborative filtering** – a term coined by the developers of Tapestry, the first ever recommender system. In Tapestry, collaborative filtering was proposed for handling email documents, where "people collaborate to help one another perform filtering by recording their reactions to documents they read" [Goldberg et al., 1992]. In our application we want to filter movies by recording the ratings (that is, reactions) that other people have to the movies they watch – a different application, but the underlying principle is the same.

To extend our factor graph to handle multiple people, we add a new plate over people and put all variables inside it except the `trait` variable (which is shared across people). The resulting factor graph is shown in Figure 5.11. Looking at this factor graph, you can see that it is symmetric between people and movies. In other words, we could swap over people and movies and we would end up with exactly the same model!

In this model we have chosen to threshold the `noisyAffinity` at zero, roughly corresponding to the assumption that half the ratings will be "like" and half will be "dislike". This is quite a strong assumption to be making, so we could instead learn this threshold value as we did for the classifier model. Instead we will do something better – we will make a change that effectively allows different thresholds to be learned for each movie and for each person. We will add a bias variable per movie

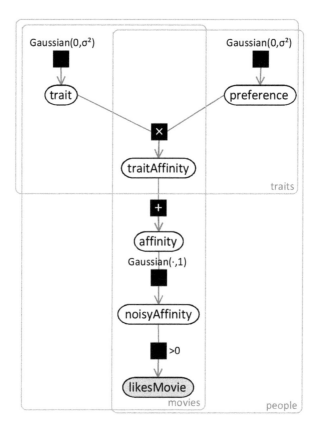

Figure 5.11 Factor graph for a recommender model which can learn from like/dislike data pooled across many people.

and a bias variable per user and include these two variables in the sum when we compute the total `affinity`. Introducing biases in this way allows the model to capture the general popularity of a movie and the degree to which each person likes movies in general. For example, if a user likes nearly every movie then they will get a high user bias. Similarly, if a movie is liked by nearly every user, then it will get a high movie bias.

We can add in biases without changing the factor graph from the one in Figure 5.11 – all we do is use a traits plate that is two bigger than the desired number of traits and fix the first `preference` value and the second `trait` value to be exactly 1.0. Then, the first `trait` value will be the bias for a movie and the second `preference` value will be the bias for a person. We will use this trick to include biases in all models in this chapter, but they will not be shown explicitly in the factor graphs to keep them uncluttered.

Our final assumption is that we do not need any more variables in our model – or to put it another way:

⑤ Whether a person will like or dislike a movie depends only on their preferences for the movie's traits and not on *anything* else.

We will assess the validity of this assumption shortly, but first let's put all of our assumptions together in one place so that we can review them all (Table 5.2).

Assumption ① seems reasonable since we can theoretically make trait space as large as we like, in order to completely characterise any movie – for smaller numbers of traits this assumption will hold less well, but still hopefully be a good enough assumption for practical purposes. Assumption ② assumes that a person's tastes can be well represented by a single point in trait space. Quite possibly, people could occupy multiple points in trait space, for example a person may like both

Table 5.2 The assumptions encoded in our recommender model.

① Each movie can be characterised by its position in trait space, represented as a continuous number for each trait.

② A person's preferences can be characterised by a position in trait space, again represented as a continuous number for each trait.

③ A positive preference value means that a person prefers movies with positive values of the trait (and vice versa for negative values). The absolute size of the preference value indicates the strength of preference, where zero means indifference.

④ The effect of one trait value on whether a person likes or dislikes a movie is the same, no matter what other trait values that movie has.

⑤ Whether a person will like or dislike a movie depends only on their preferences for the movie's traits and not on *anything* else.

children's cartoons and very violent movies, but nothing in between. However, it may be reasonable to assume that such people are rare and so a person occupying a single point is a decent assumption in most cases.

Assumption ③ and Assumption ④ relate to how movie and person traits combine together to give an affinity. Perhaps the most questionable assumption here is Assumption ④ which says that the effect of each trait does not depend on the other traits. In practice, we might expect some traits to override others or to combine in unusual ways. For example, if someone only likes action movies that star Arnold Schwarzenegger, but dislikes all the other kinds of movies that he appears in – then this would be poorly modelled by these assumptions because the "stars Arnold Schwarzenegger" trait would have a positive effect in some cases and a negative effect in others.

Finally, we have Assumption ⑤ which says that whether someone likes or dislikes a movie will depend only on their preferences for the movie's traits – in fact it may depend on many other things. For example, the time of year may be a factor – someone may love Christmas movies in December but loathe them in January. An-

A person may only like some movies at particular times of year.

other factor could be the other people that are watching the movie – whether someone enjoys a movie could well depend on who is watching it with them. Following this line of thought, we could imagine a recommendation system that recommends movies for groups of people – this has in fact been explored by, for example, Zhang et al. [2015]. Other things that could influence a person's enjoyment could include: the time of day or time of week, their emotional state (do they want a happy movie or a sad one? do they want to be distracted from real life or challenged?) and so on. In short, there is plenty to question about Assumption ⑤ – but it's fine to stick with it for now and then consider extending the model to capture additional cues later on.

So let's keep the model as it is and use it to make some recommendations!

REVIEW OF CONCEPTS

trait space   A multi-dimensional space where each point in the space corresponds to an item with a particular set of trait values. Nearby points will correspond to items with similar traits, whereas points that are further apart represent items with less in common. A trait space is useful for identifying similar items and also for making item recommendations. See Figure 5.9 for a visualisation of a two-dimensional trait space.

collaborative filtering   A means of filtering items for one user of a system based on the implicit or explicit rating of items by other users of that system. For example, filtering emails based on others' responses to the same emails or recommending movies based on others' ratings of those movies.

5.3   TRAINING OUR RECOMMENDER

Before we can train our model, we need some data to train it on. The good news here is that there are some high-quality public data sets which can be used for training recommender models. We will use one of the excellent MovieLens data sets by GroupLens Research at the University of Minnesota [Harper and Konstan, 2015]. We will use a data set that has been made freely available for education and development purposes – thank you, MovieLens!

5.3.1   Getting to know our data

As with any new data set, our first task is to get to know the data. First of all, here is a sample of 10 ratings from the data set:

Table 5.3 A sample of ratings from the MovieLens data set.

User	Movie	Rating
1	Willow (1988)	2
1	Antz (1998)	2
1	Fly, The (1986)	2.5
1	Time Bandits (1981)	1
1	Blazing Saddles (1974)	3
2	GoldenEye (1995)	4
2	Sense and Sensibility (1995)	5
2	Clueless (1995)	5
2	Seven (a.k.a. Se7en) (1995)	4
2	Usual Suspects, The (1995)	4

The sample shows that each rating gives the ID of the person providing the rating, the movie being rated, and the number of stars that the person gave the movie. In addition to ratings, the data set also contains some information about each movie – we'll look at this later on, in Section 5.6.

It's a good idea to view a new data set in many different ways, to get a deeper understanding of the data and to identify any possible data issues as early as possible. As an example, let's make a plot to understand what kind of ratings people are giving. The above sample suggests that ratings go up to five stars and that half stars are allowed.

To confirm this and to understand how frequently each rating is given, we can plot a histogram of all the ratings in the data set.

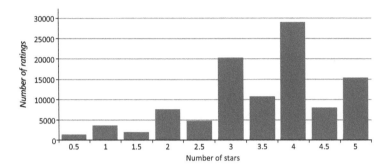

Figure 5.12 The number of ratings given for each possible number of stars (from half a star up to five stars).

We can learn a few things about the ratings from Figure 5.12. The first is that whole star ratings are given more than nearby ratings with half stars. Secondly, the plot is biased to the right, showing that people are much more likely to give a rating above three stars than below. This could perhaps be because people are generous to the movies and try to give them decent ratings. Another possibility is that people only rate movies that they watch and they only watch movies that they expect to like. For example, someone might hate horror movies and so would never watch them, and so never rate them. If they were forced to watch the movie, they would likely give it a very low rating. Since people are not usually forced to watch movies, such ratings would not appear in the data set, leading to the kind of rightward bias seen in Figure 5.12.

This issue of missing data is an important one and we will discuss it in detail in Section 6.2.1 of the next chapter. For now we will just have to bear in mind that this missing data will likely have a negative effect on our prediction accuracy – since we have less data about the movies a person does not like.

5.3.2 Training on MovieLens data

The model we have developed allows for two possible ratings: "like" or "dislike". If we want to use the MovieLens data set with this model, we need a way to convert each star rating into a like or a dislike (we'll look at how we can use the star ratings directly later). Guided by Figure 5.12, we will assume that 3 or more stars means that a person liked the movie, and that 2.5 or fewer stars means they did not like the movie. Applying the transformation gives us a data set of like/dislike ratings.

We need to split this like/dislike data into a training set for training our model, and a validation set to evaluate recommendations coming from the model. For each person we will use 70% of their likes/dislikes to train on and leave 30% to use for validation. We also remove ratings from the validation set for any movies that do not appear anywhere in the training set (since the trait position for these movies cannot be learned). The result of this process is:

- a training set of 69,983 ratings (57,383 likes/12,600 dislikes) covering 8,032 movies,

- a validation set of 28,831 ratings (23,952 likes/4,879 dislikes) covering 4,761 movies.

Both data sets contain ratings from 671 different people.

To train the model, we attach the training set data to the `likesMovie` variable and once again use expectation propagation to infer the `trait` values for each movie and the `preference` values for each person. However, when we try to do this, the posterior distributions for these variables remain broad and centered at zero. What is going on here?

To understand the cause of this problem, let's look again at the picture of trait space from Figure 5.9,

Symmetries can cause inference problems.

which we've repeated in Figure 5.13a. The choice of having emotion on the left and action on the right was completely arbitrary. We could flip these over so that action is on the left and emotion is on the right, whilst also flipping the positions of all the people and movies correspondingly, as shown in Figure 5.13b. The result is a flipped trait space that gives exactly the same predictions. We could also swap the action/emotion trait with the escapist/realist trait, as shown in Figure 5.13c. Again the result would give exactly the same predictions. Notice that Figure 5.13c is also the same as Figure 5.13b rotated by 90-degrees to the left. We can also apply other rotations so that the axes of the plot no longer lined

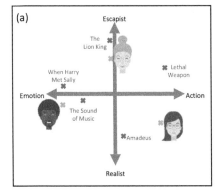
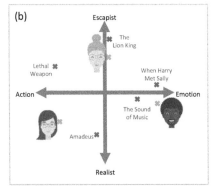

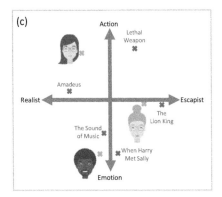
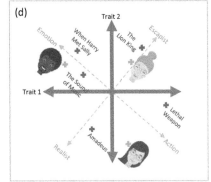

Figure 5.13 Examples of symmetries in our recommender model. (a) Original trait space (b) A left–right flip symmetry (c) A flip symmetry caused by swapping the axes (d) A rotational symmetry.

up with our original traits (Figure 5.13d) and we *still* get the same predictions! When a model's variables can be systematically transformed without changing the resulting predictions, the model is said to contain **symmetries**. During inference, these symmetries cause the posterior distributions to get very broad, as they try to capture all rotations and flips of trait space simultaneously. Not helpful!

To solve this inference problem, we need to do some kind of **symmetry breaking**. Symmetry breaking is any modification to the model or inference algorithm with the aim of removing symmetries from the posterior distributions of interest. For a two-trait version of our model, we can break symmetry by fixing the position of two points in trait space – for example, fixing the positions of the first two movies in the training set. We choose to fix the first movie to (1,0) and the second to $(0,1)$. These two points mean that rotations and flips of the trait space now lead to different results, since these two movies cannot be rotated/flipped correspondingly – and so we have removed the symmetries from our model.

With symmetry breaking in place, EP now converges to a meaningful result. However, the EP message–passing algorithm runs extremely slowly due to the high cost of computing messages relating to the product ($\times$) factor. In Stern et al. [2009] a variation of the EP message calculation is used for these messages (as shown in equation (6) in the paper), which has the effect of speeding up the message calculation dramatically.

This faster inference algorithm gives posteriors over the position in trait space for each movie and each person. In many cases, these posteriors are quite broad because there were not enough ratings to place the movie or person accurately in trait space. In Figure 5.14,

Figure 5.14 Learned positions of movies in trait space. For readability, only a subset of points have been labelled with the name of the movie (centered on the corresponding point). The two "anchor" movies, *The Usual Suspects* and *Mulholland Drive* are shown in red at $(0,1)$ and $(1,0)$.

we plot the inferred positions of those movies where the posterior was narrow enough to locate the movie reasonably precisely. Specifically, we plot a point at the posterior mean for each movie where the posterior variance is less than 0.2 in each dimension – this means that points are plotted for only 158 of our 8,032 movies. The learned positions of people in trait space are distributed in broadly similar fashion to the positions of movies, and so we will not show a plot of their positions.

This plot shows that our model has been able to learn two traits and assign values for these traits to some movies, entirely using ratings – a pretty incredible achievement! We can see that the learned trait values have some reassuring characteristics – for example, movies in the same series have been placed near each other (such as the two *Lord of the Rings* movies or the two *Ace Ventura* movies). This alone is pretty incredible – our system had no idea that these movies were from the same series, since it was not given the names of the movies. Just using the like/dislike ratings alone, it has placed these movies close together in trait space! Beyond these characteristics, it is hard to interpret much about the traits themselves at this stage. Instead, we'll just have to see how useful they are when it comes to making recommendations.

REVIEW OF CONCEPTS

symmetries   A symmetry in a model is where parts of the model are interchangeable or can act as equivalent to each other. When a model contains symmetries, this means there are multiple configurations of the models variables that give rise to the same data. During inference, such symmetries cause problems, since the posterior distributions will try to capture all these equivalent configurations simultaneously, usually with unhelpful results. When a model contains symmetries, it is usually necessary to do some kind of symmetry breaking.

symmetry breaking   Modifications to a model or inference algorithm that allow symmetries to be removed, leading to more useful posterior distributions. A typical method of symmetry breaking involves adding perturbations to the initial messages in a message passing algorithms. Other approaches involve making changes to the model to remove the symmetries, such as fixing the values of certain latent variables or adding ordering constraints.

5.4 OUR FIRST RECOMMENDATIONS

With our trained two-trait model in hand, we are now ready to make some recommendations! During training we learned the (uncertain) position of each movie and each person in trait space. We can now make a prediction for each of the held out ratings in our validation set. We do this one rating at a time – that is, for one person and one

movie at a time. First, we set the priors for the movie `trait` and the person `preference` to the posteriors learned during training. Then we run expectation propagation to infer the posterior distribution over `likesMovie` to compute the probability that the person would like the movie. Repeating this over all ratings in the validation set gives a probability of "like" for each rating, which we can compare with the ground truth like/dislike label. Figure 5.15 shows the predicted like probability and the ground truth for the ratings from the first 25 people in the validation set with more than five ratings.

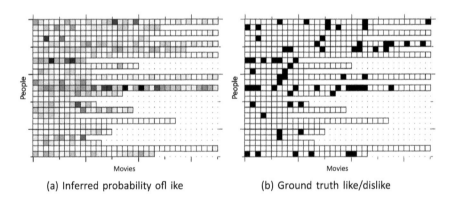

(a) Inferred probability ofl ike (b) Ground truth like/dislike

Figure 5.15 Initial results of our recommender model. (a) Computed probability of each person liking each movie. White squares correspond to probability 1.0, black to probability 0.0 and shades of grey indicate intermediate probability values. (b) Ground truth – where white indicates that the person liked the movie, black indicates they disliked it.

The first thing that stands out from Figure 5.15b is that people mostly like movies, rather than dislike them. In a sense then, the task that we have set our recommender is to try and work out which are the few movies that a person does not like. Looking at the predicted probabilities in Figure 5.15a, we can see some success in this task – because some of the darker squares do correctly align with black squares in the ground truth. In addition, some rows are generally darker or lighter than average indicating that we are able to learn how likely each person is to like or dislike movies in general. However, the predictions are not perfect – there are many disliked movies that are missed and some predictions of dislike that are incorrect. But before we make any improvements to the model, we need to decide which evaluation metrics we will use to measure and track these improvements.

5.4.1 Evaluating our predictions

In order to evaluate these predictions, we need to decide on some evaluation metrics. As discussed in Chapter 2, it makes sense to consider multiple metrics to avoid falling into the trap described by Goodhart's law. For the first metric, we will just use the fraction of correct predictions, when we predict the most probable value of `likesMovie`. For the two-trait experiment above, we see that we get 84.8% of predictions correct. This metric is helpful for tracking the raw accuracy of our recommender, but it does not directly tell us how good our recommendation experience will be for users. To do this, we will need a second metric more focused on how the recommender will actually be used.

The most common use of a recommender system is to provide an ordered list of recommendations to the user. We can use our predicted probabilities of "like" to make such a list by putting the movie with the highest probability first, then the one with the second highest probability and so on. In this scenario, a reasonable assumption is that the user will scan through the list looking for a recommendation that appeals – but that they may give up at some point during this scan. It follows that it is most important that the first item in the list is correct, then the second, then the third and so on through to the end of the list. We would like to use an evaluation metric which rewards correct predictions at the start of the list more than at the end (and penalises mistakes at the start of the list more than mistakes at the end).

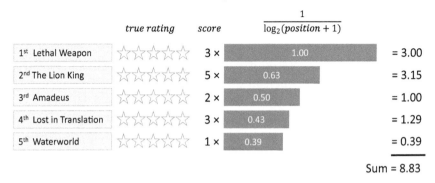

Figure 5.16 Calculation of Discounted Cumulative Gain (DCG) for a list of five movie recommendations.

A metric that has this behaviour is **Discounted Cumulative Gain** (DCG) which is defined as the sum of scores for individual recommendations, each weighted by a discount function that depends on the position of the recommendation in the list. Figure 5.16 shows the calculation of DCG for a list of five recommendations. In this figure, the discount function used is $\frac{1}{\log_2(position+1)}$ where *position* the position in the list, starting at 1. This function is often used because it smoothly decreases with list position, as shown by the blue bars in the figure. The score that we will use for a recommendation is the ground truth number of stars that the person gave that movie. So if they gave three stars then the score will be 3. Since we are calculating DCG for a list of five recommendations, we sometimes write this as DCG@5.

We can only evaluate a recommendation when we know the person's actual rating for the movie being recommended. For our data set, this means that we will only be able to make recommendations for movies from the 30% of ratings in the validation set. Effectively we will be ordering these from "most likely to like the movie" to "least likely to like the movie", taking the top 5 and using DCG to evaluate this ordering.

One problem with DCG is that the maximum achievable value varies depending on the ratings that the person gave to the validation set movies. If there are 5 high ratings, then the maximum achievable DCG@5 will be high. But if there are only 2 high ratings then the maximum achievable DCG@5 will be lower. To interpret the metric, all we really want to know is how close we got to the maximum achievable DCG. We can achieve this by computing the maximum DCG (as shown in Figure 5.17) and then dividing our DCG value by this max-

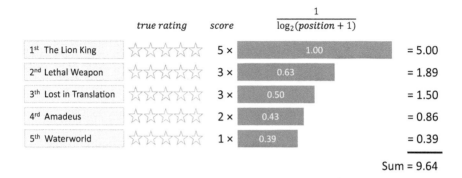

Figure 5.17 Calculation of the maximum possible DCG for the five movies from Figure 5.16. The maximum DCG is for the movies in decreasing order of the number of stars in the ground truth rating.

imum possible value. This gives a new metric called the **Normalised Discounted Cumulative Gain** (NDCG). An NDCG of 1.0 always means that the best possible set of recommendations were made. Using the maximum value from Figure 5.17, the NDCG for the recommendations in Figure 5.16 is equal to $8.83/9.64 = 0.916$.

We produce a list of recommendations for each person in our validation set, and so can compute an NDCG for each of these lists. To summarise these in a single metric, we then take an average of all the individual NDCG values. For the experiment we just ran, this gives an average NDCG@5 of 0.857.

5.4.2 How many traits should we use?

The metrics computed above are for a model with two traits. In practice, we will want to use the number of traits that gives the best recommendations according to our metrics. We can run the model with 1, 2, 4, 8 and 16 traits to see how changing the number of traits affects the accuracy of our recommendations. We can also run the model with zero traits, meaning that it gives the same recommendations to everyone – this provides a useful baseline and indicates how much we are gaining by using traits to personalise our recommendations to individual people. Note that when using zero traits, we do still include the movie and user biases in the model.

Figure 5.18 shows how our two metrics vary as we change the number of traits. Looking at the like/dislike accuracy in Figure 5.18a shows

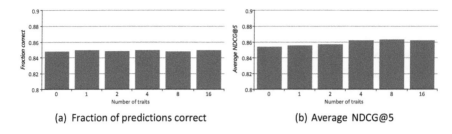

(a) Fraction of predictions correct   (b) Average NDCG@5

Figure 5.18 Accuracy and NDCG metrics computed for different numbers of traits. To make the change in metrics visible in these bar charts, we have had to start the y-axis at 0.8 rather than zero. In general, this practice should be avoided since it falsely exaggerates the differences between the bars. Since we have chosen to use it here and in some later charts, please do bear in mind that the actual differences are smaller than the charts might suggest.

that the accuracy is essentially unchanged as we change the number of traits. But the NDCG in Figure 5.18b tells a very different story, with noticeable gains in NDCG@5 as we increase the number of traits up to around 4 or 8. Beyond this point adding additional traits does not seem to help (and maybe even reduces the accuracy slightly). You might think that adding more traits would always help, but with more traits we need more data to position movies in trait space. With a fixed amount of data, the increase in position uncertainty caused by adding traits can actually reduce overall recommendation accuracy.

You may be wondering why we see an increase in average NDCG when there is no increase in prediction accuracy. The answer is that NDCG is a more sensitive metric because it makes use of the original ground truth star ratings, rather than these ratings converted into likes/dislikes. This sensitivity suggests that we would benefit by training our model on the full range of star ratings rather than just on a binary like or dislike. In the next section, we will explore what model changes we need to make to achieve this.

REVIEW OF CONCEPTS

Discounted Cumulative Gain   A metric for a list of recommendations that is defined as the sum of scores for each individual recommendation, weighted by a discount function that depends on the position of that recommendation in the list. The discount function is selected to give higher weights to recommendations at the start of the list and lower weights towards the end. Therefore, the DCG is higher when good recommendations are put at the start of the list than when the list is reordered to put them at the end. See Figure 5.16 for a visual example of calculating DCG.

Normalised Discounted Cumulative Gain A scaled version of the Discounted Cumulative Gain, where the scaling makes the maximum possible value equal to 1. This scaling is achieved by dividing by the actual DCG by the maximum possible DCG. See Figures 5.16 and 5.17 for visual examples of calculating a DCG and a maximum possible DCG.

5.5 MODELLING STAR RATINGS

Our model turns the full range of star ratings into a simple like or dislike, which means it is throwing away a lot of useful information. There is a world of difference between rating a movie at 3 stars and rating it at 5 stars, yet we are treating both of these cases the same. In order to make use of the different star ratings, we need to change our model to work with the full range of ratings rather than a binary like/dislike. Not only will this let us train on star ratings, but we will also be able to predict star ratings – a double benefit!

We can make this change by building on the binary like/dislike model that we have already designed. Inside this model, we have an `affinity` variable which is a continuous number representing how much a person likes a movie. We currently threshold this `affinity` at zero and say that values above zero mean the person likes the movie and values below zero mean that they do not like the movie. To model different star ratings, we can assume that a higher affinity means that a person will give a higher star rating. More precisely, rather than thresholding only at zero, we can now introduce thresholds for each star rating. If a person's affinity for a movie is above the threshold for a particular number of stars, then we expect them to give the movie at least that number of stars.

To add these thresholds into our model, we need to make one additional assumption. We need to decide whether the same thresholds should be used for everyone, or whether different people can have different thresholds. Allowing different thresholds might be useful – for example, it is possible that some people give a really bad movie a rating of two stars, while other people give a really bad movie a rating of one star or even half a star. If we want to model these different behaviours, we would need to allow different people to have different thresholds. This can be done but it would introduce problems of data scarcity since some people might not have any ratings for particular thresholds. Rather than tackle these problems, we will make the simplifying assumption that the thresholds are the same for everyone. We can express this assumption precisely, like so:

⑥ When two people have the same affinity for a movie, they will give it the same number of stars.

Figure 5.19 shows the factor graph for an extended model that encodes this assumption. In this model, we have added a new variable **starThreshold** which is inside a **stars** plate, meaning that there is a threshold for each number of stars.

For each movie and person, the observed variable in this graph is now called **hasStar**. This variable lies inside the **stars** plate and so has a value for each number of stars. In other words, each single star rating is represented as a set of binary variables. The binary variable for a particular number of stars is **true** if the rating has *at least* that number of stars. As an example, a rating of three stars means that

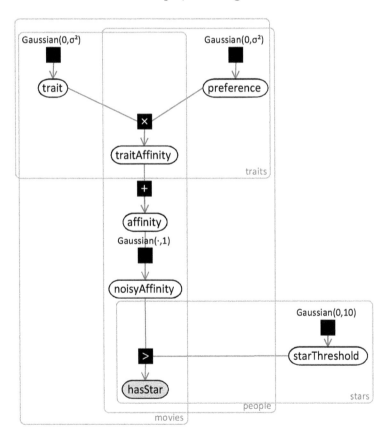

Figure 5.19 Factor graph for a recommender model that can consume and predict star ratings. Ratings are indirectly represented using binary values of the variable **hasStar** as discussed in the text.

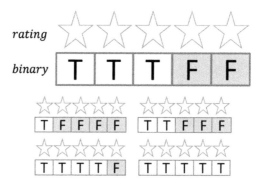

Figure 5.20 Relationship between different star ratings and the binary values used for the `hasStar` variable in the factor graph of Figure 5.19.

the first three binary variables are `true` and the other two are `false`. Figure 5.20 shows the relationship between the star rating and the binary values used for the observation of `hasStar`.

When we train this model, we set `hasStar` to the observed values given in Figure 5.20 for the corresponding rating. When using the model to make a recommendation, we get back a posterior probability of each binary variable being true. These can be converted into the probability of having a particular number of stars using subtraction. For example, if we predict the probability of having 3 or more stars is 70% and the probability of having 4 or more stars is 60%, then the probability of having exactly 3 stars must be 70% − 60% = 10%. Using this trick, we can convert the individual binary probabilities back into separate probabilities for each star rating.

There are a few more details we need to work out before we can train this model. First, in our data set we need to be able to work with half-star ratings, such as $3\frac{1}{2}$ stars. We can handle these by doubling the number of thresholds, so that there are thresholds for both whole and half star ratings. Second, there is a symmetry between the star thresholds and the biases – adding a constant value to all user or movie biases and subtracting that value off all thresholds leads to the same predictions. This can be solved by fixing one of the thresholds to be zero – for our experiments we choose to fix the three star threshold to be zero. Finally, if you look at Figure 5.20, you will note that the first binary value is always `true`. This means that the affinity must always be greater than the lowest threshold, so we can simply remove it from the model. In our case, that means there will be no threshold for a $\frac{1}{2}$

star and so the lowest threshold will be for 1 star. With these changes in place, we are now ready to train!

5.5.1 Results with star ratings

Now that we can train on star ratings, we can use the same training data as before (Section 5.3) but without converting ratings to like/dislike. When we do this training, we expect that the extra information coming from the star ratings will allow us to locate movies more precisely in trait space. Back in Figure 5.14 we found that, after training on like/dislike, 158 of the movies had a posterior variance of less than 0.2 in each dimension of trait space. After training on star ratings, the number of movies with such low posterior variance increases to 539, showing that we have indeed managed to locate movies more precisely.

As part of training the model, we also learn Gaussian posterior thresholds for each star rating – these are shown in Figure 5.21.

These threshold posteriors are worth looking at. The first thing to note is that the thresholds are ordered correctly from 1 star through to 5 stars, as we would expect. This ordering was not enforced directly in the model since the priors for all the thresholds were the same – instead, the ordering has arisen from the way the model has been trained. Another thing to note is that the posterior distribution for 1 star is much broader than for other thresholds. This is because there are very few half stars and one stars in the training set (to confirm this look back at Figure 5.12). It is these ratings which are used to learn the 1 star threshold and so their relative scarcity leads to higher uncertainty in the threshold location. A final note is that the half star thresholds are

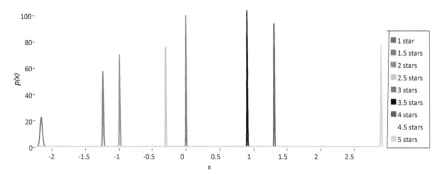

Figure 5.21 Posterior distributions for star ratings thresholds from 1 star to 5 stars. The threshold for 3 stars is fixed to be exactly zero – all other thresholds have been learned.

generally closer to the star rating above than the one below. For example, the $3\frac{1}{2}$ star threshold is much closer to the 4 star threshold than to the 3 star threshold. This implies that when a person gives $3\frac{1}{2}$ stars to a movie, in their minds they consider that to be almost as good as a 4 star movie, rather than just better than a 3 star movie. Another explanation is that some people may never use half stars (which would explain why they are relatively scarcer than the surrounding whole stars), which would introduce some bias in the inferred thresholds. It is an interesting exercise to think about how the model could be changed to reflect the fact that some people never use half stars.

Using our newly trained model, we can make predictions for exactly the same people and movies as we did in Section 5.4. Now our model is predicting star ratings, we can plot the most probable star rating, instead of posterior probabilities of like.

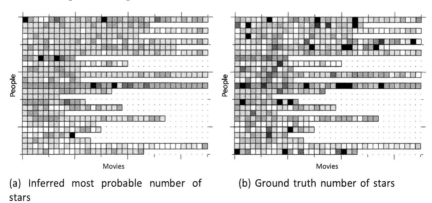

(a) Inferred most probable number of stars

(b) Ground truth number of stars

Figure 5.22 Results of our recommender model with star ratings. (a) Predicted most probable ratings, where white squares correspond to five stars, black to half a star and shades of grey represent intermediate numbers of stars. (b) Ground truth ratings using the same colour key.

Figure 5.22a shows nicely that we are now able to predict numbers of stars, rather than just like or dislike. Comparing the two plots, we can see that there are sometimes darker or lighter regions in our predictions corresponding to those in the ground truth – but that equally often there are not. It is almost impossible to look at Figure 5.22 and say whether the new model is making better recommendations than the old one. Instead we need to make a quantitative comparison, by recomputing the same metrics as before and comparing the results. For

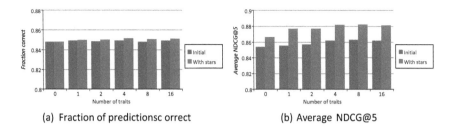

(a) Fraction of predictionsc orrect   (b) Average NDCG@5

Figure 5.23 Comparison of two metrics for the old like/dislike model and the new model with star ratings. The star ratings model gives a significant boost to NDCG, and even shows a small improvement in like/dislike accuracy.

NDCG, we can rank our recommendations by star rating and compute the metric exactly as before. For like/dislike accuracy, we need to convert our star predictions back into binary like/dislike predictions. We can do this by summing up the probabilities of all ratings of 3 stars or higher – if this sum is greater than 0.5, then we predict that the person will like the movie, otherwise that they will dislike it. Figure 5.23 shows that our new model has a significantly improved NDCG than the previous model, demonstrating the value of using the full star ratings. The improvement even shows up in our relatively insensitive fraction-correct metric, although the change is much smaller.

Because we add together probabilities of different star ratings when computing that the like/dislike accuracy metric, we are throwing away information about our recommendations. For example, we are throwing away whether we predicted 3, 4 or 5 stars. The result will be to make the metric less sensitive to improvements in accuracy. We only computed it for Figure 5.23 so that we could compare to the results of the initial model. Now that we have predictions of star ratings, we need to replace this metric with a new one that can make use of ratings. For this new metric, we could look at the fraction of times that the predicted rating correctly matched the ground truth rating. However, this would mean that a prediction that is half a star out would be treated the same as one that is four stars out. Instead, we can look at how far the predicted number of stars was from the actual number of stars, so that the error is:

$$\text{Error} = |\text{Predicted star rating} - \text{Ground truth star rating}|. \quad (5.1)$$

In equation (5.1), the vertical bars mean that we take the absolute size of the difference. For example, if the prediction is two stars and the ground truth is five stars, the error will be 3.0. The error will also be

3.0 if we swap these over so that the prediction is five stars and the ground truth is two stars. Because we use this absolute size, we call this error the **absolute error**. To compute a metric over all predictions, we average the absolute errors of each prediction, giving a metric called the **mean absolute error** (MAE).

Figure 5.24 shows this metric computed for varying numbers of traits in our new model. Taking all three metrics together, having more traits generally seems to give better quality recommendations. So we can choose to use the 16-trait version of our latest model which gives an NDCG@5 of 0.881 and an MAE of 0.663. While this gives us our best performing recommender system yet, it would still be good to make further improvements. In the next section, we'll diagnose where we are still making mistakes and look at one way to further improve our recommendation accuracy.

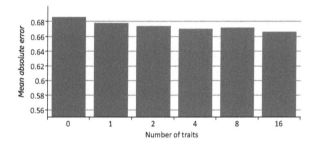

Figure 5.24 Mean absolute error for different numbers of traits in our new star rating model. The MAE generally decreases slightly as we increase the number of traits.

REVIEW OF CONCEPTS

absolute error   The difference between a predicted value and the corresponding ground truth value, ignoring the sign of the result. The absolute error between 2 stars and 5 stars is 3. The absolute error between 5 stars and 2 stars is also 3. Because we ignore the sign, the absolute error is always positive (or zero).

mean absolute error   The average (mean) of the absolute error between a predicted value and the ground truth value, across all predictions. The best possible value for this metric is 0. All other values will be positive numbers, with smaller values considered better than larger ones.

5.6 ANOTHER COLD START PROBLEM

When we plotted the position of movies in trait space (Figure 5.14), we showed only those movies where the position was known reasonably accurately (that is, where the posterior variance was low). It follows that there are many movies where the posterior variance is larger, possibly much larger. This means that we essentially do not know where some movies are in trait space. We might expect these to be the movies which do not have many ratings. If we do not know where some movies are in trait space, then we might also expect the accuracy of recommendations relating to such movies to be low. How can we diagnose if this is the case?

First, it would be useful to understand how many ratings each movie typically has. Figure 5.25 shows the number of ratings for each movie in the data set as a whole, with the movies ordered from most ratings on the left to least ratings on the right.

From Figure 5.25, we can see that only about 500 of the 9,000 movies have more than 50 ratings. Looking more closely, only around 2,000 movies have more than 10 ratings. This leaves us with 7,000 movies that have 10 or fewer ratings – of which about 3,000 have only a single rating! It would not be surprising if such movies cannot be placed accurately in trait space, using rating information alone. As a result, we might expect that our prediction accuracy would be lower for those movies with few ratings than for those with many.

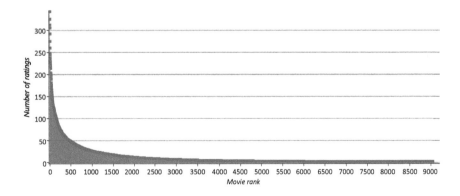

Figure 5.25 The number of ratings given for each movie in the data set as a whole. The movies are ordered from most ratings on the left to least ratings on the right.

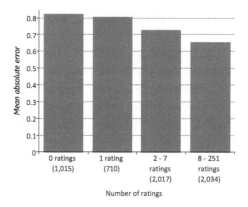

Figure 5.26 Mean absolute error for movies with different numbers of ratings in the training set, for a model with 16 traits. Each bar is labelled with the range of ratings and, in brackets, the number of movies that fall into that range. For example, the left-hand bar gives the MAE for movies with no ratings in the training set, of which there are 1,015. Comparing the four bars shows that movies with many ratings have substantially lower prediction errors than those with few or zero ratings.

To confirm this hypothesis, we can plot the mean absolute error across the movies divided into groups according to the number of ratings they have in the training set. This plot is shown in Figure 5.26 for an experiment with 16 traits. For this experiment, we added into the validation set the movies that do not have any ratings in the training set (the left-hand bar in Figure 5.26). This provides a useful reference since it shows what the MAE is for movies with no ratings at all. The plot shows that when we have just one rating (second bar), we do not actually reduce the MAE much compared to having zero ratings (first bar). For movies with more and more ratings, the mean absolute error drops significantly, as shown by the third and fourth bars in Figure 5.26. Overall, this figure shows clearly that we are doing better at predicting ratings for movies that have more ratings – and very badly for those movies with just one.

Figure 5.26 confirms that we have an accuracy problem for movies with few ratings. This is particularly troubling in practice since newly released movies are likely to have relatively few ratings but are also likely to be the most useful recommendations for users. So how can we solve this problem? Recalling Section 4.6 from the previous chapter,

Table 5.4 A sample of the additional information available for each movie.

Name	Year	Genres
GoldenEye	1995	{Action, Adventure, Thriller}
Sense and Sensibility	1995	{Drama, Romance}
Willow	1988	{Action, Adventure, Fantasy}
Antz	1998	{Adventure, Animation, Children, Comedy, Fantasy}
Fly, The	1986	{Drama, Horror, SciFi, Thriller}
Time Bandits	1981	{Adventure, Comedy, Fantasy, SciFi}
Blazing Saddles	1974	{Comedy, Western}
Clueless	1995	{Comedy, Romance}
Seven (a.k.a. Se7en)	1995	{Mystery, Thriller}
Usual Suspects, The	1995	{Crime, Mystery, Thriller}

we can think of this as another cold start problem. We need to be able to make recommendations about a movie even though we have few or even zero ratings for that movie.

Apart from ratings, what other information do we have that could be used to improve our recommendations? Looking at our data set, we see that it also includes the year of release and the genres that each movie belongs to. A sample of this additional information is shown in Table 5.4.

If we could use this information to place our movies more accurately in trait space, perhaps that would improve our recommendations for movies where we only have a few ratings. We can try this out by adding this information to our model using features, just like we did in the previous chapter.

5.6.1 Adding features to our model

To add features to our recommender model, we can re-use a chunk of the classification model from Section 4.3. Specifically, we will introduce variables for the `featureValue` for each movie and feature, along with a `weight` for each feature and trait. As before, the product of these will give a `featureScore`. The sum of these feature scores will now be used as the mean for the trait prior – which we shall call `traitMean`. It follows that the prior position of the movie in trait space can now change, depending on the feature values, before any ratings have been

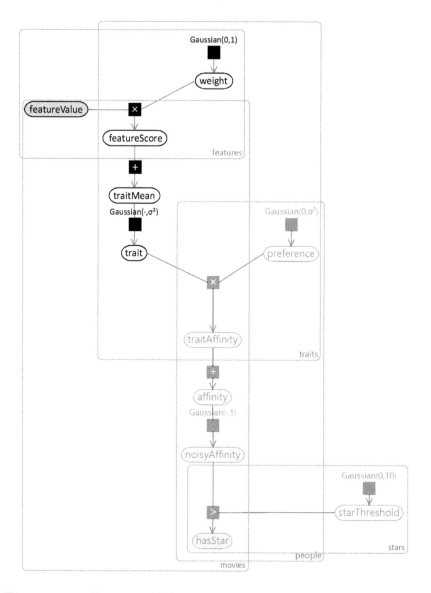

Figure 5.27 Factor graph for a recommender model that can consume feature values for individual movies. To emphasise the variables and factors which have been added, the remaining parts of the graph have been faded out.

seen! The resulting factor graph is shown in Figure 5.27 – the unchanged part of the graph has been faded out to make the newly-added part stand out.

In taking this chunk of model from the previous chapter, we must remember that we have also inherited the corresponding assumptions. Translated into the language of our model, these are:

⑦ The feature values can always be calculated, for any movie.

⑧ If a movie's feature value changes by x, then each trait mean will move by *weight* $\times x$ for some fixed, continuous, trait-specific weight.

⑨ The weight for a feature and trait is equally likely to be positive or negative.

⑩ A single feature normally has a small effect on a trait mean, sometimes has an intermediate effect and occasionally has a large effect.

⑪ A particular change in one feature's value will cause the same change in each trait mean, no matter what the values of the other features are.

We explored these assumptions extensively in the previous chapter, so will not discuss them again here. However, it would be a worthwhile exercise to spend some time reflecting on how each assumption will affect the behaviour of our recommender system.

As in the previous chapter, we need to decide how to represent our movie information as features. The features that we will use are:

1. A constant feature set to 1.0 for all movies used to capture any fixed bias.

2. A *Release Year* feature which is represented using buckets, much like the *BodyLength* feature we designed in Section 4.4. We choose the buckets to be every ten years until 1980 and then every five years after that – giving 17 buckets in total.

3. A *Genres* features which has the same design as the *Recipients* feature from Section 4.5. That is, a total feature value of 1.0 is split evenly among the genres that a movie has. So if a movie is a Drama and a Romance, the Drama bucket will have a value of 0.5 and the Romance bucket will also have a value of 0.5.

This data set contains additional information about the movies but not about the people giving the ratings (such as age or gender). If we had such additional information we could incorporate it into our model using features, just as we did for movies. All we would need to do is add a features model for the mean of the **preference** prior of the same form as the one used for the **trait** prior in Figure 5.27. The resulting model would then be symmetrical between the movies/traits and people/preferences.

5.6.2   Results with features

Let's see what effect using movie features has on our accuracy metrics. Figure 5.28 shows the mean absolute error for models with and without features, for groups of movies with different numbers of ratings. We can see that adding features has improved accuracy for all four groups, with the biggest improvements in the groups with zero ratings. While there is still better accuracy for movies with more ratings, using features has helped narrow the gap between these movies and movies where few ratings are available.

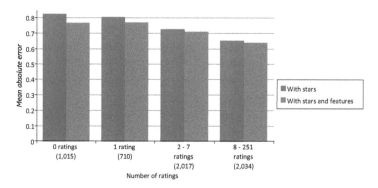

Figure 5.28 Including feature information in our model has reduced the prediction error, particularly for movies with only no ratings in the training set.

We can also look at the effect of using features on our overall metrics. These are shown for different numbers of traits in Figure 5.29. For comparison with previous results, we once again exclude ratings for movies that do not occur in the training set (that is, the left-hand bar of Figure 5.28). The chart shows that features increase accuracy whichever metric we look at. Interestingly, this increase is greater when more traits are used. The explanation for this effect is that we are not directly using features to make recommendations but instead we are using them indirectly to position movies in trait space. Using more

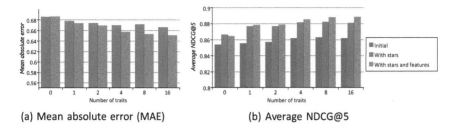

(a) Mean absolute error (MAE)   (b) Average NDCG@5

Figure 5.29 Comparison of MAE and NDCG metrics for each of our models. Note that MAE cannot be calculated for the initial model because it does not predict star ratings. According to these metrics, feature increases accuracy for any model with at least one trait, with the increase being larger as more traits are used.

traits helps us to capture the feature information more precisely, since a position in trait space conveys more information when there are more traits.

Overall, using features has provided a good increase in accuracy, particularly for items with few ratings. This means that our model should now do a much better job of making recommendations for new movies – which is a very desirable characteristic!

5.6.3 Final thoughts

In this chapter, we have developed a recommender model that can consume either like/dislike labels or full star ratings. The model can also make use of additional information about the items being recommended. As a result, this model is already enough to be valuable for many customers of Azure machine learning – and indeed is very close to the one that was actually used in Azure ML. The main difference is that the Azure ML model can also learn personalised star ratings thresholds. This was achieved by moving the `starThreshold` variable inside the people plate and giving each threshold a suitably informative prior, to allow for data scarcity.

In developing our model, we have assumed that a good recommendation is one where the user will rate the item highly, but in fact this may not be the case. A science fiction fan may rate Star Wars highly, but it would be a poor recommendation since they would almost certainly already seen it. In other words, a good recommendation is for a movie that you are likely to enjoy but not to have already seen. Real recommendation systems keep a record of what movies a person has seen through the system and these are automatically removed from any list of recommendations. But such systems have no knowledge of what movies have been watched *outside* of the system. We could modify our model to predict both whether someone would like a movie and whether they are likely to have seen it. Using both of these predictions together would lead to more valuable recommendations.

By learning the positions of items in trait space, we have also learned which items are similar, since these will be close to each other. Given a target item, we can find similar items by searching for

Similar items are nearby in trait space.

nearby items in trait space. More precisely, we can do this by making recommendations for an imaginary person located at the same position in trait space as the target item. The result of this process is useful for making item-specific recommendations, such as "people who liked this movie, also liked". Item relatedness can also be used to improve the diversity in a set of recommendations. For example, we might not want to have two very similar movies in a list of recommendations (such as two movies in the same series). We could use the distance between the movies in trait space to remove such similar movies and so create a more diverse list of recommendations.

There are further model extensions that could usefully be made. One would be to make use of *implicit* feedback about an item. For example, many people never rate any movie, but instead just watch them. Even in this case, there is still useful information about the movies that the person likes. We may assume that they watch movies that they expect to like – so watching a movie is an implicit signal that the person liked the movie. It is harder to get an implicit signal that a person did not like a movie and so often implicit feedback provides positive-only data. In other words, we have only the good ratings and none of the bad ones. Having a model that can cope with such positive-only data would be very useful – the most common approach today is to treat a random sample of unrated movies as if they were negatively rated.

Even when we do have ratings, the information about which ratings we have and which we do not have is very valuable. Having a rating is a bit like watching a movie – it provides a positive signal about liking the movie. The best performing recommender systems make use of missing ratings to provide information about what a person likes or dislikes. With any piece of data that can be missing, we can model whether or not it is missing, as well as modelling the data itself. In the next chapter, we will discuss different kinds of missing data and how to handle them – in the very different scenario of understanding childhood asthma.

CHAPTER 6

Understanding asthma

Globally around 450,000 people die each year from asthma. If we could better understand what causes people to develop asthma, it would have a hugely beneficial impact on asthma detection, diagnosis and treatment. Can model-based machine learning help provide this deeper understanding?

Asthma is a very common disease which affects around 5% of people in the UK [Anderson et al., 2007] and about 7% in the US [Fanta, 2009]. Asthma can have extremely serious outcomes for those who suffer from it. One known risk factor for developing asthma is if a person has allergies, but the relationship between allergies and asthma is not well understood. An improved understanding of this relationship could potentially allow early detection of the kind of severe asthma that can lead to hospitalisation or worse.

DOI: 10.1201/9780429192685-7

The Manchester Asthma and Allergy Study (MAAS) is a study designed to help understand the causes of childhood asthma and allergies [Custovic et al., 2002]. In particular, the study aims to understand why some children with allergies develop asthma while others do not. MAAS is a birth cohort study – in other words, people were recruited into the study at birth – and consists of around 1,000 people. The study began in 1995 and continues to this day, collecting ongoing data about the study participants, who are now young adults. As you might imagine, a huge amount of dedication and commitment is required of these participants and their families – we and the study team are immensely grateful to them all!

In this chapter, we will look at how to apply model-based machine learning to data collected in this study, to model the onset of childhood allergies and see how this relates to the development of asthma. This kind of machine learning application is different from those we have looked at in previous chapters, because we are interested in improving understanding as a primary goal of the project, rather than predicting who will develop asthma without any understanding of why. It's worth looking at these two contrasting goals in a bit more detail:

- **Predictive machine learning** – the goal is to make predictions, without requiring an explanation of the predictions. This kind of goal is common when building automated systems where explanations are not needed.

- **Explanatory machine learning** – the goal is to explain or understand patterns in the data. This kind of goal is common when doing scientific or medical research, where there is a human in the loop who wishes to understand the processes that give rise to the data.

Often there are elements of both of these goals in a particular machine learning project. For example, when doing predictions it may be useful to provide some explanation of those predictions. And even when the primary goal is improved understanding, such as in this asthma project, it may still be useful to apply that understanding to make predictions, such as predicting whether a child will develop asthma.

The model developed in this chapter was created as part of a collaboration with the MAAS team, particularly Professors Adnan Custovic and Angela Simpson, as described in Simpson et al. [2010] and Lazic et al. [2013].

You can create results like those in this chapter using the companion source code [Diethe et al., 2019]. Since we cannot distribute the actual medical data used in this work, we have provided a synthetic data set that gives similar results to the true data.

6.1 A MODEL OF ALLERGIES

Our primary goal is to improve our understanding of allergy development, as it relates to childhood asthma, by looking for patterns in the MAAS data. To understand the relevant data in the study, we need to learn a little bit about diagnosing allergies. The doctors in the study used two types of test to try to detect if a person is allergic to a specific **allergen**, such as cat hair or peanuts. The two types of test were:

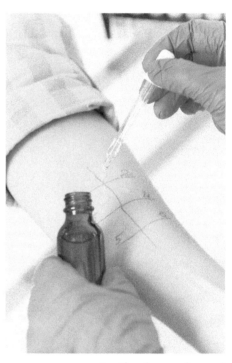

- A **skin prick test** where a drop of allergen solution is placed on the patient's skin (see image) which is then pricked with a needle. If the skin shows an immune response in the form of a red bump of a certain size, then the test is positive, otherwise it is negative.

- An allergen-specific **IgE test** – this is a blood test that looks for a kind of antibody called Immunoglobulin E (IgE) that specifically targets a particular allergen. The presence of this antibody is an indicator that the patient is allergic to that allergen. If this antibody is present in sufficient quantities the test is positive, otherwise negative.

If a child has a positive skin prick test or IgE test for an allergen, then they are said to be *sensitised* to that allergen.

For the children taking part in this study, both of these tests were performed for eight allergens: dust mite, cat, dog, pollen, mould, milk, egg and peanut. So that the development of allergies could be tracked over time, the tests were repeated at different ages (1, 3, 5 and 8). Therefore, the available data points are the two test results for each allergen, for each child, at each of the four ages.

The clinicians on the study believe that different patterns of allergies make children susceptible to different diseases, some of which may have significant impact on the child's health (such as severe asthma) and some of which may be more benign (such as mild hayfever). The goal of the project is to identify such patterns and see if they are indicative of developing particular diseases and of the severity of the disease. Our task is to develop a model of the allergen data set that can achieve this.

6.1.1 Modelling test results

To start with, let's consider a model of a child's test results for one allergen at one point in time. First, we need variables for the results of each test – we will call these `skinTest` and `igeTest`. These variables will be `true` if the corresponding test is positive and `false` if the test is negative.

Remember that the purpose of these tests is to try and detect whether a child is actually sensitised (allergic) to a particular allergen. However, the tests are not perfectly consistent – for example, it is not unusual for a child to have a positive IgE test but a negative skin test. To cope with such inconsistencies, we can have a variable representing whether the child is truly sensitised to the allergen, which we will call `sensitised`. This variable will be `true` if the child is actually sensitised to the allergen and false if they are not sensitised. We then allow for the results of the tests to occasionally disagree with the value of this variable. In other words, we assume that each test can give a false positive (where the test is positive but the child is not sensitised) or a false negative (where the test is negative but the child is sensitised).

If a child is sensitised to a particular allergen (`sensitised=true`), then a skin prick test will be positive (`skinTest=true`) with some probability, which we will call `probSkinIfSens`. Since we expect the test to be mostly correct we would expect this probability to be high but less than one, since a skin prick test can give false negatives. Conversely, even if a child is <u>not</u> sensitised to a particular allergen (`sensitised=false`), then we might occasionally expect a skin prick test to be positive, but with some low probability `probSkinIfNotSens`. Although this probability is low, we still expect it to be greater than zero because a skin prick test can give false positives.

These two probabilities together define a conditional probability table for `skinTest` conditioned on `sensitised` (Table 6.1).

We have introduced these two probabilities as random variables in our model because we will want to learn them from data, in order

Table 6.1 The conditional probability table for $P(\texttt{skinTest}\mid$ $\texttt{sensitised})$ Table columns correspond to values of the conditioned variable `skinTest`, rows correspond to values of the conditioning variable `sensitised`, and table cells contain the conditional probability values.

sensitised	skinTest=true (positive)	skinTest=false (negative)
true	probSkinIfSens	1 - probSkinIfSens
false	probSkinIfNotSens	1 - probSkinIfNotSens

to determine the false positive and false negative rates for the skin prick test. In order to learn their values, we must provide suitable prior distributions for each variable, that encode our assumptions about them. Let's write down those assumptions:

① If a child is sensitised to a particular allergen, there is a high probability that they will get a positive test.

② If a child is NOT sensitised to a particular allergen, there is a low probability that they will get a positive test.

As in Section 2.6, we can use beta distributions as prior distributions over probabilities that can represent these assumptions. Assumption ① says that we expect `probSkinIfSens` to be high so we can use a $Beta(2,1)$ prior which favours higher probability values. Assumption ② says that we expect `probSkinIfNotSens` to be low so we can use a $Beta(1,2)$ prior which favours low probability values. Armed with these prior probabilities, we can now draw a factor graph for a skin test, using the *Table* factor that we introduced back in Section 2.6.

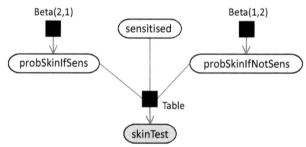

Figure 6.1 A model relating the result of a skin prick test (`skinTest`) to the underlying allergic sensitisation state (`sensitised`). The `skinTest` variable is observed to equal the actual outcome of the test and so is shown shaded.

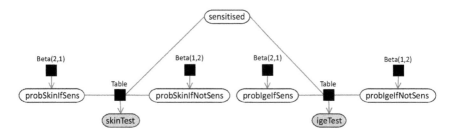

Figure 6.2 A model relating the results of both kinds of allergy test to the underlying allergic sensitisation state. Each type of test has its own probability variables which means that each test can have different false positive and false negative rates. The test results are observed and so are shown shaded.

Now that we have a model for a skin test, we can add in the corresponding model for an IgE test. We again need probability variables for the probability of a positive test if sensitised `probIgeIfSens` and if not sensitised `probIgeIfNotSens` with the corresponding beta distribution priors. The `sensitised` variable is shared between the two tests, because both tests are attempting to detect the same underlying sensitisation. The resulting factor graph for both tests is shown in Figure 6.2.

Inference in this model enables us to fuse the outcomes of both tests into a single underlying sensitisation state. Learning the probabilities of true and false positives will let the model learn which test to pay most attention to. For example, if a test has a high false positive probability, then a positive outcome would influence the inference of the sensitisation state less than a positive outcome for a test with a low false positive probability.

6.1.2 Modelling tests through time

For each child, we have test measurements at multiple points in time – ages 1, 3, 5 and 8. Such a collection of measurements is known as a **time series**, and analysis of such data is known as **time series analysis**. To understand the development of allergies, we need to build a model of a time series of allergy test results.

We could start building a time series model by duplicating the factor graph of Figure 6.2 at each time point. This would introduce a separate `sensitised` variable at each age, which we could call `sensitised1`, sensitised3, sensitised5 and sensitised8. It would also introduce separate test result variables at each age, which we could similarly call skinTest1, igeTest1, skinTest3, igeTest3 and so on. However, directly duplicating the factor graph would also mean having separate variables at each time point for the probability of a positive test given sensitised/not sensitised. Do we really expect the false positive and false negative rates for the tests to change over time? If exactly the same tests were done at each age, it would be reasonable to assume that the false positive and false negative rates did not change over time. Let's write down this assumption:

③ For each type of test, the false positive and false negative rates are the same for all such tests carried out in the study.

The consequence of this assumption is that the skin test probability variables (probSkinIfSens, probSkinIfNotSens) and the IgE test probability variables (probIgeIfSens, probIgeIfNotSens) will be shared across all time points. The result of this sharing is the factor graph of Figure 6.3.

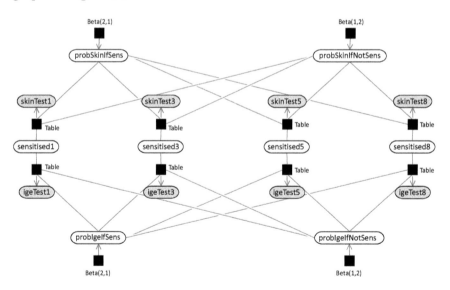

Figure 6.3 An initial model of a time series of allergy test results, which are explained by a series of underlying sensitisations. The false positive/false negative probability variables for each test are shared across all time points.

You might wonder why we have drawn out the variables for each time point, rather than use a plate to collapse them all together. This is because, when modelling time series, we expect variables later in time to depend on the values of variables earlier in time. By drawing out all variables, we can now add factors connecting variables across time. But what should these factors be?

At age 1, there is a certain initial probability that a child will already be sensitised to a particular allergen – let's call this `probSens1`. Now, suppose the child is not sensitised at age 1 (`sensitised1=false`), there is some probability that they will become sensitised by age 3 – let's call this `probGain3`. Conversely, if the child is sensitised at age 1 (`sensitised1=true`), there is some probability that they retain that sensitisation to age 3 – let's call this `probRetain3`. We can model this using a *Table* factor, just as we did for modelling the skin and IgE tests.

When we consider age 5, we need to ask ourselves a question: do we think that the sensitisation at age 5 depends on both previous sensitisations (at ages 1 and 3), or just the most recent one (at age 3). Similarly, do we think that sensitisation at age 8 depends on all three previous sensitisations (at ages 1, 3 and 5) or just the most recent one (at age 5). Either of these assumptions might be reasonable, depending on the details of how the immune system functions. For now, we will assume that just the most recent sensitisation is relevant since that simplifies the model the most:

④ Whether a child is sensitised to an allergen at a particular time point depends only on whether they were sensitised to that allergen at the previous time point.

This kind of assumption is so common in time series modelling that it even has a name – it is called a **Markov assumption** after the Russian mathematician Andrey Markov. Our Markov assumption means that we can model sensitisation at ages 5 and 8 just like we did at age 3. So for age 5, we have variables `probGain5` and `probRetain5` for the probabilities of gaining or retaining sensitisation between the ages of 3 and 5. Similarly, for age 8, we have variables `probGain8` and `probRetain8` for the probabilities of gaining or retaining sensitisation between the ages of 5 and 8. As for age 3, we can model sensitivity at ages 5 and 8 using a *Table* factor, giving the factor graph of Figure 6.4.

Looking at Figure 6.4, you can see the chain of factors connecting the sensitisation variables through time, from `sensitised1` through

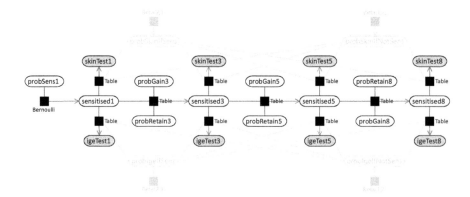

Figure 6.4 An improved time series model where the allergic sensitisation at each point in time, depends on the sensitisation at the previous point in time. The variables and factors relating to the test false positive/false negative rates have been dimmed, to emphasise the new factors added in the model.

to `sensitised8`. This kind of chain structure is a common feature of time series model that make Markov assumptions, and so is called a **Markov chain**.

6.1.3 Completing the model

To complete our time series model, we need to extend it to cover multiple allergens and multiple children. We can add plates for allergens and children and place the sensitisation and skin/IgE test variables inside both plates, since there are tests and sensitisation states for every child and allergen. Assumption ③ says that the false positive and false negative rates of our tests are the same throughout the study, and so the variables `probSkinIfSens`, `probIgeIfSens`, `probSkinIfNotSens` and `probIgeIfNotSens` lie outside both plates. This leaves only the variables relating to the probability of initial having, gaining and retaining sensitisation. We want these variables to be able to vary between allergens, so we can learn if different allergies are gained or lost at different points in time. So these variables must lie *inside* the **allergens** plate. But if we are trying to learn patterns of gaining or losing sensitisation that are common to multiple children, we must have these probability variables shared across children. Right now, the only way of doing this is to place them outside the **children** plate. This corresponds to the following assumption, which is the final assumption of the model:

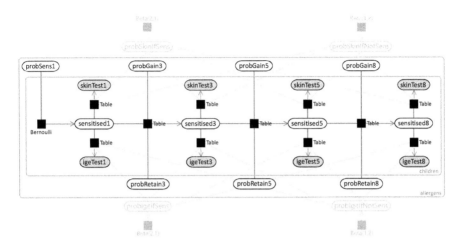

Figure 6.5 A complete model of a set of allergy tests for multiple children and multiple allergens. Plates are used to duplicate certain variables across children and allergens (see text for discussion). As in Figure 6.4, the variables and factors relating to the test false positive/false negative rates have been dimmed, to make the factor graph easier to read and to emphasise the Markov chain.

⑤ The probabilities relating to initially having, gaining or retaining sensitisation to a particular allergen are the same for all children.

Given this assumption, we can now draw the factor graph with plates, where the variables have been appropriately placed inside or outside each plate (see Figure 6.5).

Reviewing Figure 6.5, you can see that:

- the test false positive/false negative probabilities are outside both plates and so are shared across all children and allergens;

- the probabilities of initially having, gaining and retaining sensitisation are inside the allergens plate but outside the children plate, so are shared across children but can differ across allergens;

- the test results and sensitisation are inside both plates, since there are tests and sensitisation states for each child and allergen.

Given these plates, we now have a complete model that we can use with our data set of skin and IgE test results.

6.1.4 Reviewing our assumptions

As in previous chapters, we should take a moment to review our modelling assumptions. They are shown all together in Table 6.2.

Assumption ① and Assumption ② seem to be safe assumptions – doctors would not use these tests if they were not correct most of the time. Assumption ③ seems like a plausible assumption, but we might worry that the tests have different false positive/false negative rates for different allergens. It might also be possible that the test was improved or updated during the study and so that the rates would change over time. To check this out we consulted with the MAAS clinicians and they confirmed that the tests were performed exactly the same way throughout the study – the same test methodology, the same allergen solutions, even the same person doing the tests! So it seems like this assumption is a relatively safe one.

Assumption ④ is our Markov assumption – this is a common simplifying assumption but is also commonly criticised as being too simplistic. For example, in our case, it says that the probability of gaining/retaining sensitisation depends only the sensitisation state at the previous time point and not, for example, on how long the child has had

Table 6.2 The five assumptions encoded in our allergy model.

① If a child is sensitised to a particular allergen, there is a high probability that they will get a positive test.

② If a child is NOT sensitised to a particular allergen, there is a low probability that they will get a positive test.

③ For each type of test, the false positive and false negative rates are the same for all such tests carried out in the study.

④ Whether a child is sensitised to an allergen at a particular time point depends only on whether they were sensitised to that allergen at the previous time point.

⑤ The probabilities relating to initially having, gaining or retaining sensitisation to a particular allergen are the same for all children.

the sensitisation (or lack of sensitisation). Nonetheless, this assumption keeps the model simple and so we will stick with it.

Finally, Assumption ⑤ says that all children have the same patterns of gaining and losing sensitisation. This assumption goes against the very purpose of the project, which is to identify how these patterns vary between children. We will spend much of the rest of this chapter looking at how to improve on this assumption, but it is useful to keep it in place for now so we explore the behaviour of our new model.

REVIEW OF CONCEPTS

allergen   A substance which someone can be allergic to, such as cat hair or peanuts.

skin prick test   A test where a drop of allergen solution is placed on the patient's skin, which is then pricked with a needle. If the skin shows an immune response in the form of a red bump of a certain size, then the test is positive, otherwise it is negative.

IgE test   A blood test that looks for a kind of antibody called Immunoglobulin E (IgE) that specifically targets a particular allergen. If this antibody is present in sufficient quantities the test is positive, otherwise negative.

time series   A series of data points, listed in time order, that represent the measurement of some quantity over time – such as a stock price, blood pressure or population counts.

time series analysis   Analysis of a time series, so as to understand the time-varying process underlying the time series data.

Markov assumption   The assumption that a state of a process depends only on the previous state of that process, and not any earlier states. Named after the Russian mathematician Andrey Markov.

Markov chain   A random process such that the probability distribution of the next state depends only on the previous state and not on any earlier state. In a factor graph, a Markov chain appears as a chain of time series variables with adjacent variables connected by factors.

6.2 TRYING OUT THE MODEL

Now that we have a complete model, we are ready to try it out on some study data. As we've emphasised many times before in this book, when using a real data set, it is *essential* to look carefully at the data set to make sure that it is complete, correct and has the form that you expect. Remember that many common machine learning problems are caused by problems with data (such as those listed in Section 2.5). A good way to check your data set is to construct visualisations that let you to see at a glance what it looks like. In this case, we need to create visualisations of the test results for each child, allergen and time point. However, this study data set contains private medical data and so we cannot share the data publicly in this book, even in the form of a visualisation. The most important thing that we learned from doing this visualisation is that there are a lot of test results missing from the data set.

When there are **missing data**, it is always worth analysing to understand why they are missing. In Figure 6.6, we plot the number of test results in the data set (whether positive or negative) for each age and type of test.

You can see several different patterns of missing data in Figure 6.6. First, the plot shows that there are ages and test types that have no data for particular allergens. For example, peanut has no results at all for ages 1 and 3, and only IgE results at age 5. Mould has no IgE results at all, and no skin test results at age 1. Second, there is a lot more missing data at early ages, particularly age 1. Third, the plot

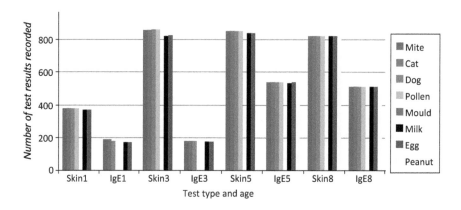

Figure 6.6 The test results recorded for each of the two types of tests, split by age of child.

shows that there is a lot more missing data overall for IgE tests than skin tests. We need to take into consideration the effect of all these missing data points.

6.2.1 Working with missing data

Missing data can introduce bias into the posterior distributions computed by running inference on a model, leading to incorrect or misleading results. Whether or not this effect will occur, and how big the bias will be, depends on why the data points are missing in the first place. In statistics, it is common to consider three kinds of missingness, which are referred to using the following (quite confusing!) terms:

Missing data can obscure or distort the patterns in a data set.

- **missing completely at random** (MCAR) – where the missing data points occur entirely at random. In other words, the fact that the data is missing is independent of the value of the missing data point (the test result that would have been given had the test actually happened).

  When data is MCAR, the remaining, non-missing, data points are effectively just a random subset of the overall data set. In this case, the posterior distributions computed by probabilistic inference will be unbiased by the missing data. Unfortunately, in reality, missing data is rarely missing completely at random. However, it may be an acceptable approximation to assume that it is – in which case, this assumption should be made with full understanding of the possibility of introducing biases.

- **missing at random** (MAR) – where the missingness is not random, but where other known data values fully account for the fact that the data is missing. For example, suppose that boys are more likely to refuse an IgE test than girls. Considering the fact that boys are more likely to have allergies, this would introduce a bias in our results, since the missing tests would be more likely to be positive than the non-missing tests.

  When data is MAR, it is possible to correct for the bias, at least to some extent, by changing the model appropriately to account for why the data is missing. This extension requires creating a new variable in the model for each data point, which is `true` if the data point is missing and `false` otherwise, and then building a suitable sub model to explain this new variable. For example, if boys are more likely than girls to skip an IgE test, then to correct for bias we would need to extend our model to represent this effect, such as by adding a new `gender` variable connected to the missingness variable. We would also need to allow this `gender` variable to affect the probability of sensitisation in an appropriate way. The degree to which this approach corrects the bias introduced by missing data, depends on how good the model of missingness is. As ever, a better model will give better results.

- **missing not at random** (MNAR) – where the missingness is not either MCAR or MAR. In this case, the fact that a data point is missing depends on the value of that data point. For example, this would occur if children with lots of allergies were more likely to skip a skin prick test because of concerns about the discomfort involved in having a positive test. Or such children might be more used to medical interventions and so may be less likely to skip a blood test due to fear of needles.

  When data is MNAR, it is not possible to correct for the bias without making modelling assumptions about the nature of the bias (which could be dangerous as there would be no data to verify such assumptions). One possible approach would be to try and collect additional information relevant to why the data is missing, in the hope that this would now make it missing at random (MAR).

For more information on handling missing data, see Little and Rubin [2014].

For our study, we need to find out why the various patterns of missing data arose. Consulting again with the MAAS team, we find that:

1. The clinicians chose to omit mould tests at age 1, since this is a rare allergy and there was a desire to minimise the number of tests performed on babies. Similarly, a decision was made half way through the study to add in peanut tests.

2. The reduced number of tests at age 1 are due to manpower limitations as the study was ramped up – not all children could be brought in for testing by age 1.

3. The greater number of missing IgE tests are due to children not wanting to give blood, or parents not wanting babies or young children to have blood taken.

For 1, we know why the data is missing–because the clinicians chose not to do certain tests. Such data can be assumed to be missing completely at random, since the choice of which tests to perform at each age was made independently of any test results. For 2, the study team chose whether to invite a child in for testing by age 1 and so could choose in a way that was not influenced by the child's allergies (such as at random). So again, we could assume such data to be missing completely at random. For 3, we might be more concerned, as now it is a decision of the child or the parents that is influencing whether the test is performed. This is more likely to be affected by the child's allergies, as we discussed above, and so it is possible that such missing data is not missing completely at random. For the sake of simplicity, we will assume that it is – this is such an important assumption that we should record it:

⑥ Missing test results are missing completely at random.

Having made this assumption, we should bear in mind that our inference results may contain biases. One reassuring point is that where we do not have an IgE test result, we often have a skin test result. This means that we still have some information about the underlying sensitisation state even when an IgE test result is missing, which is likely to diminish any bias caused by its missingness.

There is another impact of missing data. Even when missing data is not introducing bias, if there is a lot of missing data it can lead to uncertainty, in the form of very broad posterior distributions. For example, at several time points we have no data for mould or peanut and so the gain/retain probabilities for those ages would be very uncertain, and so have broad posterior distributions. When included in results plots, such broad distributions can distract from the remaining meaningful results. To keep our plots as clear as possible, we will simply drop the mould and peanut allergens from our data set and consider only the remaining six allergens.

6.2.2 Some initial results

Having decided to treat our missing data as missing completely at random, we are now in a position to apply expectation propagation to our model and get some results. Where we have a missing data point, we simply do not observe the value of the corresponding random variable.

Having run our inference algorithm, the first posterior distributions we will look at are those for `probSkinIfSens`, `probSkinIfNotSens`, `probIgeIfSens` and `probIgeIfNotSens`. These posteriors are beta distributions, which we can summarise using a mean plus or minus a value indicating the width of the beta distribution, as shown in Table 6.3.

The results in Table 6.3 show that the two types of test are complementary: the skin prick test has a very low false positive rate (¡1%) but as a result has a reduced true positive rate ($\sim 79\%$); in contrast, the IgE test has a high true positive rate ($\sim 93\%$) but as a result has a higher false positive rate ($\sim 4\%$). The complementary nature of the two tests show why they are both used together – each test brings additional information about the underlying sensitisation state of the child. During inference, our model will automatically take these true and false positive rates into account when inferring the sensitisation state at each time point, so it will gain the advantage of the strengths of both tests, whilst being able to minimise the weaknesses.

Next let's look at the inferred probabilities of initially having, gaining and retaining sensitisation for each allergen. Figure 6.7a shows the probability of initially having a sensitisation (age 1) and then the probability of gaining sensitisation (ages 3, 5, 8). Similarly, Figure 6.7b shows

Table 6.3 The probability of a positive test for each test type and for each sensitisation state The plus/minus values indicate the uncertainty in the probability given by the posterior beta distributions. The table shows that the skin test has a low false positive probability, but also a lower true positive probability. Conversely, the IgE test has a higher false positive probability, but a very high true positive probability. These results show that, taken together, the tests have complementary strengths and weaknesses.

	If Sensitised	If Not Sensitised
Prob. of Pos. Skin Test	79.0%±0.7%	0.5%±0.04%
Prob. of Pos. IgE Test	93.0%±0.6%	3.7%±0.1%

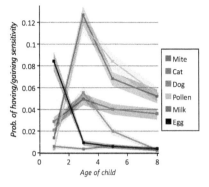

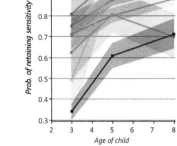

(a) The probability of having sensitivity (age 1) or subsequently gaining sensitivity (ages 3, 5 and 8).

(b) The probability of retaining sensitivity since the previous time point at ages 3, 5 and 8.

Figure 6.7 Plots showing the probabilities for (a) having/gaining and (b) retaining sensitisation for each time point and allergen.

the probability of retaining sensitisation since the previous time point (for ages 3, 5 and 8 only). Since each probability has a beta posterior distribution, the charts show the uncertainty associated with the probability values, using the lower and upper quartiles of each beta distribution.

Looking at Figure 6.7a and Figure 6.7b together, we can see that different allergens have different patterns of onset and loss of sensitisation. For example, there is a high initial probability of sensitivity to egg but, after that, a very low probability of gaining sensitivity. Egg also has the lowest probability of retaining sensitisation, meaning that children tend to have egg sensitivity very early in life and then rapidly lose it. As another example, mite and pollen have very low initial probabilities of sensitisation, but then very high probabilities of gaining sensitisation by age 3. Following sensitisation to mite or pollen, the probability of retaining that sensitisation is very high. In other words, children who gain sensitisation to mite or pollen are most likely to do so between ages 1 and 3 and will then likely retain that sensitisation (at least to age 8). Cat and dog have similar patterns of gain and loss to each other, but both have a higher initial probability of sensitisation and a lower peak than mite and pollen. Milk shows the lowest probabilities of sensitisation, meaning that it is a rare allergy in this cohort of children. As a result, the probability of retaining a milk sensitisation is more uncertain, since it is learned from relatively few children. This uncertainty is shown by the broad shaded region for milk in Figure 6.7b.

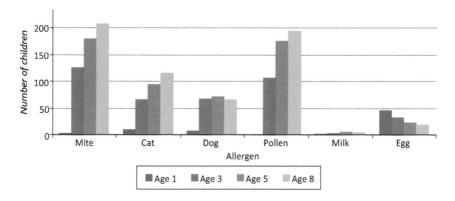

Figure 6.8 The number of children with inferred sensitisations for each allergen, at each point in time.

Another way of visualisaing these results is to look at the inferred sensitisations. We have inferred the posterior probability of each child having a sensitisation to each allergen at each time point. We can then count the number of children who are more likely to be sensitised than not sensitised (that is, where the probability is >50%). Plotting this count of sensitisations for each allergen and age gives Figure 6.8.

Figure 6.8 shows the patterns of gaining and losing sensitisation in a different way, by showing the count of sensitised children. The chart shows that egg allergies start off common and disappear over time. The chart also shows that mite and pollen allergies start between ages 1 and 3 and the total number of allergic children only increases with age. In many ways, this chart is easier to read than the line charts of Figure 6.7a and Figure 6.7b because it looks directly at the counts of sensitisations rather than at changes in sensitisations. Also, all the information appears on one chart rather than two. For this reason, we will use this kind of chart to present results as we evolve the model later in the chapter.

To summarise, we have built a model that can learn about the patterns of gaining and losing allergic sensitisation. The patterns that we have found apply to the entire cohort of children – effectively they are patterns for the population as a whole. What the model does not tell us is whether there are groups of children within the cohort that have different patterns of allergic sensitisation, which might give rise to different diseases. By looking at all children together, this information is lost. Reviewing our assumptions, the problematic assumption is this one:

⑤ The probabilities relating to initially having, gaining or retaining sensitisation to a particular allergen are the same for all children.

We'd really like to change the assumption to allow children to be in different groups, where each group of children can have different patterns of sensitisation. Let's call these groups "sensitisation classes". The assumption would then be:

⑤ The probabilities relating to initially having, gaining or retaining sensitisation to a particular allergen are the same for all children in each sensitisation class.

The problem is that we do not know which child is in which sensitisation class. We need a model that can represent alternative processes for gaining and losing sensitisation, and which can determine which process took place for each individual child. In other words, we need to be able to compare alternative models for each child's data and determine which is likely to be the one that gave rise to the data. To achieve this will require some new tools for modelling and inference, which we will introduce in the next section.

REVIEW OF CONCEPTS

missing data In a data set, a missing data point is one where no value is available for a variable in an observation. The reason for the value being missing is important and can affect the validity of probabilistic inference using the remaining non-missing values. See Section 6.2.1.

missing completely at random Where missing data points occur entirely at random. In other words, the fact that the data is missing is independent of the value of the missing data point.

missing at random Where missing data points do not occur at random, but where other known data values fully account for the fact that the data is missing.

missing not at random Where missing data is neither missing completely at random (MCAR) not missing at random (MAR). In this case, the fact that a data point is missing depends on the value of that data point. Where data is missing not at random, it is very difficult to avoid biases in the results of inference.

6.3 COMPARING ALTERNATIVE MODELS

In all the previous chapters, we have assumed that the data arose from a single underlying process. But now we can no longer presume this, since we expect there to be different processes for children who do develop allergies and asthma and for those who do not. To handle these kinds of alternative processes, we need to introduce a new modelling technique.

This technique will allow us to:

- Represent multiple alternative processes within a single model;

- Evaluate the probability that each alternative process gave rise to a particular data item (such as the data for a particular child);

- Compare two or more different models to see which best explains some data.

To introduce this new technique, we will need to put the asthma project to one side for now and instead look at a simple example of a two-process scenario (if you'd prefer to stay focused on the asthma project, skip ahead to Section 6.5). Since we are in the medical domain, there is a perfect two-process scenario available: the **randomised controlled trial**. A randomised controlled trial is a kind of clinical trial commonly used for testing the effectiveness of various types of medical intervention, such as new drugs. In such a trial, each subject is randomly assigned into either a

The goal of our randomised controlled trial will be to find out if a new drug is effective.

treated group (which receives the experimental intervention) or a control group (which does not receive the intervention). The purpose of the trial is to determine whether the experiment intervention has an effect on one or more outcomes of interest and to understand the nature of that effect.

Let's consider a simple trial to test the effectiveness of a new drug on treating a particular illness. We will use one outcome of interest – whether the patient made a full recovery from the illness. In modelling terms, the purpose of this trial is to determine which of the following two processes occurred:

1. A process where the drug <u>had no effect</u> on whether the patient recovered.

2. A process where the drug <u>did have an effect</u> on whether the patient recovered.

To determine which process took place, we need to build a model of each process and then compare them to see which best fits the data. In both models, the data is the same: whether or not each subject recovered. We can attach the data to each model using binary variables which are `true` if that subject recovered and `false` otherwise. We'll put these binary variables into two arrays: `recoveredControl` contains the variables for each subject in the control group and `recoveredTreated` similarly contains the variables for each subject in the treated group.

Model where the drug had no effect

Let's start with a model of the first process, where the drug had no effect. In this case, because the drug had no effect, there is no difference between the treated group and the control group. So we can use an assumption like this one:

① The (unknown) probability of recovery is the same for subjects in the treated and control groups.

It is perfectly possible that a subject could recover from the illness without any medical intervention (or with a medical intervention that does nothing). In this model, we assume that the drug has no effect and therefore all recoveries are of this kind. We do not know what the probability of such a spontaneous recovery is and so we can introduce a random variable `probRecovery` to represent it, with a uniform $Beta(1,1)$ prior. Then for each variable in the `recoveredControl` and `recoveredTreated` arrays, we assume that they were drawn from a Bernoulli distribution whose parameter is `probRecovery`. The resulting model is shown as a factor graph in Figure 6.9 – for a refresher on beta Bernoulli models like this one, take a look back at Chapter 2.

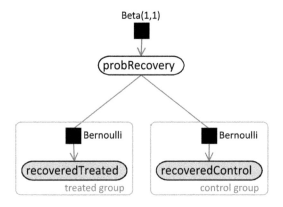

Figure 6.9 Factor graph for a process where the experimental drug has no effect. In this case, the probability of recovery is the same for the treated and control groups.

Model where the drug did have an effect

Now let's turn to the second process, where the drug did have an effect on whether the patient recovered. In this case, we need to assume that there is a different probability of recovery for the treated group and for the control group. We hope that there is a higher probability of recovery for the treated group, but we are not going to assume this. We are only going to assume that the probability of recovery changes if the drug is taken.

② The probability of recovery is different for subjects in the treated group and for subjects in the control group.

To encode this assumption in a factor graph, we need two variables: `probTreated` which is the probability of recovery for subjects who were given the drug and `probControl` which is the probability of recovery for subjects in the control group who were not given the drug. Once again, we choose uniform $Beta(1,1)$ priors over each of these variables. Then for each variable in the `recoveredControl` array, we assume that they were drawn from a Bernoulli distribution whose parameter is `probControl`. Conversely, for each variable in the `recoveredTreated` array, we assume that they were drawn from a Bernoulli distribution whose parameter is `probTreated`. The resulting model is shown in Figure 6.10.

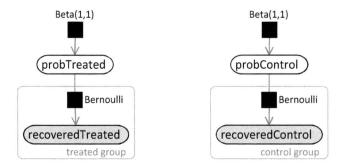

Figure 6.10 Factor graph for a process where the experimental drug does have an effect, and so the probability of recovery is different for the treated group and for the control group.

Compare the models of the two different processes given in Figures 6.9 and 6.10. You can see that the factor graphs are pretty similar. The only difference is that the "no effect" model has a single shared probability of recovery whilst the "has effect" model has different probabilities of recovery for the treated and control groups.

Selecting between the two models

We now need to decide which of these two models gave rise to the actual outcomes measured in the trial. The task of choosing which of several models best fits a particular data set is called **model selection**. In model-based machine learning, if we want to know the value of an unknown quantity, we introduce a random variable for that quantity and infer a posterior distribution over the value of the variable. We can use exactly this approach to do model selection. Let's consider a random variable called model which has two possible values NoEffect if the "no effect" model gave rise to the data and HasEffect if the "has effect" model gave rise to the data. Notice the implicit assumption here:

③ Either the "no effect" model or the "has effect" model gave rise to the data. No other model will be considered.

For brevity, let's use data to refer to all our observed data, in other words, the two arrays recoveredTreated and recoveredControl. We can then use Bayes' rule (Panel 1.1) to infer a posterior distribution over model given the data.

$$P(\text{model}|\text{data}) = \frac{P(\text{model})P(\text{data}|\text{model})}{P(\text{data})}. \qquad (6.1)$$

Unsurprisingly, this technique of using Bayes's rule to do model selection is called **Bayesian model selection**. In equation (6.1), the left–hand side is the posterior distribution over models that we want to compute. On the right–hand side, $P(\texttt{model})$ encodes our prior belief about which model is more probable –

Models can be compared using model evidence, in a process called Bayesian model selection.

usually, this prior is chosen to be uniform so as not to favour any one model over another. Also on the right–hand side, $P(\texttt{data}|\texttt{model})$ gives the probability of the data conditioned on the choice of model. This is the data-dependent term that varies from model to model and so provides the evidence for or against each model. For this reason, this quantity is known as the **model evidence** or sometimes just as the **evidence**.

With a uniform prior over models, the result is that the posterior distribution over `model` is equal to the model evidence values normalised to add up to 1. In other words, the posterior probability of a model is proportional to the model evidence for that model. For this reason, when comparing two models, it is common to look at the ratio of their model evidences – a quantity known as a **Bayes factor**. For example, the Bayes factor comparing the "has effect" model evidence to the "no effect" model evidence is:

$$\text{Bayes factor} = \frac{P(\texttt{data}|\texttt{model} = \texttt{HasEffect})}{P(\texttt{data}|\texttt{model} = \texttt{NoEffect})} \qquad (6.2)$$

The higher the Bayes factor, the stronger the evidence that the top model (in this case the "has effect" model) is a better model than the bottom model (the "no effect" model). For example, Kass and Raftery [1995] suggest that a Bayes factor between 3 and 20 is positive evidence for the top model, a Bayes factor between 20 and 150 is strong evidence, and a Bayes factor above 150 is very strong evidence. However, it is important to bear in mind that this evidence is only *relative* evidence that the top model is better than the bottom one – it is not evidence that this is the true model of the data or even that it is a good model of the data.

You might worry that the "has effect" model will *always* be favoured over the "no effect" model, because the "has effect" model includes the "no effect" model as a special case (when `probTreated` is equal to `probControl`). This means that the "has effect" model can always fit any data generated by the "no effect" model. So, even if the drug has no effect, the "has effect" model will still fit the data well. As we will see when we start computing Bayes factors, if the drug has no effect the Bayes factor will correctly favour the "no effect" model.

So why is the "no effect" model favoured in this case? It is because of a principle known as **Occam's razor** (named after William of Ockham who popularised it) which can be expressed as "where multiple explanations fit equally well with a set of observations, favour the simplest". Bayesian model selection applies Occam's razor automatically by favouring simple models (generally those with fewer variables) over complex ones. This arises because a more complex model can generate more different data sets than a simpler model, and so will place lower probability on any particular data set. It follows that, where a data set could have been generated by either model, it will have higher probability under the simpler model – and so a higher model evidence. We will see this effect in action in the next section, where we show how to compute model evidences and Bayes factors for different trial outcomes.

6.3.1 Comparing the two models using Bayesian model selection

⚓ **Inference deep-dive**
In this optional section, we show the inference calculations needed to do Bayesian model selection for the two models we just described. If you want to focus on modelling, feel free to skip this section.

Next we can look at how to perform Bayesian model selection between the two models in our randomised controlled trial. As an example, we will consider a trial with 40 people: 20 in the control group and 20 in the treated group. In this example trial, we found that 13 out of 20 people recovered in the treated group compared to just 8 out of 20 in the control group. To do model selection for this trial, we will need to compute the model evidence for each of our two models.

Computing the evidence for the "no effect" model

Let's first compute the evidence for the "no effect" model, which is given by $P(\text{data}|\text{model} = \text{NoEffect})$. Remembering that `data` refers to the two arrays `recoveredTreated` and `recoveredControl`, we can write this more precisely as $P($`recoveredTreated`, `recoveredControl` $|$`model` $=$ `NoEffect`$)$.

If we write down the joint probability for the "no effect" model, it looks like this:

$$P(\texttt{recoveredTreated}, \texttt{recoveredControl}, \texttt{probRecovery}|$$
$$\texttt{model} = \texttt{NoEffect}) = Beta(\texttt{probRecovery}; 1, 1)$$
$$\times \prod_{i \in \text{treated}} Bernoulli(\texttt{recoveredTreated}[i]|\texttt{probRecovery})$$
$$\times \prod_{i \in \text{control}} Bernoulli(\texttt{recoveredControl}[i]|\texttt{probRecovery}) \quad (6.3)$$

In equation (6.3), the notation $\prod_{i \in \text{treated}}$ means a product of all the contained terms where i varies over all the people in the treated group. Notice that there is a term in the joint probability for each factor in the factor graph of Figure 6.9, as we learned back in Section 2.1. Also notice that when working with multiple models, we write the joint probability conditioned on the choice of model, in this case `model` $=$ `NoEffect`. This conditioning makes it clear which model we are writing the joint probability for.

We can simplify this joint probability quite a bit. First, we can note that $Beta(\texttt{probRecovery}; 1, 1)$ is a uniform distribution and so we can remove it (because multiplying by a uniform distribution has no effect). Second, we can use the fact that `recoveredTreated` and `recoveredControl` are both observed variables, so we can replace the Bernoulli terms by `probRecovery` for each subject that recovered and by $(1 - \texttt{probRecovery})$ for each subject that did not recover. It is helpful at this point to define some counts of subjects. Let's call the number of treated group subjects that recovered T_T and the number which did not recover T_F. Similarly, let's call the number of control group subjects that recovered C_T and the number which did not recover C_F.

$$P(\texttt{recoveredTreated}, \texttt{recoveredControl}, \texttt{probRecovery} |$$
$$\texttt{model} = \texttt{NoEffect})$$
$$= \texttt{probRecovery}^{T_T}(1 - \texttt{probRecovery})^{T_F}$$
$$\times \texttt{probRecovery}^{C_T}(1 - \texttt{probRecovery})^{C_F}$$
$$= \texttt{probRecovery}^{(T_T+C_T)}(1 - \texttt{probRecovery})^{(T_F+C_F)} \qquad (6.4)$$

This joint probability $P(\texttt{recoveredTreated}, \texttt{recoveredControl}, \texttt{probRecovery} | \texttt{model} = \texttt{NoEffect})$ is quite similar to the model evidence that we are trying to compute $P(\texttt{recoveredTreated}, \texttt{recoveredControl} | \texttt{model} = \texttt{NoEffect})$. The difference is that the joint probability includes the $\texttt{probRecovery}$ variable. In order to compute the model evidence, we need to remove this variable by marginalising (integrating) it out.

$$P(\texttt{recoveredTreated}, \texttt{recoveredControl} | \texttt{model} = \texttt{NoEffect})$$
$$= \int P(\texttt{recoveredTreated}, \texttt{recoveredControl}, \texttt{probRecovery} |$$
$$\texttt{model} = \texttt{NoEffect}) \, d\texttt{probRecovery}$$
$$= \int \texttt{probRecovery}^{(T_T+C_T)}(1 - \texttt{probRecovery})^{(T_F+C_F)}$$
$$d\texttt{probRecovery} \qquad (6.5)$$

To evaluate this integral, we can compare it to the probability density function of the beta distribution, that we introduced back in equation (2.19):

$$Beta(x; \alpha, \beta) = \frac{x^{\alpha-1}(1-x)^{\beta-1}}{\mathrm{B}(\alpha, \beta)} \qquad (6.6)$$

We know that the integral of this density function is 1, because the area under any probability density function must be 1. Our model evidence in equation (6.5) looks like the integral of a beta distribution with $\alpha = T_T + C_T + 1$ and $\beta = T_F + C_F + 1$, except that it is not being divided by the normalising beta function $\mathrm{B}(\alpha, \beta)$. If we did divide by $\mathrm{B}(\alpha, \beta)$, the integral would be 1. Since we are not, the integral must equal $\mathrm{B}(\alpha, \beta)$ for the above values of α and β. In other words, the model evidence is equal to $\mathrm{B}(T_T + C_T + 1, T_F + C_F + 1)$.

For the counts in our example, this model evidence is $\mathrm{B}(13 + 8 + 1, 7 + 12 + 1)$, which equals $\mathrm{B}(22, 20)$.

Computing the evidence for the "has effect" model

The computation of the model evidence for the "has effect" model is actually quite similar. Again, we write down the joint distribution

$$P(\texttt{recoveredTreated}, \texttt{recoveredControl}, \texttt{probTreated},$$
$$\texttt{probControl}|\texttt{model} = \texttt{HasEffect})$$
$$= Beta(\texttt{probTreated}; 1, 1)$$
$$\times Beta(\texttt{probControl}; 1, 1)$$
$$\times \prod_{i \in \text{treated}} Bernoulli(\texttt{recoveredTreated}[i]|\texttt{probTreated})$$
$$\times \prod_{i \in \text{control}} Bernoulli(\texttt{recoveredControl}[i]|\texttt{probControl}) \quad (6.7)$$

We now condition the joint distribution on $\texttt{model} = \texttt{HasEffect}$, which shows that this is the joint distribution for the "has effect" model. We can simplify this expression by removing the uniform beta distributions and again using the counts of recovered/not recovered subjects in each group:

$$P(\texttt{recoveredTreated}, \texttt{recoveredControl}, \texttt{probTreated},$$
$$\texttt{probControl}|\texttt{model} = \texttt{HasEffect})$$
$$= \texttt{probTreated}^{T_T}(1 - \texttt{probTreated})^{T_F}$$
$$\times \texttt{probControl}^{C_T}(1 - \texttt{probControl})^{C_F} \quad (6.8)$$

Notice that in this model we have two extra variables that we need to get rid of by marginalisation: $\texttt{probTreated}$ and $\texttt{probControl}$. To integrate this expression over these extra variables, we can use the same trick as before except that now we have two beta densities: one over $\texttt{probTreated}$ and one over $\texttt{probControl}$. The resulting model evidence is:

$$P(\texttt{recoveredTreated}, \texttt{recoveredControl}|\texttt{model} = \texttt{HasEffect})$$
$$= \mathrm{B}(T_T + 1, T_F + 1) \times \mathrm{B}(C_T + 1, C_F + 1) \quad (6.9)$$

For the counts in our example, this model evidence is $B(13 + 1, 7 + 1)B(8 + 1, 12 + 1)$, which simplifies to $B(14, 8)B(9, 13)$.

Computing the Bayes factor for the "has effect" model over the "no effect" model

We now have the model evidence for each of our two models:

- $P(\text{data}|\text{model} = \text{NoEffect}) = B(T_T + C_T + 1, T_F + C_F + 1)$

- $P(\text{data}|\text{model} = \text{HasEffect}) = B(T_T + 1, T_F + 1) \times B(C_T + 1, C_F + 1)$

These model evidence values can be plugged into equation (6.1) to compute a posterior distribution over the model variable.

Let's compute the Bayes factor for our example trial, where $8/20$ of the control group recovered, compared to $13/20$ of the treated group:

$$\text{Bayes factor} = \frac{P(\text{data}|\text{model} = \text{HasEffect})}{P(\text{data}|\text{model} = \text{NoEffect})}$$

$$= \frac{B(14, 8)B(9, 13)}{B(22, 20)} = 1.25 \qquad (6.10)$$

A Bayes factor of just 1.25 shows that the "has effect" model is very slightly favoured over the "no effect" model but that the evidence is very weak. Note that this does not mean that the drug has no effect, but that we have not yet shown reliably that it does have an effect. The root problem is that the trial is just too small to provide strong evidence for the effect of the drug. We'll explore the effect on the Bayes factor of increasing the size of the trial in the next section.

Earlier, we claimed that the Bayes factor will correctly favour the "no effect" model in the case where the drug really has no effect. To prove this, let's consider a trial where the drug does indeed have no effect, which leads to an outcome of $8/20$ recovering in both the control and treated groups. In this case, the Bayes factor is given by:

$$\text{Bayes factor} = \frac{P(\text{data}|\text{model} = \text{HasEffect})}{P(\text{data}|\text{model} = \text{NoEffect})}$$

$$= \frac{B(9, 13)B(9, 13)}{B(17, 25)} = 0.37 \qquad (6.11)$$

Now we have a Bayes factor of less than 1 which means that the "no effect" model has been favoured over the "has effect" model, despite them both fitting the data equally well. This tendency of Bayesian model selection to favour simpler models is crucial to selecting the correct model in real applications. As this example shows, without it, we would not be able to tell that a drug doesn't work! For more explanation of this preference for simpler, less flexible models take a look at Section 7.3.2 in the next chapter.

The model evidence calculations we have just seen have a familiar form. We introduced a random variable called `model` and then used Bayes' rule to infer the posterior distribution over that random variable. However, the random variable `model` did not appear in any factor graph and we manually computed its posterior distribution, rather than using a general-purpose message passing algorithm. It would be simpler, easier and more consistent if the posterior distribution could be calculated by defining a model containing the `model` variable and running a standard inference algorithm on that model. In the next section, we show that this can be achieved using a modelling structure called a *gate*.

REVIEW OF CONCEPTS

randomised controlled trial A randomised controlled trial is a kind of clinical trial commonly used for testing the effectiveness of various types of medical intervention, such as new drugs. In such a trial, each subject is randomly assigned into either a treated group (which receives the experimental intervention) or a control group (which does not receive the intervention). The purpose of the trial is to determine whether the experimental intervention has an effect or not on one or more outcomes of interest, and to understand the nature of that effect.

model selection The task of choosing which of several models best fits a particular data set. Model selection is helpful not only because it allows the best model to be used, but also because identifying the best model helps to understand the processes that gave rise to the data set.

Bayesian model selection The process of doing model selection by computing a posterior distribution over the choice of model conditioned on a given data set. Rather than given a single "best" model, Bayesian model selection returns a probability for each model and the relative size of these probabilities can be used to assess the relative quality of fit of each model.

model evidence   The probability of the data conditioned on the choice of model, in other words $P(\mathtt{data}|\mathtt{model})$. This conditional probability provides evidence for or against each model being the one that gave rise to the data set, thus the name "model evidence". Comparing model evidence values for different models allows for Bayesian model selection. Because it is a frequently used concept, model evidence is often called just the "evidence".

Bayes factor   The ratio of the model evidence for a particular model of interest to the model evidence for another model, usually a baseline or "null" model. The higher the Bayes factor, the greater the support for the proposed model relative to the a baseline model.

Occam's razor   Where multiple explanations fit equally well with a set of observations, favour the simplest. It is named after William of Ockham who used it in his philosophical arguments. He did not invent the concept, however, there are references to it as early as Aristotle (384–322 BC).

6.4 MODELLING WITH GATES

In the previous section, we saw how to compare alternative processes by manually inferring the posterior distribution over a random variable that selects between them. What we will now see is how to do the same calculation by defining an appropriate model and performing inference within that model. To do this, we need a new modelling structure that allows alternatives to be represented within a model. The modelling structure that we can use to do this is called a **gate**, as described in Minka and Winn [2009].

A gate allows part of a factor graph to be turned on or off.

A gate encloses part of a factor graph and switches it on or off depending on the state of a random variable called the **selector variable**. The gate is on when the selector variable has a particular value, called the *key*, and off for all other values. An example gate is shown in the factor graph of Figure 6.11. The gate is shown as a dashed rectangle with the key value (**true**) in the top left corner. The selector variable **selector** has an edge connecting it to the gate – the arrow on the edge shows that the gate is considered to be a child of the selector variable. When **selector** equals **true**, the gate is on and so x has a *Bernoulli*(0.2) distribution. Otherwise, the gate is off and x has a uniform distribution, since it is not connected to any factors.

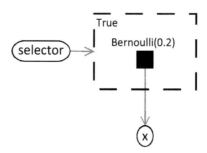

Figure 6.11 An example of a factor graph which contains a gate, shown as a dashed rectangle. When **selector** equals the key value **true** (shown in the top left of the gate), the gate is on and the variable x has a *Bernoulli*(0.2) distribution. When **selector** is **false**, the gate is off and x has a uniform distribution since it is not connected to any factors.

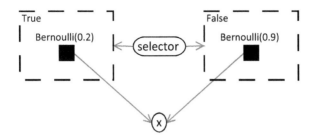

Figure 6.12 An example of a factor graph which contains a gate block. When `selector` equals `true`, the left gate is on and the right gate is off and so x has a *Bernoulli*(0.2) distribution. When `selector` equals `false`, the left gate is off and the right gate is on and so x has a *Bernoulli*(0.9) distribution.

When writing the joint distribution for a factor graph with a gate, all terms relating to the part of the graph inside the gate need to be switched on or off according to whether the selector variable takes the key value or not. Such terms can be turned off by raising them to the power zero and left turned on by raising to the power one. For example, the joint distribution for Figure 6.11 is

$$P(\texttt{selector}, \texttt{x}) \propto Bernoulli(x; 0.2)^{\delta(\texttt{selector=true})} \qquad (6.12)$$

where the function $\delta()$ equals one if the expression in brackets is true and zero otherwise. If `selector` is not `true`, the *Bernoulli*$(x; 0.2)$ term will be raised to the power zero, making the term equal to one – equivalent to removing it from the product (i.e. turning it off).

When using gates inside a model, it is common to have a gate for each value of the selector variable. In this case, the resulting set of gates is called a **gate block**. Because the selector variable can only have one value, only one gate in a gate block can be on at once. An example gate block is shown in the factor graph of Figure 6.12. In this example, the selector variable is binary and so there are two gates in the gate block, one with the key value `true` and one with the key value `false`. It is also possible to have selector variables with any number of values, leading to gate blocks containing the corresponding number of gates.

The joint probability distribution for this factor graph is

$$P(\texttt{selector}, \texttt{x}) \propto Bernoulli(x; 0.2)^{\delta(\texttt{selector=true})}$$
$$Bernoulli(x; 0.9)^{\delta(\texttt{selector=false})}. \qquad (6.13)$$

Looking at this joint probability, you might be able to spot that the gate block between `selector` and `x` represents a conditional probability table, like so:

Table 6.4 The conditional probability table represented by the gate block in Figure 6.12.

selector	x=true	x=false
true	0.200	0.800
false	0.900	0.100

As another example, we can represent the conditional probability table for the skin test (Figure 6.1) using gates like this:

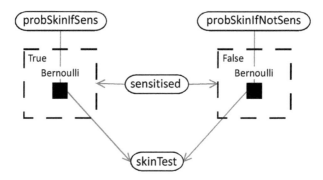

Figure 6.13 The conditional probability table for the skin test (Figure 6.1) represented using a gate block. If `sensitised` is `true`, the left–hand gate is on and the right–hand gate is off. The skin test result `skinTest` then has a Bernoulli distribution with the probability of true given by `probSkinIfSens`. If `sensitised` is `false`, then `skinTest` has a Bernoulli distribution with the probability of true given by `probSkinIfNotSens`.

Representing this conditional probability table using a gate block is less compact than using a *Table* factor (as we did in Figure 6.1) but has the advantage of making the relationship between the parent variable and child variable more clear and precise. When a variable has multiple parents, using a gate block to represent a conditional probability table can also lead to more accurate or more efficient inference.

6.4.1 Using gates for model selection

Representing a conditional probability table is just the start of what can be achieved using gates. For example, they can also be used to do model selection. To see how, let's return to our model selection problem from the previous section. Remember that we wanted to select between a "has effect" model and a "no effect" model, by inferring the posterior distribution of a random variable called `model`. Using gates, we can represent this model selection problem as a single large factor graph,

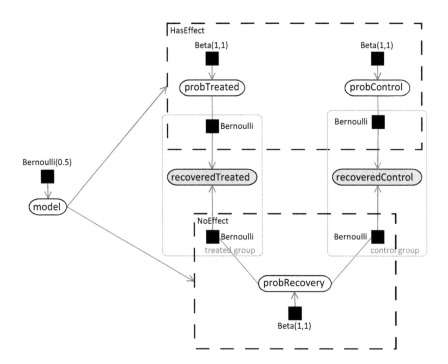

Figure 6.14 A factor graph which uses gates to do model selection between two models. The "has effect" model is in the top gate and the "no effect" mode is in the bottom gate. The observed data variables lie outside both gates, since they are common to both models. When the selector variable `model` has the value `HasEffect` the top gate is on and the bottom gate is off and so the "has effect" model applies. When the selector variable `model` has the value `NoEffect` the top gate is off and the bottom gate is on and so the "no effect" model applies. Because `model` is a random variable with unknown value, inferring its posterior distribution is equivalent to doing Bayesian model selection between the two models.

using a gate block where the selector variable is `model`. We then place the entire "no effect" model inside a gate whose key value is `NoEffect` and the entire "has effect" model inside the other gate of the block whose key value is `HasEffect`. The observed variables are left outside of both gates because they are common to both models and so are always on. The result is the factor graph in Figure 6.14.

This factor graph may look a bit scary, but it can be interpreted in pieces. The top gate contains exactly the model from Figure 6.10 with the observed variables outside the gate. The bottom gate contains exactly the model from Figure 6.9 drawn upside down and sharing the same observed variables. Finally, we have one new variable which is our `model` variable used to do model selection.

Given this factor graph, we just need to run expectation propagation to infer the posterior distribution over `model`. Right? Well, almost – it turns out that first we need to make some extensions to expectation propagation to be able to handle gates. The good news is that these modifications allow expectation propagation to be applied to any factor graph containing gates.

6.4.2 Expectation propagation in factor graphs with gates

⚓ Inference deep-dive

In this optional section, we see how to use expectation propagation to compute model evidence and then how to extend expectation propagation to work on graphs containing gates. If you want to focus on modelling, feel free to skip this section.

To run expectation propagation in a factor graph which contains gates, we first need to be able to compute the model evidence for a factor graph without gates. It turns out that we can compute an approximation to the model evidence by using existing EP messages to compute evidence contributions for each variable and factor individually, and then multiplying them together. For example, the evidence contribution for a variable x is given by:

$$\text{evidence}_x = \sum_x \text{product of all messages into x} \qquad (6.14)$$

This equation states that to compute the evidence for a variable x, first take the product of all incoming messages on edges connected to the variable, then sum the result over the values that x can take (this is what the notation $\sum_x$ means). Because of this sum, the result is a single number rather than a distribution – this number is the local contribution to the model evidence.

The evidence contribution for a factor f connected to multiple variables Y is given by:

$$\text{evidence}_f = \frac{\sum_Y f(Y) \times \text{product of all messages into } f}{\sum_Y \text{product of all messages into or out of } f} \qquad (6.15)$$

In this equation, the notation $\sum_Y$ means the sum over all joint configurations of the connected variables Y.

We can use equations (6.14) and (6.15) to calculate evidence contributions for every variable and factor in the factor graph. The product of all these contributions gives the EP approximation to the model evidence. For a model M, this gives:

$$\text{evidence}_M = \prod_{x \text{ in } M} \text{evidence}_x \times \prod_{f \text{ in } M} \text{evidence}_f \qquad (6.16)$$

In equation (6.16), the first term means the product of the evidence contributions from every variable in model M and the second term means the product of evidence contributions from every factor in model M.

Adding in gates

If we now turn to factor graphs which contains gates, there is a new kind of evidence contribution that comes from any edge that crosses over a gate boundary. If such an edge connects a variable x to a factor f, then the evidence contribution is:

$$\text{evidence}_{fx} = \sum_x \text{message from x to } f \times \text{message from } f \text{ to x} \qquad (6.17)$$

In other words, we take the product of the two messages passing in each direction over the edge and then sum the result over the values of the variable x.

The advantage of computing evidence contributions locally on parts of the factor graph is that, as well as computing evidence for the model as a whole, we can also compute evidence for any particular gate. The evidence for a gate is the product of the evidence contributions for all variables and factors inside the gate, along with the contributions from any edges crossing the gate boundary. For a gate g, this product is given by:

$$\text{evidence}_g = \prod_{x \text{ in } g} \text{evidence}_x \times \prod_{f \text{ in } g} \text{evidence}_f$$

$$\times \prod_{fx \text{ crossing } g} \text{evidence}_{fx} \tag{6.18}$$

If there are no edges crossing the gate boundary – in other words, the gate contains an entire model disconnected from the rest of the graph – then this equation reduces to the model evidence equation (6.16), and so gives the evidence for the contained model.

Given these evidence contributions, we can now define an extended version of expectation propagation which works for factor graphs that contain gates. The algorithm requires that gates only occur in gate blocks and that any variable connecting to a factor in one gate of a gate block, also connects to factors in all other gates of the gate block. This "gate balancing" can be achieved by connecting the variable to uniform factors in any gate where it does not already connect to a factor. We need this gate balancing because messages will be defined as going to or from gate blocks, rather than to or from individual gates.

When sending messages from a factor f inside a gate g to a variable x outside the gate, we will need to weight the message appropriately, using a weight defined as:

$$\text{weight}_{gfx} = \frac{\text{evidence}_g}{\text{evidence}_{fx}} \times \text{message from the selector variable[key]} \tag{6.19}$$

where the notation [key] indicates that we are evaluating the probability of the gate's key value under the distribution given by the message from the selector variable. Using these weights, we can define our extended expectation propagation algorithm as shown in Algorithm 6.1.

The full derivation of this algorithm is given in Minka and Winn [2009], along with some additional details that we have omitted here (such as how to handle nested gates).

Algorithm 6.1: Expectation Propagation with Gates

Input: factor graph with gate blocks, list of target variables to compute marginals for, message-passing schedule, initial message values (optional), choice of approximating distributions for each edge.

Output: marginal distributions for target variables.

Initialise all messages to uniform (or initial values, if provided).

repeat

    foreach *edge in the message-passing schedule* **do**

        Send the appropriate message below:

        - Selector variable to gate block: the product of all messages received on the other edges connected to the selector variable;

        - Gate block to selector variable: a distribution over the selector variable where the probability of each value is proportional to the evidence for the gate with that key value;

        - Factors in gate block to variable outside gate block: Compute weighted sum of messages from the factor in each gate using weights given by (6.19). Multiply by the context message (the message coming from the variable to the gate block). Project into the desired distribution type using moment matching. Divide out the context message.

        - All other messages: the normal EP message (defined in Algorithm 3.1);

    end

until *all messages have converged*

Compute marginal distributions as the product of all incoming messages at each target variable node.

Now that we have a general-purpose inference algorithm for gated graphs, we can use it to do Bayesian model selection and to infer posterior distributions over variables of interest, both at the same time! For example, recall the example trial from Section 6.3. In this trial, 13 out of 20 people in the treated group recovered compared to 8 out of 20 in the control group. Attaching this data to the gated factor graph of Figure 6.14, we can apply expectation propagation to compute posteriors over the model selection variable `model` and also over other variables such as `probTreated` and `probControl`. The results are shown in Figure 6.15.

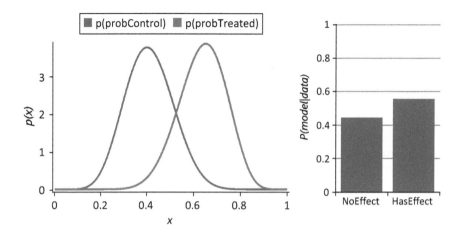

Figure 6.15 Inferred posterior distributions for the example trial with 20 people in each group. The left plot shows posteriors over `probControl` and `probTreated` in the `HasEffect` model. The right plot shows the posterior distribution over the `model` variable.

Figure 6.15 shows that the posterior distribution over `model` puts slightly higher probability on the "has effect" model than on the "no effect" model. The exact values are 0.5555 for `model=HasEffect` and 0.4445 for `model=NoEffect`. The ratio of these probabilities is the Bayes factor, which in this case is 1.25. This is the same value that we computed manually in Section 6.3, showing that for this model the expectation propagation posterior is exact. The posterior distributions over `probControl` and `probTreated` give an indication of why the Bayes factor is so small. The plots show that there is a lot of overlap between the two distributions, meaning that is possible that both probabilities are the same value, in other words, that the "no effect" model applies.

Let's see what happens when we increase the size of the trial, but leave the proportions of people who recovered the same in each group. For a trial of three times the size, this would see 39 out of 60 recovered in the treated group compared to 24 out of 60 in the control group. Plugging this new data into our model gives the results shown in Figure 6.16.

Figure 6.16 shows that, after tripling the size of the trial, the "has effect" model has a much higher probability of 0.904, giving a Bayes factor of 9.41. Since this factor lies in the range 3–20, the outcome of this trial can now be considered positive evidence in favour of the

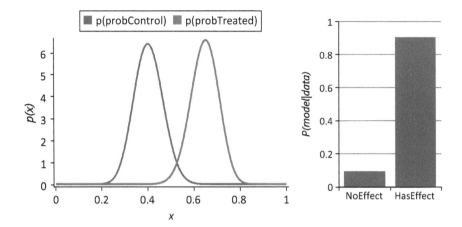

Figure 6.16 Inferred posterior distributions for the example trial with 60 people in each group. The left plot shows posteriors over `probControl` and `probTreated` in the `HasEffect` model. The right plot shows the posterior distribution over the `model` variable.

"has effect" model. The posterior distributions over `probControl` and `probTreated` show why the Bayes factor is now much larger: the two curves have much less overlap, meaning that the chances of the two probabilities being the same is much reduced. We can take this further and increase the trial size again so that it is five times the size of the original trial. In this larger trial, 65 out of 100 recovered in the treated group compared to 40 out of 100 in the control group, giving the results as shown in Figure 6.17.

In Figure 6.17, the posterior distributions over `probControl` and `probTreated` hardly overlap at all. As a result, the "has effect" model now has a probability of 0.989, giving a Bayes factor of 92.4. Since this factor lies in the range 20–150, the outcome of this trial can now be considered strong evidence in favour of the "has effect" model. These results show the importance of running a large enough clinical trial if you want to prove the effectiveness of your new drug!

Now that we understand how gates can be used to model alternatives in our randomised controlled trial model, we are ready to use gates to model alternative sensitisation classes in our allergy model, as we will see in the next section.

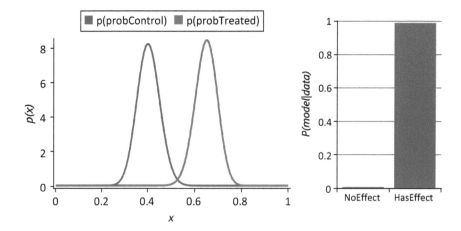

Figure 6.17 Inferred posterior distributions for the example trial with 100 people in each group. The left plot shows posteriors over `probControl` and `probTreated` in the `HasEffect` model. The right plot shows the posterior distribution over the `model` variable.

REVIEW OF CONCEPTS

gate A container in a factor graph that allows the contained piece of the graph to be turned on or off, according to the value of another random variable in the graph (known as the selector variable). Gates can be used to create alternatives within a model and also to do model selection. More details of gates can be found in Minka and Winn [2009] or in the expanded version Minka and Winn [2008].

selector variable A random variable that controls whether a gate is on or off. The gate will specify a particular key value – when the selector variable has that value then the gate is on; for any other value it is off. For an example of a selector variable, see Figure 6.11.

gate block A set of gates each with a different key value corresponding to the possible values of a selector variable. For any value of the selector variable, one gate in the gate block will be on and all the other gates will be off. An example gate block is shown in the factor graph of Figure 6.12.

6.5 DISCOVERING SENSITISATION CLASSES

Now that we have gates in our modelling toolbox, we can extend our allergy model so that different children can have different patterns of allergy gain and loss. As you may recall from Section 6.2, the model change that we want to make is to encode this modified assumption:

⑤ The probabilities relating to initially having, gaining or retaining sensitisation to a particular allergen are the same for all children in each sensitisation class.

This assumption requires that each child belongs to some sensitisation class, but we do not know which class each child belongs to. We can represent this unknown class membership using a `sensClass` random variable for each child, which takes a value in $0, 1, 2, \ldots$ depending on whether the child is in class 0, class 1 and so on. Because this variable can take more than two values, we cannot use a *Bernoulli* distribution to represent its uncertain value. Instead we need a **discrete distribution**, which is a generalisation of a Bernoulli distribution to variables with more than two values.

Our aim is to do unsupervised learning of this `sensClass` variable – in other words, we want to learn which class each child is in, even though we have no idea what the classes are and we have no labelled examples of which child is in which class. Grouping data items together using unsupervised learning is sometimes called **clustering**. The term clustering can be misleading, because it suggests that data items naturally sit together in unique clusters and we just need to use machine learning to reveal these clusters. Instead, data items can usually be grouped together in many different ways, and we choose a particular kind of grouping to meet the needs of our application. For example, in this asthma project, we want to group together children that have similar patterns of allergic sensitisation. But for another project, we could group those same children in a different way, such as by their genetics, by their physiology and so on. For this reason, we will avoid using the terms "clustering" and "clusters" and use the more precise term "sensitisation class".

Each sensitisation class needs to have its own patterns of gaining and losing allergic sensitisations, with the corresponding probabilities for gaining and losing sensitisations at each time point. For example, each class should have its own value of `probSens1` which gives the prob-

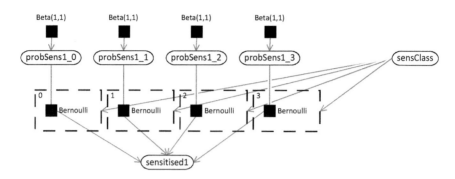

Figure 6.18 A factor graph with four different probabilities of sensitisation at age 1, where the appropriate probability is selected according to the value of the `sensClass` variable (0, 1, 2 or 3). For any value of `sensClass`, one gate is on and all other gates are off.

ability of sensitisation at age 1 for children in that particular sensitisation class. To achieve this in our model, we need the sensitisation state at age 1 (`sensitised1`) to be connected to the appropriate `probSens1` corresponding to the sensitisation class of the child. We can achieve this by replicating the connecting *Bernoulli* factor for each sensitisation class, and then using a gate block to ensure that only one of these factors is turned on, as shown in Figure 6.18.

In Figure 6.18, we have assumed that there are four sensitisation classes and duplicated `probSens1` into separate probabilities for each class ($probSens1_0$, $probSens1_1$ ...). There is a gate for each class keyed by the number of the class (0, 1, 2 or 3). Because each key is different, any value of `sensClass` leads to one gate being on and all the other gates being off. In this way, the value of `sensClass` determines which of the four initial sensitisation probabilities to use.

The factor graph of Figure 6.18 is quite cluttered because of the repeated factors and variables for each sensitisation class. We can represent the same model more compactly if we introduce a plate across the sensitisation classes and put the repeated elements inside the plate, as shown in Figure 6.19.

Using the compact notation of Figure 6.19, we can modify our allergy model of Figure 6.5 to have different probabilities for each sensitisation class. We take all our probability variables `probSens1`, `probGain3` and so on and duplicate them across classes using a plate. We then place each factor in the Markov chain inside a gate and plate,

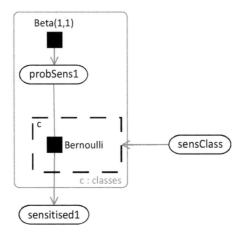

Figure 6.19 The same model as Figure 6.18, shown more compactly by using a plate across sensitisation classes. The initial sensitisation probabilities, gates and corresponding factors are duplicated for each sensitisation class.

where the gates are all connected to a **sensClass** selector variable. Finally, we choose a uniform prior over **sensClass**, giving the factor graph of Figure 6.20.

6.5.1 Testing the model with two classes

To test out our model in its simplest form, we can set the number of sensitisation classes to two. With just two classes, we would expect the model to divide the children into a group which have no sensitisations and a second group that contains those children with sensitisations. However, when we run expectation propagation in the model, we get an unexpected result. The posterior distributions over the sensitisation class are all uniform, for every child! In addition, when we look at the learned probabilities of gaining/retaining sensitisations, they are also all the same for each class – and look just like the one-class probabilities shown in Figure 6.7. What has happened here?

The issue is that our model defines every sensitisation class in exactly the same way – each class has the same set of variables which all have exactly the same priors. We could reorder the sensitisation classes in any order and the model would be unchanged. This self-similarity is a symmetry of the model, very similar to the symmetry we encountered in Section 5.3 in the previous chapter. During inference, this symmetry

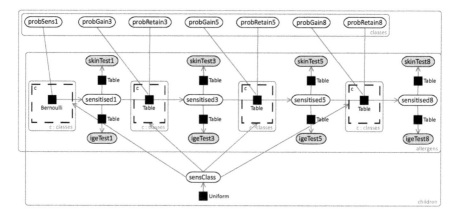

Figure 6.20 Modified factor graph which has different probabilities of having, gaining and retaining sensitisation for each sensitisation class. The random variables for these probabilities are duplicated by a `classes` plate at the top of the factor graph. These probabilities are then connected into the rest of the model by factors each contained in a gate and a plate. The `sensClass` variable is connected to all gates and switches between the different sets of probabilities, according to the sensitisation class of the child. In this figure, the probability variables relating to skin and IgE tests have been omitted for clarity.

causes problems because the posterior distributions will not favour any particular ordering of classes and so will end up giving an average of all classes – in other words, the same results as the one-class model. Not helpful!

As in the previous chapter, we need to apply some kind of symmetry breaking to get useful inference results. In this case, we can break symmetry by providing initial messages to our model, such that the messages differ from class to class. A simple approach is to provide an initial message into each `sensClass` variable which is a point mass at a randomly selected value. The effect of these initial messages is to randomly assign children to sensitisation classes for the first iteration of expectation propagation. This randomisation affects the messages going to the class-specific variables (such as `probSens1`) in the first iteration, which in turn means that the messages to each `sensClass` variable are non-uniform in the next iteration and so on. The end result is that the class-specific variables eventually converge to describe

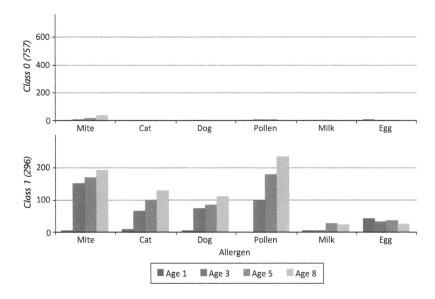

Figure 6.21 Plots for each class showing the number of children with inferred sensitisations for each allergen/time. The first class contains roughly three-quarters of the children who have almost no sensitisations. The remaining children in the second class are those with sensitisations.

different underlying sensitisation classes and the `sensClass` variables converge to assign children to these different classes.

With symmetry breaking in place, we can now run inference successfully in a two-class model. We can visualise the results using a chart like Figure 6.8 for each class. To do this, we assign each child to the sensitisation class with the highest posterior probability, giving the plots of Figure 6.21 for the two classes. The figure shows that the model has picked up on a large class of 757 children who have virtually no sensitisations and a smaller class of 296 children who do have sensitisations. In other words, the two-class model has behaved as expected and separated out the children who have sensitisations from those who do not.

6.5.2   Exploring more sensitisation classes

The results for two classes provide a useful sanity check that the model is doing something reasonable. However, we are really interested in what happens when we have more than two classes, since we hope additional

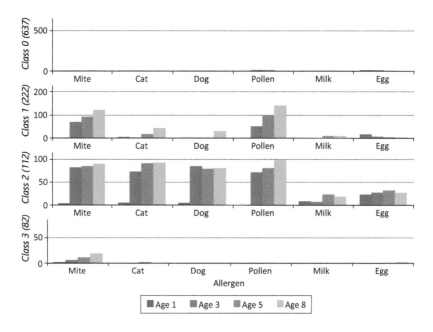

Figure 6.22 Plots for each of four classes showing the number of children with inferred sensitisations for each allergen/time. The first class contains roughly three-quarters of the children who have almost no sensitisations. The remaining children, with sensitisations, are divided into three classes according to which sensitisations they have and when they acquired them, as discussed in the text.

classes would uncover new patterns of sensitisation. Let's consider running the model with five possible classes. We say five "possible" classes, because there is no guarantee that all classes will be used. That is, it is possible to run the inference algorithm and find that there are classes with no children assigned to them. With our model and data set, we find that it is common when running with five classes, that only four of them are actually in use. Effectively the number of classes in the model defines a maximum on the number of classes found – which allows for the number of classes itself to be learned. Different random initialisations give slightly different sensitisation classes, but often these contain very similar looking classes. Figure 6.22 shows some typical results for the four classes found when up to five were allowed in the model.

As you can see from Figure 6.22, model has divided the children with sensitisations into three separate classes. The largest of these,

Class 1, contains 222 children who predominantly have mite and pollen allergies, but have few other allergies. In contrast, Class 2 contains 112 children who have allergies to cat and dog as well as mite and pollen. This class also contains those children who have milk and egg allergies. It is also worth noting that the children in this class acquire their allergies early in life – in most cases by age 3. The final class, Class 3, is relatively small and contains 82 children who predominantly have mite allergies.

These results demonstrate the strength of unsupervised learning – it can discover patterns in the data that you did not expect in advance. Here we have uncovered three different patterns of sensitisation that we were not previously aware of. The next question to ask is "how does this new knowledge help our understanding of asthma?". To answer this question, we can see if there is any link between which sensitisation class a child belongs to and whether they went on to develop asthma.

For each child, our data set contains a measurement of whether they had developed asthma by age 8. For each of the two class and four class models, we can use these measurements to plot the percentage of children in each sensitisation class that went on to develop asthma. The results are shown in Figure 6.23.

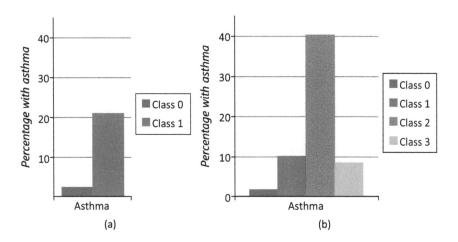

Figure 6.23 Percentage of children in each class who developed asthma by age 8, for (a) the two–class model (b) the four–class model. In the four–class model, class 2 has a much higher percentage of children with asthma than any other class, in either model.

Let's start by looking at plots for the two–class model. As we might expect, the percentage of children with asthma is higher in the class with sensitisations (class 1) than the class without sensitisations (class 0). Indeed, the presence of allergic sensitisations is used as a predictor of developing asthma. But when we look at the results for the four–class model, we see a very interesting result – whilst all the classes with sensitisations show an increased percentage of children developing asthma, class 2 shows a *much* higher percentage than any other class. It seems that children who have the broad set of allergies characterised by class 2 are more than four times as likely to develop asthma than children who have other patterns of allergies! This is a very exciting and clinically useful result. Indeed, when we looked further we found that this pattern of allergies also led to an increased chance of severe asthma with an associated increased risk of hospital admission [Simpson et al., 2010]. Being able to detect such severe asthma early in life could help prevent such life-threatening episodes from occurring.

In summary, in this chapter, we have seen how unsupervised learning discovered new patterns of allergic sensitisation in our data set. In this case, these patterns have led to a new understanding of childhood asthma with the potential of significant clinical impact. Although, in general, unsupervised learning can be more challenging than supervised learning, the value of the new understanding that it delivers frequently justifies the extra effort involved.

REVIEW OF CONCEPTS

discrete distribution   A probability distribution over a many-valued random variable which assigns a probability to each possible value. The parameters of the distribution are these probabilities, constrained to add up to 1 across all possible values. This distribution is also known as a categorical distribution.

An example of a discrete distribution is the outcome of rolling a fair dice, which can be written as $Discrete(\frac{1}{6}, \frac{1}{6}, \frac{1}{6}, \frac{1}{6}, \frac{1}{6}, \frac{1}{6})$. The Bernoulli distribution is actually a special case of a discrete distribution for when there are only two possible values.

clustering   A form of unsupervised learning where data items are automatically collected into a number of groups, which are known as clusters. Each cluster is then assumed to contain items which are in some way similar.

CHAPTER 7

Harnessing the crowd

In 2010 a magnitude 7.0 earthquake struck Haiti, causing massive loss of life and widespread devastation. The ensuing humanitarian aid effort was hampered by damage to communication systems, transport facilities and electrical networks. Messages from people in the affected area proved to be a vital source of information for aid workers. But these messages needed to be triaged and categorised – by volunteer workers with varying abilities, biases and attention to detail. In a future crisis, could model-based machine learning make use of such conflicting and noisy information to infer the true situation on the ground?

A round the world people are increasingly connected through their mobile phones, even in remote locations. People close to a crisis event are a vital source of information for providing disaster relief, humanitarian aid or conflict analysis. In 2008, tensions over the Kenyan presidential election erupted into outbreaks of violence, resulting in eyewitness reports sent by email

DOI: 10.1201/9780429192685-8

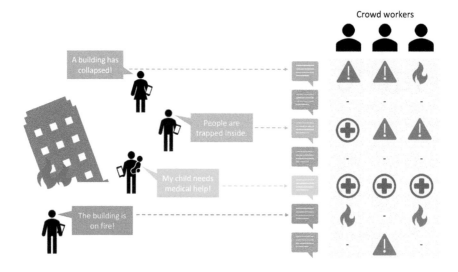

Figure 7.1 In a crisis situation, people on the ground send messages describing the situation or asking for help. Crowd workers then place messages into different categories (such as emergency or medical), or mark the messages as irrelevant. Different crowd workers may assign different category labels to the same message.

and text message. A new crowd-sourcing platform was created to map these reports and determine where the violence was occurring – the platform was named *Ushahidi* which translates to "testimony" in Swahili [Ushahidi, 2008].

The Ushahidi platform was used during the Haiti earthquake to collect and disseminate information. As reported by Norheim-Hagtun and Meier [2010], "the tool quickly became the go-to place for up-to-date crisis information, with a range of military, United Nations, and non-governmental organizations using the map as part of their needs assessment process. Preliminary feedback from these responders suggests that the project saved hundreds of lives".

Tens of thousands of tweets, text messages and pictures were contributed by ordinary individuals in the field to Ushahidi Haiti, and this enabled humanitarian crisis professionals to quickly get a picture of the disaster and to start to build a disaster map. Messages were translated and categorised by volunteer crowd workers, much as shown in Figure 7.1.

Given the quantity of messages needing categorisation and the urgency of the work, it is inevitable that crowd workers sometimes categorised the same message differently. These differences may be due to, for example, differences in judgement, insufficient training or lack of clarity in guidelines given to crowd workers. In some cases, workers deliberately misclassified messages "because of a concern that messages not associated with a specific classified need might be ignored" [Morrow et al., 2011]. The net effect was that different workers exhibited different biases is how they labelled messages.

One of the recommendations coming out of the use of Ushahidi in Haiti was to "Implement more rigorous quality assurance techniques to monitor accuracy of classifications in near real-time". In this chapter, we will look at how to automatically improve classifications by modelling worker biases, using both the crowd worker assessments and the messages themselves. The goal will be to work out the best category label for each message, taking into account the abilities and biases of individual crowd workers. The hope is that any increase in categorisation accuracy that we can achieve could lead to lives being saved in the next humanitarian crisis.

The model developed in this chapter is based on the models described in Venanzi et al. [2012] and Venanzi et al. [2014]. You can also refer to the source code for the chapter [Diethe et al., 2019].

7.1 A MODEL OF A CROWD WORKER

Messages sent during the Haiti earthquake were labelled according to the nine primary categories shown in Table 7.1. Each category was further divided into a number of sub-categories – for example, "Infrastructure Damage" had sub-categories of "Collapsed building", "Unstable structures", "Roads blocked", "Compromised bridge" and "Communication lines down". The result is 50 possible subcategory labels that could be applied to any given message, although messages could also be labelled only with a primary category.

Table 7.1 The nine primary categories which could be used to label each message Primary categories were further subdivided into a total of 50 secondary categories (see Morrow et al. [2011] for details).

Label	Description
Emergency	Emergencies requiring rapid response, such as fire, trapped people or medical emergencies.
Vital Lines	Supply line issues such as power outages or shortages of food, water or fuel.
Public Health	Medical issues such as infectious diseases or shortages of medical supplies.
Security Threats	Security issues such as looting, violence or rioting.
Infrastructure Damage	Collapsed buildings, blocked roads, damaged bridges or communication lines.
Natural Hazards	Floods, landslides, after shocks or missing people.
Services Available	Services such as clinics, food or aid distribution points or shelters.
Other	Other relevant messages not falling into the above categories.
Not Relevant	Messages not relevant to the situation.

In addition, each message was permitted to have multiple labels, for example "Water Shortage" and "Medical Emergency" – which were allowed to be a mix of primary and secondary categories. These labelling complexities would make developing a model more difficult, without adding a lot of value. Instead of working with such complexities, it makes sense to use a simpler setting for model development where each message has a single label from a set of possible labels.

7.1.1 A simpler setting

The problem of inferring high–quality labels from a large number of noisy crowd-sourced annotations arises in many applications. To investigate how well different approaches work at scale a company called CrowdFlower (now Appen) ran the CrowdScale Shared Task Challenge, back in 2013. In this competition, different systems competed to see who could infer the best labels for a set of messages given a large number of noisy annotations. For the purposes of the competition, CrowdFlower created a data set of tweets about the weather, along with around 550K annotations from different crowd workers (which was

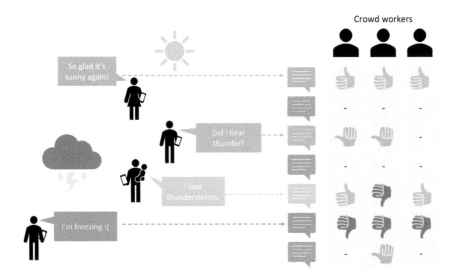

Figure 7.2 In the CrowdFlower competition, crowd workers annotated tweets as being positive about the weather, negative about the weather, neutral about the weather or unrelated to the weather. Note the similarity between this setting and that of Figure 7.1.

an unprecedented number at the time). To assess the quality of the inferred labels, CrowdFlower also provided a high–quality set of labels to be used as ground truth. In the context of crowd sourcing, such labels are often called **gold labels** to distinguish them from labels provided by the workers.

Figure 7.2 shows the setting that CrowdFlower created for their competition. Crowd workers were presented with tweets selected so as to be mostly about the weather. The task given to each crowd worker was to read a tweet and annotate with one of the labels from Table 7.2. Crowd workers were also given the option to say "Cannot tell" – rather than treat this as a label, we will take it to mean that the worker could not provide a meaningful label and so we will discard such labels. This

Table 7.2 The categories which could be used to label a tweet in the CrowdFlower data set. This is a much simpler set of labels than those of Table 7.1.

Label	Description
Positive	Positive sentiment about the weather – for example, "It's lovely and sunny today".
Negative	Negative sentiment about the weather – for example, "I'm fed up with all the rain".
Neutral	Neutral about the weather – for example, "When do you think we will get some snow?".
Unrelated	Messages that are unrelated to the weather – for example, "I love Snow Patrol!".

kind of task, where the aim is to infer an author's feelings from a piece of text is called **sentiment analysis** [Liu, 2012].

The full CrowdFlower data set consists of:

- 98,920 tweets, selected so that a high proportion are about the weather;

- 540,021 labels provided by 1,958 crowd workers;

- 975 gold labels provided by expert labellers.

A small sample of the data set is shown in Table 7.3.

7.1.2 Using more than two labels

In this weather setting, the true label for each tweet can have one of four possible values: `Positive`, `Negative`, `Neutral` or `Unrelated`. We will need to have a variable in our model for this true label, which we'll call `trueLabel`. As usual, we will keep track of all the assumptions we are making in building this model. So our first assumption is:

① Each tweet has a true label which is one of the following set: `Positive`, `Negative`, `Neutral` or `Unrelated`.

Table 7.3 Sample data from the CrowdFlower data set, consisting of (a) tweets selected to be likely to be about the weather (b) worker labels and (c) gold labels.

Tweet Id	Text
81989448	How about an internet special for this sunny Wednesday? Halfpriced bottles of beer (excludes hig...
81989449	@mention Aloha! I love Snow Patrol, so this is right up my street. They are going to be HUGE. {link}
81989450	Hey baby the skys on fire, I'm dying ain't I. I'm going to Carolina in my mind. In my mind I'm goingt...
81989451	Have you ever wondered how to find a good weather forecast? Now you can: {link}
81989452	#NEWMUSIC Superstar 9000 feat. Stuey Rock Thunderstorm by Superstar 9000.. {link}
81989453	Frozen rain... And no, I don't mean snow.
81989454	today was a good sunny day had to hoop a lil bit but now Im to the lab for a hr or 2 or 3...
81989455	Game Day Preview 5.11: Omaha Storm Chasers 1814 1st Place + 4 G

(a) Example tweets

Tweet Id	Worker Id	Worker Label
81988817	W397	Unrelated
81988817	W87	Unrelated
81988817	W39	Neutral
81988817	W315	Positive
81988817	W267	Neutral
81988817	W540	Positive
81988817	W99	Positive
81988818	W96	Negative
81988818	W541	Negative

Tweet Id	Gold Label
79197903	Negative
79197928	Positive
80050064	Neutral
80050108	Unrelated
80050144	Neutral

(b) Example crowd worker labels   (c) Example gold labels

Because `trueLabel` can take more than two values, we need to use a discrete distribution as a prior or posterior distribution for this variable. Recall that we first encountered discrete distributions back in Section 6.5 when working with a sensitisation class variable that could also take on more than two values. The important thing to remember is that the discrete distribution is an extension of the Bernoulli distribution for variables with more than two possible values.

When working out which label a tweet has, it is very useful to know whether some labels are more common than others. For example, if the set of tweets has been selected to be as relevant as possible, we might expect the `Unrelated` label to be less common. We can incorporate this knowledge into our model by learning the probability of a tweet taking on each of the labels – effectively this means learning the parameters of a discrete distribution. We have encountered a similar situation before in Section 2.6, where we used a beta distribution to learn the probability of true for a Bernoulli distribution. Here, we want to learn the probabilities associated with each possible value in a discrete distribution. We need an extended form of a beta distribution, that can handle learning a set of probability values that add up to 1. Happily, such a distribution exists: it is called the **Dirichlet distribution** – and has a probability density function given by:

$$Dirichlet(\mathbf{x}; \alpha) = \frac{x_1^{\alpha_1} x_2^{\alpha_2} \dots x_K^{\alpha_K}}{\mathrm{B}(\alpha)} \tag{7.1}$$

where K is the number of values that the variable can have, $\mathbf{x}$ is an array of K probability values adding up to 1 and α is the array of K counts that are the parameters of the distribution. Here, B() is the multivariate form of the beta function that we encountered in the density of the beta distribution (Section 2.6). When K is 2, equation (7.1) becomes identical to the beta density given back in equation (2.19) – this means that the beta distribution is exactly the same as a Dirichlet distribution with $K = 2$.

For our setting, we have four possible labels and so K is equal to 4. We want to learn an array of four probabilities for each of the four possible labels. Since we want to learn this array, we need to create a random variable for it – which we shall call `probLabel`. Note that the value of this variable is an array of probability values, rather than just one value. We need to choose a prior distribution for `probLabel` to encode our knowledge about this array of probabilities before we have seen any data. Since we don't want to assume anything about the probabilities ahead of time, we can choose a uniform Dirichlet distribution

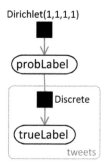

Figure 7.3 A model where the probability of the true label for a tweet taking each possible value is given by the array of probabilities `probLabel`.

that gives equal probability to any array of probability values that sum to 1. Such a uniform Dirichlet can be created by setting all the count parameters α to 1, which can be written as $Dirichlet(1,1,1,1)$.

We've now defined two variables for our model: a `trueLabel` variable for each tweet and a single, global `probLabel` variable giving the probabilities for each label. We can connect these variables in a factor graph as shown in Figure 7.3, where the *Discrete* factor defines a discrete distribution over `trueLabel` whose parameters are the probability array `probLabel`. Because there is a label for each tweet, the `trueLabel` variable sits inside a plate across the tweets.

In the model of Figure 7.3, neither of the two variables are observed. In particular, we do not observe the `trueLabel` because we need to infer this from the workers' labels. We need to extend our model then to include the crowd workers and their labels.

7.1.3 Incorporating crowd worker labels

In this chapter, we will find ourselves re-using pieces of models that we have developed in previous chapters. The ability to draw on existing model components is a very useful advantage of model-based machine learning. It means that we can often construct our models out of large pre-existing pieces rather than having to design them from scratch each time.

We can use pieces of models from previous chapters as building blocks for our new model.

We need to model the situation where a crowd worker is trying to work out the correct label for a tweet. This is similar to the situation in Chapter 2 where a candidate was trying to work out the correct answer for a question. In that model, we assumed that either the candidate had the skills to answer a question or not. Here, we will make a similar assumption:

② When a worker looks at a tweet, they will either be able to work out what the true label is or not.

To model this assumption, we will use a variable for whether the worker can work out the true label, or not. We'll call this `isCorrect` and it will be `true` if the worker can work out the correct label or `false` otherwise.

Next we need to decide what the worker does to choose a label for the tweet. Let's call this label `workerLabel` and allow it to take any of the four label values, just like `trueLabel`. Building on our previous assumption, if the worker can work out the true label, then we may reasonably assume that this is the label that they will provide.

③ If a worker can determine the true label, they will give this as their label.

If they cannot work out the true label, then they still need to provide *some* label – so we need to decide what they do in this case. In Chapter 2, we assumed that if someone did not know the answer to a question, then they would just guess at random. We can make the same assumption here:

④ If a worker cannot determine the true label, they will choose a label uniformly at random.

According to Assumption ③, if `isCorrect` is `true`, then `workerLabel` will simply be a copy of `trueLabel`. But according to Assumption ④, if `isCorrect` is `false`, then `workerLabel` must instead have a uniform distribution. To switch between these two difference ways of modelling `workerLabel`, we can use gates just like we did in the previous chapter (Section 6.4). For Assumption ③, we need a gate which is on when `isCorrect` is `true` and which contains a *Copy* factor that copies the value of `trueLabel` into `workerLabel`. The *Copy* factor is a deterministic factor which gives probability 1.0 to the child variable having the same value as the parent variable

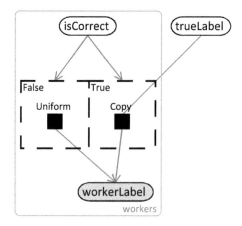

Figure 7.4 Model of all the worker labels for a single tweet. Each worker can either correctly work out the true label or not, as indicated by isCorrect. If they can work out the true label then they copy it into their label (right hand gate), otherwise they pick a label uniformly at random (left hand gate). The resulting label is stored in workerLabel – this is shown shaded because the values of these labels are known to the system.

and probability 0.0 to all other values. To model Assumption ④, we need a second gate which is on when isCorrect is false and contains a *Uniform* factor that gives a uniform discrete distribution to workerLabel. The resulting factor graph for a single tweet is shown in Figure 7.4.

7.1.4   Completing the model

The model of Figure 7.4 does not provide a prior for the isCorrect variable. We could just pick one and assume, say, that worker are correct 90% of the time. Instead, we will be a bit more sophisticated and allow the model to learn the probability of each worker being correct. We will call this the ability of the worker and put it inside a plate over the workers to give each worker there own ability. The assumption we will make is:

⑤ Some workers will be able to determine the true label more often than others, but most will manage most of the time.

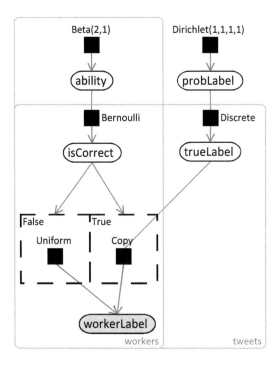

Figure 7.5 The overall model of a set of crowd workers labelling a set of tweets. Each worker has a different `ability` indicating the proportion of tweets that they will label correctly.

Since we expect most workers to determine the true label most of the time, we will give `ability` a prior distribution that favours probabilities above 50%. A *Beta*(2,1) distribution is a reasonable choice here.

We can now put together factor graphs Figures 7.3 and 7.4, along with this new `ability` variable to give the overall factor graph of Figure 7.5. Here we have placed the single tweet model of Figure 7.4 inside a plate over tweets, added in `probLabel` from Figure 7.4 and added the `ability` variable as a parent to `isCorrect`.

As usual, we should now take a moment to review our modelling assumptions. They are shown all together in Table 7.4.

Assumption ① is given by the setting, so is a safe assumption. Assumption ② also seems safe since surely the worker can either work out the correct label or not. Assumption ③ is a reasonable assumption if we believe that workers are genuinely trying to be helpful and not deliberately providing incorrect values. If we instead believe that there are workers trying to undermine the correct labelling, then we

Table 7.4 The five assumptions encoded in our crowd worker model.

---

① Each tweet has a true label which is one of the following set: `Positive`, `Negative`, `Neutral` or `Unrelated`.

② When a worker looks at a tweet, they will either be able to work out what the true label is or not.

③ If a worker can determine the true label, they will give this as their label.

④ If a worker cannot determine the true label, they will choose a label uniformly at random.

⑤ Some workers will be able to determine the true label more often than others, but most will manage most of the time.

---

would need to revisit this assumption. Assumption ④ is a simplifying assumption – in practice, workers will rarely pick at random but might instead make a best guess – this assumption may well be worth refining later. Finally, Assumption ⑤ seems like a reasonable assumption as long as we believe that the labelling task is easy enough for most workers most of the time. If this is not true, then we are probably in trouble anyway!

We now have a complete model and are ready to try it out – read on to see how well it works.

REVIEW OF CONCEPTS

gold labels Very high–quality labels used as a "gold standard" when deciding whether labels provided by crowd workers are correct.

sentiment analysis The task of determining a person's feelings, attitudes or opinions from a piece of written text.

Dirichlet distribution A probability distribution over a set of continuous probability values that add up to 1. The Dirichlet distribution is an extension of the beta distribution that can handle variables with more than two values. The probability density function for the Dirichlet distribution is:

$$Dirichlet(\mathbf{x}; \alpha) = \frac{x_1^{\alpha_1} x_2^{\alpha_2} \ldots x_K^{\alpha_K}}{B(\alpha)}$$

where K is the number of values that the variable can have, $\mathbf{x}$ is an array of K probability values adding up to 1 and α is the array of K counts that are the parameters of the distribution. Here, $B()$ is the multi-variate form of the beta function that we encountered in the density of the beta distribution (Section 2.6). When K is 2, the Dirichlet distribution reduces to a beta distribution.

The mean of the Dirichlet distribution is the count array α scaled so that the sum of its elements adds up to 1 – in other words it is $\frac{\alpha}{\sum_i \alpha_i}$. The mean value gives the position of the centre of mass of the distribution and the sum of the counts $\sum_i \alpha_i$ controls how spread out the distribution is, where a larger sum means a narrower distribution.

7.2 TRYING OUT THE WORKER MODEL

To try out the model, we must define some training and validation sets. For the validation set, we need to know the correct label, in order to be able to evaluate our model. So our validation set must consist only of tweets where we have gold labels. We will use 70% of the 950 gold labelled tweets as our validation set, so that some gold labels are available for training, if we want to use them. For the training set, we will use the remaining 30% of gold labelled tweets, plus a random selection of the remaining tweets to bring us to a totals of 20,000 tweets. The full statistics of the data sets are:

- **Training set:** 20,000 tweets with 54,440 labels from 1,788 workers;

- **Validation set:** 683 tweets with 3,637 labels from 764 workers.

To train our model, we will use the 20,000 training set tweets as our observed data. For now, we will not make any use of the gold labels during training. As we have throughout the book, we will use expectation propagation to infer posterior distributions over all unobserved variables.

For validation, we will apply the model to each validation tweet individually. The posteriors learned during training for the probability of each label `probLabel` and the `ability` of each worker will used as priors for these variables during validation. Expectation propagation will then be used to give posteriors over the `trueLabel` for the validation set tweet. The label with the highest probability under this posterior distribution will be considered to be the true label inferred by the model.

Since we have gold labels for all tweets in our validation set, we can use them to evaluate whether the inferred true label is correct. We can then compute the accuracy of our model, as the percentage of inferred labels that are correct. For this initial model, we find that our accuracy is 91.5%, which seems like a pretty good start!

Majority vote: the label with the most votes wins!

But before we break out the champagne, it would be helpful to know how good this accuracy really is. To do this, we should compare to a simple **baseline method**. We will use a simple method where the label assigned to a tweet is the one that the most workers chose, breaking ties at random. This method is called **majority vote**. If we use majority vote to label our validation set, then we get an accuracy of 90.3%. So, in fact, our model is giving us an improvement over this baseline, but only of 1.2%.

It's informative to consider why our model is able to do better than majority vote. The main reason is that we are learning the abilities of each worker. This allows us to let the votes of good workers count more than the votes of bad workers. To explore this a bit more, let's look at the inferred abilities of our workers. Figure 7.6 shows a histogram of the inferred abilities of our crowd workers.

We can see from Figure 7.6 that almost all abilities are above 50%, showing that most workers are able to provide correct labels – this is reassuring given that we assumed this in Assumption ⑤. The histogram also shows that there is a wide variety of abilities ranging from a bit over 10% up to around 95%. Being able to discount the weaker workers on the left of the histogram and pay more attention to the stronger workers on the right allows our model to achieve this 1.2% improvement in accuracy.

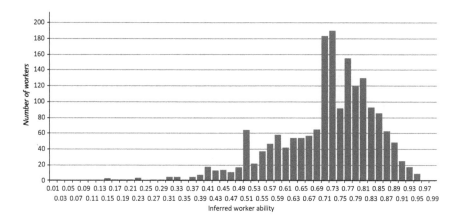

Figure 7.6 Histogram of inferred worker abilities, showing the number of workers with abilities in each bucket of the histogram. The workers have a wide range of abilities, but most have abilities above 50%.

	Negative (Inferred True)	Neutral (Inferred True)	Positive (Inferred True)	Unrelated (Inferred True)
Negative (True)	144	8	1	3
Neutral (True)	4	135	9	22
Positive (True)	0	6	136	3
Unrelated (True)	1	0	1	210

Figure 7.7 A confusion matrix showing the counts of tweets with each possible true and inferred label. Counts on the diagonal show where the inferred label matches the true label. Off-diagonal counts show various kinds of errors.

For our application, we want to push the accuracy as high as we can – as every correct label could have real benefit and every incorrect label could cause resources to be wasted. To increase our accuracy, it would be helpful to get a more detailed picture of the mistakes our model is making. If we had only two possible labels, we could count the true and false positives and the true and false negatives to produce a table in the structure of Table 2.7. In that table, each row corresponds to a true label and each column corresponds to an inferred label. Even though we have more than two labels, we can use the exact same table structure and put in each cell the count of tweets with the true label of the row and the inferred label of the column. This table is then called a **confusion matrix**. The confusion matrix for our initial model results is shown in Figure 7.7.

When working with a confusion matrix like this one, it can be hard to compare cells since the number of tweets with each true label varies. We can correct for this by dividing the value in each cell by the sum of the row and so express it as a percentage. A cell then shows the percentage of items with this true label that are predicted to have the particular inferred label. Figure 7.8 gives the same results as above expressed as a confusion matrix with percentages.

Looking at Figure 7.8, we can now see more clearly where the main sources of error are. For example, the most common error is that we are inferred the label Unrelated when the true label is Neutral. Another kind of error is incorrectly labelling Positive or Negative tweets as being Neutral – and, to a lesser extent, vice versa.

Our model is making these errors because of labelling errors made by individual crowd workers. So, it would also be useful to understand

	Negative (Inferred True)	Neutral (Inferred True)	Positive (Inferred True)	Unrelated (Inferred True)
Negative (True)	92.3%	5.1%	0.6%	1.9%
Neutral (True)	2.4%	79.4%	5.3%	12.9%
Positive (True)	0.0%	4.1%	93.8%	2.1%
Unrelated (True)	0.5%	0.0%	0.5%	99.1%

Figure 7.8 A confusion matrix where each cell contains the percentage of items with the true label that have the particular inferred label. Because all cells contain percentages, it is now easier to compare the values in different cells.

the kinds of errors that particular crowd workers make by plotting a confusion matrix for each individual worker. The problem is that each worker labels relatively few tweets and it is likely that few, or even none, of these have gold labels. Instead of limiting ourselves to just gold labels, we can also use the inferred true label, as we expect that this will generally be more correct than any individual worker. The resulting confusion matrices will be an approximation, but hopefully a good enough for us to get insights into the kinds of errors that workers make.

Figure 7.9 shows confusion matrices for three workers with different patterns of errors. For each of these three patterns, there were many workers with similar confusion matrices – we chose a representative example in each case. Figure 7.9a shows a worker who often gives the Neutral label to tweets that should have one of the other labels. Figure 7.9b shows a worker that makes relatively few mistakes – such a worker will have a high ability. Figure 7.9c shows a worker that often incorrectly gives the Unrelated label, while also giving the Neutral label to tweets that should be labelled as Positive or Negative.

Rather than just learn the overall ability of a worker, it would be helpful if we could learn the individual biases of the worker so that we can more accurately correct for different patterns of errors. We will look at how to do this in the next section.

	Negative (Worker)	Neutral (Worker)	Positive (Worker)	Unrelated (Worker)
Negative (True)	68.6%	24.5%	2.0%	4.9%
Neutral (True)	1.7%	87.5%	0.8%	10.0%
Positive (True)	5.9%	18.8%	68.3%	6.9%
Unrelated (True)	5.0%	24.5%	2.5%	67.9%

(a) Confusion matrix for worker #393

	Negative (Worker)	Neutral (Worker)	Positive (Worker)	Unrelated (Worker)
Negative (True)	95.4%	1.8%	2.8%	0.0%
Neutral (True)	6.4%	88.3%	3.2%	2.1%
Positive (True)	0.9%	3.7%	95.4%	0.0%
Unrelated (True)	4.6%	6.9%	1.5%	86.9%

(b) Confusion matrix for worker #128

	Negative (Worker)	Neutral (Worker)	Positive (Worker)	Unrelated (Worker)
Negative (True)	67.9%	15.4%	0.0%	16.7%
Neutral (True)	2.4%	77.6%	1.2%	18.8%
Positive (True)	0.0%	11.0%	68.5%	20.5%
Unrelated (True)	0.0%	0.0%	0.0%	100.0%

(c) Confusion matrix for worker #50

Figure 7.9 Confusion matrices for three different workers, showing that each makes different kinds of labelling errors.

REVIEW OF CONCEPTS

baseline method A method for doing a task that can be used to provide some comparative metrics. Such baseline metrics help us to understand just how good a model is at performing a task. We would generally hope that a new model would produce better metrics than a baseline model. If a model does not do much better than baseline then this suggests that either there is a bug in the model implementation or the model needs redesigning. A baseline method is often one that is simple to implement, so that not much effort is needed to run it and compute its metrics.

majority vote A method for labelling items where the winning label is the one with the most "votes" – that is, the one that was given by the most crowd workers.

confusion matrix A table (matrix) giving the results of a label prediction problem. Each row of the table corresponds to a true label and each column of the table corresponds to a predicted label. The cells of the table then contain counts of items with the true label of the row and the inferred label of the column.

Here is an example confusion matrix from Figure 7.7.

	Negative (Inferred True)	Neutral (Inferred True)	Positive (Inferred True)	Unrelated (Inferred True)
Negative (True)	144	8	1	3
Neutral (True)	4	135	9	22
Positive (True)	0	6	136	3
Unrelated (True)	1	0	1	210

7.3 CORRECTING FOR WORKER BIASES

We have discovered that some crowd workers are biased towards certain wrong labels for tweets with a particular true label. For example, some workers tend to give the label Neutral for tweets which should be labelled Positive or Negative. This contradicts our Assumption ④, which stated that:

④ If a worker cannot determine the true label, they will choose a label uniformly at random.

In fact, workers do not choose labels at random. They instead choose labels in a biased way that depends on the true label. If we look at the confusion matrices in Figure 7.9, then we can see each worker makes different kinds of mistakes. The confusion matrices provide a clear description of the mistakes that each worker makes. If only we could get our model to learn the confusion matrix for each worker, then it could use this to improve its accuracy. For example, for workers that incorrectly give label Neutral for tweets with true label Negative, our model could learn that when the worker provides the label Neutral then this is actually evidence for label Negative.

How can we get our model to learn a confusion matrix for each worker? First, we need to throw away all of our previous assumptions about how workers provide labels (Assumption ② through to Assumption ⑤). We can then make a new assumption:

② Each worker gives a tweet a particular label with a worker-specific probability that depends on the true label of the tweet.

Here, we are assuming that each worker has their own conditional probability table, which gives the probability of the worker assigning each label to a tweet, conditioned on the true label of the tweet. This conditional probability table has the same rows and columns as the worker's confusion matrix and the conditional probabilities in the cells correspond to the percentage entries in the confusion matrix. In other words, the conditional probability table will represent the confusion matrix – and so learning the table for a worker will effectively mean that we are learning their personal confusion matrix.

To learn the conditional probability table for a worker, we will need to represent it using random variables. Recall from Section 1.1 that the probabilities in each row of a conditional probability table must add up to 1. That means each row of a conditional probability table is an array of probabilities summing to 1, just like for probLabel! So

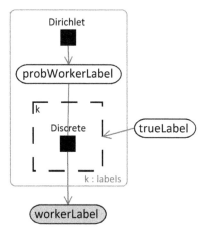

Figure 7.10 A model for learning a worker's conditional probability table. Each `probWorkerLabel` variable represents a row of the table. The `trueLabel` selects one row of the table which then provides the probabilities for choosing each possible value for the `workerLabel`.

we can create a similar random variable called `probWorkerLabel` to contain the probabilities for a row. If we put this variable inside a plate over the labels, we will get a row per label – in other words, an entire table. To make use of this table, we need a gate for row which is turned on only when `trueLabel` has that value. Each gate then connects the corresponding row of the table to a *Discrete* factor to generate the `workerLabel`. The resulting factor graph is shown in Figure 7.10 – notice that it looks just like the factor graph of Figure 6.19 but with discrete/Dirichlet factors instead of Bernoulli/Beta ones.

In Figure 7.10 we have used a Dirichlet prior over `probWorkerLabel`, just like we did for `probLabel`. We can choose this prior for each row of the conditional probability table to encode any assumptions we want to make about the probabilities in that row. Specifically, we will assume:

③ Most workers will have a higher probability of giving the correct label than an incorrect one.

This assumption states that we expect the conditional probability of the correct label for a tweet to be higher than that for an incorrect label, for most workers. We can encode this assumption in our model by using a Dirichlet prior for each row with a higher count parameter for the correct label than for incorrect labels combined. If we choose the three incorrect labels in a row to have a count parameter of 1, then we could give the correct label a count parameter of 6, which is twice the combined counts of the three incorrect labels. These counts mean we would use *Dirichlet*(6,1,1,1) for the prior for the first row, *Dirichlet*(1,6,1,1) for the second row, *Dirichlet*(1,1,6,1) for the third row and *Dirichlet*(1,1,1,6) for the last row. These prior distributions favour having high probabilies on the diagonal entries of the CPT than on the off-diagonal entries, which is just what we want in order to satisfy Assumption ③.

If we use the factor graph of Figure 7.10 to replace the corresponding piece of our initial model, we get the new model of Figure 7.11. This kind of model was first developed by Kim and Ghahramani. [2012] who called it the Independent Bayesian Classifier Combination (IBCC) model.

We expect that the model of Figure 7.11 will be able to learn about the biases of each worker and so correct for them. The general problem of correcting for data set bias is a very important one in machine learning. Bias in data sets has been shown to lead to a form of automated discrimination, where machine learning systems have given biased out-

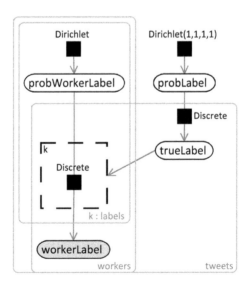

Figure 7.11 A biased worker model which assumes that each worker has their own biases which can be captured by a conditional probability table. The hope is that the model can learn each worker's biases and appropriately correct for them when inferring the true label of a tweet.

puts, for example, with respect to gender, race or economic status. A core assumption of many machine learning systems is that the training set is representative of how the system will be applied – in practice, this is often far from true. For example, face recognitions systems have often been trained on data sets with predominantly white-skinned people. Overcoming these problems to make fairer machine learning systems is a very important problem and the focus of much current work (see Holstein et al. [2019], for example). The approach we are using in this chapter shows one possible way of correcting for these kinds of biases.

7.3.1 Evaluating our biased worker model

We believe that our new model will be able to learn and correct for the biases of our workers and so give improved accuracy when inferring the true labels of tweets. To see if this is true, we can evaluate our new model and compare results to our initial model and to majority vote. Figure 7.12 shows the accuracy of each of our models. Looking at this figure, you can see that our new model is actually doing much worse than our initial model! In fact, its accuracy is almost down to the level of majority vote.

How can our new model be doing so much worse than the initial one? This is surprising because we expect our new model to be able to learn the biases of each crowd worker and so do better. This result is particularly counter-intuitive because the initial model is actually a

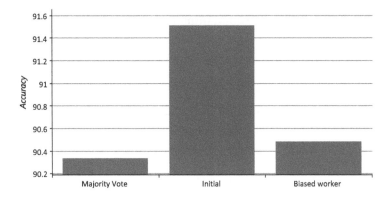

Figure 7.12 Accuracy of our new biased worker model compared to the initial model and to majority vote. Unfortunately, our new model is less accurate than our initial model and only slightly more accurate than our majority vote baseline.

special case of the biased worker model. We can choose a conditional probability table whose diagonal values are the `ability` from the previous model and zero elsewhere, and then add in a uniform distribution to each row to represent the crowd worker guessing when they do not know the true label. With these settings our new model exactly reproduces the old model. We would therefore expect that the new model would be at least as good as the old, since it could learn to fall back on the old model's settings if necessary. Because the new model is actually doing less well, there must be some kind of problem in learning a good enough conditional probability table in `probWorkerLabel`. But what could this problem be?

Here, it is useful to consider what we are asking our model to learn, and from what data. For each worker, we are trying to learn a 4×4 conditional probability table – in other words, 16 probability values. But since each row has to add up to 1, we only really need to learn 12 of these 16 values, because one value in each row can be computed by subtracting the remaining values from 1.0. Each of these 12 values is a conditional probability of the worker giving some label for a tweet with some true label. If we were asked to estimate such a probability, we'd want to see examples of tweets with each true label and each possible worker label. For example, if we wanted to estimate the probability of a worker giving label Neutral to tweets with true label Negative, then we'd want to see lots of examples of Negative tweets so that we could estimate the proportion of these labelled as Neutral. The more examples we were given, the more accurately we'd expect to estimate the probability – so we would want lots of labels for each combination of true and worker labels. But how many do we actually have? Figure 7.13 shows how many workers provided differ amounts of labels in our training set.

The plot shows that the majority of workers have labelled less than 50 tweets – and many have labelled far fewer. Even for workers with 50 labels, if these were split evenly amongst 12 values we are trying to learn, we would only have four or so labels per probability value – not enough to accurately estimate the probabilities. In reality, the labels are not split evenly and so it is likely that we would have no data at all for many probability values. In short, we do not have enough data to learn the conditional probability tables for most of the workers. Therefore, most worker conditional probability tables will end up very uncertain – and so we will, in turn, become less certain about the true label for a tweet.

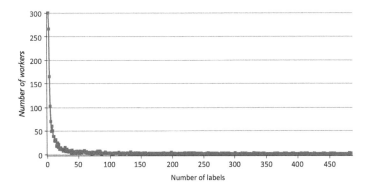

Figure 7.13 Histogram of the number of workers who have given different numbers of labels. The histogram shows that the majority of workers have labelled fewer than 50 tweets and many have labelled far fewer than that.

Another way of looking at this problem is that our model is too flexible. It allows for too many possible kinds of workers. For example, it allows for workers that always give the label `Positive`, for workers that always pick labels at random, for workers that deliberately give `Positive` for tweets that are `Negative` and vice versa, indeed for workers that give every possible wrong label for each true label and with every possible probability, and so on. This is a huge number of possibilities! If we believe that workers are generally well intentioned, then many of these possibilities will

When working with data, being too flexible can be bad!

likely not occur. Yet our model is requiring us rule out each unlikely possibility, and to do this for each worker individually. This task is asking too much of the available data.

7.3.2 Comparing more and less flexible models

A visualisation of this situation is shown in Figure 7.14, which is heavily inspired by a figure from David MacKay's excellent book [MacKay, 2003, p. 344]. In this figure, the x-axis represents all possible data sets, so we can think of each point on the axis as a particular data set, such as the marked data sets D_A and D_B. The y-axis represents the

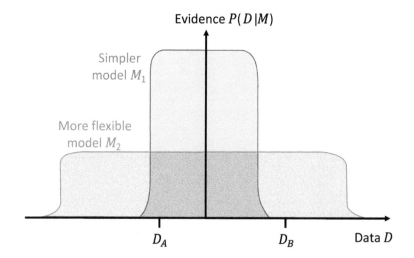

Figure 7.14 A visualisation of a simpler model M_1 and a more flexible model M_2. The x-axis represents all possible data sets and the y-axis gives the probability of each data set under the model (the evidence). The simpler model M_1 can explain fewer data sets and so gives higher probability to each one than the more flexible model M_2. So for a data set that fits both models, like D_A, the simpler model is more probable. Where the additional flexibility of M_2 is needed to explain the data set, as is the case for D_B, then the more complex model becomes more probable.

probability of a data set given a model, which is the model evidence (see Section 6.3). The simpler model M_1 can only explain a limited range of possible data sets – which includes D_A but excludes D_B. Our initial model is like this – for example, it cannot explain data sets where crowd workers have strong biases and so these will have very low probability under the model. However, because a simpler model explains fewer data sets, it can put higher probability on each one and so have higher model evidence. So for a data set like D_A, the simpler model M_1 is more probable, even though it could also be explained by the more flexible model M_2. The result is that predictions under M_1 would be more accurate than under M_2 – exactly the situation that we are seeing with our two models.

The figure also shows another data set D_B which can be explained by the more flexible model M_2, but not by the simpler model M_1. Here the additional flexibility of M_2 is essential for explaining the data set and so will have much higher model evidence than M_1. In general, the more restrictive the assumptions encoded by the model, the smaller the range of data sets that will be explained well by the model. If the actual data set lies in this range then this restrictive model will work better than a model with less restrictive assumptions.

> **A model with more restrictive assumptions will perform better, as long as those assumptions hold true for the data.**

So the reason that the new model is working less well, is that it is too flexible. The model is trying to learn a conditional probability table for every single worker and there is just insufficient data to do this well. We need to find a way to learn our conditional probability tables from much more data – to learn how we can do this, read on!

7.4 COMMUNITIES OF WORKERS

In the previous section, our biased worker model failed to improve our accuracy, due to lack of data. More specifically, each worker does not have enough data for the model to learn a personalised conditional probability table to represent their biases. To consider how to solve this problem, think back to Section 6.5 where we were learning how children gain or lose allergies. Rather than learning the probabilities of each individual child gaining or losing each allergy, we grouped the children into classes and learned probabilities for all children in a class. We can use exactly the same trick here!

It seems reasonable to group our workers together, as we may expect that there are communities of workers that have similar behaviour. We saw this when selecting worker confusion matrices for Figure 7.9 – many workers had very similar confusion matrices. For example, there seemed to be a community of workers who are very careful and give very good quality labels, another community who make mistakes about which tweets are relevant or not, a smaller community of workers who confuse the labels **Neutral** and **Negative** and so on. If we switch our model to learning conditional probability tables for whole communities, rather than for individual workers, then we will have much more data to train each CPT. More data will mean more certain inferred CPTs and so hopefully better accuracy. This was the approach taken by Venanzi et al. [2014] who developed a model very similar to the one we will now explore.

To change our model to learn CPTs for communities instead of workers, we need to modify our assumptions:

② Each worker in a particular community will give a tweet a particular label with a ~~worker~~ community-specific probability that depends on the true label of the tweet.

③ Most ~~workers~~ communities will have a higher probability of giving the correct label than an incorrect one.

and add a new one:

④ Each worker belongs to a single community.

To encode these new assumptions in a model, we need to move the `probWorkerLabel` variable out of the plate over the workers and into a new plate over communities. Each worker will also need a new

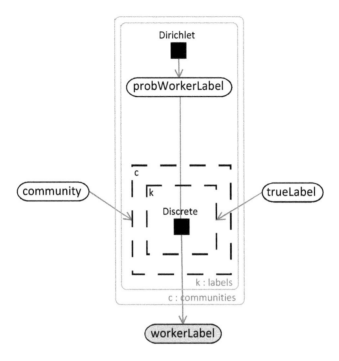

Figure 7.15 Community model for a single label. The two nested gates show that the conditional probability for the worker label is selected by both the `community` of the worker and the `trueLabel` of the tweet.

`community` variable to indicate which community that workers belongs to: 0, 1, 2 ... and so on. We will need a new gate inside the communities plate which is switched on and off by this `community` variable. Given that we already have a gate connected to the `trueLabel` variable, this means that we now have two gates – one inside the other. The conditional probability for a label is therefore selected by both the `community` of the worker and the `trueLabel` of the tweet. Figure 7.15 shows the resulting factor graph for a single label with the two nested gates and the new `community` variable and plate.

We expect some communities to be much larger than others, and so it will be useful to learn the probability that a worker belongs to each available community. We can use exactly the same approach as for learning the probability of each true label and create a new variable `probCommunity` that holds an array of probabilities that add up to 1 – and once again give this a *Dirichlet* prior. Putting everything together gives us the overall model of Figure 7.16.

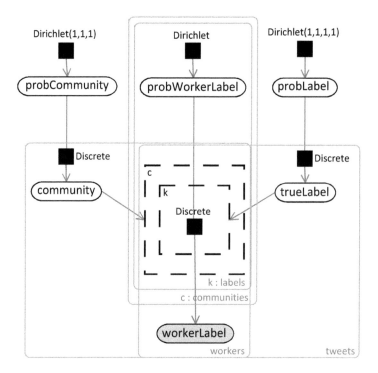

Figure 7.16 The community model in full. Notice that this model has ended up having a symmetry between the two sides – the `community` variable and its parent `probCommunity` are connected just like the `trueLabel` variable and its parent `probLabel`.

7.4.1 Results of the community model

We can try out our model for different numbers of communities – say, between 1 and 3. For any of these, we can look at the inferred CPTs for each community given by the posterior over `probWorkerLabel`. These CPTs should give us a good understanding of the entire population of workers – what patterns of mistakes are made and how many workers fall into each pattern. For example, Figure 7.17 shows the inferred CPTs for a three-community model, along with the number of workers in the training set assigned to each community. The three CPTs show three different patterns of errors, much like the three example worker confusion matrices in Figure 7.9.

Understanding the kinds of mistakes different workers make can be useful by itself. For example, it provides insights in how to improve the training given to the workers. In our case, Figure 7.9 suggests that we

	Negative (Worker)	Neutral (Worker)	Positive (Worker)	Unrelated (Worker)
Negative (True)	71.9%	22.0%	1.9%	4.2%
Neutral (True)	3.1%	89.0%	2.0%	5.8%
Positive (True)	2.0%	15.2%	78.3%	4.5%
Unrelated (True)	1.6%	10.4%	1.4%	86.6%

(a)CPT of the largest community with 842 workers

	Negative (Worker)	Neutral (Worker)	Positive (Worker)	Unrelated (Worker)
Negative (True)	90.3%	3.9%	3.8%	2.0%
Neutral (True)	13.6%	76.1%	6.9%	3.3%
Positive (True)	3.2%	3.1%	91.4%	2.3%
Unrelated (True)	3.8%	7.2%	4.0%	85.0%

(b) CPT of the middle community with 561 workers

	Negative (Worker)	Neutral (Worker)	Positive (Worker)	Unrelated (Worker)
Negative (True)	73.6%	9.7%	2.9%	13.8%
Neutral (True)	5.7%	71.1%	4.1%	19.1%
Positive (True)	2.0%	7.1%	78.1%	12.8%
Unrelated (True)	1.6%	2.2%	1.5%	94.7%

(c) CPT of the smallest community with 385 workers

Figure 7.17 Learned conditional probability tables for our community model, run with three communities. Each CPT shows a different crowd worker bias. For example, the top CPT shows a community of workers which tend to label tweets incorrectly as Neutral – this bias is visible in the second column of the CPT where there is a relatively high probability of giving the label Neutral for the three rows where the true label is not Neutral. Similarly, the bottom CPT shows a community of workers that tend to label tweets incorrectly as Unrelated.

should have additional training to show what tweets should be labelled as Neutral or Unrelated perhaps by showing workers real examples of tweets that have been incorrectly labelled. Hopefully, these kind of changes alone would lead to improvements in labelling accuracy. We could even provide customised training for each worker, tailored to the community that the worker belongs to!

Even without improved worker training, now that we are modelling the error patterns of our workers, we may hope for improved accuracy. The accuracies for models with 1, 2 and 3 communities are shown in Figure 7.18, compared to the accuracies of previous models. The chart shows that our community model is now leading to improved

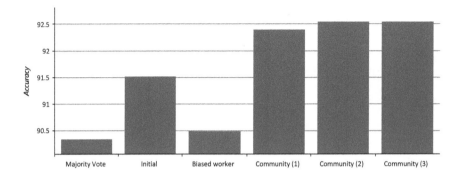

Figure 7.18 Accuracies for community models with 1, 2 and 3 communities, along with previous models for comparison. The community model is giving a good improvement in accuracy over the previous models. Surprisingly, having more communities does not seem to help the accuracy much.

accuracy, whether we choose 1, 2 or 3 communities. Interestingly, the numbers of communities does not seem to have much affect on the overall accuracy. This may be because the communities are similar enough that modelling one big community really well is nearly as good as modelling communities separately. It is also possible that having more communities means that there is less data per community and so more uncertainty in each community CPT. This uncertainty could be negatively affecting the accuracy.

7.4.2 Results with less training data

We've seen that our new community model works better than our previous models, and we believe this is because it makes better use of the available training data. In our application, we care deeply about how quickly we can get accurate labels – we want our system to be as accurate as possible even early on when there are relatively few labelled tweets. We can check how well our system performs with little training data by artificially reducing the size of our training set and seeing what effect this has on our accuracy. To do this, we will use training sets ranging from 10% of the original size up to 100% of the original size, in 10% increments. Figure 7.19 shows how the accuracy of each model varies as we increase the amount of training data.

The plot in Figure 7.19 is very encouraging for our community model. It shows that the accuracy of the model remains high even with

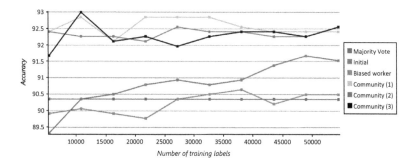

Figure 7.19 Plot showing how the accuracy of each model varies with the number of training labels. As the training data is reduced to 10% of its original size, the community models show only a small reduction in accuracy. In contrast, the accuracy of both the initial model and the biased worker model drop to below that of majority vote. As a result the communities models do even better than the other models when there are few training labels, since the gap is larger on the left of the plot than on the right.

only 10% of the training data (the left-hand end of the graph). This suggests that the model will do well early on, when there are relatively few labels, and also continue to give the best performance later, when more tweets have been labelled. Interestingly, we see that the initial model copes particularly badly with little training data: its accuracy drops rapidly as the training data is reduced and at 10% training data it is worse than both the biased worker model and the majority vote baseline! It seems we were very wise to move away from this model.

It is fantastic that our community model works well even when there are relatively few labels – but it would be even better if we could make our model useful before we have any labels at all! We will explore this idea in the next section.

7.5 MAKING USE OF THE TWEETS

Our community model makes good use of the labels being provided by our crowd workers. But there is some information that our model is not making use of: the tweets themselves. We do not expect to be able to build a model that could accurately label tweets – if we could do this, then we would not need the human crowd workers! However, we *can* build a model to label tweets somewhat accurately, although less accurately than a human worker. Such a model is useful because it can triage the tweets – in other words, work out if a tweet is likely to be about an emergency situation and, if so, send it to be labelled with high priority.

To predict the label for each tweet we can construct a classifier model. We could use the one from Chapter 4 but instead we will use an even simpler classifier based on the following assumption:

⑤ The probability that a tweet contains a particular word depends only on the true label of the tweet.

To model this assumption, we will need a variable to represent an observed word in a tweet. To represent a word, we assume that we have a vocabulary of all words that we want to represent. Then, a word in a tweet will be represented as an index into this vocabulary – 0 for the first word in the vocabulary, 1 for the second, and so on. We will use a variable called `word` to represent each word and put it inside a plate across the words in a tweet and also inside the existing tweets plate, since there are different words in each tweet.

We will also need a variable `probWords` to hold the probability of each word. Since we need a word probability for each possible true label, `probWords` needs to lie in a plate across the labels. Figure 7.20 shows the resulting model which includes these two variables and connects them to the `trueLabel` variable. This model is a kind of **naive Bayes classifier** since it assumes that the probability of each word does not depend on the presence or absence of other words in the tweet. This is not a particularly good assumption to make about words since certain words often occur together, such as in phrases. We will work with it for now and then discuss how it could be improved later.

Gold labels are rare!

An important question is: What data should we use to train this model? We could use the gold labels, but there are relatively few tweets

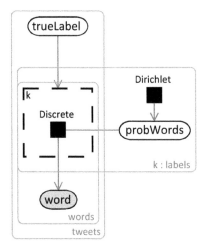

Figure 7.20 A model of the words in each tweet, where the probability of a word being included in a tweet depends only on the true label of that tweet.

with gold labels. Training our classifier only on tweets with gold labels would mean ignoring most of the tweets. But we would like to be able to train on all of the tweets!

Our community model gives us inferred labels for all tweets, whether or not they have gold labels. If we could use this inferred label from this model, we could train our classifier on all of the tweets. To achieve this, we can embed the words model of Figure 7.20 inside our existing community model, and share the **trueLabel** variable between them – making one unified model. The resulting combined model is shown in Figure 7.21.

7.5.1 Results with words

Because our combined model can use inferred labels for training, we are able to train it on all 20,000 tweets in our training set. We use a vocabulary consisting of all words that occur at least ten times in this training set, to ensure there is a reasonable amount of data for each word. To see how well our model works for triage, we then apply it to the validation set, but without supplying any worker labels. Unlike earlier models, this model can provide meaningful predictions without any worker labels, by making use of the words in each tweet. The resulting predictions have an accuracy of 66.5%. As expected, this is much lower

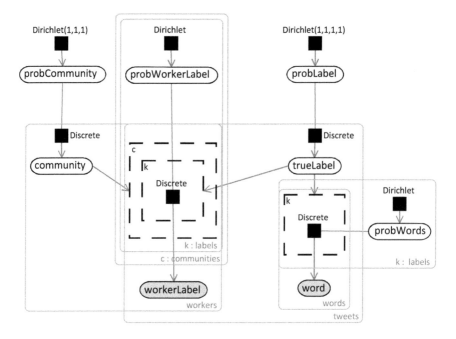

Figure 7.21 Our combined model, which infers the tweet labels by using information both from the crowd worker judgements and from the words in the tweet.

than the accuracy of 92.5% we achieved when making use of worker labels. Nonetheless, it may still be useful for triaging tweets. To explore how useful it can be, let's take a look at the confusion matrix, shown in Figure 7.22.

The confusion matrix shows that our accuracy differs for different types of tweet. For example, the accuracy at predicting the label of **Negative** tweets is much higher than for **Neutral** tweets. Suppose we wanted to detect **Negative** tweets urgently, as we would for emergency

	Negative (Inferred True)	Neutral (Inferred True)	Positive (Inferred True)	Unrelated (Inferred True)
Negative (True)	75.6%	1.9%	10.3%	12.2%
Neutral (True)	17.1%	51.2%	5.3%	26.5%
Positive (True)	17.9%	0.7%	66.9%	14.5%
Unrelated (True)	18.9%	4.7%	4.7%	71.7%

Figure 7.22 Confusion matrix for our words-only model.

tweets in a crisis situation. If we prioritise tweets that our words model infers to be `Negative`, then three times out of four the crowd workers will confirm this tentative labelling – showing that our model could provide a pretty useful form of triage.

It is informative to explore how our words model is making its predictions. One way to do this is to look at the posterior distribution over `probWords` for a label. Specifically, we are interested in words that are more common for tweets with a particular label than for tweets in general. To find such words, we can compute the ratio of the probability of each word in `probLabel` to the probability of the word in the data set as a whole. Table 7.5 shows the ten words with the highest such ratio for each of the four labels.

The words in Table 7.5 tell a fascinating story. The `Positive` column is a good place to start looking – the top words here are all words of positive sentiment and "finally" which suggests relief at some bad weather being over at last. But, surprisingly, words about it being "hot" or "sunny" do not appear in this column. In fact, "hot" instead appears in the `Negative` column, along with many swear words. Interestingly, the `Negative` column also includes "I" which indicates that people may tend to use more personal language when complaining about the weather ("I hate the rain") than when being positive ("What a lovely day today"). The `Neutral` column has the kinds of words that a formal weather forecasting tweet might contain, such as temperatures and wind speeds – just what you might expect from a neutral tweet about

Table 7.5 For each label, the ten words with the highest probability in tweets of that label, relative to their probability in tweets in general.

Negative	Neutral	Positive	Unrelated
its	{number}f	beautiful	patrol
outside	{number}mph	nice	check
hot	f	perfect	snow
f***	pm	enjoy	video
cold	wind	loving	song
it	feels	great	you
i	mph	enjoying	blizzard
freezing	humidity	love	white
hell	severe	finally	she
d***	cdt	gorgeous	via

the weather. Finally, the `Unrelated` column seems to have identified words that go with weather words in tweets that are not about the weather, such as "Snow Patrol" (a rock band) or "Snow White".

This table helps us to understand how our words model is making predictions and also suggests the kinds of mistakes it might make. For example, an unrelated tweet about a "hot dog" would likely lead our model to give an incorrect prediction of `Negative`. An interesting exercise is to consider how to modify Assumption ⑤ to address these kinds of mistakes. For example, we could consider assumptions about the probability of words co-occurring, such as "hot" and "dog" occurring together, conditioned on the true label of the tweet.

7.5.2 Wrapping up

In this chapter, we have developed a model that can learn about the biases of crowd workers by assigning them to communities of similar workers. The model can then appropriately correct for worker biases to give high accuracy labels. Where tweets are being labelled, the model can also make use of the words in the tweet to perform triage, in order to prioritise labelling the most important messages. Importantly, along the way we have learned that more flexible models are not necessarily better models!

There are a number of ways in which this model could be further improved. For example, the model could be extended to infer the difficulty of labelling each tweet, somewhat like we did for quiz questions in Chapter 2. It could also incorporate other kinds of information, such as how long it took for the annotator to produce a label. Nonetheless, the model is already competitive: Venanzi et al. [2012] used a version of this model to take part in the CrowdScale Shared Task Challenge described at the start of the chapter. Because the model can combine labels from the crowd workers with information from the words in the tweet, they were able to achieve joint first place in this challenge. What's more, Simpson et al. [2015] compared variants of this model with a number of crowd sourcing models and found that the model with words was most accurate on two different, challenging data sets. So, at the time, the model developed in this chapter really was a competitive solution to processing crowd-sourced labels.

Even more exciting, an extension of this model by Ramchurn et al. [2015] was actually used to analyse live streams of emergency tweets received during environmental disasters in the Philippines – an excellent application of model-based machine learning!

REVIEW OF CONCEPTS

naive Bayes classifier A classification model that has the label variable as a parent variable and separate child variables for each feature value. These classifiers are "naive" because they make the assumption that each feature value is independent given the label – this is usually a poor assumption since feature values are often correlated with each other.

CHAPTER 8

How to read a model

We've now created several models by piecing together the assumptions needed to solve a particular problem. But there is a vast ecosystem of models and algorithms already out there that other people have built. It would be great to make use of this work to avoid reinventing the wheel. Can model-based machine learning help us to pick up someone else's model and understand what assumptions it is making, so that we can make good use of it?

S O far in the book, we've designed a variety of different models in order to solve a range of real world problems. But this isn't the only way to apply the skills of model-based machine learning. As well as designing models, model-based machine learning also enables us to understand and interpret models created by other people. This understanding is useful for:

- seeing whether it makes sense to apply someone else's model to a particular task;

We do not want to re-invent the wheel.

- explaining the behaviour of such a model – for example, on a particular data item;

- diagnosing problems that arise when applying an existing model to a new problem;

DOI: 10.1201/9780429192685-9

- exploring how best to extend a model to encode new assumptions or to modify existing ones.

In this chapter, we will demonstrate how to interpret models by example – we will take a number of popular models and show how to understand the assumptions represented in each model. We will explore what these assumptions mean in terms of what data and tasks each model is, and is not, suitable for. We will also identify assumptions that limit where the model can be applied. By relaxing these assumptions, we will create extended models which can be applied more broadly than the original.

In some cases, we will start with an algorithm rather than a model. Here, we will first have to translate the algorithm into a corresponding model before we can begin the process of analysis. This is also a very useful skill – as well as allowing for analysis of the resulting model, it also allows the full range of inference algorithms to be applied, often unlocking new capabilities that the original algorithm lacked.

The models and algorithms that we will explore are:

- **Latent Dirichlet Allocation** – a model of the topics mentioned in a set of documents;

- **Decision Tree** – a classification algorithm based on very different assumptions to the classifier we developed in Chapter 4;

- **Principal Component Analysis** – an algorithm for transforming a set of observations of correlated variables into a set of values of uncorrelated variables, known as principal components;

- **k-means clustering** – a popular algorithm for discovering clusters of related data points.

To explore our first model, Latent Dirichlet Allocation, read on...

8.1 LATENT DIRICHLET ALLOCATION

Latent Dirichlet Allocation (LDA) is a model of the words in a set of documents or of other kinds of data with similar structure, such as sets of genetic sequences or images. LDA is a kind of **topic model** – a model which aims to discover the topics being written about in a set of documents, and also annotate each piece of text with the topics mentioned in it. This model was first developed by citetPritchard:2000 in the context of population genetics, and then independently rediscovered by Blei et al. [2003] who named it LDA. The relative simplicity of the model, along with its applicability to a broad range of data types, has made it one of the most popular and widely used machine learning models, particularly for analysing textual data.

In previous chapters, we have built up a factor graph by making a series of assumptions about the problem domain. In this chapter, we will reverse this process: we will start with a factor graph and analyse it to understand the assumptions that it is making – much as we might do for any published model that we would like to understand. Following this process, we need the factor graph for LDA so that we can analyse it. This factor graph can be found in Blei et al. [2003], a version of which is shown in Figure 8.1.

To analyse this factor graph, we can start by exploring what each variable is – what type it has and what the variable means in the problem domain. It is usually easiest to start with observed variables since they correspond to the data being processed. In this model,

LDA is a model of multiple documents.

there is one observed variable: `word`. This `word` variable lies in a plate over words inside a plate over document, so the observed data is all the words in some set of documents. The type of `word` is discrete (a.k.a. categorical) which here means that its value identifies a particular word – we can think of this as the index of the word in a particular vocabulary of words.

From the factor graph, we can see that `probWord` is a probability distribution over the words in the vocabulary. We can also see that probWord lies inside a plate over topics – so there is one such distribution for each topic. Since this is the only topic-specific variable, it shows that a topic is entirely characterised by its distribution over words. The gate structure in the middle shows that the `topic` variable switches between these topic-specific distributions. Because the `topic` variable lies inside plates over words and documents, we can see that this topic switching happens for each word individually. In other words, each word has its own topic label.

Finally, `probTopic` is a probability distribution over topics. It lives inside the plate over documents, showing that each document has its own distribution over the topics in that document.

8.1.1 Exploring the assumptions in LDA

We've described the factor graph of Figure 8.1 at a factual level – now let's see how to read off the assumptions being made in this graph. Again, let's start with the observed variable `word`. We can see from the graph that the only parent of `word` that is word- or document-specific is the `topic` variable. So the model is assuming that the topic is the

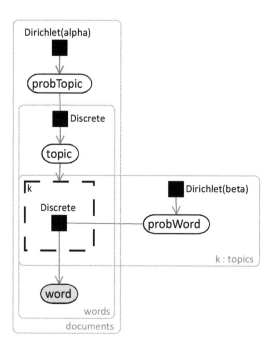

Figure 8.1 Factor graph for the Latent Dirichlet Allocation model.

only characteristic of the word or document that affects the choice of word used. More precisely, the assumption is:

(1) The probability of writing a particular word depends only on the topic being written about.

Our goal is to understand what the LDA model does and where it can be applied. So, let's consider situations where this assumption would and would not hold. We could start by considering what, other than the topic, might affect word choice – for example:

- **The author** – two different people are likely to use different words when talking about the same topic;

- **The kind of document** – the choice of word is also likely to vary depending on the kind of document being written. For example, a technical paper on a topic might use different words to a news article on the same topic – and a tweet about the topic would likely use yet different words again.

- **When the document was written** – use of words changes slowly over time. Two documents about the same topic written many years apart would be very likely to have differing distributions of words, even if written by the same person.

- **The language** – writing about the same topic in different languages would definitely lead to very different words being used!

All of these variables could cause a change to the distribution of words unrelated to the topic being written about. If we want our inferred topic variable to actually correspond to the topic of the document, then we would need to keep all such variables fixed. For example, we would want to run LDA on documents of the same kind, in the same language, written by the same author at around the same time. The first two of these are usually quite easy to achieve. There are many collections of documents available where all documents are the same kind and written in the same language – for example, news articles. However, such documents collections are not usually written by a single author and may have been written over many years. The risk of using LDA in such cases is that the inferred topics might start to depend on the author or time as well as the actual topic (or on some combination of these), rather than on the topic alone.

Let's explore some more assumptions – looking at the factor graph, we can see that the `topic` and `word` variables sit inside a plate over the words. This means that the process for generating the topic for each word, and for generating the word itself, is identical for every word in the document. To put this another way, you could re-order the words in a document and the topics inferred for each word would remain exactly the same. There are two underlying assumptions here:

② Changing the order of words in a document has no affect on the topic being talked about.

③ The topics of two words are just as likely to be the same if the words are adjacent, as if they are far away.

Assumption ② is a very poor assumption as a model of text. If you re-order the words in a document then it will likely make very little sense, and should definitely not be considered equivalent to the original document! Yet, for the purpose of identifying topics, re-ordering may not be so bad – the relevant question is "do we expect to be able to tell the topic of a word, even if we ignore the surrounding words?". In many cases, the word alone may be enough to clearly define the topic. An exception would be for phrases where we several words in order have a meaning that the individual words lack. Back in Section 7.5, we found our model trying to distinguish between tweets about "snow" and about "snow patrol". Distinguishing between these two topics is going to be very sensitive to word order! LDA would struggle to provide correct topic labels in such cases.

Assumption ③ may also be a poor assumption in practice, if the goal is to have words reliably labelled with topics. In most documents, we may expect entire sentences, or even entire paragraphs, to be about the same topic. But LDA is unlikely to give the same topic label to all the words in a sentence or paragraph, since it is making independent choices for each word. For example, the phrase "track and field" is likely related to the topic of athletics, but the middle word "and" by itself is not. Even if "track" and "field" were correctly labelled, it is most likely that "and" would be inferred to have an entirely different topic label. In practice, such neutral words like "and" often end up assigned to a general-purpose topic, for words that are used in many contexts. If the goal is to infer the topics of the *document*, rather than the topic of individual words or sentences, then LDA can work well despite this assumption – the overall distribution of topic labels can be usefully accurate even if the labels for individual words are not.

Moving up to the top of the factor graph, we can consider what assumptions are being made about the topics overall. One assumption is:

④ The overall number of topics is known.

The size k of the topic plate is fixed and so we are assuming that this number of topics is known. In practice, LDA is often used in an unsupervised way, to discover topics in a set of documents. In such an application, there is no reason to believe that the number of topics would be known. This assumption can be sidestepped to an extent by exploring many different values of k and seeing which is best for the intended application.

A more concerning assumption arises because of the Dirichlet prior on `probTopic`:

⑤ Any pair of topics are equally likely to be talked about in the same document.

On the surface, Assumption ⑤ is a very odd assumption. There are topics which

A document is unlikely to talk about both patisserie and politics.

are very unlikely to be addressed in the same document (such as political commentary and patisserie recipes) and others which are much more likely to be mentioned together (such as political commentary and economic analysis). The symmetry between topics in the Dirichlet prior means the LDA model treats both equally. What's more, with the parameter `alpha` fixed, the model cannot even learn which topics are more or less common! As with many questionable choices of prior distribution, the hope here is that the data will overwhelm the prior. In other words, it doesn't matter if the model assumes that all topics are equally likely to co-occur, since the observed words will provide plenty of evidence as to which topics are being talked about. For reasonably long documents, it is likely that the prior would indeed be overwhelmed in this way. For shorter documents, such as tweets, having a more carefully designed prior would likely have a significant benefit.

In summary, our analysis of the assumptions suggest that LDA is likely to work well for similar kinds of documents, written in the same language and style, where the documents are not too short and not too dependent on multi-word phrases. Such conditions apply moderately well to many common data sets of documents, which no doubt explains why LDA is a popular model in many such cases.

8.1.2 Extensions to LDA

As we have seen, the LDA model makes a number of assumptions which limit either its applicability or its accuracy. Happily, the model can be extended in a variety of ways to overcome these assumptions. For example, Assumption ⑤, that any pair of topics are equally likely to be talked about in the same document, arises from the choice of a Dirichlet distribution over `probTopic`. We can change this assumption by changing the form of the prior. In the Correlated Topic Model [Blei and Lafferty, 2006], the authors replace the Dirichlet prior with a logistic-normal prior capable of representing correlations between topics. The resulting model then gives much higher log-likelihood scores than LDA when the number of topics is large, where learning the correlations between topics is going to be particularly beneficial. The learned correlations between topics also means that topics connect to each other, forming a graph. Such a topic graph identifies related topics, providing a useful way to browse a set of topics, along with their associated documents.

Other extensions to LDA have been made when applying it to different kinds of data. The computer vision community explored making use of LDA by defining "documents" to be images or regions of images and "words" to be patches of the image. Various extensions were then developed to tailor the LDA model to make it more suitable to imaging applications. For example, the Spatial Latent Dirichlet Allocation model [Wang and Grimson, 2007] attempted to divide an image into regions (documents) containing patches (words) of similar appearance. This model is a particularly interesting use of LDA since it assumes that the allocation of words to documents is unknown, and so needs to be inferred at the same as time as the topic appearances and distributions over topics.

Over the years, there have been a variety of other extensions to LDA, each changing some part of the original model so as to replace or modify one of the assumptions being made. The result is an excellent demonstration of the modularity of probabilistic models – such models really can have pieces added, removed or replaced to meet the requirements of the problem domain where they are being applied.

REVIEW OF CONCEPTS

Latent Dirichlet Allocation A model of the words in a set of documents which assumes each word has an associated topic and that each document has an associated distribution over topics. In typical use, the topics and their distributions are inferred unsupervised given a set of documents. Latent Dirichlet Allocation can also be applied to other kinds of data with similar structure, such as sets of genetic sequences or images.

topic model A model which aims to discover topics in text (or other kinds of data) and also annotate text with the topics being written about.

8.2 DECISION TREE

A **decision tree** is a classifier that makes use of a tree structure to make predictions over a desired target variable. The tree starts at a root node and then contains multiple branching points, where a binary feature is applied at each branching point. Each "leaf" of the tree contains the predictive distribution used for data items that reach that leaf. For example, Figure 8.2 shows a decision tree which predicts whether an email will be replied to – the problem that we explored back in Chapter 4.

To use this decision tree to make a prediction for a particular email, we start by evaluating the top (root) feature for the email. In Figure 8.2, the first feature is: "is the user is on the To line for the email?". If the user is on the To line, we follow the "yes" path to the left, otherwise we follow the "no" path to the right. Suppose we followed the "yes" path – we then get to the feature "is the user first on the To line?". Suppose the user is indeed first on the To line, we again follow the "yes" path to the first leaf node. This leaf node contains a probability of reply of 20%, so the tree predicts a 20% probability of replying to this particular email. We will see later how these probabilities, and the structure of the tree itself, can be learned from data.

We'd like to understand the assumptions baked into this prediction process. Unlike for Latent Dirichlet Allocation, there is no standard factor graph for us to analyse. A decision tree is normally described as an algorithm, rather than as a probabilistic model. So our first challenge is to try and represent a decision tree as a prob-

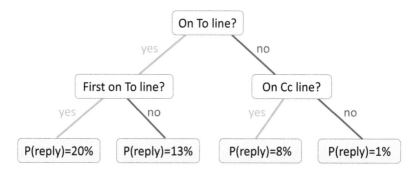

Figure 8.2 Decision tree for predicting whether an email will be replied to.

abilistic model, by constructing a factor graph corresponding to the algorithm.

8.2.1 Factor graph for a decision tree

In a decision tree, the root feature controls whether to use the left half of the tree or the right half of the tree. Effectively it switches off the half that is not being used. Similarly, each feature below the root can be thought of as switching off one half of the tree below it. If we switch off half the graph sequentially down from the root, we end up with a single leaf node being left switched on.

Viewing a decision tree this way, we can model its behaviour using gates. The root feature is the selector for a pair of gates, each containing half of the tree. The pair of gates are set up so that one is on when the root feature is `true` and the other is on when the root feature is `false`. Within the gate for the left–hand side of the tree, we then repeat this idea. We have a variable for the left–hand feature controlling a pair of gates nested inside the top level gate. Similarly, the gate for the right-hand side of the tree has another pair of gates controlled by the right-hand feature. This construction continues recursively down to the bottom of the tree. When a leaf is reached, we place a factor corresponding to the predictive distribution for that leaf, such as a *Bernoulli* distribution. All such leaf node factors connect to the single variable which is being predicted.

Applying this construction to the decision tree of Figure 8.2 gives the factor graph of Figure 8.3.

In this factor graph, the feature variables are shown as observed (shaded), since the features can be calculated from the email and so are known. The only other variable is the unobserved `reply` variable that we want to make a prediction for. The nested gates are set up so that only one of the four factor nodes is switched on, depending on the values of the feature variables. This switched-on factor directly provides the predictive distribution for the `reply` variable.

In Figure 8.3, the leaf probabilities are fixed by the four *Bernoulli* factors. If we want to learn these probabilities, we need to make them into variables, as shown in Figure 8.4. With the leaf probabilities observed, we can apply a standard inference algorithm to this factor graph to make predictions. Conversely, if the `reply` variable is observed, we can use the exact same algorithm to learn the leaf probabilities. We could further extend the factor graph to learn which feature to use at

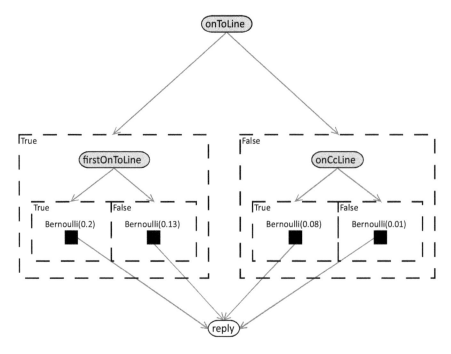

Figure 8.3 Factor graph for the decision tree of Figure 8.2.

each branching point, by adding a gate in a plate that switches between all possible features. Inference of the selector variable for that
gate would correspond to learning which feature to apply at that point
in the tree. For now though, we will limit ourselves to using the current
factor graph to analyse the assumptions that it contains.

8.2.2 What assumptions are being made?

We can use our factor graph to understand the assumptions encoded in
a decision tree classifier. It will be informative to compare these assumptions to the ones we made when designing the classifier of Chapter 4.
Since both models make use of features of the data, they both make
the core assumption that feature values can always be calculated for
any data item. But beyond this, the two models make very different
assumptions about how feature values combine to give a predictive distribution.

In Chapter 4, the effect of changing the value of one feature was
always the same, no matter what the values of other features were (see
Table 4.3). This is not true for a decision tree – the leaf node that is
reached depends on the value of every feature in the path leading to

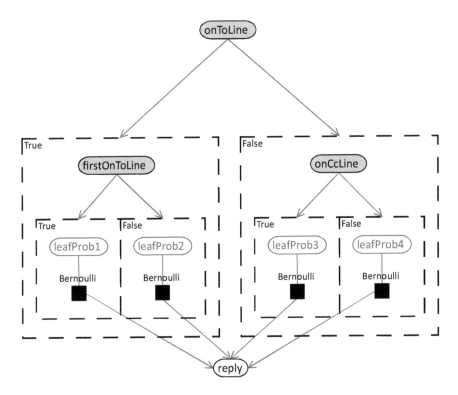

Figure 8.4 Factor graph for the decision tree of Figure 8.2 but where the leaf probabilities have been made into random variables in the model (shown in blue). This change allows for the leaf probabilities to be learned (at training time) or observed (for making predictions).

that leaf. Changing a feature may even do nothing at all, if the feature is not on the path from the root to the currently switched-on leaf. In fact, given that the number of features is usually large compared to the depth of the tree (the number of features from the root to a leaf), changing a randomly selected feature is likely to have no effect! The relevant assumption that the decision tree is making is:

① The predicted probability will only change if one of a small subset of features changes.

To explore this assumption further, consider the set of features we might wish to use for our email prediction problem. Our small initial feature set in Table 4.4 had six features, many of which had multiple buckets. To use these features in a decision tree, they would have to be converted into binary features. For example, if we created one binary feature for each bucket, we would have around 30 binary features. When learning a decision tree, we would need to select one of these features at each branching point. A decision tree with depth five would have $2^5 - 1 = 31$ branching points, each of which would need to be assigned a feature. However, for any given email, only five features would lie on the path from the root to the selected leaf for that email. Changing any feature apart from those five would have no effect on the predicted probability of reply.

It follows from Assumption ① that the decision tree classifier completely ignores any useful information contained in features other than those on the selected path. Whilst we might expect a few features to dominate in making a prediction, that does not mean we would expect other features to contain no useful information whatsoever. The consequence of this assumption is that the decision tree is likely less accurate than it could be, because it is not making use of all the available information.

Now let's suppose we change the value of a feature that is one of the few affecting the predicted reply probability. How much do we expect the reply probability to change? In Table 4.3 we assumed that a change in a single feature normally has a small effect on the reply probability, sometimes has an intermediate effect and occasionally has a large effect. But for a decision tree, the assumption is again very different. A change in a feature which is on the path to the root will cause a different leaf node to switch on. This node could have a completely different probability of reply. So for a decision tree, the assumption would be:

② Changing a feature value can completely change the predicted probability.

This assumption also has significant consequences. It means that a change in the value of a single feature can totally change the predicted probability. In the context of reply prediction, if the email length is used as a feature, adding a single character to the email could possibly change the leaf node reached. This in turn would change the predicted probability of reply, potentially by a large amount. In practice, we would want the probability to change smoothly as the length of an email changed. This would require a very large decision tree with many leaf nodes, so that we could transition through a series of leaf nodes with slightly different probabilities. In addition, training such a tree would require a great deal of data, in order to accurately learn the reply probability for each of the tree's many leaves.

So, both of the above assumptions are problematic in terms of making full use of the available data and ensuring that the predicted probability changes appropriately as feature values change. These problems are not just theoretical – decision tree classifiers do indeed suffer from these issues in practice. The solution to both problems is to use more than one decision tree, combined together into a **decision forest**.

8.2.3 Decision forest

A decision forest is made up of a collection of decision trees, known as an **ensemble**. Decision forests were first developed by Ho [1995] and then later extended and popularised by Breiman [2001]. Trees in a decision forest are trained so as to be different to one other – for example, by training

A forest is much better than a single tree.

each tree using different subsets of features or different subsets of the training data. The result of such training is that each tree will give similar, but different, predictive distributions for the same input. To apply the forest, we compute the predictive distribution for each individual tree, and then average them together. A decision forest can also be represented as a factor graph – see Figure 8.5.

A decision forest can overcome both of the issues that arise when using a single decision tree. The first issue, of not making full use of the data, is addressed by including many trees in the forest. Although each tree only makes use of a small subset of features for any data item, these are unlikely to be the same subset from tree to tree. As long as we have sufficient trees, then together they will likely use a large proportion of the available features between them. Overall then the forest will be able to make use of all available information.

Similarly, a change in the value of a single feature is now unlikely to cause a large change in the predictive probability. This is because many of the trees will not have this feature in the switched-on set, and so their predictive probability will remain unchanged. The few trees that do have the feature active could completely change their predictive

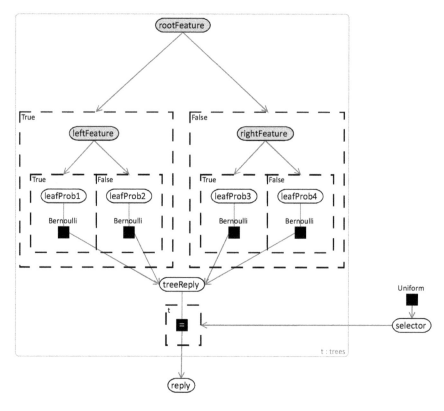

Figure 8.5 Factor graph for a decision forest. In this graph, a new plate duplicates the decision tree factor graph from Figure 8.4 to give a set of decision trees. Since these trees may have different features, we define `rootFeature` to be an array of the values of the root features for each tree – bearing in mind that the root feature can differ from tree to tree. Similarly, `leftFeature` and `rightFeature` are the values of the left and right features in each tree, whatever those features actually are. To make an overall prediction, we use a `selector` variable to select one tree at random, and copy its prediction. Since selector is unobserved, at inference time this has the effect of averaging over the predictions given by individual trees.

probabilities, but when we average all probabilities together, the overall change is more likely be small. So, using the decision forest has the effect of smoothing the predictive distribution. However, if there is lots of data to suggest that the probability should change rapidly in response to changing a particular feature, then the trees will end up using the same feature and the probability can change sharply. In practice, use of decision forests improves both accuracy and calibration compared to a single decision tree. The relative simplicity and interpretability of decision forests has led to their use for a wide range of applications. To learn more about using decision forests for a variety of machine learning tasks, take a look at Criminisi et al. [2012].

REVIEW OF CONCEPTS

decision tree A classifier that uses a tree structure to make predictions for a desired target variable. Each branching point in the tree is associated with a binary feature and each leaf node of the tree is associated with a predictive distribution. To apply the tree, we start at the root and take the left or right path according to the value of the binary feature. This procedure is repeated at each branching point until a leaf node is reached. The output of the classifier is then the predictive distribution at that leaf node.

decision forest A classifier that makes use of a number of decision trees. When making a classification, the predicted probabilities for each decision tree are averaged together to give the prediction for the forest as a whole.

ensemble A collection of models used together to give better predictive performance than any one of the individual models.

8.3 PRINCIPAL COMPONENT ANALYSIS

Principal component analysis (PCA) assumes that a data set arose from mixing together some underlying signals in different ways. PCA then attempts to "un-mix" the data, so as to recover these original signals. More precisely, PCA is a procedure for transforming a set of observation of **correlated variables** into a set of uncorrelated variables called **principal components**. PCA was invented back in 1901 by the mathematician Karl Pearson [Pearson, 1901] and, since that time, has been rediscovered and reformulated by numerous people for a variety of applications in fields from mechanical engineering to meteorology.

The intent of applying PCA is usually to try to determine the underlying causes affecting a measured data set. For example, in speech recognition, it is important to be able to separate the sounds from different sources, such as different speakers or background sources of noise. An array of microphones will pick up sound from each source to a different extent, so the audio signals reaching the microphones will likely be correlated. To try and separate out the individual audio signals from different sources, someone may try to use a method like PCA, under the assumption that the individual sources are uncorrelated. Importantly, "uncorrelated" in PCA means *linearly* uncorrelated – whilst there will be no linear dependency between the principal components, there may well remain a nonlinear dependency. We will see later that this definition of uncorrelated has significant implications in the behaviour of PCA.

Multiple microphones will hear the same sounds but at different volumes.

Other applications of PCA include applying it to stock market data, to try and understand underlying causes that affect many stocks at once. PCA has also been used to process readings from correlated sensors, such as in neuroscience applications when sensing neural activation. More generally, PCA is used for visualising high dimensional data – for example, by plotting only the largest few principal components, which are assumed to capture the most important aspects of the data.

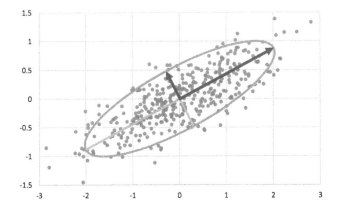

Figure 8.6 A visualisation of the principal components of a two dimensional data set. If we fit an ellipse to our data, the axes of the ellipse give the directions of the principal components, as indicated by the red arrows.

8.3.1 Computing the principal components

In two dimensions, PCA can be thought of as fitting an ellipse to the data where each axis of the ellipse represents a principal component. This idea is illustrated in Figure 8.6.

In $n > 2$ dimensions, PCA can similarly be thought of as fitting an n-dimensional ellipsoid. The process for fitting the ellipsoid is:

1. Subtract the mean of each variable from each value to centre the data set at zero;

2. Compute the **covariance matrix** of the centred data set;

3. Calculate the principal components as the eigenvectors of this covariance matrix, as described in Bishop [2006, section 12.1].

When the number of dimensions is large, it is common for some axes of the fitted ellipsoid to become quite small. The corresponding principal directions have small variance and so can be collapsed without losing much information in the original signals. In our microphone array, for example, we might hope that collapsing directions with small variance would leave only those directions corresponding to distinct sources of sound – that is, each individual speaker, whilst reducing general background noise.

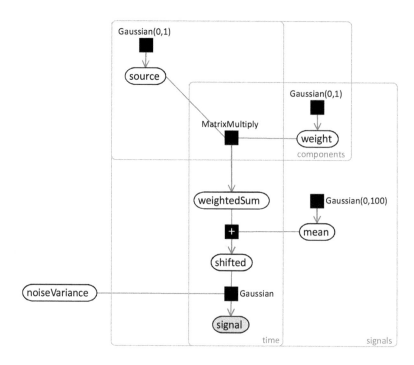

Figure 8.7 Factor graph for probabilistic principal component analysis.

8.3.2 A factor graph for PCA

It is far from obvious how to construct a factor graph to get random variables corresponding to the principal components of a set of observed data. Happily, this task has already been done for us by Tipping and Bishop [1999], where the authors develop a probabilistic model which achieves exactly this. The factor graph for this model is shown in Figure 8.7. In this model, maximum likelihood inference of the `weight` matrix gives the principal components of the observed `signal` data.

Let's have a look at what's going on in this factor graph. The graph contains three plates:

- **The number of signals**, such as the number of microphones in the microphone array;

- **The number of components**, the number of principal components to find;

- **The number of data points**, which we've called `time` since it is common for these to be measurements across time. However, they could be any set of measurements, such as measurements of pixels in an image.

The core idea of PCA is to transform the signal dimensions into a smaller number of underlying principal component directions. We can see this in the coarse structure of the graph – the observed `signal` and most variables near it live in the `signals` plate, but further up the graph the variables lie in the `components` plate. More specifically, we start at the top with a variable for the uncorrelated `source` components which, unsurprisingly, lies in the `components` plate. The `weight` variable is the only one in both the `components` and `signals` plates and it is responsible for transforming between the two. The `weightedSum` variable holds a weighted sum of components that approximately reconstructs the centered signal. This is then "un-centered" by shifting it by the `mean` to get the `shifted` form. Finally, we add noise with variance `noiseVariance` to give the observed `signal`. This noise accounts for differences between the reconstruction and the actual measured signal.

In Figure 8.7, we have chosen *Gaussian*(0,1) priors for the uncorrelated `source` components and the elements of the `weight` matrix. This assumes that the signals have approximately unit variance – in other words, that the signal variation is on the order of ±1. If this is not the case, then it is common to re-scale the signal before applying PCA – for example, to ensure it has unit variance. Because we are using a probabilistic model, we have the option of changing the priors instead – for example, by making the `source` components have a prior matched to the observed signal. The factor graph also shows a broad *Gaussian*(0,100) prior for the `mean`. This prior assumes that the mean lies somewhere roughly in the range 0 ± 10 on each dimension. With PCA it is common to subtract the mean – but with this model you do not have to as long as the prior on `mean` is sufficiently broad to include the actual mean of the data.

Representing PCA as a probabilistic model allows us to use standard inference algorithms to infer the principal components. This can be useful in situations where the normal algorithm cannot be applied. For example, if there is missing data, we cannot compute the covariance matrix and so the normal PCA algorithm cannot be used. However, in the probabilistic model, an inference algorithm can still be run when some of the `signal` variables are not observed. We can even use the inference algorithm to compute posterior distributions over such unobserved variables to fill in missing values!

8.3.3 The assumptions built in to PCA

With the factor graph for PCA in hand, we can now read off the assumptions being made. As before, we'll start at the bottom with the observed `signal` variable. We are assuming that this observation consists of an underlying component coming from the shared sources (`shifted`) and some signal-specific variability which we are modelling as Gaussian measurement noise. So our first assumption is:

① The measurement noise is Gaussian.

For some kinds of sensors, the noise really is approximately Gaussian, and so this will be a perfectly fine assumption. The problem comes if the sensor noise is non-Gaussian and occasionally gives large noise values, which will show up as outliers in the data. Since the PCA model assumes that there are no outliers, these will be assumed to be valid data points and will strongly affect the inferred principal components. Informally, they will drag the fitted ellipsoid toward the outlier – not a good thing!

Moving up the graph, we get to where the `weightedSum` is being reconstructed by multiplying the underlying source components by the `weight` matrix. This is where the really interesting assumptions are being made, starting with:

② All underlying sources affect all signals.

Elements in the `weight` matrix have a $Gaussian(0,1)$ prior, which does not encourage the elements to be zero or near-zero. As a result, we may expect weights to be generally non-zero and so every source will have an effect on every signal. For our microphone array, this may be a perfectly reasonable assumption. The microphones are close together and we might expect that any sound source heard by one of the microphones would be audible to the other

An event may cause one stock to go up, but another to go down.

microphones. In other settings, however, this assumption may not be so reasonable. For example, if modelling stock prices, we might expect certain underlying events to only affect stocks in a particular industry, but to have almost no effect at all on stocks in other industries. The PCA model would likely fail to capture such a localised effect.

Another assumption about the `weight` matrix is:

③ Weights can be positive or negative.

In some applications, we may want the weights to represent the degree to which a source affects a particular signal. For example, in a microphone array we want the weights to represent how loud the source signal is at each microphone. In such cases, it only makes sense for the weights to be positive, since there is no physical mechanism for inverting the effect of the source. When modelling stock prices, however, it is perfectly reasonable to assume that some underlying event has a positive effect on some stocks and a negative effect on others. For example, the outbreak of a pandemic may cause video conference stocks to rise but airline stocks to fall. The result of incorrectly allowing negative weights is that the inferred source signals may get inverted. In addition, it introduces a symmetry in the model which can cause problems during inference, as discussed in Section 5.3.

A related assumption is:

④ Sources can be positive or negative.

As with the previous assumption, there are applications where it makes sense for the underlying sources to be positive or negative (such as when they are audio signals) and applications where it does not (such as where the underlying causes are events). As before, getting this assumption wrong can lead to symmetries that make inference problematic.

We'll look at one more assumption, which turns out to be quite critical:

⑤ Sources are Gaussian-distributed.

This assumption is critical in order for the model to discover uncorrelated principal components. Because principal directions are orthogonal (at right angles to each other), this means that the rows of the weight matrix will be orthogonal. This causes a major problem in many applications. For example, in our microphone array we might expect the rows in the weight matrix to be similar for nearby microphones. However, they cannot be similar if they need to be at right angles to each other!

Figure 8.8 illustrates this problem. In this figure, data from two non-Gaussian sources has been mixed using a non-orthogonal weight matrix,

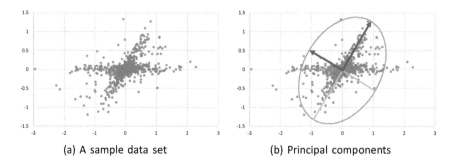

(a) A sample data set (b) Principal components

Figure 8.8 (a) A sample data set where the underlying signals are picked up by different amounts in two sensors. Here, the weight matrix is non-orthogonal and so the direction of variation of the two signals are not at right angles. (b) Since PCA assumes Gaussian sources, it will always find principal directions which are at right angles, even if these do not match the underlying signals in the data.

much as might happen when two sound signals arrive at a nearby pair of microphones. Figure 8.8b shows the principal components of this data set, which are required to be at right angles to each other and so do not capture the directions of the underlying sources. Simply put, this assumption often makes PCA unusable – we instead have to use extensions to PCA that make different assumptions about the sources.

8.3.4 Extensions to PCA

PCA is such a well-known and useful method that people have extended it to fix the problems caused by each of the above assumptions. For example, to overcome issues caused by Assumption ①, **robust PCA** methods have been developed that infer the principal components reliably, even in the presence of outliers. Such robustness can be achieved by changing the measurement noise to be non-Gaussian. For example, Luttinen et al. [2012] use a distribution called a Student-t distribution to model the noise. This distribution has more probability mass in its tails than a Gaussian distribution and so is much more robust to outliers.

Assumption ② is not appropriate for applications where measured signals will be affected by only some of the underlying sources. In such cases, variants of **sparse PCA** have been created which allow the weight matrix to contain many zero elements – see, for example, Tipping [2001].

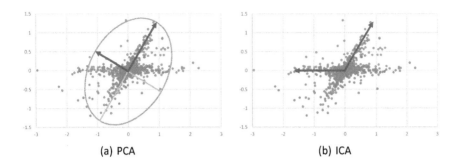

(a) PCA   (b) ICA

Figure 8.9 Illustration of the difference between PCA and ICA. (a) As we saw in Figure 8.8, PCA will always find principal directions which are at right angles, since it assumes Gaussian sources. (b) ICA instead allows for sources to be non-Gaussian and so can recover the true directions of the sources.

In applications where the sources and weights are known to be positive (or zero), it is preferable to avoid Assumption ③ and Assumption ④. Here, **non-negative matrix factorisation** (NMF) methods can be applied instead. These methods constrain the weights and sources to be non-negative. For example, NMF can be achieved by changing the priors on `weight` and `source` to distributions that only allow non-negative values. It follows that the prior on `source` must now be non-Gaussian and so Assumption ⑤ no longer holds, allowing for non-orthogonal weight matrices. Indeed, NMF does lead to a weight matrices with non-orthogonal rows.

We may want to have a non-orthogonal weight matrix *without* constraining our sources to be non-negative. To achieve this we can use some form of **independent component analysis** (ICA), which aims to infer latent sources that are not just linearly uncorrelated but actually statistically independent of each other. One way to do ICA is to change the prior over the `source` variable to a suitable non-Gaussian prior, thus changing Assumption ⑤. For example, the prior can be a mixture of Gaussians, as in Chan et al. [2003].

Figure 8.9 illustrates the difference in behaviour of ICA compared to PCA. As we saw in Figure 8.8, PCA finds principal directions at right angles (Figure 8.9a), whereas ICA discovers the underlying source directions, even though they are not orthogonal (Figure 8.9b). For our example task of separating out the different audio sources reaching a microphone array, ICA is clearly a better choice than PCA.

REVIEW OF CONCEPTS

Principal component analysis   A procedure for transforming a set of observations of correlated variables into a set of values of uncorrelated variables, known as principal components. Importantly, "uncorrelated" here is linearly uncorrelated – in other words, whilst there is no linear dependency between the principal components, there may well remain a nonlinear dependency.

correlated variables   Variables such that there is a statistical relationship between the two variables. Generally, this could be any statistical relationship, but most commonly, "correlation" is used to refer to *linear* correlation – the degree to which a pair of variables are linearly related. The difference between general correlation and linear correlation is often a cause of confusion, since there are many ways two variables can be correlated in the general sense, whilst not being linearly correlated.

principal components   The uncorrelated variables produced by applying principal component analysis.

covariance matrix   A matrix computed from a set of random variables where the element in the (i, j) position is the covariance between the ith and jth random variables.

robust PCA   A variant of principal component analysis that allows for the presence of outliers in the data.

sparse PCA   A variant of principal component analysis where the weight matrix has sparse structure – that is, contains many zero elements.

non-negative matrix factorisation   A method which factorises a non-negative matrix $\mathbf{A}$ into two matrices $\mathbf{B}$ and $\mathbf{C}$, such that $\mathbf{B}$ and $\mathbf{C}$ have no negative elements. Here "factorises" means that $\mathbf{A} = \mathbf{BC}$.

independent component analysis   A procedure for transforming observations of dependent variables into a set of underlying sources which are statistically independent.

8.4   K-MEANS CLUSTERING

K-means clustering (or simply "k-means") is an algorithm for dividing a set of data points into k different clusters, where each cluster is defined by the mean of the points in the cluster. Data points are assigned to the cluster with the closest mean. K-means clustering is a popular method for data analysis when the goal is to identify underlying structure in a data set. The hope is that the resulting clusters will align with some underlying structure of interest. For example, suppose we have a medical data set where each data point consists of a set of relevant measurements for a person. The hope would then be that k-means clustering would result in clusters that identify useful sub-populations of people – for example, groups of people who may respond differently to treatment. K-means clustering has been around for a while – it was named "k-means" in 1967 by James MacQueen [MacQueen, 1967], but the algorithm itself was developed ten years earlier by Stuart Lloyd in Bell Labs [Lloyd, 1957].

We have seen an example of doing clustering before – in Section 6.5, we used a carefully constructed model to cluster children into different sensitisation classes. In doing so, we made a number of assumptions about how the children should be clustered together, to ensure that the resulting sensitisation classes made sense. Had we made different assumptions, the children could have been partitioned into very different clusters. Put simply, the clusters that you get out of a clustering method depend strongly on the assumptions underlying that method. This is such an important point, and one so often ignored, that it is worth repeating:

The clusters you get out of a clustering method depend heavily on the assumptions being made by that method.

So when performing any kind of clustering, it is crucially important to understand what assumptions are being made. In this section, we will explore the assumptions underlying k-means clustering. These assumptions will allow us to understand whether clusters found using k-means will correspond well to the underlying structure of a particular data set, or not.

8.4.1 The k-means algorithm

The standard k-means algorithm involves alternating between two steps:

- **Update assignments:** given the cluster means, assign each point to the cluster with the closest mean;

- **Update means:** given the assignment of points to clusters, set each cluster mean to be the mean of all points assigned to that cluster.

To start alternating between these steps, you need either an initial set of means or an initial assignment of points to clusters. One common way to get an initial set of means, is to randomly select k data points to be the starting cluster means. Alternatively, to get an initial assignment of points, each point can be assigned to a randomly selected cluster. This second approach is the one we will use here.

Figure 8.10a shows some an example set of data points, where the points have been randomly assigned to one of two clusters (red and blue). Given this initial assignment, the first cluster centre was set to be the mean of all blue points, and the second cluster centre to be the mean of all red points. Each data point was then assigned to the cluster with the closest centre, giving the result in Figure 8.10b. Already you

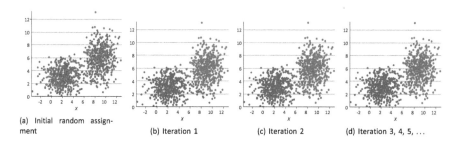

(a) Initial random assignment

(b) Iteration 1

(c) Iteration 2

(d) Iteration 3, 4, 5, ...

Figure 8.10 Results of applying the k-means algorithm to an example data set. (a) Initially, points are randomly assigned to two clusters (red or blue) (b) After just one iteration of k-means, the two underlying clusters in the data are already fairly well discovered. (c) A second iteration causes some data points near the boundary to be re-assigned to the correct underlying cluster. (d) A third iteration gives a good final assignment of points to clusters, which is unchanged by any further iterations.

can see that the colours are reasonably well aligned with the underlying clusters in the data. A further iteration gives Figure 8.10c where one data cluster is now almost entirely blue and the other almost entirely red. One more iteration causes a single data point to change colour, as shown in Figure 8.10d. Further iterations have no effect, since the assignment of points to clusters does not change.

In this example, the clusters given by k-means have done a good job at identifying the underlying structure of the data set. But will this always be the case? To answer this question, we need to express this algorithm as a model, so that we can uncover and analyse the assumptions made by the k-means algorithm.

8.4.2   A model for k-means

A model for the k-means algorithm needs to have variables for:

- the **data**, inside plates for the number of data points and for the number of dimensions;

- the **mean** for each cluster, inside plates for the number of clusters (K) and for the number of dimensions;

- the **assignment** for each data point, inside a plate across the data points.

Since we don't know anything about the **mean** ahead of time, the prior must be uniform across all real values. Similarly, since we don't know anything about each **assignment**, the prior must be uniform across the clusters. The **assignment** controls which of the k means the corresponding data point comes from – so we use it to turn on a gate connecting the kth **mean** to the observed **data**.

The trickiest part is how to choose the factor connecting the assigned **mean** to each data point. To get the same result as k-means, we need a factor which gives higher probability to data points closer in distance to the cluster mean. A Gaussian factor achieves this, so long as the variance is kept fixed for all dimensions and for all clusters. Putting all this together gives the model in Figure 8.11. This factor graph is a form of a well-known model called a **mixture of Gaussians**.

To be exactly equivalent to k-means, we need the message from the gates to the **assignment** variable to be a point mass ("hard" assignment). Applying a probabilistic inference method such as expectation propagation results in a message which is a distribution over the clusters ("soft" assignment). Although soft assignment is generally preferable

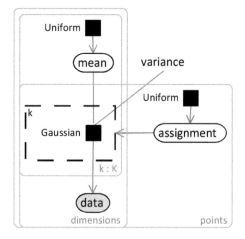

Figure 8.11 A mixture of Gaussians model which gives the same clusters as the k-means algorithm. The variance of each Gaussian is fixed across clusters and across dimensions of the data.

in practice, hard assignment can be achieved by setting the variance of the Gaussian factor to be extremely small. This causes the message to `assignment` to collapse to a point mass. Alternatively, we can just re-define the inference algorithm so that the message to `assignment` is defined to be a point mass at the most probable value under the distribution message. Either approach will give results identical to that of the k-means algorithm

8.4.3 Some hidden assumptions in k-means

The factor graph of Figure 8.11 reveals a number of assumptions hidden inside the k-means algorithm. For example, because the variance is outside the plate over the clusters, the model assumes that all the clusters have the same variance. In other words:

① All clusters are the same size.

This assumption would not hold in a data set where the measurements vary more in one cluster than another. In a medical data set, for example, the weight of someone who has severe disease may fluctuate more than the weight of someone with milder disease and this assumption would be violated.

In Figure 8.11, the variance is also outside the plate over dimensions, which means that we assume the same amount of variability in each data dimension. Put simply:

② Clusters have the same extent in every direction.

This assumption would not be true in a data set where different measurements are in different units. In a medical data set, the units of body temperature would be different from the units of weight, and so the variation in these measurements would be on a different scale.

We'll look at one more assumption, corresponding to the choice of prior over `assignment` variable. Because this prior is uniform, the model is assuming that all clusters are equally probable. This can be expressed as the assumption that:

③ Clusters have similar numbers of points assigned to them.

This assumption would not hold in a data set where the underlying variable causing the clusters is not equally likely to choose any cluster. For example, in a medical data set, one underlying cluster may correspond to the most severely ill people and another to people with a milder form of the disease. If severe cases are rare compared to mild cases then this assumption would not hold.

8.4.4 Problems with k-means

Now that we understand the assumptions that the k-means algorithm is making, we can construct synthetic data sets to illustrate the problems these assumptions can cause. Assumption ① is that the clusters are all the same size. So, if we make a data set with two very different size clusters, we should expect to see k-means having problems. Figure 8.12a shows a synthetic data set with one large and one small cluster. If we run k-means clustering on this data set, we get the result shown in Figure 8.12b, where k-means has failed to discover the two clusters in the data. Instead, nearby points in the large cluster are incorrectly assigned to the small cluster, due to this incorrect assumption.

To address this problem, we can modify the factor graph to make the variance into a random variable, give it a suitable broad prior, and move it inside the plate over the clusters. With this modification, we can learn a per cluster variance and so allow clusters to be different sizes. The result of applying this model is shown in Figure 8.12c, where the two data clusters have now been correctly identified.

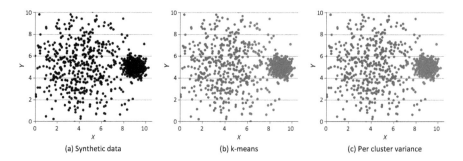

(a) Synthetic data   (b) k-means   (c) Per cluster variance

Figure 8.12 (a) Data with different size clusters. (b) k-means does not correctly discover the two clusters. (c) If we modify the mixture of Gaussians model to allow a cluster variance to be learned for each cluster, then the two clusters are correctly discovered.

Assumption ② is that clusters have the same extent in every direction. So if we make a data set with clusters that have different extents in different directions, then we would again expect k-means to have problems. Figure 8.13a shows such a data set, where the two clusters have been squashed vertically. Figure 8.13b shows the result of running k-means on this dataset. This result is particularly bad – k-means gives two clusters separated by a diagonal line which are not at all aligned with the actual data clusters!

We can further modify the factor graph to address the problem, by moving the `variance` variable inside the gate over the dimensions. This modification allows the variance to be learned per dimension, as well

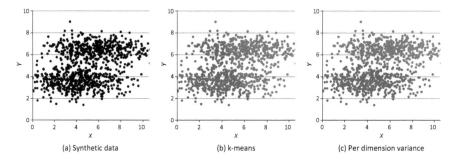

(a) Synthetic data   (b) k-means   (c) Per dimension variance

Figure 8.13 (a) Data with "squashed" clusters that have different widths in different directions. (b) k-means clustering gives poor results that do not align with the data clusters, (c) Extending the model to allow a per dimension variance addresses the problem.

as per cluster. Figure 8.13c shows the result of running this modified model – now the squashed clusters in the data are correctly matched to the inferred assignments. This modification only works because the data clusters are squashed in an axis-aligned direction. To allow for the data to be squashed in any direction, we would need to change the model to learn a full covariance matrix for each cluster.

Our final assumption was that each cluster has a similar number of points (Assumption ③). Figure 8.14a shows a synthetic data set with two identically-sized clusters, but where the left–hand cluster has 90% of the data points. This imbalance makes the left–hand cluster look bigger, even though its variance is actually the same as the right–hand cluster. Because the left cluster is much more probable than the right one, points half-way between are much more likely to belong to the left cluster. If we look at the result of running k-means (Figure 8.14b), then you can see that it incorrectly assigns such points to the right–hand cluster.

We can modify our model to solve this problem by introducing a new probability vector **probs**, to represent the probability associated with each cluster. This modified model gives the result shown in Figure 8.14c, where the two data clusters are again nicely separated. Putting all of the above modifications together gives the factor graph of Figure 8.15. This model which makes none of these three assumptions and so has none of the associated problems.

Even this improved model is still making assumptions about the data which will not be true for some real data sets – for example, that

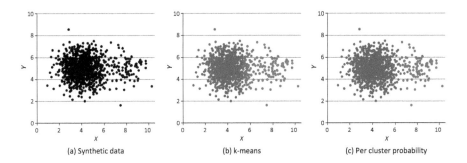

Figure 8.14 (a) Two same-size clusters where the left contains 90% of the data points. (b) k-means clustering incorrectly assigns mid-way data points to the right–hand cluster (c) Learning the probability of a data point being in each cluster addresses this problem.

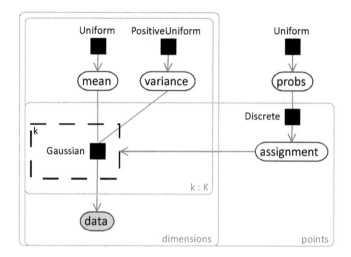

Figure 8.15 An improved mixture of Gaussians model which addresses three problematic assumptions made by the k-means algorithm.

the number of clusters is known or that the clusters are elliptical in shape. Further changes could be made to address these assumptions. For example, gates could be used to learn the number of clusters. We can continue this process of identifying assumptions and improving the model until it is sufficiently powerful and flexible to represent the structure of the desired data set. This ability to identify and address assumptions is the very essence of what it means to do model-based machine learning.

REVIEW OF CONCEPTS

K-means clustering An algorithm for dividing a set of data points into k different clusters, where each cluster is defined by the mean of the points that belong to it. Data points are assigned to the cluster with the closest mean.

mixture of Gaussians A well-known model where each data point is generated by first selecting one of several Gaussian distributions and then sampling from that distribution.

Afterword

Ten years ago, when I first started thinking about this book, machine learning was mostly an academic study. It was primarily an intellectual exercise whose goal was to push ahead and see what a computer could be made to learn: to understand what tasks were within the capabilities of our current techniques and which ones lay outside. The focus was to try and move this boundary – to test the limits and break through, as a popular children's song might have it.

My goal then was to write a book to help people to understand that machine learning models and algorithms are not abstract mathematical concepts, but mathematical descriptions of the real world. By explaining the assumptions hidden away in machine learning algorithms, I hoped to make them easier to understand, both to beginners and to those with more experience. The idea was to show by example how each choice about the structure of the mathematical model has a real effect on the behaviour of the resulting machine learning system.

In the intervening decade, the role of machine learning in the world has fundamentally changed. It is no longer a purely intellectual discipline. Instead, use of machine learning has expanded ten-fold, a hundred-fold, in a myriad of applications across every aspect of our digital lives. Increasingly, machine learning is affecting everything we see online, what is drawn to our attention and what is hidden. Machine learning influences what we watch, what we listen to, the things that we buy, even the people that we date. More worryingly, machine learning is starting to influence who gets hired for a job, who gets access to medical treatments, even where police get deployed and who gets sent to jail.

Understanding how the assumptions in a machine learning model affect its behaviour is no longer just a useful skill for developing machine learning systems. It has become a critically important way of making sure that a machine learning system is transparent, interpretable and fair. As people's lives are influenced by machine-made decisions to an ever greater extent, the call to understand the reasoning behind these systems is going to become deafeningly loud. The assumptions in these systems need to be clear, transparent and available for all to see – and made accessible through clear explanations of each decision or prediction. Model-based machine learning is a crucial tool in ensuring that transparency and fairness lie at the foundations of all machine learning systems.

So, to those who are designing the next generation of machine learning systems, think carefully about every assumption you make and about every data set you train on. Your modelling decisions are not abstract: they will have very real effects on the lives of real people. Machine learning will affect the lives of your family, your friends, of you yourself. Remember that if you use gender as a variable in your model, it will likely make sexist predictions. If you use race as a variable, your model will likely be racist. Training on data sets which record the status quo will entrench past inequalities and propagate them to the future. So apply your skills with thought, with care and, above all, with empathy.

May all your assumptions be good ones.

John Winn
June 2020

Bibliography

Abadi, M., Barham, P., Chen, J., Chen, Z., Davis, A., Dean, J., Devin, M., Ghemawat, S., Irving, G., Isard, M., et al. (2016). Tensorflow: A system for large-scale machine learning. In *12th USENIX Symposium on Operating Systems Design and Implementation (OSDI 16)*, pages 265–283. USENIX Association.

Anderson, H. R., Gupta, R., Strachan, D. P., and Limb, E. S. (2007). 50 years of asthma: UK trends from 1955 to 2004. *Thorax*, 62(1):85–90.

Bai, J., Lu, F., Zhang, K., et al. (2019). ONNX: Open Neural Network Exchange.

Bayes, T. (1763). An Essay towards Solving a Problem in the Doctrine of Chances. By the Late Rev. Mr. Bayes, F. R. S. Communicated by Mr. Price, in a Letter to John Canton, A. M. F. R. S. *Philosophical Transactions*, 53:370–418.

Bishop, C. M. (2006). *Pattern Recognition and Machine Learning*. Springer.

Blackstone, W. (1765). Commentaries on the laws of England.

Blei, D. M. and Lafferty, J. D. (2006). Correlated topic models. In *Proceedings of the 23rd International Conference on Machine Learning*, pages 113–120. MIT Press.

Blei, D. M., Ng, A. Y., and Jordan, M. I. (2003). Latent Dirichlet Allocation. *Journal of Machine Learning Research*, 3(4–5):993–1022.

Bliss, C. I. (1934). The Method of Probits. *Science*, 79(2037):38–39.

Breiman, L. (2001). Random Forests. *Machine Learning*, 45:5–32.

Chan, K., Lee, T.-W., and Sejnowski, T. (2003). Variational Bayesian Learning of ICA with Missing Data. *Neural Computation*, 15:1991–2011.

Criminisi, A., Shotton, J., and Konukoglu, E. (2012). Decision Forests: A Unified Framework for Classification, Regression, Density Estimation, Manifold Learning and Semi-Supervised Learning. *Foundations and TrendsÂő in Computer Graphics and Vision*, 7(2–3):81–227.

Custovic, A., Simpson, B. M., Murray, C. S., Lowe, L., and Woodcock, A. (2002). The national asthma campaign Manchester asthma and allergy study. *Pediatric Allergy and Immunology*, 13:32–37.

Dangauthier, P., Herbrich, R., Minka, T., and Graepel, T. (2007). Trueskill through time: Revisiting the history of chess. In Platt, J. C., Koller, D., Singer, Y., and Roweis, S. T., editors, *NIPS*, pages 931–938. Curran Associates, Inc.

Dawid, A. P. (1982). The Well-Calibrated Bayesian. *Journal of the American Statistical Association*, 77(379):605–610.

Diethe, T., Guiver, J., Zaykov, Y., Kats, D., Novikov, A., and Winn, J. (2019). Model-Based Machine Learning book, accompanying source code. https://github.com/dotnet/mbmlbook.

Fanta, C. H. (2009). Asthma. *New England Journal of Medicine*, 360(10):1002–1014. PMID: 19264689.

Fawcett, T. (2006). An introduction to ROC analysis. *Pattern Recognition Letters*, 27(8):861–874.

Frey, B. and MacKay, D. (1998). A Revolution: Belief Propagation in Graphs With Cycles. In *Proceedings of the 10th International Conference on Neural Information Processing Systems*, pages 479–485. MIT Press.

Goldberg, D., Nichols, D., Oki, B. M., and Terry, D. (1992). Using collaborative filtering to weave an information tapestry. *Communications of the ACM*, 35:61–70.

Graepel, T., Lauter, K., and Naehrig, M. (2013). ML Confidential: Machine Learning on Encrypted Data. In Kwon, T., Lee, M.-K., and Kwon, D., editors, *Information Security and Cryptology - ICISC 2012*, volume 7839 of *Lecture Notes in Computer Science*, pages 1–21. Springer Berlin Heidelberg.

Harper, F. M. and Konstan, J. A. (2015). The MovieLens Datasets: History and Context. *ACM Trans. Interact. Intell. Syst.*, 5(4):1–19.

Herbrich, R., Graepel, T., and Campbell, C. (2001). Bayes Point Machines. *Journal of Machine Learning Research*, 1:245–279.

Herbrich, R., Minka, T., and Graepel, T. (2007). TrueSkill(TM): A Bayesian Skill Rating System. In *Advances in Neural Information Processing Systems 20*, pages 569–576. MIT Press.

Ho, T. K. (1995). Random Decision Forests. In *Proceedings of the 3rd International Conference on Document Analysis and Recognition*, pages 278–282. IEEE Computer Society.

Holstein, K., Vaughan, J. W., DaumÃľ III, H., DudÃŋk, M., and Wallach, H. M. (2019). Improving fairness in machine learning systems: What do industry practitioners need? In *ACM CHI Conference on Human Factors in Computing Systems*, pages 1âĂŞ–16. Association for Computing Machinery.

Junker, B. W. and Sijtsma, K. (2001). Cognitive assessment models with few assumptions, and connections with nonparametric item response theory. *Applied Psychological Measurement*, 25:258–272.

Kass, R. E. and Raftery, A. E. (1995). Bayes factors. *Journal of the American Statistical Association*, 90(430):773–795.

Kim, H.-C. and Ghahramani., Z. (2012). Bayesian classifier combination. *Journal of Machine Learning Research*, 22:619–627.

Krizhevsky, A., Sutskever, I., and Hinton, G. (2012). ImageNet Classification with Deep Convolutional Neural Networks. In *Neural Information Processing Systems*, volume 25, pages 1097âĂŞ–1105.

Kschischang, F. R., Frey, B. J., and Loeliger, H. (2001). Factor graphs and the sum-product algorithm. *IEEE Transactions on Information Theory*, 47(2):498–519.

Lauritzen, S. L. and Spiegelhalter, D. J. (1988). Local Computations with Probabilities on Graphical Structures and Their Application to Expert Systems. *Journal of the Royal Statistical Society, Series B*, 50(2): 157–224.

Lazic, N., Roberts, G., Custovic, A., Belgrave, D., Christopher Bishop, J. W., Curtin, J., Arshad, S. H., and Simpson, A. (2013). Multiple atopy phenotypes and their associations with asthma: Similar findings from two birth cohorts. *Allergy*, 68, No. 6:764âĂŞ770.

Little, R. and Rubin, D. (2014). *Statistical Analysis with Missing Data, Second Edition*. John Wiley & Sons.

Liu, B. (2012). Sentiment Analysis and Opinion Mining. *Synthesis Lectures on Human Language Technologies*, 5(1):1–167.

Lloyd, S. P. (1957). Least square quantization in PCM. Technical report, Bell Telephone Laboratories.

Lunn, D., Thomas, A., Best, N., and Spiegelhalter, D. (2000). WinBUGS – a Bayesian modelling framework. *Statistics and Computing*, 10:325–337. MRC Biostatistics Unit. http://www.mrc-bsu.cam.ac.uk/software/bugs.

Luttinen, J., Ilin, A., and Karhunen, J. (2012). Bayesian Robust PCA of Incomplete Data. *Neural Processing Letters*, 36(2):189–202.

MacKay, D. C. J. (2003). *Information Theory, Inference & Learning Algorithms*. Cambridge University Press.

MacQueen, J. B. (1967). Some Methods for Classification and Analysis of Multivariate Observations. In *Proceedings of 5th Berkeley Symposium on Mathematical Statistics and Probability*, pages 281–297. University of California Press.

Maybeck, P. S. (1982). Stochastic models, estimation, and control. In *Volume 2*, volume 141, Part 2 of *Mathematics in Science and Engineering*, chapter Chapter 12 Nonlinear estimation, pages 212–271. Elsevier.

Minka, T. (2005). Divergence Measures and Message Passing. Technical Report MSR-TR-2005-173, Microsoft Research.

Minka, T., Cleven, R., and Zaykov, Y. (2018). TrueSkill 2: An improved Bayesian skill rating system. Technical Report MSR-TR-2018-8, Microsoft.

Minka, T. and Winn, J. (2008). Gates: A graphical notation for mixture models. Technical report, Microsoft Research.

Minka, T. and Winn, J. (2009). Gates. In *Proceedings of the 21st International Conference on Neural Information Processing Systems*, page 1073âĂŞ1080. Curran Associates Inc.

Minka, T., Winn, J., Guiver, J., Webster, S., Zaykov, Y., Yangel, B., Spengler, A., and Bronskill, J. (2014). Infer.NET 2.6. Microsoft Research Cambridge. http://research.microsoft.com/infernet.

Minka, T. P. (2001). Expectation propagation for approximate Bayesian inference. In *Uncertainty in Artificial Intelligence*, volume 17, pages 362–369. Morgan Kaufmann Publishers Inc.

Morrow, N., Mock, N., Papendieck, A., and Kocmich, N. (2011). Independent Evaluation of the Ushahidi Haiti Project.

Moser, J. (2010). The Math behind TrueSkill. http://www.moserware.com/2010/03/computing-your-skill.html.

Norheim-Hagtun, I. and Meier, P. (2010). Crowdsourcing for Crisis Mapping in Haiti. *Innovations: Technology, Governance, Globalization*, 5(4):81–89.

Opper, M. (1998). A Bayesian approach to on-line learning. In Saad, D., editor, *On-line Learning in Neural Networks*, chapter A Bayesian Approach to On-line Learning, pages 363–378. Cambridge University Press, New York, NY, USA.

Outlook team (2008). Internal email study.

Paszke, A., Gross, S., Massa, F., Lerer, A., Bradbury, J., Chanan, G., Killeen, T., Lin, Z., Gimelshein, N., Antiga, L., Desmaison, A., Kopf, A., Yang, E., DeVito, Z., Raison, M., Tejani, A., Chilamkurthy, S., Steiner, B., Fang, L., Bai, J., and Chintala, S. (2019). PyTorch: An Imperative Style, High-Performance Deep Learning Library. In *Advances in Neural Information Processing Systems 32*, pages 8024–8035. Curran Associates, Inc.

Patil, D. J. (2012). *Data Jujitsu: The Art of Turning Data into Product.* O'Reilly Media.

Pearl, J. (1982). Reverend Bayes on Inference Engines: A Distributed Hierarchical Approach. In *Proceedings of the Second AAAI Conference on Artificial Intelligence*, AAAI'82, pages 133âĂŞ–136. AAAI Press.

Pearl, J. (1985). Bayesian networks: A model of self-activated memory for evidential reasoning. In *Proc. of Cognitive Science Society (CSS-7)*, pages 329–334.

Pearl, J. (1988). *Probabilistic Reasoning in Intelligent Systems.* Morgan Kaufmann, San Francisco.

Pearson, K. (1901). On Lines and Planes of Closest Fit to Systems of Points in Space. *Philosophical Magazine*, 2(11):559–572.

Powers, D. (2008). Evaluation: From Precision, Recall and F-Factor to ROC, Informedness, Markedness and Correlation. *Machine Learning Technologies.*, 2:37–63.

Radicati, S. and Hoang, Q. (2010). Microsoft Exchange Server and Outlook Market Analysis, 2010-2014. Technical report, The Radicati Group, Inc.

Ramchurn, S., Dong Huynh, T., Ikuno, Y., Flann, J., Wu, F., Moreau, L., R. Jennings, N., Fischer, J., Jiang, W., Rodden, T., Simpson, E., Reece, S., and Roberts, S. (2015). HAC-ER: A disaster response system based on human-agent collectives. *Journal of Artificial Intelligence Research*, 1:533–541.

Simpson, A., Tan, V., Winn, J., Svensen, M., Bishop, C., Heckerman, D., Buchan, I., and Custovic, A. (2010). Beyond atopy: Multiple patterns of sensitization in relation to asthma in a birth cohort study. *American Journal of Respiratory and Critical Care Medicine*, 181:1200–1206.

Simpson, E., Venanzi, M., Reece, S., Kohli, P., Guiver, J., Roberts, S., and Jennings, N. R. (2015). Language understanding in the wild: Combining crowdsourcing and machine learning. In *24th International World Wide Web Conference (WWW 2015)*, pages 992–1002. International World Wide Web Conferences Steering Committee.

Stan Development Team (2014). Stan: A C++ Library for Probability and Sampling, Version 2.5.0.

Stern, D., Herbrich, R., and Graepel, T. (2009). Matchbox: Large Scale Bayesian Recommendations. In *Proceedings of the 18th International World Wide Web Conference*, pages 111âĂŞ-120. Association for Computing Machinery.

Suermondt, H. and Cooper, G. F. (1990). Probabilistic inference in multiply connected belief networks using loop cutsets. *International Journal of Approximate Reasoning*, 4(4):283–306.

Sutskever, I., Vinyals, O., and Le, Q. V. (2014). Sequence to Sequence Learning with Neural Networks. In *Proceedings of the 27th International Conference on Neural Information Processing Systems - Volume 2*, pages 3104–3112. MIT Press.

The CALO Project (2004). Enron email data set. http://www.cs.cmu.edu/~enron.

Tipping, M. E. (2001). Sparse Kernel Principal Component Analysis. In Leen, T. K., Dietterich, T. G., and Tresp, V., editors, *Advances in Neural Information Processing Systems 13*, pages 633–639. MIT Press.

Tipping, M. E. and Bishop, C. (1999). Probabilistic Principal Component Analysis. *Journal of the Royal Statistical Society, Series B*, 21(3):611–622.

Tufte, E. R. (1986). *The Visual Display of Quantitative Information*. Graphics Press, Cheshire, CT, USA.

Ushahidi (2008). http://www.ushahidi.com/.

Venanzi, M., Guiver, J., Kazai, G., and Kohli, P. (2012). Bayesian Combination of Crowd-Based Tweet Sentiment Analysis Judgments. In *Crowdscale Shared Task Challenge*.

Venanzi, M., Guiver, J., Kazai, G., Kohli, P., and Shokouhi, M. (2014). Community-based Bayesian Aggregation Models for Crowdsourcing. In *Proceedings of the 23rd International Conference on World Wide Web*, WWW '14, pages 155–164, New York, NY, USA. ACM.

Wang, X. and Grimson, E. (2007). Spatial Latent Dirichlet Allocation. In *Proceedings of the 20th International Conference on Neural Information Processing Systems*, NIPS'07, pages 1577–1584. Curran Associates Inc.

Zhang, C., Guiver, J., Minka, T., and Zaykov, Y. (2015). Groupbox: A generative model for group recommendation. Technical report, Microsoft Research.

Index

For Product Safety Concerns and Information please contact our EU
representative GPSR@taylorandfrancis.com
Taylor & Francis Verlag GmbH, Kaufingerstraße 24, 80331 München, Germany